SECRET
SOCIETIES
& SUBVERSIVE MOVEMENTS

SECRET
SOCIETIES

COVER CONCEPT: *ACT GRAPHIX*
LETTERING: *INDUSTRIAL FONTS X GRAPHIX*

Webster, Nesta, Helen.
 Secret Societies and subversive movements/ Nesta H. Webster.
  p. cm.
 Originally published: London: Boswell Print. & Co., 1924
 Includes bibliographical references (p.   ) and index.
 ISBN: 1-881316-88-2
  1. Secret Societies—History.   2. Freemasonry—History.
3. Subversive activities—History.   I. Title.
HS126.W4   1998
366'.009—dc21   98-3343
                                                                           CIP

02   03   04   05   5   4   3

Printed in Canada

A&B PUBLISHERS GROUP
Brooklyn, New York
11238
(718) 783-7808

SECRET
SOCIETIES
& SUBVERSIVE MOVEMENTS

Nesta H. Webster

A&B PUBLISHERS GROUP
1000 ATLANTIC AVENUE
BROOKLYN, NEW YORK

BY THE SAME AUTHOR

The Chevalier de Boufflers
The French Revolution
World Revolution
The Socialist Network
The Surrender of an Empire
Louis XVI and Marie Antoinette: Before the Revolution
Louis XVI and Marie Antoinette: During the Revolution
Spacious Days

" There is in Italy a power which we seldom mention in this House
. . . I mean the secret societies. . . . It is useless to deny, because
it is impossible to conceal, that a great part of Europe—the whole
of Italy and France and a great portion of Germany, to say nothing of
other countries—is covered with a network of these secret societies,
just as the superficies of the earth is now being covered with railroads.
And what are their objects? They do not attempt to conceal them.
They do not want constitutional government; they do not want
ameliorated institutions . . . they want to change the tenure of land,
to drive out the present owners of the soil and to put an end to
ecclesiastical establishments. Some of them may go further. . . ."
(DISRAELI in the House of Commons, July 14, 1856.)

PREFACE

IT is a matter of some regret to me that I have been so far unable to continue the series of studies on the French Revolution of which *The Chevalier de Boufflers* and *The French Revolution, a Study in Democracy* formed the first two volumes. But the state of the world at the end of the Great War seemed to demand an enquiry into the present phase of the revolutionary movement, hence my attempt to follow its course up to modern times in *World Revolution*. And now before returning to that first cataclysm I have felt impelled to devote one more book to the Revolution as a whole by going this time further back into the past and attempting to trace its origins from the first century of the Christian era. For it is only by taking a general survey of the movement that it is possible to understand the causes of any particular phase of its existence. The French Revolution did not arise merely out of conditions or ideas peculiar to the eighteenth century, nor the Bolshevist Revolution out of political and social conditions in Russia or the teaching of Karl Marx. Both these explosions were produced by forces which, making use of popular suffering and discontent, had long been gathering strength for an onslaught not only on Christianity, but on all social and moral order.

It is of immense significance to notice with what resentment this point of view is met in certain quarters. When I first began to write on revolution a well-known London publisher said to me, " Remember that if you take an anti-revolutionary line you will have the whole literary world against you." This appeared to me extraordinary. Why should the literary world sympathize with a movement which from the French Revolution onwards has always been directed against literature, art, and science, and has openly proclaimed its aim to exalt the manual workers over the intelligentsia? " Writers must be proscribed as the most dangerous enemies of the people," said Robespierre; his colleague Dumas said all clever men should be guillotined. " The system of perse-cution against men of talents was organized. . . . They cried

out in the sections of Paris , ' Beware of that man for he
has written a book!'"[1] Precisely the same policy has been
followed in Russia. Under Moderate Socialism in Germany
the professors, not the " people," are starving in garrets.
Yet the whole press of our country is permeated with subversive influences. Not merely in partisan works, but in
manuals of history or literature for use in Schools, Burke is
reproached for warning us against the French Revolution and
Carlyle's panegyric is applauded. And whilst every slip on
the part of an anti-revolutionary writer is seized on by the
critics and held up as an example of the whole, the most
glaring errors not only of conclusions but of facts pass un-
challenged if they happen to be committed by a partisan of the
movement. The principle laid down by Collot d'Herbois
still holds good: "Tout est permis pour quiconque agit dans
le sens de la révolution."

All this was unknown to me when I first embarked on my
work. I knew that French writers of the past had distorted
facts to suit their own political views, that a conspiracy of
history is still directed by certain influences in the masonic
lodges and the Sorbonne; I did not know that this conspiracy was being carried on in this country. Therefore the
publisher's warning did not daunt me. If I was wrong either
in my conclusions or facts I was prepared to be challenged.
Should not years of laborious historical research meet either
with recognition or with reasoned and scholarly refutation?
But although my book received a great many generous and
appreciative reviews in the press, criticisms which were hostile
took a form which I had never anticipated. Not a single
honest attempt was made to refute either my *French Revolution* or *World Revolution* by the usual methods of controversy;
statements founded on documentary evidence were met with
flat contradiction unsupported by a shred of counter evidence.
In general the plan adopted was not to disprove, but to
discredit by means of flagrant misquotations, by attributing
to me views I had never expressed, or even by means of
offensive personalities. It will surely be admitted that this
method of attack is unparalleled in any other sphere of literary
controversy.

It is interesting to notice that precisely the same line was
adopted a hundred years ago with regard to Professor Robison
and the Abbé Barruel, whose works on the secret causes of the
French Revolution created an immense sensation in their

[1] *Moniteur* for the 14th Fructidor, An II.

day. The legitimate criticisms that might have been made on their work find no place in the diatribes levelled against them; their enemies content themselves merely with calumnies and abuse. A contemporary American writer, Seth Payson, thus describes the methods employed to discredit them:

The testimony of Professor Robison and Abbé Barruel would doubtless have been considered as ample in any case which did not interest the prejudices and passions of men against them. The scurrility and odium with which they have been loaded is perfectly natural, and what the nature of their testimony would have led one to expect. Men will endeavour to invalidate that evidence which tends to unveil their dark designs: and it cannot be expected that those who believe that "the end sanctifies the means" will be very scrupulous as to their measures. Certainly he was not who invented the following character and arbitrarily applied it to Dr. Robison, which might have been applied with as much propriety to any other person in Europe or America. The character here referred to, is taken from the American *Mercury*, printed at Hartford, September 26, 1799, by E. Babcock. In this paper, on the pretended authority of Professor Ebeling, we are told "that Robison had lived too fast for his income, and to supply deficiencies had undertaken to alter a bank bill, that he was detected and fled to France; that having been expelled the Lodge in Edinburgh, he applied in France for the second grade, but was refused; that he made the same attempt in Germany and afterwards in Russia, but never succeeded; and from this entertained the bitterest hatred to masonry; and after wandering about Europe for two years, by writing to Secretary Dundas, and presenting a copy of his book, which, it was judged, would answer certain purposes of the ministry, the prosecution against him was stopped, the Professor returned in triumph to his country, and now lives upon a handsome pension, instead of suffering the fate of his predecessor Dodd.[1]

Payson goes on to quote a writer in *The National Intelligencer* of January 1801, who styles himself a " friend to truth " and speaks of Professor Robison as " a man distinguished by abject dependence on a party, by the base crimes of forgery and adultery, and by frequent paroxysms of insanity." Mounier goes further still, and in his pamphlet *De l'influence attribuée aux Philosophes, . . . Francs-maçons et . . . Illuminés*, etc., inspired by the Illuminatus Bode, quotes a story that Robison suffered from a form of insanity which consisted in his believing that the posterior portion of his body was made of glass![2]

[1] Seth Payson, *Proofs of the Real Existence and Dangerous Tendency of Illuminism* (Charleston, 1802), pp. 5–7.   [2] Ibid., p. 5 note.

In support of all this farrago of nonsense there is of course
no foundation of truth; Robison was a well-known savant
who lived sane and respected to the end of his days. On his
death Watt wrote of him: " He was a man of the clearest
head and the most science of anybody I have ever known."[1]
John Playfair, in a paper read before the Royal Society of
Edinburgh in 1815, whilst criticizing his *Proofs of a Conspiracy*
—though at the same time admitting he had himself never
had access to the documents Robison had consulted!—paid
the following tribute to his character and erudition:

> His range in science was most extensive; he was familiar with
> the whole circle of the accurate sciences. . . . Nothing can add
> to the esteem which they [i.e. "those who were personally
> acquainted with him"] felt for his talents and worth or to the
> respect in which they now hold his memory.[2]

Nevertheless, the lies circulated against both Robison and
Barruel were not without effect. Thirteen years later we find
another American, this time a Freemason, confessing "with
shame and grief and indignation" that he had been carried
away by "the flood of vituperation poured upon Barruel and
Robison during the past thirty years," that the title pages of
their works "were fearful to him," and that although "wishing
calmly and candidly to investigate the character of Freemasonry he refused for months to open their books." Yet
when in 1827 he read them for the first time he was astonished
to find that they showed "a manifest tendency towards Freemasonry." Both Barruel and Robison, he now realized, were
"learned men, candid men, lovers of their country, who had
a reverence for truth and religion. They give the reasons
for their opinions, they quote their authorities, naming the
author and page, like honest people; they both had a wish to
rescue British Masonry from the condemnation and fellowship of continental Masonry and appear to be sincerely actuated
by the desire of doing good by giving their labours to the
public."[3]

That the author was right here in his description of Barruel's

[1] Quoted in the Life of John Robison (1739–1805) by George Stronach in
the *Dictionary of National Biography*, Vol. XLIX. p. 58.

[2] *Transactions of the Royal Society of Edinburgh*, Vol. VII, pp. 538, 539
(1815).

[3] *Freemasonry, its Pretensions Exposed* . . . by a Master Mason, p. 275 (New
York. 1828).

attitude to Freemasonry is shown by Barruel's own words on the subject:

England above all is full of those upright men, excellent citizens, men of every kind and in every condition of life, who count it an honour to be masons, and who are distinguished from other men only by ties which seem to strengthen those of benevolence and fraternal charity. It is not the fear of offending a nation amongst which I have found a refuge which prompts me to make this exception. Gratitude would prevail with me over all such terrors and I should say in the midst of London: "England is lost, she will not escape the French Revolution if the masonic lodges resemble those I have to unveil. I would even say more: government and all Christianity would long ago have been lost in England if one could suppose its Freemasons to be initiated into the last mysteries of the sect."[1]

In another passage Barruel observes that Masonry in England is "a society composed of good citizens in general whose chief object is to help each other by principles of equality which for them is nothing else but universal fraternity."[2] And again: "Let us admire it [the wisdom of England] for having known how to make a real source of benefit to the State out of those same mysteries which elsewhere conceal a profound conspiracy against the State and religion."[3]

The only criticism British Freemasons may make on this verdict is that Barruel regards Masonry as a system which originally contained an element of danger that has been eliminated in England whilst they regard it as a system originally innocuous into which a dangerous element was inserted on the Continent. Thus according to the former conception Freemasonry might be compared to one of the brass shell-cases brought back from the battle-fields of France and converted into a flower-pot holder, whilst according to the latter it resembles an innocent brass flower-pot holder which has been used as a receptacle for explosives. The fact is that, as I shall endeavour to show in the course of this book, Freemasonry being a composite system there is some justification for both these theories. In either case it will be seen that Continental Masonry alone stands condemned.

The plan of representing Robison and Barruel as the enemies

[1] *Mémoires sur le Jacobinisme,* II. 195 (1818 edition).
[2] Barruel, op. cit., II. 208.
[3] Ibid., II. 311.

of British Masonry can therefore only be regarded as a method for discrediting them in the eyes of British Freemasons, and consequently for bringing the latter over to the side of their antagonists. Exactly the same method of attack has been directed against those of us who during the last few years have attempted to warn the world of the secret forces working to destroy civilization; in my own case even the plan of accusing me of having attacked British Masonry has been adopted without the shadow of a foundation. From the beginning I have always differentiated between British and Grand Orient Masonry, and have numbered high British Masons amongst my friends.

But what is the main charge brought against us? Like Robison and Barruel, we are accused of raising a false alarm, of creating a bogey, or of being the victims of an obsession. Up to a point this is comprehensible. Whilst on the Continent the importance of secret societies is taken as a matter of course and the libraries of foreign capitals teem with books on the question, people in this country really imagine that secret societies are things of the past—articles to this effect appeared quite recently in two leading London newspapers—whilst practically nothing of any value has been written about them in our language during the last hundred years. Hence ideas that are commonplaces on the Continent here appear sensational and extravagant. The mind of the Englishman does not readily accept anything he cannot see or even sometimes anything he can see which is unprecedented in his experience, so that like the West American farmer, confronted for the first time by the sight of a giraffe, his impulse is to cry out angrily: " I don't believe it! "

But whilst making all allowance for honest ignorance and incredulity, it is impossible not to recognize a certain method in the manner in which the cry of " obsession " or " bogey " is raised. For it will be noticed that people who specialize on other subjects are not described as " obsessed." We did not hear, for example, that the late Professor Einstein had Relativity " on the brain " because he wrote and lectured exclusively on this question, nor do we hear it suggested that Mr. Howard Carter is obsessed with the idea of Tutankhamen and that it would be well if he were to set out for the South Pole by way of a change. Again, all those who warn the world concerning eventualities they conceive to be a danger are not accused of creating bogeys. Thus although Lord Roberts was denounced as a scaremonger for urging the country to prepare for defence

against a design openly avowed by Germany both in speech
and print, and in 1921 the Duke of Northumberland was
declared the victim of a delusion for believing in the existence
of a plot against the British Empire which had been proclaimed
in a thousand revolutionary harangues and pamphlets. People
who, without bothering to produce a shred of documentary
evidence, had sounded the alarm on the menace of " French
Imperialism " and asserted that our former Allies were engaged
in building a vast fleet of aeroplanes in order to attack
our coasts. They were not held to be either scaremongers
or insane. On the contrary, although some of these same people
were proved by events to have been completely wrong in their
prognostications at the beginning of the Great War, they are
still regarded as oracles and sometimes even described as
" thinking for half Europe."

Another instance of this kind may be cited in the case of
Mr. John Spargo, author of a small book entitled *The Jew
and American Ideals.* On page 37 of this work Mr. Spargo
in refuting the accusations brought against the Jews observes:

Belief in widespread conspiracies directed against individuals or
the state is probably the commonest form assumed by the human
mind when it loses its balance and its sense of proportion.

Yet on page 6 Mr. Spargo declares that when visiting this
country in September and October 1920:

I found in England great nation-wide organizations, obviously
well financed, devoted to the sinister purpose of creating anti-
Jewish feeling and sentiment. I found special articles in influ-
ential newspapers devoted to the same evil purpose. I found at
at least one journal, obviously well financed again, exclusively devoted
to the fostering of suspicion, fear, and hatred against the
Jew . . . and in the bookstores I discovered a whole library of books
devoted to the same end.

It will be seen then that a belief in widespread conspiracies
is not always to be regarded as a sign of loss of mental balance,
even when these conspiracies remain completely invisible
to the general public. For those of us who were in London
during the period of Mr. Spargo's visit saw nothing of the
things he here describes. Where, we ask, were these " great
nation-wide organizations " striving to create anti-Jewish
sentiments? What were their names? By whom were they
led? It is true, however, that there were nation-wide organi-

zations in existence here at this date instituted for the purpose
of combating Bolshevism. Is anti-Bolshevism then synonymous with "anti-Semitism"?[1] This is the conclusion to
which one is inevitably led. For it will be noticed that anyone
who attempts to expose the secret forces behind the revolutionary movement, whether he mentions Jews in this connexion or
even if he goes out of his way to exonerate them, will incur
the hostility of the Jews and their friends and will still be
described as "anti-Semite." The realization of this fact has
led me particularly to include the Jews in the study of secret
societies.

The object of the present book is therefore to carry further
the enquiry I began in *World Revolution*, by tracing the course
of revolutionary ideas through secret societies from the earliest
times, indicating the rôle of the Jews only where it is to be
clearly detected, but not seeking to implicate them where
good evidence is not forthcoming. For this reason I shall
not base assertions on merely "anti-Semite" works, but
principally on the writings of the Jews themselves. In the
same way with regard to secret societies I shall rely as far as
possible on the documents and admissions of their members,
on which point I have been able to collect a great deal of
fresh data entirely corroborating my former thesis. It should
be understood that I do not propose to give a complete history
of secret societies, but only of secret societies in their relation
to the revolutionary movement. I shall therefore not attempt
to describe the theories of occultism nor to enquire into the
secrets of Freemasonry, but simply to relate the history of these
systems in order to show the manner in which they have been
utilized for a subversive purpose. If I then fail to convince
the incredulous that secret forces of revolution exist, it will not
be for want of evidence.

NESTA H. WEBSTER.

[1] I use the word "anti-Semitism" here in the sense in which it has come
to be used—that is to say, anti-Jewry, but place it in inverted commas
because it is in reality a misnomer coined by the Jews in order to create a
false impression. The word anti-Semite literally signifies a person who
adopts a hostile attitude towards all the descendants of Shem—the Arabs,
and the entire twelve tribes of Israel. To apply the term to a person who
is merely antagonistic to that fraction of the Semitic race known as the
Jews is therefore absurd, and leads to the ridiculous situation that one may
be described as "anti-Semitic and pro-Arabian." This expression actually
occurred in *The New Palestine* (New York), March 23, 1923. One might
as well speak of being "anti-British and pro-English."

CONTENTS

PART I   *THE PAST*

1

THE ANCIENT SECRET TRADITION

THE East is the cradle of secret societies. For whatever end they may have been employed, the inspiration and methods of most of those mysterious associations which have played so important a part behind the scenes of the world's history will be found to have emanated from the lands where the first recorded acts of the great human drama were played out—Egypt, Babylon, Syria, and Persia. On the one hand Eastern mysticism, on the other Oriental love of intrigue, framed the systems later on to be transported to the West with results so tremendous and far-reaching.

In the study of secret societies we have then a double line to follow—the course of associations enveloping themselves in secrecy for the pursuit of esoteric knowledge, and those using mystery and secrecy for an ulterior and, usually, a political purpose.

But esotericism again presents a dual aspect. Here, as in every phase of earthly life, there is the *revers de la médaille*—white and black, light and darkness, the Heaven and Hell of the human mind. The quest for hidden knowledge may end with initiation into divine truths or into dark and abominable cults. Who knows with what forces he may be brought in contact beyond the veil? Initiation which leads to making use of spiritual forces, whether good or evil, is therefore capable of raising man to greater heights or of degrading him to lower depths than he could ever have reached by remaining on the purely physical plane. And when men thus unite themselves in associations, a collective force is generated which may exercise immense influence over the world around. Hence the importance of secret societies.

Let it be said once and for all, secret societies have not always been formed for evil purposes. On the contrary, many have arisen from the highest aspirations of the human mind—the desire for a knowledge of eternal verities. The

3

evil arising from such systems has usually consisted in the perversion of principles that once were pure and holy. If I do not insist further on this point, it is because a vast literature has already been devoted to the subject, so that it need only be touched on briefly here.

Now, from the earliest times groups of Initiates or "Wise Men" have existed, claiming to be in possession of esoteric doctrines known as the "Mysteries," incapable of apprehension by the vulgar, and relating to the origin and end of man, the life of the soul after death, and the nature of God or the gods. It is this exclusive attitude which constitutes the essential difference between the Initiates of the ancient world and the great Teachers of religion with whom modern occultists seek to confound them. For whilst religious leaders such as Buddha and Mohammed sought for divine knowledge in order that they might impart it to the world, the Initiates believed that sacred mysteries should not be revealed to the profane but should remain exclusively in their own keeping. So although the desire for initiation might spring from the highest aspiration, the gratification, whether real or imaginary, of this desire often led to spiritual arrogance and abominable tyranny, resulting in the fearful trials, the tortures physical and mental, ending even at times in death, to which the neophyte was subjected by his superiors.

THE MYSTERIES

According to a theory current in occult and masonic circles, certain ideas were common to all the more important "Mysteries," thus forming a continuous tradition handed down through succeeding groups of Initiates of different ages and countries. Amongst these ideas is said to have been the conception of the unity of God. Whilst to the multitude it was deemed advisable to preach polytheism, since only in this manner could the plural aspects of the Divine be apprehended by the multitude, the Initiates themselves believed in the existence of one Supreme Being, the Creator of the Universe, pervading and governing all things. Le Plongeon, whose object is to show an affinity between the sacred Mysteries of the Mayas and of the Egyptians, Chaldeans, and Greeks, asserts that "The idea of a sole and omnipotent Deity, who created all things, seems to have been the universal belief in early ages, amongst all the nations that had reached a high degree of civilization. This was the doctrine of the

Egyptian priests."[1]   The same writer goes on to say that the
" doctrine of a Supreme Deity composed of three parts distinct
from each other, yet forming one, was universally prevalent
among the civilized nations of America, Asia, and the
Egyptians," and that the priests and learned men of Egypt,
Chaldea, India, or China " . . . kept it a profound secret and
imparted it only to a few select among those initiated in the
sacred mysteries."[2]   This view has been expressed by many
other writers, yet lacks historical proof.

That monotheism existed in Egypt before the days of Moses
is, however, certain. Adolf Erman asserts that " even in early
times the educated class " believed all the deities of the
Egyptian religion to be identical and that " the priests did not
shut their eyes to this doctrine, but strove to grasp the idea
of the one God, divided into different persons by poesy and
myth. . . . The priesthood, however, had not the courage to take
the final step, to do away with those distinctions which they
declared to be immaterial, and to adore the one God under the
one name."[3]   It was left to Amenhotep IV, later known as
Ikhnaton, to proclaim this doctrine openly to the people.
Professor Breasted has described the hymns of praise to the
Sun God which Ikhnaton himself wrote on the walls of the
Amarna tomb-chapels:

They show us the simplicity and beauty of the young king's
faith in the sole God. He had gained the belief that one God
created not only all the lower creatures but also all races of men,
both Egyptians and foreigners. Moreover, the king saw in his
God a kindly Father, who maintained all his creatures by his
goodness. . . . In all the progress of men which we have followed
through thousands of years, no one had ever before caught such
a vision of the great Father of all.[4]

May not the reason why Ikhnaton was later described as a
" heretic " be that he violated the code of the priestly hierarchy
by revealing this secret doctrine to the profane? Hence, too,
perhaps the necessity in which the King found himself of
suppressing the priesthood, which by persisting in its exclusive
attitude kept what he perceived to be the truth from the minds
of the people.

The earliest European centre of the Mysteries appears to
have been Greece, where the Eleusinian Mysteries existed at

[1] Augustus le Plongeon, Sacred Mysteries among the Mayas and the Quiches,
p. 53 (1909).
[2] Ibid., pp. 56, 58.
[3] Adolf Erman, Life in Ancient Egypt, p. 45 (1894).
[4] J. H. Breasted, Ancient Times: a History of the Early World, p. 92 (1916).

a very early date. Pythagoras, who was born in Samos about 582 B.C., spent some years in Egypt, where he was initiated into the Mysteries of Isis. After his return to Greece, Pythagoras is said to have been initiated into the Eleusinian Mysteries and attempted to found a secret society in Samos; but this proving unsuccessful, he journeyed on to Crotona in Italy, where he collected around him a great number of disciples and finally established his sect. This was divided into two classes of Initiates—the first admitted only into the exoteric doctrines of the master, with whom they were not allowed to speak until after a period of five years' probation; the second consisting of the real Initiates, to whom all the mysteries of the esoteric doctrines of Pythagoras were unfolded. This course of instruction, given, after the manner of the Egyptians, by means of images and symbols, began with geometrical science, in which Pythagoras during his stay in Egypt had become an adept, and led up finally to abstruse speculations concerning the transmigration of the soul and the nature of God, who was represented under the conception of a Universal Mind diffused through all things. It is, however, as the precursor of secret societies formed later in the West of Europe that the sect of Pythagoras enters into the scope of this book. Early masonic tradition traces Free-masonry partly to Pythagoras, who is said to have travelled in England, and there is certainly some reason to believe that his geometrical ideas entered into the system of the operative guilds of masons.

The Jewish Cabala[1]

According to Fabre d'Olivet, Moses, who "was learned in all the wisdom of the Egyptians," drew from the Egyptian Mysteries a part of the oral tradition which was handed down through the leaders of the Israelites.[2] That such an oral tradition, distinct from the written word embodied in the Pentateuch, did descend from Moses and that it was later committed to writing in the Talmud and the Cabala is the opinion of many Jewish writers.[3]

This word is spelt variously by different writers thus: Cabala, Cabbala, Kabbala, Kabbalah, Kabalah. I adopt the first spelling as being the one employed in the *Jewish Encyclopœdia*.

[2] Fabre d'Olivet, *La Langue Hébraïque*, p. 28 (1815).

[3] " According to the Jewish view God had given Moses on Mount Sinai alike the oral and the written Law, that is, the Law with all its interpretations and applications."—Alfred Edersheim, *The Life and Times of Jesus the Messiah*, I. 99 (1883), quoting other Jewish authorities.

The first form of the Talmud, called the Mischna, appeared in about the second or third century A.D.; a little later a commentary was added under the name of the Gemara. These two works compose the Jerusalem Talmud, which was revised in the third to the fifth centry. This later edition was named the Babylonian Talmud and is the one now in use.

The Talmud relates mainly to the affairs of everyday life—the laws of buying and selling, of making contracts—also to external religious observances, on all of which the most meticulous details are given. As a Jewish writer has expressed it:

. . . the oddest rabbinical conceits are elaborated through many volumes with the finest dialectic, and the most absurd questions are discussed with the highest efforts of intellectual power; for example, how many white hairs may a red cow have, and yet remain a *red* cow; what sort of scabs require this or that purification; whether a louse or a flea may be killed on the Sabbath—the first being allowed, while the second is a deadly sin; whether the slaughter of an animal ought to be executed at the neck or the tail; whether the high priest put on his shirt or his hose first; whether the *Jabam,* that is, the brother of a man who died childless, being required by law to marry the widow, is relieved from his obligation if he falls off a roof and sticks in the mire.[1]

But it is in the Cabala, a Hebrew word signifying " reception," that is to say " a doctrine orally received," that the speculative and philosophical or rather the theosophical doctrines of Israel are to be found. These are contained in two books, the *Sepher Yetzirah* and the *Zohar.*

The *Sepher Yetzirah,* or Book of the Creation, is described by Edersheim as " a monologue on the part of Abraham, in which, by the contemplation of all that is around him, he ultimately arrives at the conclusion of the unity of God "[2]; but since this process is accomplished by an arrangement of the Divine Emanations under the name of the Ten Sephiroths, and in the permutation of numerals and of the letters of the Hebrew alphabet, it would certainly convey no such idea—nor probably indeed any idea at all—to the mind uninitiated into Cabalistic systems. The Sepher Yetzirah is in fact admittedly a work of extraordinary obscurity[3] and almost certainly of extreme antiquity. Monsieur Paul Vulliaud, in

[1] *Solomon Maimon: an Autobiography,* translated from the German by J. Clark Murray, p. 28 (1888). The original appeared in 1792.
[2] Alfred Edersheim, *The Life and Times of Jesus the Messiah,* II. 689 (1883).
[3] " There exists in Jewish literature no book more difficult to understand than the Sepher Yetzirah."—Phineas Mordell in the *Jewish Quarterly Review,* New Series, Vol. II. p. 557.

his exhaustive work on the Cabala recently published,[1] says
that its date has been placed as early as the sixth century
before Christ and as late as the tenth century A.D., but that
it is at any rate older than the Talmud is shown by the fact
that in the Talmud the Rabbis are described as studying it
for magical purposes.[2] The Sepher Yetzirah is also said to
be the work referred to in the Koran under the name of the
" Book of Abraham."[3]

The immense compilation known as the *Sepher-Ha-Zohar*,
or Book of Light, is, however, of greater importance to the
study of Cabalistic philosophy. According to the Zohar itself,
the " Mysteries of Wisdom " were imparted to Adam by God
whilst he was still in the Garden of Eden, in the form of a
book delivered by the angel Razael. From Adam the book
passed on to Seth, then to Enoch, to Noah, to Abraham, and
later to Moses, one of its principal exponents.[4] Other Jewish
writers declare, however, that Moses received it for the first
time on Mount Sinai and communicated it to the Seventy
Elders, by whom it was handed down to David and Solomon,
then to Ezra and Nehemiah, and finally to the Rabbis of the
early Christian era.[5]

Until this date the Zohar had remained a purely oral
tradition, but now for the first time it is said to have been
written down by the disciples of Simon ben Jochai. The.
Talmud relates that for twelve years the Rabbi Simon and his
son Eliezer concealed themselves in a cavern, where, sitting
in the sand up to their necks, they meditated on the sacred
law and were frequently visited by the prophet Elias.[6] In
this way, Jewish legend adds, the great book of the Zohar was
composed and committed to writing by the Rabbi's son Eliezer
and his secretary the Rabbi Abba.[7]

[1] Paul Vulliaud, *La Kabbale Juive: histoire et doctrine*, 2 vols. (Émile
Nourry, 62 Rue des Écoles, Paris, 1923). This book, neither the work of a
Jew nor of an " anti-Semite," but of a perfectly impartial student, is invaluable for a study of the Cabala rather as a vast compendium of opinions than
as an expression of original thought.

[2] " Rab Hanina and Rab Oschaya were seated on the eve of every Sabbath
studying the Sepher Ietsirah; they created a three-year-old heifer and ate
it."—Talmud treatise Sanhedrim, folio 65.

[3] Koran, Sura LXXXVII. 10.

[4] Zohar, section Bereschith, folio 55, and section Lekh-Lekha, folio 76
(De Pauly's translation, Vol. I. pp. 431, 446).

[5] Adolphe Franck, *La Kabbale,* p. 39; J. P. Stehelin, *The Traditions of
the Jews*, I. 145 (1748).

[6] Adolphe Franck, op. cit., p. 68, quoting Talmud treatise Sabbath,
folio 34; Dr. Christian Ginsburg, *The Kabbalah*, p. 85; Drach, *De l'Harmonie entre l'Église et la Synagogue*, I. 457.

[7] Adolphe Franck, op. cit., p. 69.

The first date at which the Zohar is definitely known to have appeared is the end of the thirteenth century, when it was committed to writing by a Spanish Jew, Moses de Leon, who, according to Dr. Ginsburg, said he had discovered and repro- duced the original document of Simon ben Jochai; his wife and daughter, however, declared that he had composed it all himself.[1] Which is the truth? Jewish opinion is strongly divided on this question, one body maintaining that the Zohar is the comparatively modern work of Moses de Leon, the other declaring it to be of extreme antiquity. M. Vulliaud, who has collated all these views in the course of some fifty pages, shows that although the name Zohar might have originated with Moses de Leon, the ideas it embodied were far older than the thirteenth century. How, he asks perti- nently, would it have been possible for the Rabbis of the Middle Ages to have been deceived into accepting as an ancient document a work that was of completely modern origin?[2] Obviously the Zohar was not the composition of Moses de Leon, but a compilation made by him from various documents dating from very early times. Moreover, as M. Vulliaud goes on to explain, those who deny its antiquity are the anti-Cabalists, headed by Graetz, whose object is to prove the Cabala to be at variance with orthodox Judaism. Theodore Reinach goes so far as to declare the Cabala to be " a subtle poison which enters into the veins of Judaism and wholly infests it "; Salomon Reinach calls it " one of the worst aberrations of the human mind."[3] This view, many a student of the Cabala will hardly dispute, but to say that it is foreign to Judaism is another matter. The fact is that the main ideas of the Zohar find confirmation in the Talmud. As the *Jewish Encyclopædia* observes, " the Cabala is not really in opposition to the Talmud," and " many Talmudic Jews have supported and contributed to it."[4] Adolphe Franck does not hesitate to describe it as " the heart and life of Judaism."[5] " The greater number of the most eminent Rabbis of the seventeenth and eighteenth centuries believed firmly in the sacredness of the Zohar and the infallibility of its teaching."[6]

[1] Dr. Christian Ginsburg (1920), *The Kabbalah*, pp. 172, 173.
[2] Vulliaud, op. cit., I. 253.
[3] Ibid., p. 20, quoting Theodore Reinach, *Historie des Israelites*, p. 221, and Salomon Reinach, *Orpheus*, p. 299.
[4] *Jewish Encyclopædia*, article on Cabala.
[5] Adolphe Franck, op. cit., p. 288.
[6] Vulliaud, op. cit., I. 256, quoting Greenstone, *The Messiah Idea*, p. 229.

The question of the antiquity of the Cabala is therefore in reality largely a matter of names. That a mystical tradition existed amongst the Jews from remote antiquity will hardly be denied by anyone[1]; it is therefore, as M. Vulliaud observes, " only a matter of knowing at what moment Jewish mysticism took the name of Cabala."[2] Edersheim asserts that—

It is undeniable that, already at the time of Jesus Christ, there existed an assemblage of doctrines and speculations that were carefully concealed from the multitude. They were not even revealed to ordinary scholars, for fear of leading them towards heretical ideas. This kind bore the name of Kabbalah, and as the term (of Kabbalah, to receive, transmit) indicates, it represented the spiritual traditions transmitted from the earliest ages, although mingled in the course of time with ʲmpure or foreign elements.[3]

Is the Cabala, then, as Gougenot des Mousseaux asserts, older than the Jewish race, a legacy handed down from the first patriarchs of the world?[4] We must admit this hypothesis to be incapable of proof, yet it is one that has found so much favour with students of occult traditions that it cannot be ignored. The Jewish Cabala itself supports it by tracing its descent from the patriarchs—Adam, Noah, Enoch, and Abraham—who lived before the Jews as a separate race came into existence. Eliphas Lévi accepts this genealogy, and relates that " the Holy Cabala " was the tradition of the children of Seth carried out of Chaldea by Abraham, who

---

[1] H. Loewe, in an article on the Kabbala in Hastings' *Encyclopædia of Religion and Ethics*, says: " This secret mysticism was no late growth. Difficult though it is to prove the date and origin of this system of philosophy and the influences and causes which produced it, we can be fairly certain that its roots stretch back very far and that the mediæval and Geonic Kabbala was the culmination and not the inception of Jewish esoteric mysticism. From the time of Graetz it has been the fashion to decry the Kabbala and to regard it as a later incrustation, as something of which Judaism had reason to be ashamed." The writer goes on to express the opinion that " the recent tendency requires adjustment. The Kabbala, though later in form than is claimed by its adherents, is far older in material than is allowed by its detractors."

[2] Vulliaud, op. cit., I. 22.

[3] Ibid., I. 13, 14, quoting Edersheim, *La Société Juive au temps de Jésus-Christ* (French translation), pp. 363–4.

[4] See chapters on this question by Gougenot des Mousseaux in *Le Juif, le Judaïsme et la Judaïsation des Peuples Chrétiens*, pp. 499 and following (2nd edition, 1886). The first edition of this book, published in 1869, is said to have been bought up and destroyed by the Jews, and the author died a sudden death before the second edition could be published.

was "the inheritor of the secrets of Enoch and the father of initiation in Israel."[1]

According to this theory, which we find again propounded by the American Freemason, Dr. Mackey,[2] there was, besides the divine Cabala of the children of Seth, the magical Cabala of the children of Cain, which descended to the Sabeists, or star-worshippers, of Chaldea, adepts in astrology and necromancy. Sorcery, as we know, had been practised by the Canaanites before the occupation of Palestine by the Israelites; Egypt, India, and Greece also had their soothsayers and diviners. In spite of the imprecations against sorcery contained in the law of Moses, the Jews, disregarding these warnings, caught the contagion and mingled the sacred tradition they had inherited with magical ideas partly borrowed from other races and partly of their own devising. At the same time the speculative side of the Jewish Cabala borrowed from the philosophy of the Persian Magi, of the Neo-Platonists,[3] and of the Neo-Pythagoreans. There is, then, some justification for the anti-Cabalists' contention that what we know to-day as the Cabala is not of purely Jewish origin.

Gougenot des Mousseaux, who had made a profound study of occultism, asserts that there were therefore two Cabalas: the ancient sacred tradition handed down from the first patriarchs of the human race; and the evil Cabala, wherein this sacred tradition was mingled by the Rabbis with barbaric superstitions, combined with their own imaginings and henceforth marked with their seal.[4] This view also finds expression in the remarkable work of the converted Jew Drach, who refers to—

The ancient and true Cabala, which . . . we distinguish from the modern Cabala, false, condemnable, and condemned by the Holy See, the work of the Rabbis, who have also falsified and perverted the Talmudic tradition. The doctors of the Synagogue trace it back to Moses, whilst at the same time admitting that the principal truths it contains were those known by revelation to the first patriarchs of the world.[5]

[1] Eliphas Lévi, *Histoire de la Magie*, pp. 46, 105. (Eliphas Lévi was the pseudonym of the celebrated nineteenth-century occultist the Abbé Constant.)
[2] *Lexicon of Freemasonry*, p. 323.
[3] Ginsburg, op. cit., p. 105; *Jewish Encyclopædia*, article on Cabala.
[4] Gougenot des Mousseaux, *Le Juif, le Judaïsme et la Judaïsation des Peuples Chrétiens*, p. 503 (1886).
[5] P. L. B. Drach, *De l'Harmonie entre l'Église et la Synagogue*, Vol. I. p. xiii (1844). M. Vulliaud (op. cit., II. 245) points out that, as far as he can discover, Drach's work has never met with any refutation from the Jews, by whom it was received in complete silence. The *Jewish Encyclopædia*

Further on Drach quotes the statement of Sixtus of Sienna, another converted Jew and a Dominican, protected by Pius V:

> Since by the decree of the Holy Roman Inquisition all books appertaining to the Cabala have lately been condemned, one must know that the Cabala is double; that one is true, the other false. The true and pious one is that which . . . elucidates the secret mysteries of the holy law according to the principle of anagogy (i.e. figurative interpretation). This Cabala therefore the Church has never condemned. The false and impious Cabala is a certain mendacious kind of Jewish tradition, full of innumerable vanities and falsehoods, differing but little from necromancy. This kind of superstition, therefore, improperly called Cabala, the Church within the last few years has deservedly condemned.[1]

The modern Jewish Cabala presents a dual aspect—theoretical and practical; the former concerned with theosophical speculations, the latter with magical practices. It would be impossible here to give an idea of Cabalistic theosophy with its extraordinary imaginings on the Sephiroths, the attributes and functions of good and bad angels, dissertations on the nature of demons, and minute details on the appearance of God under the name of the Ancient of Ancients, from whose head 400,000 worlds receive the light. "The length of this face from the top of the head is three hundred and seventy times ten thousand worlds. It is called the 'Long Face,' for such is the name of the Ancient of Ancients."[2] The description of the hair and beard alone belonging to this gigantic countenance occupies a large place in the Zoharic treatise, Idra Raba.[3]

According to the Cabala, every letter in the Scriptures contains a mystery only to be solved by the initiated.[4] By means of this system of interpretation passages of the Old Testament are shown to bear meanings totally unapparent to the ordinary reader. Thus the Zohar explains that Noah was lamed for life by the bite of a lion whilst he was in the ark,[5] the adventures of Jonah inside the whale are related with an extraordinary wealth of imagination,[6] whilst the

has an article on Drach in which it says he was brought up in a Talmudic school and afterwards became converted to Christianity, but makes no attempt to challenge his statements.

[1] Drach, op. cit., Vol. II. p. xix.
[2] Franck, op. cit., p. 127.
[3] De Pauly's translation, Vol. V. pp. 336–8, 343–6.
[4] Zohar, treatise Beschalah, folio 59b (De Pauly, III. 265).
[5] Zohar, Toldoth Noah, folio 69a (De Pauly, I. 408).
[6] Zohar, treatise Beschalah, folio 48a (De Pauly, III. 219).

beautiful story of Elisha and the Shunnamite woman is travestied in the most grotesque manner.[1]

In the practical Cabala this method of " decoding " is reduced to a theurgic or magical system in which the healing of diseases plays an important part and is effected by means of the mystical arrangement of numbers and letters, by the pronunciation of the Ineffable Name, by the use of amulets and talismans, or by compounds supposed to contain certain occult properties.

All these ideas derived from very ancient cults; even the art of working miracles by the use of the Divine Name, which after the appropriation of the Cabala by the Jews became the particular practice of Jewish miracle-workers, appears to have originated in Chaldea.[2] Nor can the insistence on the Chosen People theory, which forms the basis of all Talmudic and Cabalistic writings, be regarded as of purely Jewish origin; the ancient Egyptians likewise believed themselves to be " the peculiar people specially loved by the gods."[3] But in the hands of the Jews this belief became a pretension to the exclusive enjoyment of divine favour. According to the Zohar, "all Israelites will have a part in the future world,"[4] and on arrival there will not be handed over like the *goyim* (or non-Jewish races) to the hands of the angel Douma and sent down to Hell.[5] Indeed the *goyim* are even denied human attributes. Thus the Zohar again explains that the words of the Scripture " Jehovah Elohim made man " mean that He made Israel.[6] The seventeenth-century Rabbinical treatise Emek ha Melek observes: " Our Rabbis of blessed memory have said: ' Ye Jews are men because of the soul ye have from the Supreme Man (i.e. God). But the nations of the world are not styled men because they have not, from the Holy and Supreme Man, the Neschama (or glorious soul), but they have the Nephesch (soul) from Adam Belial, that is the malicious and unnecessary man, called Sammael, the Supreme Devil.' "[7]

In conformity with this exclusive attitude towards the rest of the human race, the Messianic idea which forms the dominat-

---

[1] Ibid., folio 44a (De Pauly, III. 200).
[2] *Jewish Encyclopædia*, article on Cabala.
[3] Adolf Erman, *Life in Ancient Egypt*, p. 32.
[4] Zohar, treatise Toldoth Noah, folio 59b (De Pauly, I, 347).
[5] Zohar, treatise Lekh-Lekha, folio 94a (De Pauly, I. 535).
[6] Zohar, treatise Bereschith, folio 26a (De Pauly, I. 161).
[7] The *Emek ha Melek* is the work of the Cabalist Napthali, a disciple of Luria.

ing theme of the Cabala is made to serve purely Jewish intere᷄ ᷄.
Yet in its origins this idea was possibly not Jewish. It is ᷄aid
by believers in an ancient secret tradition common to other
races besides the Jews, that a part of this tradition related to
a past Golden Age when man was free from care and evil non-
existent, to the subsequent fall of Man and the loss of this
primitive felicity, and finally to a revelation received from
Heaven foretelling the reparation of this loss and the coming
of a Redeemer who should save the world and restore the
Golden Age. According to Drach:

> The tradition of a Man-God who should present Himself as the
> teacher and liberator of the fallen human race was constantly
> taught amongst all the enlightened nations of the globe. *Vetus et
> constans opinio,* as Suetonius says. It is of all times and of all
> places.[1]

And Drach goes on to quote the evidence of Volney, who
had travelled in the East and declared that—

> The sacred and mythological traditions of earlier times had spread
> throughout all Asia the belief in a great Mediator who was to
> come, of a future Saviour, King, God, Conqueror, and Legislator
> who would bring back the Golden Age to earth and deliver men
> from the empire of evil.[2]

All that can be said with any degree of certainty with regard
to this belief is that it did exist amongst the Zoroastrians of
Persia as well as amongst the Jews. D'Herbelot, quoting
Abulfaraj, shows that five hundred years before Christ,
Zerdascht, the leader of the Zoroastrians, predicted the coming
of the Messiah, at whose birth a star would appear. He also
told his disciples that the Messiah would be born of a virgin,
that they would be the first to hear of Him, and that they
should bring Him gifts.[3]

Drach believes that this tradition was taught in the ancient
synagogue,[4] thus explaining the words of St. Paul that unto
the Jews " were committed the oracles of God "[5]:

This oral doctrine, which is the Cabala, had for its object the
most sublime truths of the Faith which it brought back incessantly

---

[1] Drach, *De l'Harmonie entre l'Église et la Synagogue,* I. 272.
[2] Ibid., p. 273.
[3] D'Herbelot, *Bibliothèque Orientale* (1778), article on Zerdascht.
[4] Ibid., I. 18.
[5] Rom. iiⁱ. 2.

to the promised Redeemer, the foundation of the whole system of the ancient tradition.[1]

Drach further asserts that the doctrine of the Trinity formed a part of this tradition:

Whoever has familiarized himself with that which was taught by the ancient doctors of the Synagogue, particularly those who lived before the coming of the Saviour, knows that the Trinity in one God was a truth admitted amongst them from the earliest times.[2]

M. Vulliaud points out that Graetz admits the existence of this idea in the Zohar: " It even taught certain doctrines which appeared favourable to the Christian dogma of the Trinity!" And again: " It is incontestable that the Zohar makes allusions to the beliefs in the Trinity and the Incarnation."[3] M. Vulliaud adds: " The idea of the Trinity must therefore play an important part in the Cabala, since it has been possible to affirm that ' the characteristic of the Zohar and its particular conception is its attachment to the principle of the Trinity,' "[4] and further quotes Edersheim as saying that " a great part of the explanation given in the writings of the Cabalists resembles in a surprising manner the highest truths of Christianity."[5] It would appear, then, that certain remnants of the ancient secret tradition lingered on in the Cabala. The *Jewish Encyclopædia*, perhaps unintentionally, endorses this opinion, since in deriding the sixteenth-century Christian Cabalists for asserting that the Cabala contained traces of Christianity, it goes on to say that what appears to be Christian in the Cabala is only ancient esoteric doctrine.[6] Here, then, we have it on the authority of modern Jewish scholars that the ancient secret tradition was in harmony with Christian teaching. But in the teaching of the later synagogue the philosophy of the earlier sages was narrowed down to suit the exclusive system of the Jewish hierarchy, and the ancient hope of a Redeemer who should restore Man

[1] Drach, *De l'Harmonie entre l'Église et la Synagogue*, II. 19.
[2] Ibid., I. 280.
[3] Vulliaud, op. cit., II. 255, 256.
[4] Ibid., p. 257, quoting Karppe, *Études sur les Origines du Zohar*, p. 494.
[5] Ibid., I. 13, 14. In Vol. II. p. 411, M. Vulliaud quotes Isaac Meyer's assertion that " the triad of the ancient Cabala is Kether, the Father; Binah, the Holy Spirit or the Mother; and Hochmah, the Word or the Son." But in order to avoid the sequence of the Christian Trinity this arrangement has been altered in the modern Cabala of Luria and Moses of Cordovero, etc.
Jewish Encyclopædia, article on Cabala, p. 478.

to the state of felicity he had lost at the Fall was transformed into the idea of salvation for the Jews alone[1] under the ægis of a triumphant and even an avenging Messiah.[2] It is this Messianic dream perpetuated in the modern Cabala which nineteen hundred years ago the advent of Christ on earth came to disturb.

THE COMING OF THE REDEEMER

The fact that many Christian doctrines, such as the conception of a Trinity, the miraculous birth and murder of a Deity, had found a place in earlier religions has frequently been used as an argument to show that the story of Christ was merely a new version of various ancient legends, those of Attis, Adonis, or of Osiris, and that consequently the Christian religion is founded on a myth. The answer to this is that the existence of Christ on earth is an historic fact which no serious authority has ever denied. The attempts of such writers as Drews and J. M. Robertson to establish the theory of the " Christ-Myth," which find an echo in the utterances of Socialist orators,[3] have been met with so much able criticism as to need no further refutation. Sir James Frazer, who will certainly not be accused of bigoted orthodoxy, observes in this connexion:

The doubts which have been cast on the historical reality of Jesus are, in my judgement, unworthy of serious attention. . . . To dissolve the founder of Christianity into a myth, as some would do, is hardly less absurd than it would be to do the same for Mohammed, Luther, and Calvin.[4]

[1] ". . . All that Israel hoped for, was national restoration and glory. Everything else was but means to these ends; the Messiah Himself only the grand instrument in attaining them. Thus viewed, the picture presented would be of Israel's exaltation, rather than of the salvation of the world. . . . The Rabbinic ideal of the Messiah was not that of ' a light to lighten the Gentiles, and the glory of His people Israel '—the satisfaction of the wants of humanity, and the completion of Israel's mission—but quite different, even to contrariety."—Edersheim, The Life and Times of Jesus the Messiah, I. 164 (1883).

[2] Zohar, section Schemoth, folio 8; cf. ibid., folio 9b: " The period when the King Messiah will declare war on the whole world " (De Pauly, III. 32, 36).

[3] A blasphemous address entitled The God Man, given by Tom Anderson, the founder of the Socialist Sunday Schools, on Glasgow Green to an audience of over 1,000 workers in 1922 and printed in pamphlet form, was founded entirely on this theory.

[4] J. G. Frazer, The Golden Bough, Part VI. " The Scapegoat," p. 412 (1914 edition); E. R. Bevan endorses this view.

May not the fact that certain circumstances in the life of Christ were foreshadowed by earlier religions indicate, as Eliphas Lévi observes, that the ancients had an intuition of Christian mysteries?[1]

To those therefore who had adhered to the ancient tradition, Christ appeared as the fulfilment of a prophecy as old as the world. Thus the wise men came from afar to worship the Babe of Bethlehem, and when they saw His star in the East they rejoiced with exceeding great joy. In Christ they hailed not only Him who was born King of the Jews, but the Saviour of the whole human race.[2]

In the light of this great hope, that wondrous night in Bethlehem is seen in all its sublimity. Throughout the ages the seers had looked for the coming of the Redeemer, and lo! He was here; but it was not to the mighty in Israel, to the High Priests and the Scribes, that His birth was announced, but to humble shepherds watching their flocks by night. And these men of simple faith, hearing from the angels " the good tidings of great joy " that a Saviour, " Christ the Lord " was born, went with haste to see the babe lying in the manger, and returned " glorifying and praising God." So also to the devout in Israel, to Simeon and to Anna the prophetess, the great event appeared in its universal significance, and Simeon, departing in peace, knew that his eyes had seen the salvation that was to be " a light to lighten the Gentiles " as well as the glory of the people of Israel.

But to the Jews, in whose hands the ancient tradition had been turned to the exclusive advantage of the Jewish race, to the Rabbis, who had, moreover, constituted themselves the sole guardians within this nation of the said tradition, the manner of its fulfilment was necessarily abhorrent. Instead of a resplendent Messiah who should be presented by them to the people, a Saviour was born amongst the people themselves and brought to Jerusalem to be presented to the Lord; a Saviour moreover who, as time went on, imparted His divine message to the poor and humble and declared that His Kingdom was not of this world. This was clearly what Mary meant when she said that God had " scattered the proud in the imagination of their hearts," that He had " put down the mighty from their seats, and exalted them of low degree." Christ was therefore doubly hateful to the Jewish

[1] *Histoire de la Magie*, p. 69.
[2] The Magi or Wise Men are generally believed to have come from Persia this would accord with the Zoroastrian prophecy quoted above.

hierarchy in that He attacked the privilege of the race to which they belonged by throwing open the door to all mankind, and the privilege of the caste to which they belonged by revealing sacred doctrines to the profane and destroying their claim to exclusive knowledge.

Unless viewed from this aspect, neither the antagonism displayed by the Scribes and Pharisees towards our Lord nor the denunciations He uttered against them can be properly understood. " Woe unto you, Lawyers! for ye have taken away the key of knowledge: ye entered not in yourselves, and them that were entering in ye hindered. . . . Woe unto you, Scribes and Pharisees, hypocrites! for ye shut up the kingdom of heaven against men: for ye neither go in your- selves, neither suffer ye them that are entering to go in." What did Christ mean by the key of knowledge? Clearly the sacred tradition which, as Drach explains, foreshadowed the doctrines of Christianity.[1] It was the Rabbis who per- verted that tradition, and thus " the guilt of these perfidious Doctors consisted in their concealing from the people the traditional explanation of the sacred books by means of which they would have been able to recognize the Messiah in the person of Jesus Christ."[2] Many of the people, however, did recognize Him; indeed, the multitude acclaimed Him, spreading their garments before Him and crying, "Hosanna to the Son of David! Blessed is He that cometh in the name of the Lord!" Writers who have cited the choice of Barabbas in the place of Christ as an instance of misguided popular judgement, overlook the fact that this choice was not spon- taneous; it was the Chief Priests who delivered Christ " from envy " and who " moved the people that Pilate should rather release unto them Barabbas." *Then* the people obediently cried out, " Crucify Him!"

So also it was the Rabbis who, after hiding from the people the meaning of the sacred tradition at the moment of its fulfil- ment, afterwards poisoned that same stream for future genera- tions. Abominable calumnies on Christ and Christianity occur not only in the Cabala but in the earlier editions of the Talmud. In these, says Barclay—

Our Lord and Saviour is "that one," "such a one," "a fool," " the leper," "the deceiver of Israel," etc. Efforts are made to prove that He is the son of Joseph Pandira before his marriage with Mary. His miracles are attributed to sorcery, the secret of

Drach, op. cit., II. p. 32.   [2] Ibid., II. p. xxiii.

which He brought in a slit in His flesh out of Egypt. He is said
to have been first stoned and then hanged on the eve of the Pass-
over. His disciples are called heretics and opprobrious names.
They are accused of immoral practices, and the New Testament
is called a sinful book. The references to these subjects manifest
the most bitter aversion and hatred.[1]

One might look in vain for passages such as these in
English or French translations of the Talmud, for the reason
that no complete translation exists in these languages. This
fact is of great significance. Whilst the sacred books of every
other important religion have been rendered into our own
tongue and are open to everyone to study, the book that
forms the foundation of modern Judaism is closed to the
general public. We can read English translations of the
Koran, of the Dhammapada, of the Sutta Nipata, of the Zend
Avesta, of the Shu King, of the Laws of Manu, of the Bhaga-
vadgita, but we cannot read the Talmud. In the long series
of Sacred Books of the East the Talmud finds no place.
All that is accessible to the ordinary reader consists, on one
hand, in expurgated versions or judicious selections by Jewish
and pro-Jewish compilers, and, on the other hand, in "anti-
Semitic" publications on which it would be dangerous to
place reliance. The principal English translation by Rodkinson is very incomplete, and the folios are nowhere indicated,
so that it is impossible to look up a passage.[2] The French
translation by Jean de Pavly professes to present the entire
text of the Venetian Talmud of 1520, but it does nothing
of the kind[3] The translator, in the Preface, in fact admits
that he has left out "sterile discussions" and has throughout
attempted to tone down "the brutality of certain expressions
which offend our ears." This of course affords him infinite
latitude, so that all passages likely to prove displeasing to
the "Hébraïsants," to whom his work is particularly dedicated,
are discreetly expunged. Jean de Pauly's translation of the
Cabala appears, however, to be complete.[4] But a fair and
honest rendering of the whole Talmud into English or French
still remains to be made.

Moreover, even the Hebrew scholar is obliged to exercise
some discrimination if he desires to consult the Talmud in

[1] Joseph Barclay, The Talmud, pp. 38, 39; cf. Drach, op. cit., I. 167.
[2] The Talmud, by Michael Rodkinson (alias Michael Levy Rodkinssohn).
[3] Le Talmud de Babylone (1900).
[4] Le Zohar, translation in 8 vols. by Jean de Pauly, published in 1909 by
Emile Lafuma-Giraud. Wherever possible in quoting the Talmud or the
Cabala I shall give a reference to one of the translations here mentioned.

its original form. For by the sixteenth century, when the study of Hebrew became general amongst Christians, the anti-social and anti-Christian tendencies of the Talmud attracted the attention of the Censor, and in the Bâle Talmud of 1581 the most obnoxious passages and the entire treatise Abodah Zara were suppressed.[1]

In the Cracow edition of 1604 that followed, these passages were restored by the Jews, a proceeding which aroused so much indignation amongst Christian students of Hebrew that the Jews became alarmed. Accordingly a Jewish synod, assembled in Poland in 1631, ordered the offending passages to be expunged again, but—according to Drach—to be replaced by circles which the Rabbis were to fill in orally when giving instruction to young Jews.[2] After that date the Talmud was for a time carefully bowdlerized, so that in order to discover its original form it is advisable to go back to the Venetian Talmud of 1520 before any omissions were made, or to consult a modern edition. For now that the Jews no longer fear the Christians, these passages are all said to have been replaced and no attempt is made, as in the Middle Ages, to prove that they do not refer to the Founder of Christianity.[3]

Thus the *Jewish Encyclopædia* admits that Jewish legends concerning Jesus are found in the Talmud and Midrash and in " the life of Jesus (Toledot Yeshu) that originated in the Middle Ages. It is the tendency of all these sources to belittle the person of Jesus by ascribing to Him illegitimate birth, magic, and a shameful death."[4]

The last work mentioned, the *Toledot Yeshu,* or the *Sepher Toldos Jeschu,* described here as originating in the Middle Ages, probably belongs in reality to a much earlier period. Eliphas Lévi asserts that " the Sepher Toldos, to which the Jews attribute a great antiquity and which they hid from the Christians with such precautions that this book was for a long while unfindable, is quoted for the first time by Raymond

---

[1] *Jewish Encyclopædia,* article Talmud.

[2] Drach, op. cit., I. 168, 169. The text of this encyclical is given by Drach in Hebrew and also in translation, thus: " This is why we enjoin you, under pain of excommunication major, to print nothing in future editions, whether of the Mischna or of the Gemara, which relates whether for good or evil to the acts of Jesus the Nazarene, and to substitute instead a circle like this O, which will warn the Rabbis and schoolmasters to teach the young these passages only viva voce. By means of this precaution the savants amongst the Nazarenes will have no further pretext to attack us on this subject." Cf. Abbé Chiarini, *Le Talmud de Babylone,* p. 45 (1831).

[3] On this point see Appendix I.

[4] *Jewish Encyclopædia,* article on " Jesus."

Martin of the Order of the Preaching Brothers towards the
end of the thirteenth century. . . . This book was evidently
written by a Rabbi initiated into the mysteries of the Cabala."[1]
Whether then the Toledot Yeshu had existed for many centuries before it was first brought to light or whether it was a
collection of Jewish traditions woven into a coherent narrative
by a thirteenth-century Rabbi, the ideas it contains can be
traced back at least as far as the second century of the Christian
era. Origen, who in the middle of the third century wrote
his reply to the attack of Celsus on Christianity, refers to a
scandalous story closely resembling the Toledot Yeshu, which
Celsus, who lived towards the end of the second century,
had quoted on the authority of a Jew.[2] It is evident, therefore, that the legend it contains had long been current in
Jewish circles, but the book itself did not come into the hands
of Christians until it was translated into Latin by Raymond
Martin. Later on Luther summarized it in German under
the name of *Schem Hamphorasch*; Wagenseil in 1681 and
Huldrich in 1705 published Latin translations.[3] It is also to
be found in French in Gustave Brunet's *Evangiles Apocryphes*.

However repugnant it is to transcribe any portion of this
blasphemous work, its main outline must be given here in
order to trace the subsequent course of the anti-Christian
secret tradition in which, as we shall see, it has been
perpetuated up to our own day. Briefly, then, the Toledot
Yeshu relates with the most indecent details that Miriam, a
hairdresser of Bethlehem,[4] affianced to a young man named
Jochanan, was seduced by a libertine, Joseph Panther or
Pandira, and gave birth to a son whom she named Johosuah
or Jeschu. According to the Talmudic authors of the Sota
and the Sanhedrim, Jeschu was taken during his boyhood to
Egypt, where he was initiated into the secret doctrines of the
priests, and on his return to Palestine gave himself up to the
practice of magic.[5] The Toledot Yeshu, however, goes on to
say that on reaching manhood Jeschu learnt the secret of his
illegitimacy, on account of which he was driven out of the
Synagogue and took refuge for a time in Galilee. Now, there
was in the Temple a stone on which was engraved the Tetragrammaton or Schem Hamphorasch, that is to say, the Ineffable

[1] Eliphas Lévi, *La Science des Esprits*, p. 40.
[2] Origen, *Contra Celsum*.
[3] S. Baring-Gould, *The Counter-Gospels*, p. 69 (1874).
[4] Cf. Baring-Gould, op. cit., quoting Talmud, treatise Sabbath, folio 104.
[5] Ibid., p. 55, quoting Talmud, treatise Sanhedrim, folio 107, and Sota, folio 47; Eliphas Lévi, *La Science des Esprits*, pp. 32, 33.

Name of God; this stone had been found by King David when the foundations of the Temple were being prepared and was deposited by him in the Holy of Holies. Jeschu, knowing this, came from Galilee and, penetrating into the Holy of Holies, read the Ineffable Name, which he transcribed on to a piece of parchment and concealed in an incision under his skin. By this means he was able to work miracles and to persuade the people that he was the son of God foretold by Isaiah. With the aid of Judas, the Sages of the Synagogue succeeded in capturing Jeschu, who was then led before the Great and Little Sanhedrim, by whom he was condemned to be stoned to death and finally hanged.

Such is the story of Christ according to the Jewish Cabalists, which should be compared not only with the Christian tradition but with that of the Moslems. It is perhaps not sufficiently known that the Koran, whilst denying the divinity of Christ and also the fact of His crucifixion,[1] nevertheless indignantly denounces the infamous legends concerning Him perpetuated by the Jews, and confirms in beautiful language the story of the Annunciation and the doctrine of the Miraculous Conception.[2] " Remember when the angels said, ' O Mary! verily hath God chosen thee and purified thee, and chosen thee above the women of the worlds.' . . . Remember when the angels said, ' O Mary! verily God announceth to thee the Word from Him : His name shall be Messiah, Jesus the son of Mary, illustrious in this world, and in the next, and one of those who have near access to God."

The Mother of Jesus is shown to have been pure and to have " kept her maidenhood "[3]; it was the Jews who spoke against Mary " a grievous calumny."[4] Jesus Himself is described as " strengthened with the Holy Spirit," and the Jews are reproached for rejecting " the Apostle of God,"[5] to whom was given " the Evangel with its guidance and light confirmatory of the preceding Law."[6]

Thus during the centuries that saw the birth of Christianity,

---

[1] According to the Koran, it was the Jews who said, " ' Verily we have slain the Messiah, Jesus the son of Mary, an apostle of God.' Yet they slew him not, and they crucified him not, but they had only his likeness. . . . No sure knowledge had they about him, but followed an opinion, and they did not really slay him, but God took him up to Himself."—Sura iv. 150. See also Sura iii. 40. The Rev. J. M. Rodwell, in his translation of the Koran, observes in a footnote to the latter passage: " Muhammad probably believed that God took the dead body of Jesus to Heaven—for three hours, according to some—while the Jews crucified a man who resembled him."

[2] Sura iii. 30, 40.   [3] Sura xxi. 90.   [4] Sura iv. 150.
[5] Sura ii. 89, 250; v. 100.   [6] Sura v. 50.

although other non-Christian forces arrayed themselves against the new faith, it was left to the Jews to inaugurate a campaign of vilification against the person of its Founder, whom Moslems to this day revere as one of the great teachers of the world.[1]

THE ESSENES

A subtler device for discrediting Christianity and undermining belief in the divine character of our Lord has been adopted by modern writers, principally Jewish, who set out to prove that He belonged to the sect of the Essenes, a community of ascetics holding all goods in common, which had existed in Palestine before the birth of Christ. Thus the Jewish historian Graetz declares that Jesus simply appropriated to himself the essential features of Essenism, and that primitive Christianity was "nothing but an offshoot of Essenism."[2] The Christian Jew Dr. Ginsburg partially endorses this view in a small pamphlet[3] containing most of the evidence that has been brought forward on the subject, and himself expresses the opinion that "it will hardly be doubted that our Saviour Himself belonged to this holy brotherhood."[4] So after representing Christ as a magician in the Toledot Yeshu and the Talmud, Jewish tradition seeks to explain His miraculous works as those of a mere healer—an idea that we shall find descending right through the secret societies to this day. Of course if this were true, if the miracles of Christ were simply due to a knowledge of natural laws and His doctrines were the outcome of a sect, the whole theory of His divine power and mission falls to the ground. This is why it is essential to expose the fallacies and even

[1] In the masonic periodical *Ars Quatuor Coronatorum*, Vol. XXIV, a Freemason (Bro. Sydney T. Klein) observes: "It is not generally known that one of the reasons why the Mohammedans removed their Kiblah from Jerusalem to Mecca was that they quarrelled with the Jews over Jesus Christ, and the proof of this may still be seen in the Golden Gate leading into the sacred area of the Temple, which was bricked up by the Mohammedans, and is bricked up to this day, because they declared that nobody should enter through that portal until Jesus Christ comes to judge the world, and this is stated in the Koran." I cannot trace this passage in the Koran, but much the same idea is conveyed by the Rev. J. M. Rodwell, who in the note above quoted adds: "The Muhammadans believe that Jesus on His return to earth at the end of the world will slay the Antichrist, die, and be raised again. A vacant place is reserved for His body in the Prophet's tomb at Medina."

[2] Graetz, *Geschichte der Juden*, III. 216-52.

[3] *The Essenes: their History and Doctrines*, an essay by Christian D. Ginsburg, LL.D. (Longmans, Green & Co., 1864).

[4] Ibid., p. 24.

the bad faith on which the attempt to identify Him with the Essenes is based.

Now, we have only to study the Gospels carefully in order to realize that the teachings of Christ were totally different from those peculiar to the Essenes.[1] Christ did not live in a fraternity, but, as Dr. Ginsburg himself points out, associated with publicans and sinners. The Essenes did not frequent the Temple and Christ was there frequently. The Essenes disapproved of wine and marriage, whilst Christ sanctioned marriage by His presence at the wedding of Cana in Galilee and there turned water into wine. A further point, the most conclusive of all, Dr. Ginsburg ignores, namely, that one of the principal traits of the Essenes which distinguished them from the other Jewish sects of their day was their disapproval of ointment, which they regarded as defiling, whilst Christ not only commended the woman who brought the precious jar of ointment, but reproached Simon for the omission: " My head with oil thou didst not anoint: but this woman hath anointed My feet with ointment." It is obvious that if Christ had been an Essene but had departed from His usual custom on this occasion out of deference to the woman's feelings, he would have understood why Simon had not offered Him the same attention, and at any rate Simon would have excused himself on these grounds. Further, if His disciples had been Essenes, would they not have protested against this violation of their principles, instead of merely objecting that the ointment was of too costly a kind?

But it is in attributing to Christ the Communistic doctrines of the Essenes that Dr. Ginsburg's conclusions are the most misleading—a point of particular importance in view of the fact that it is on this false hypothesis that so-called " Christian Socialism " has been built up. " The Essenes," he writes, " had all things in common, and appointed one of the brethren as steward to manage the common bag; so the primitive Christians (Acts ii. 44, 45, iv. 32-4; John xii. 6, xiii. 29)." It is perfectly true that, as the first reference to the Acts testifies, some of the primitive Christians after the death of Christ formed themselves into a body having all things in common, but there is not the slightest evidence that Christ

---

[1] Edersheim (op. cit., I. 325) ably refutes both Graetz and Ginsburg on this point, and shows that " the teaching of Christianity was in a direction the opposite from that of Essenism." M. Vulliaud (op. cit., I. 71) dismisses the Essene origin of Christianity as unworthy of serious attention. " To maintain the Essenism of Jesus is a proof of frivolity or of invincible ignorance."

and His disciples followed this principle. The solitary passages in the Gospel of St. John, which are all that Dr. Ginsburg can quote in support of this contention, may have referred to an alms-bag or a fund for certain expenses, not to a common pool of all monetary wealth. Still less is there any evidence that Christ advocated Communism to the world in general. When the young man having great possessions asked what he should do to inherit eternal life, Christ told him to follow the commandments, but on the young man asking what more he could do, answered: "If thou wilt be perfect go and sell that thou hast and give to the poor." Renunciation—but not the pooling—of all wealth was thus a counsel of perfection for the few who desired to devote their lives to God, as monks and nuns have always done, and bore no relation to the Communistic system of the Essenes.

Dr. Ginsburg goes on to say: "Essenism put all its members on the same level, forbidding the exercise of authority of one over the other and enjoining mutual service; so Christ (Matt. xx. 25-8; Mark ix. 35-7, x. 42-5). Essenism commanded its disciples to call no man master upon the earth; so Christ (Matt. xxiii. 8-10)." As a matter of fact, Christ strongly upheld the exercise of authority, not only in the oft-quoted passage, "Render to Cæsar the things that are Cæsar's," but in His approval of the Centurion's speech: "I am a man under authority, having soldiers under me: and I say to this man, Go, and he goeth; and to another, Come, and he cometh; and to my servant, Do this, and he doeth it." Everywhere Christ commends the faithful servant and enjoins obedience to masters. If we look up the reference to the Gospel of St. Matthew where Dr. Ginsburg says that Christ commanded His disciples to call no man master on earth, we shall find that he has not only perverted the sense of the passage but reversed the order of the words, which, following on a denunciation of the Jewish Rabbis, runs thus: "But be not ye called Rabbi: for one is your master, even Christ, and all ye are brethren. . . . Neither be ye called masters: for one is your master, even Christ. But he that is greatest among you shall be your servant." The apostles were therefore, never ordered to call no man master, but not to be called master themselves. Moreover, if we refer to the Greek text, we shall see that this was meant in a spiritual and not a social sense. The word for "master" here given is in the first verse διδάσκαλος, i.e. teacher, in the second, καθηγγητὴς literally guide, and the word is servant is διακόνοσ. When

masters and servants in the social sense are referred
to in the Gospels, the word employed for master is κύριος
and for servant δοῦλος.   Dr. Ginsburg should have been aware
of this distinction and that the passage in question had therefore
no bearing on his argument.   As a matter of fact it would
appear that some of the apostles kept servants, since Christ
commends them for exacting strict attention to duty:

> Which of you, having a servant ploughing or feeding cattle, will
> say unto him by and by, when he is come from the field, Go and
> sit down to meat? And will not rather say unto him, Make ready
> wherewith I may sup, and gird thyself, and serve me, till I have
> eaten and drunken; and afterwards thou shalt eat and drink?
> Doth he thank that servant because he did the things that were
> commanded to him? I trow not.[1]

This passage would alone suffice to show that Christ and
His apostles did not inhabit communities where all were
equal, but followed the usual practices of the social system
under which they lived, though adopting certain rules, such
as taking only one garment and carrying no money when they
went on journeys. Those resemblances between the teaching
of the Essenes and the Sermon on the Mount which Dr.
Ginsburg indicates refer not to the customs of a sect, but to
general precepts for human conduct—humility, meekness,
charity, and so forth.

At the same time it is clear that if the Essenes in general
conformed to some of the principles laid down by Christ,
certain of their doctrines were completely at variance with
those of Christ and of primitive Christians, in particular their
custom of praying to the rising sun and their disbelief in the
resurrection of the body.[2] St. Paul denounces asceticism,
the cardinal doctrine of the Essenes, in unmeasured terms,
warning the brethren that " in the latter times some shall
depart from the faith, giving heed to seducing spirits, and
doctrines of devils, . . . forbidding to marry, and commanding
to abstain from meats, which God hath created to be received
with thanksgiving of them which believe and know the truth.
For every creature of God is good, and nothing to be refused,
if it be received with thanksgiving. . . . If thou put the brethren
in remembrance of these things, thou shalt be a good minister
of Jesus Christ."

This would suggest that certain Essenean ideas had crept

[1] Luke xvii. 7–9.   [2] Ginsburg, op. cit., pp. 15, 22, 55.

into Christian communities and were regarded by those who remembered Christ's true teaching as a dangerous perversion.

The Essenes were therefore not Christians, but a secret society, practising four degrees of initiation, and bound by terrible oaths not to divulge the sacred mysteries confided to them. And what were those mysteries but those of the Jewish secret tradition which we now know as the Cabala? Dr. Ginsburg throws an important light on Essenism when, in one passage alone, he refers to the obligation of the Essenes " not to divulge the secret doctrines to anyone, . . . carefully to preserve the books belonging to their sect and the names of the angels or the mysteries connected with the Tetra-grammaton and the other names of God and the angels, comprised in the theosophy as well as with the cosmogony which also played so important a part among the Jewish mystics and the Kabbalists."[1] The truth is clearly that the Essenes were Cabalists, though doubtless Cabalists of a superior kind. The Cabal they possessed very possibly descended from pre-Christian times and had remained uncontaminated by the anti-Christian strain introduced into it by the Rabbis after the death of Christ.[2]

The Essenes are of importance to the subject of this book as the first of the secret societies from which a direct line of tradition can be traced up to the present day. But if in this peaceful community no actually anti-Christian influence is to be discerned, the same cannot be said of the succeeding pseudo-Christian sects which, whilst professing Christianity, mingled with Christian doctrines the poison of the perverted Cabala, main source of the errors which henceforth rent the Christian Church in twain.

THE GNOSTICS

The first school of thought to create a schism in Christianity was the collection of sects known under the generic name of Gnosticism. In its purer forms Gnosticism aimed at supplementing faith by knowledge of eternal verities and at giving a wider meaning to Christianity by linking it up with earlier

[1] Ginsburg, op. cit., p. 12.
[2] Fabre d'Olivet thinks this tradition had descended to the Essenes from Moses: " If it is true, as everything attests, that Moses left an oral law, it is amongst the Essenes that it was preserved. The Pharisees, who flattered themselves so highly on possessing it, only had its outward forms (*apparences*), as Jesus reproaches them at every moment. It is from these latter that the modern Jews descend, with the exception of a few real *savants* whose secret tradition goes back to the Essenes."—*La Langue Hebraïque,* p. 27 (1815).

faiths. "The belief that the divinity had been manifested in the religious institutions of all nations"[1] thus led to the conception of a sort of universal religion containing the divine elements of all.

Gnosticism, however. as the *Jewish Encyclopædia* points out, "was Jewish in character long before it became Christian."[2] M. Matter indicates Syria and Palestine as its cradle and Alexandria as the centre by which it was influenced at the time of its alliance with Christianity. This influence again was predominantly Jewish. Philo and Aristobulus, the leading Jewish philosophers of Alexandria, "wholly attached to the ancient religion of their fathers, both resolved to adorn it with the spoils of other systems and to open to Judaism the way to immense conquests."[3] This method of borrowing from other races and religions those ideas useful for their purpose has always been the custom of the Jews. The Cabala, as we have seen, was made up of these heterogeneous elements. And it is here we find the principal progenitor of Gnosticism. The Freemason Ragon gives the clue in the words: "The Cabala is the key of the occult sciences. The Gnostics were born of the Cabalists."[4]

For the Cabala was much older than the Gnostics. Modern historians who date it merely from the publication of the Zohar by Moses de Leon in the thirteenth century or from the school of Luria in the sixteenth century obscure this most important fact which Jewish savants have always clearly recognized.[5] The *Jewish Encyclopædia,* whilst denying the certainty of connexion between Gnosticism and the Cabala, nevertheless admits that the investigations of the anti-Cabalist Graetz "must be resumed on a new basis," and it goes on to show that "it was Alexandria of the first century, or earlier, with her strange commingling of Egyptian, Chaldean, Judean, and Greek culture which furnished soil and seeds for that mystic philosophy."[6] But since Alexandria was at the same period the home of Gnosticism, which was formed from the same elements enumerated here, the connexion between the two systems is clearly evident. M. Matter is therefore right in

[1] Matter, *Histoire du Gnosticisme,* I. 44 (1844).
[2] *Jewish Encyclopædia,* article on Cabala.
[3] Matter, op. cit., II. 58.
[4] Ragon, *Maçonnerie Occulte,* p. 78.
[5] "The Cabala is anterior to the Gnosis, an opinion which Christian writers little understand, but which the erudites of Judaism profess with a legitimate assurance."—Matter, op. cit., Vol. I. p. 12.
[6] *Jewish Encyclopædia,* article on Cabala.

saying that Gnosticism was not a defection from Christianity, but a combination of systems into which a few Christian elements were introduced. The result of Gnosticism was thus not to christianize the Cabala, but to cabalize Christianity by mingling its pure and simple teaching with theosophy and even magic. The *Jewish Encyclopædia* quotes the opinion that " the central doctrine of Gnosticism—a movement closely connected with Jewish mysticism—was nothing else than the attempt to liberate the soul and unite it with God "; but as this was apparently to be effected " through the employment of mysteries, incantations, names of angels," etc., it will be seen how widely even this phase of Gnosticism differs from Christianity and identifies itself with the magical Cabala of the Jews.

Indeed, the man generally recognized as the founder of Gnosticism, a Jew commonly known as Simon Magus, was not only a Cabalist mystic but avowedly a magician, who with a band of Jews, including his master Dositheus and his disciples Menander and Cerinthus, instituted a priesthood of the Mysteries and practised occult arts and exorcisms.[1] It was this Simon of whom we read in the Acts of the Apostles that he " bewitched the people of Samaria, giving out that himself was some great one: to whom they all gave heed from the least to the greatest, saying, This man is the great power of God," and who sought to purchase the power of the laying on of hands with money. Simon, indeed, crazed by his incantations and ecstasies, developed megalomania in an acute form, arrogating to himself divine honours and aspiring to the adoration of the whole world. According to a contemporary legend, he eventually became sorcerer to Nero and ended his life in Rome.[2]

The prevalence of sorcery amongst the Jews during the first century of the Christian era is shown by other passages in the Acts of the Apostles; in Paphos the " false prophet," a Jew, whose surname was Bar-Jesus, otherwise known as " Elymas the sorcerer," opposed the teaching of St. Paul and brought on himself the imprecation: " O full of all subtlety and all mischief, thou child of the devil, thou enemy of all righteousness, wilt thou not cease to pervert the right ways of the Lord?"

Perversion is the keynote of all the debased forms

[1] John Yarker, *The Arcane Schools*, p. 167; Matter, op. cit., II. 365, quoting Irenæus.
[2] Eliphas Lévi, *Histoire de la Magie*, p. 189.

of Gnosticism. According to Eliphas Lévi, certain of the Gnostics introduced into their rites that profanation of Christian mysteries which was to form the basis of black magic in the Middle Ages.[1] The glorification of evil, which plays so important a part in the modern revolutionary movement, constituted the creed of the Ophites, who worshipped the Serpent (ὄφις) because he had revolted against Jehovah, to whom they referred under the Cabalistic term of the "demiurgus,"[2] and still more of the Cainites, so-called from their cult of Cain, whom, with Dathan and Abiram, the inhabitants of Sodom and Gomorrah, and finally Judas Iscariot, they regarded as noble victims of the demiurgus.[3] Animated by hatred of all social and moral order, the Cainites "called upon all men to destroy the works of God and to commit every kind of infamy."[4]

These men were therefore not only the enemies of Christianity but of orthodox Judaism, since it was against the Jehovah of the Jews that their hatred was particularly directed. Another Gnostic sect, the Carpocratians, followers of Carpocrates of Alexandria and his son Epiphanus—who died from his debaucheries and was venerated as a god[5]—likewise regarded all written laws, Christian or Mosaic, with contempt and recognized only the γνῶσις or knowledge given to the great men of every nation—Plato and Pythagoras, Moses and Christ—which "frees one from all that the vulgar call religion" and "makes man equal to God."[6]

So in the Carpocratians of the second century we find already the tendency towards that *deification of humanity* which forms the supreme doctrine of the secret societies and of the visionary Socialists of our day. The war now begins between the two contending principles: the Christian conception of man reaching up to God and the secret society conception of man as God, needing no revelation from on high and no guidance but the law of his own nature. And since that nature is in itself divine, all that springs from it is praiseworthy, and those acts usually regarded as sins are not to be condemned. By this line of reasoning the Carpocratians arrived at much the same conclusions as modern Communists with regard to

---

[1] Eliphas Lévi, op. cit., p. 218.
[2] Dean Milman, *History of the Jews* (Everyman's Library edition), II. 491.
[3] Matter, II. 171; E. de Faye, *Gnostiques et Gnosticisme*, p. 349 (1913).
[4] De Luchet, *Essai sur la Secte des Illuminés*, p. 6.
[5] *Manuel d'Histoire Ecclésiastique*, par R. P. Albers, S.J., adapté par René Hedde, O.P., p. 125 (1908); Matter, op. cit., II. 197.
[6] Matter, op. cit., II. 188.

the ideal social system. Thus Epiphanus held that since Nature herself reveals the principle of the community and the unity of all things, human laws which are contrary to this law of Nature are so many culpable infractions of the legitimate order of things. Before these laws were imposed on humanity everything was in common—land, goods, and women. According to certain contemporaries, the Carpocratians returned to this primitive system by instituting the community of women and indulging in every kind of licence.

The further Gnostic sect of Antitacts, following this same cult of human nature, taught revolt against all positive religion and laws and the necessity for gratifying the flesh; the Adamites of North Africa, going a step further in the return to Nature, cast off all clothing at their religious services so as to represent the primitive innocence of the garden of Eden—a precedent followed by the Adamites of Germany in the fifteenth century.[1]

These Gnostics, says Eliphas Lévi, under the pretext of "spiritualizing matter, materialized the spirit in the most revolting ways. . . . Rebels to the hierarchic order, . . . they wished to substitute the mystical licence of sensual passions to wise Christian sobriety and obedience to laws. . . . Enemies of the family, they wished to produce sterility by increasing debauchery."[2]

By way of systematically perverting the doctrines of the Christian faith the Gnostics claimed to possess the true versions of the Gospels, and professed belief in these to the exclusion of all the others.[3] Thus the Ebionites had their own corrupted version of the Gospel of St. Matthew founded on the "Gospel of the Hebrews," known earlier to the Jewish Christians; the Marcosians had their version of St. Luke, the Cainites their own "Gospel of Judas," and the Valentinians their "Gospel of St. John." As we shall see later, the Gospel of St. John is the one that throughout the war on Christianity has been specially chosen for the purpose of perversion.

Of course this spirit of perversion was nothing new; many centuries earlier the prophet Isaiah had denounced it in the words: "Woe unto them that call evil good, and good evil; that put darkness for light, and light for darkness!" But the rôle of the Gnostics was to reduce perversion to a system

[1] Matter, op. cit., II. 199, 215.
[2] Eliphas Lévi, *Histoire de la Magie*, pp. 217, 218.
[3] Matter, op. cit., II. 115, III. 14; S. Baring-Gould, *The Lost and Hostile Gospels* (1874).

by binding men together into sects working under the guise of enlightenment in order to obscure all recognized ideas of morality and religion. It is this which constitutes their importance in the history of secret societies.

Whether the Gnostics themselves can be described as a secret society, or rather as a ramification of secret societies, is open to question. M. Matter, quoting a number of third-century writers, shows the possibility that they had mysteries and initiations; the Church Fathers definitely asserted this to be the case.[1] According to Tertullian, the Valentinians continued, or rather perverted, the mysteries of Eleusis, out of which they made a " sanctuary of prostitution."[2]

The Valentinians are known to have divided their members into three classes—the Pneumatics, the Psychics, and the Hylics (i.e. materialists); the Basilideans are also said to have possessed secret doctrines known to hardly one in a thousand of the sect. From all this M. Matter concludes that:

1. The Gnostics professed to hold by means of tradition a secret doctrine superior to that contained in the public writings of the apostles.

2. That they did not communicate this doctrine to everyone. . . .

3. That they communicated it by means of emblems and symbols, as the Diagram of the Ophites proves.

4. That in these communications they imitated the rites and trials of the mysteries of Eleusis.[3]

This claim to the possession of a secret oral tradition, whether known under the name of γνῶσις or of Cabala, confirms the conception of the Gnostics as Cabalists and shows how far they had departed from Christian teaching. For if only in this idea of " one doctrine for the ignorant and another for the initiated," the Gnostics had restored the very system which Christianity had come to destroy.[4]

MANICHEISM

Whilst we have seen the Gnostic sects working for more or less subversive purposes under the guise of esoteric doctrines, we find in the Manicheans of Persia, who followed a

[1] Matter, op. cit., II. 364.
[2] Ibid., p. 365.
[3] Ibid., p. 369.
[4] *Some Notes on Various Gnostic Sects and their Possible Influence on Freemasonry*, by D. F. Ranking, republished from *Ars Quatuor Coronatorum* (Vol. XXIV, p. 202, 1911) in pamphlet form, p. 7.

century later, a sect embodying the same tendencies and approaching still nearer to secret society organization.

Cubricus or Corbicius, the founder of Manicheism, was born in Babylonia about the year A.D. 216. Whilst still a child he is said to have been bought as a slave by a rich widow of Ctesiphon, who liberated him and on her death left him great wealth. According to another story—for the whole history of Manes rests on legends—he inherited from a rich old woman the books of a Saracen named Scythianus on the wisdom of the Egyptians. Combining the doctrines these books contained with ideas borrowed from Zoroastrianism, Gnosticism, and Christianity, and also with certain additions of his own, he elaborated a philosophic system which he proceeded to teach. Cubricus then changed his name to Mani or Manes and proclaimed himself the Paraclete promised by Jesus Christ. His followers were divided into two classes —the outer circle of hearers or combatants, and the inner circle of teachers or ascetics described as the Elect. As evidence of their resemblance with Freemasons, it has been said that the Manicheans made use of secret signs, grips, and passwords, that owing to the circumstances of their master's adoption they called Manes " the son of the widow " and themselves " the children of the widow," but this is not clearly proved. One of their customs is, however, interesting in this connexion. According to legend, Manes undertook to cure the son of the King of Persia who had fallen ill, but the prince died, whereupon Manes was flayed alive by order of the king and his corpse hanged up at the city gate. Every year after this, on Good Friday, the Manicheans carried out a mourning ceremony known as the Bema around the catafalque of Manes, whose real sufferings they were wont to contrast with the unreal sufferings of Christ.

The fundamental doctrine of Manicheism is Dualism—that is to say, the existence of two opposing principles in the world, light and darkness, good and evil—founded, however, not on the Christian conception of this idea, but on the Zoroastrian conception of Ormuzd and Ahriman, and so perverted and mingled with Cabalistic superstitions that it met with as vehement denunciation by Persian priests as by Christian Fathers. Thus, according to the doctrine of Manes, all matter is absolute evil, the principle of evil is eternal, humanity itself is of Satanic origin, and the first human beings, Adam and Eve, are represented as the offspring of devils.[1] Much the same idea

[1] Hastings, *Encyclopædia of Religion and Ethics*, article on Manicheism.

may be found in the Jewish Cabala, where it is said that Adam, after other abominable practices, cohabited with female devils whilst Eve consoled herself with male devils, so that whole races of demons were born into the world. Eve is also accused of cohabiting with the Serpent.[1] In the Yalkut Shimoni it is also related that during the 130 years that Adam lived apart from Eve, " he begat a generation of devils, spirits, and hob-goblins."[2] Manichean demonology thus paved the way for the placation of the powers of darkness practised by the Euchites at the end of the fourth century and later by the Paulicians, the Bogomils, and the Luciferians.

So it is in Gnosticism and Manicheism that we find evidence of the first attempts to pervert Christianity. The very fact that all such have been condemned by the Church as " heresies " has tended to enlist sympathy in their favour, yet even Eliphas Lévi recognizes that here the action of the Church was right, for the " monstrous gnosis of Manes " was a desecration not only of Christian doctrines but of pre-Christian sacred traditions.

---

[1] Zohar, treatise Bereschith, folio 54 (De Pauly's translation, I. 315).
[2] The Yalkut Shimoni is a sixteenth-century compilation of Haggadic Midrashim.

2

THE REVOLT AGAINST ISLAM [1]

WE have followed the efforts of subversive sects hitherto directed against Christianity and orthodox Judaism; we shall now see this attempt, reduced by gradual stages to a working system of extraordinary efficiency, organized for the purpose of undermining all moral and religious beliefs in the minds of Moslems. In the middle of the seventh century an immense schism was created in Islam by the rival advocates of successors to the Prophet, the orthodox Islamites known by the name of Sunnis adhering to the elected Khalifas Abu Bakr, Omar, and Othman, whilst the party of revolt, known as the Shiahs, claimed the Khalifate for the descendants of Mohammed through Ali, son of Abu-Talib and husband of Fatima, the Prophet's daughter. This division ended in open warfare; Ali was finally assassinated, his elder son Hason was poisoned in Medina, his younger son Husain fell at the battle of Kerbela fighting against the supporters of Othman. The deaths of Hasan and Husain are still mourned yearly by the Shiahs at the Moharram.

THE ISMAILIS

The Shiahs themselves split again over the question of Ali's successors into four factions, the fourth of which divided again into two further sects. Both of these retained their allegiance to the descendants of Ali as far as Jafar-as-Sadik, but whilst one party, known as the Imamias or Isna-Asharias (i.e. the Twelvers), supported the succession through his younger son Musa to the twelfth Iman Mohammed, son of

[1] Principal authorities consulted for this chapter: Joseph von Hammer, *The History of the Assassins* (Eng. trans., 1835); Silvestre de Sacy, *Exposé de le Religion des Druses* (1838) *and Mémoires sur la Dynastie des Assassins* in *Mémoires de l'Institut Royal de France*, Vol. IV. (1818); Hastings *Encyclopædia of Religion and Ethics;* Syed Ameer Ali, *The Spirit of Islam* (1922); Dr. F. W. Bussell, *Religious Thought and Heresy in the Middle Ages* (1918).

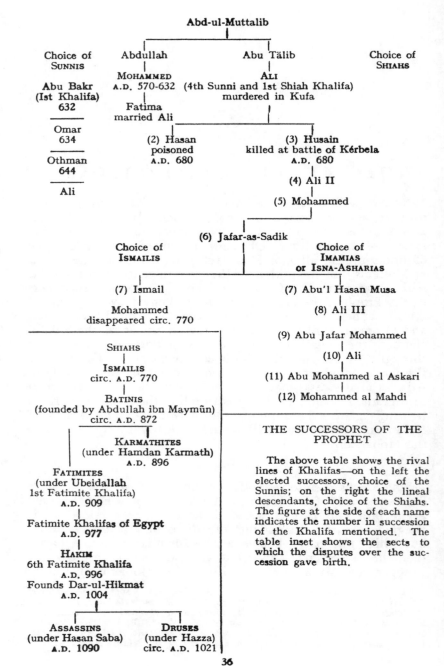

Abd-ul-Muttalib

Choice of SUNNIS	Abdullah	Abu Tälib	Choice of SHIAHS

Choice of
SUNNIS

Abu Bakr
(Ist Khalifa)
632

―――

Omar
634

―――

Othman
644

―――

Ali

Abdullah

MOHAMMED
A.D. 570-632

Fatima
married Ali

(2) Hasan
poisoned
A.D. 680

Abu Tälib

ALI
(4th Sunni and 1st Shiah Khalifa)
murdered in Kufa

(3) Husain
killed at battle of Kérbela
A.D. 680

(4) Ali II

(5) Mohammed

(6) Jafar-as-Sadik

Choice of
ISMAILIS

(7) Ismail

Mohammed
disappeared circ. 770

Choice of
IMAMIAS
or ISNA-ASHARIAS

(7) Abu'l Hasan Musa

(8) Ali III

(9) Abu Jafar Mohammed

(10) Ali

(11) Abu Mohammed al Askari

(12) Mohammed al Mahdi

SHIAHS

ISMAILIS
circ. A.D. 770

BATINIS
(founded by Abdullah ibn Maymūn)
circ. A.D. 872

KARMATHITES
(under Hamdan Karmath)
A.D. 896

FATIMITES
(under Ubeidallah
1st Fatimite Khalifa)
A.D. 909

Fatimite Khalifas of Egypt
A.D. 977

HAKIM
6th Fatimite Khalifa
A.D. 996
Founds Dar-ul-Hikmat
A.D. 1004

ASSASSINS
(under Hasan Saba)
A.D. 1090

DRUSES
(under Hazza)
circ. A.D. 1021

THE SUCCESSORS OF THE PROPHET

The above table shows the rival lines of Khalifas—on the left the elected successors, choice of the Sunnis; on the right the lineal descendants, choice of the Shiahs. The figure at the side of each name indicates the number in succession of the Khalifa mentioned. The table inset shows the sects to which the disputes over the succession gave birth.

Askeri, the Ismailis (or Seveners) adhered to Ismail, the elder son of Jafar-as-Sadik.

So far, however, in spite of divisions, no body of Shiahs had ever deviated from the fundamental doctrines of Islamism, but merely claimed that these had been handed down through a different line from that recognized by the Sunnis. The earliest Ismailis, who formed themselves into a party at about the time of the death of Mohammed, son of Ismail (i.e. circ. A.D. 770), still remained believers, declaring only that the true teaching of the Prophet had descended to Mohammed, who was not dead but would return in the fullness of time and that he was the Mahdi whom Moslems must await. But in about A.D. 872 an intriguer of extraordinary subtlety succeeded in capturing the movement, which, hitherto merely schismatic, now became definitely subversive, not only of Islamism, but of all religious belief.

This man, Abdullah ibn Maymūn, the son of a learned and free-thinking doctor in Southern Persia, brought up in the doctrines of Gnostic Dualism and profoundly versed in all religions, was in reality, like his father, a pure materialist. By professing adherence to the creed of orthodox Shi-ism, and proclaiming a knowledge of the mystic doctrines which the Ismailis believed to have descended through Ismail to his son Mohammed, Abdullah succeeded in placing himself at the head of the Ismailis.

His advocacy of Ismail was thus merely a mask, his real aim being materialism, which he now proceeded to make into a system by founding a sect known as the Batinis with seven degrees of initiation. Dozy has given the following description of this amazing project:

To link together into one body the vanquished and the con-querors; to unite in the form of a vast secret society with many degrees of initiation free-thinkers—who regarded religion only as a curb for the people—and bigots of all sects; to make tools of believers in order to give power to sceptics; to induce conquerors to overturn the empires they had founded; to build up a party, numerous, compact, and disciplined, which in due time would give the throne, if not to himself, at least to his descendants, such was Abdullah ibn Maymūn's general aim—an extraordinary conception which he worked out with marvellous tact, incomparable skill, and a profound knowledge of the human heart. The means which he adopted were devised with diabolical cunning. . . .

It was . . . not among the Shi-ites that he sought his true sup-porters, but among the Ghebers, the Manicheans, the pagans of Harran, and the students of Greek philosophy; on the last alone could he rely, to them alone could he gradually unfold the final mystery, and reveal that Imams, religions, and morality were nothing but an imposture and an absurdity. The rest of mankind—the "asses," as Abdullah called them—were incapable of understanding such doctrines. But to gain his end he by no means disdained their aid; on the contrary, he solicited it, but he took care to initiate devout and lowly souls only in the first grades of the sect. His missionaries, who were inculcated with the idea that their first duty was to conceal their true sentiments and adapt themselves to the views of their auditors, appeared in many guises, and spoke, as it were, in a different language to each class. They won over the ignorant vulgar by feats of legerdemain which passed for miracles, or excited their curiosity by enigmatical discourse. In the presence of the devout they assumed the mask of virtue and piety. With mystics they were mystical, and unfolded the inner meanings of phenomena, or explained allegories and the figurative sense of the allegories themselves. . . .

By means such as these the extraordinary result was brought about that a multitude of men of diverse beliefs were all working together for an object known only to a few of them. . . .[1]

I quote this passage at length because it is of immense importance in throwing a light on the organization of modern secret societies. It does not matter what the end may be, whether political, social, or religious, the system remains the same—the setting in motion of a vast number of people and making them work in a cause unknown to them. That this was the method adopted by Weishaupt in organizing the Illuminati and that it came to him from the East will be shown later on. We shall now see how the system of the philosopher Abdullah paved the way for bloodshed by the most terrible sect the world had ever seen.

THE KARMATHITES

The first open acts of violence resulting from the doctrines of Abdullah were carried out by the Karmathites, a new development of the Ismailis. Amongst the many Dais sent out by the leader—which included his son Ahmed and Ahmed's son— was the Dai Hosein Ahwazi, Abdullah's envoy to Irak in Persia, who initiated a certain Hamdan surnamed Karmath into the secrets of the sect. Karmath, who was a born intriguer and believed in nothing, became the leader of the Karmathites in Arabia, where a number of Arabs were soon enlisted in the society. With extraordinary skill he succeeded in persuading these dupes to make over all their money to him, first by means

[1] Reinhart Dozy, *Spanish Islam* (Eng. trans.), pp. 403–5.

of small contributions, later by larger sums, until at last he convinced them of the advantages of abolishing all private property and establish:ng the system of the community of goods and wives. This principle was enforced by the passage of the Koran: " Remember the grace of God in that whilst you were enemies, He has united your hearts, so that by His grace you have become brothers. . . ." De Sacy thus transcribes the methods employed as given by the historian Nowairi:

When Karmath had succeeded in establishing all this, and everyone had agreed to conform to it, he ordered the Dais to assemble all the women on a certain night so that they should mingle promiscuously with all the men. This, he said, was perfection and the last degree of friendship and fraternal union. Often a husband led his wife and presented her himself to one of his brothers when that gave him pleasure. When he (Karmath) saw that he had become absolute master of their minds, had assured himself of their obedience, and found out the degree of their intelligence and discernment, he began to lead them quite astray. He put before them arguments borrowed from the doctrines of the Dualists. They fell in easily with all that he proposed, and then he took away from them all religion and released them from all those duties of piety, devotion, and the fear of God that he prescribed for them in the beginning. He permitted them pillage, and every sort of immoral licence, and taught them to throw off the yoke of prayer, fasting, and other precepts. He taught them that they were held by no obligations, and that they could pillage the goods and shed the blood of their adversaries with impunity, that the knowledge of the master of truth to whom he had called them took the place of everything else, and that with this knowledge they need no longer fear sin or punishment.

As the result of these teachings the Karmathites rapidly became a band of brigands, pillaging and massacring all those who opposed them and spreading terror throughout all the surrounding districts.

Peaceful fraternity was thus turned into a wild lust for conquest; the Karmathites succeeded in dominating a great part of Arabia and the mouth of the Euphrates, and in A.D. 920 extended their ravages westwards. They took possession of the holy city of Mecca, in the defence of which 30,000 Moslems fell. " For a whole century," says von Hammer, " the pernicious doctrines of Karmath raged with fire and sword in the very bosom of Islamism, until the widespread conflagration was extinguished in blood."

But in proclaiming themselves revolutionaries the Karmathites had departed from the plan laid down by the originator of their creed, Abdullah ibn Maymūn, which had consisted not in acts of open violence but in a secret doctrine which should lead to the gradual undermining of all religious faith and a condition of mental anarchy rather than of material chaos. For violence, as always, had produced counter-violence, and it was thus that while the Karmathites were rushing to their own destruction through a series of bloody conflicts, another branch of the Ismailis were quietly reorganizing their forces more in conformity with the original method of their founder. These were the Fatimites, so-called from their professed belief that the doctrine of the Prophet had descended from Ali, husband of Fatima, Mohammed's daughter. Whilst less extreme than the Karmathites, or than their predecessor Abdullah ibn Maymūn, the Fatimites, according to the historian Makrizi, adopted the method of instilling doubts into the minds of believers and aimed at the substitution of a natural for a revealed religion. Indeed, after the establishment of their power in Egypt, it is difficult to distinguish any appreciable degree of difference in the character of their teaching from the anarchic code of Abdullah and his more violent exponent Karmath.

The Fatimites

The founder of the Fatimite dynasty of the Khalifas was one Ubeidallah, known as the Mahdi, accused of Jewish ancestry by his adversaries the Abbasides, who declared—apparently without truth—that he was the son or grandson of Ahmed, son of Adbullah ibn Maymūn, by a Jewess. Under the fourth Fatimite Khalifa Egypt fell into the power of the dynasty, and, before long, bi-weekly assemblages of both men and women known as "societies of wisdom" were instituted in Cairo. In 1004 these acquired a greater importance by the establishment of the Dar ul Hikmat, or the House of Knowledge, by the sixth Khalifa Hakim, who was raised to a deity after his death and is worshipped to this day by the Druses. Under the direction of the Dar ul Hikmat or Grand Lodge of Cairo, the Fatimites continued the plan of Abdullah ibn Maymūn's secret society with the addition of two more degrees, making nine in all. Their method of enlisting proselytes and system of initiation—which, as Claudio Jannet points out, " are absolutely those which Weishaupt, the founder of the

Illuminati, prescribed to the 'Insinuating Brothers' "[1]—
were transcribed by the fourteenth-century historian Nowairi
in a description that may be briefly summarized thus[2]:

The proselytes were broadly divided into two classes, the
learned and the ignorant.   The Dai was to agree with the
former, applauding his wisdom, and to impress the latter with
his own knowledge by asking him perplexing questions on
the Koran.   Thus in initiating him into the first degree the
Dai assumed an air of profundity and explained that religious
doctrines were too abstruse for the ordinary mind, but must
be interpreted by men who, like the Dais, had a special knowledge of this science.   The initiate was bound to absolute
secrecy concerning the truths to be revealed to him and obliged
to pay in advance for these revelations.   In order to pique his
curiosity, the Dai would suddenly stop short in the middle of
a discourse, and should the novice finally decline to pay the
required sum, he was left in a state of bewilderment which
inspired him with the desire to know more.

In the second degree the initiate was persuaded that all his
former teachers were wrong and that he must place his confidence solely in those Imams endowed with authority from
God; in the third he learnt that these Imams were those of
the Ismailis, seven in number ending with Mohammed, son
of Ismail, in contradistinction to the twelve Imams of the
Imamias who supported the claims of Ismail's brother Musa;
in the fourth he was told that the prophets preceding the
Imams descending from Ali were also seven in number—namely
Adam, Noah, Abraham, Moses, Jesus, the first Mohammed,
and finally Mohammed son of Ismail.

So far, then, nothing was said to the initiate in contradiction to the broad tenets of orthodox Islamism.   But with
the fifth degree the process of undermining his religion began,
he was now told to reject tradition and to disregard the precepts
of Mohammed; in the sixth he was taught that all religious

[1] Claudio Jannet, *Les Précurseurs de la Franc-Maçonnerie,* p. 58 (1887).
[2] The following account is given by de Sacy in connexion with Abdullah
ibn Maymūn (op. cit., I. lxxiv), and Dr. Bussell (*Religious Thought and
Heresy in the Middle Ages,* p. 353) includes it in his chapter on the Karmathites.   Von Hammer, however, gives it as the programme of the Dar ul
Hikmat, and this seems more probable since the initiation consists of nine
degrees and Abdullah's society of Batinis, into which Karmath had been
initiated, included only seven.   Yarker (*The Arcane Schools,* p. 185) says
the two additional degrees were added by the Dar ul Hikmat.   It would
appear then that de Sacy, in placing this account before his description of the
Karmathites, was anticipating.   The point is immaterial, the fact being that
the same system was common to all these ramifications of Ismailis, and that
of the Dar ul Hikmat varied but little from that of Abdullah and Karmath.

observances—prayer, fasting, etc.—were only emblematic, that in fact all these things were devices to keep the common herd of men in subordination; in the seventh the doctrines of Dualism, of a greater and a lesser deity, were introduced and the unity of God—fundamental doctrine of Islamism—was destroyed; in the eighth a great vagueness was expressed on the attributes of the first and greatest of these deities, and it was pointed out that real prophets were those who concerned themselves with practical matters—political institutions and good forms of government; finally, in the ninth, the adept was shown that all religious teaching was allegorical and that religious precepts need only be observed in so far as it is necessary to maintain order, but the man who understands the truth may disregard all such doctrines. Abraham, Moses, Jesus, and the other prophets were therefore only teachers who had profited by the lessons of philosophy. All belief in revealed religion was thus destroyed. It will be seen then that in the last degrees the whole teaching of the first five was reversed and therefore shown to be a fraud. Fraud in fact constituted the system of the society; in the instructions to the Dais every artifice is described for enlisting proselytes by misrepresentation: Jews were to be won by speaking ill of Christians, Christians by speaking ill of Jews and Moslems alike, Sunnis by referring with respect to the orthodox Khalifas Abu Bakr and Omar and criticizing Ali and his descendants. Above all, care was to be taken not to put before proselytes doctrines that might revolt them, but to make them advance step by step. By these means they would be ready to obey any commands. As the instructions express it:

If you were to give the order to whoever it might be to take from him all that he holds most precious, above all his money, he would oppose none of your orders, and if death surprised him he would leave you all that he possesses in his will and make you his heir. He will think that in the whole world he cannot find a man more worthy than you.

Such was the great secret society which was to form the model for the Illuminati of the eighteenth century, to whom the summary of von Hammer might with equal truth apply:

To believe nothing and to dare all was, in two words, the sum of this system, which annihilated every principle of religion and morality, and had no other object than to execute ambitious designs with suitable ministers, who, daring all and knowing nothing, since they consider everything a cheat and nothing forbidden, are the best tools of an infernal policy. A system which, with no other aim than the gratification of an insatiable lust for domination, instead of seeking the highest of human objects, precipitates itself into the abyss, and mangling itself, is buried amidst the ruins of thrones and altars, the wreck of national happiness, and the universal execration of mankind.[1]

THE DRUSES

The terrible Grand Lodge of Cairo before long became the centre of a new and extraordinary cult. Hakim sixth Fatimite Khalifa and founder of the Dar ul Hikmat—a monster of tyranny and crime whose reign can only be compared to that of Caligula or Nero—was now raised to the place of a divinity by one Ismail Darazi, a Turk who in 1016 announced in a mosque in Cairo that the Khalifa should be made an object of worship. Hakim, who "believed that divine reason was incarnate in him," four years later proclaimed himself a deity, and the cult was finally established by one of his viziers, the Persian mystic Hamza ibn Ali. Hakim's cruelties, however, had so outraged the people of Egypt that a year later he was murdered by a band of malcontents, led, it is said, by his sister, who afterwards concealed his body—a circumstance which gave his followers the opportunity to declare that the divinity had merely vanished in order to test the faith of believers, but would reappear in time and punish apostates. This belief became the doctrine of the Druses of Lebanon, whom Darazi had won over to the worship of Hakim.

It is unnecessary to enter into the details of this strange religion, which still persists to-day in the range of Lebanon; suffice it to say that, although the outcome of the Ismailis, the Druses do not appear to have embraced the materialism of Abdullah ibn Maymūn, but to have grafted on a primitive form of Nature-worship and of Sabeism the avowed belief of the Ismailis in the dynasty of Ali and his successors, and beyond this an abstruse, esoteric creed concerning the nature of the Supreme Deity. God they declare to be "Universal Reason," who manifests Himself by a series of "avatars." Hakim was the last of the divine embodiments, and "when evil and misery have increased to the predestined height he will again appear, to conquer the world and to make his religion supreme."

It is, however, as a secret society that the Druses enter into the scope of this book, for their organization presents several

[1] Von Hammer, op. cit. (Eng. trans.), pp. 36, 37.

analogies with that which we now know as " masonic." Instead of the nine degrees instituted by the Lodge of Cairo, the Druses are divided into only three—Profanes, Aspirants, and Wise—to whom their doctrines are gradually unfolded under seal of the strictest secrecy, to ensure which signs and passwords are employed after the manner of Freemasonry. A certain degree of duplicity appears to enter into their scheme, much resembling that enjoined to the Ismaili Dais when enlisting proselytes belonging to other religions: thus in talking to Mohammedans, the Druses profess to be followers of the Prophet; with Christians, they pretend to hold the doctrines of Christianity, an attitude they defend on the score that it is unlawful to reveal the secret dogmas of their creed to a " Black," or unbeliever.

The Druses are in the habit of holding meetings where, as in the Dar ul Hikmat, both men and women assemble and religious and political questions are discussed; the uninitiated, however, are allowed to exercise no influence on decisions, which are reached by the inner circle, to which only the " Wise " are admitted. The resemblance between this organization and that of Grand Orient Freemasonry is clearly apparent. The Druses also have modes of recognition which are common to Freemasonry, and M. Achille Laurent has observed: " The formula or catechism of the Druses resembles that of the Freemasons; one can learn it only from the *Akals* (or Akels = Intelligent, a small group of higher initiates), who only reveal its mysteries after having subjected one to tests and made one take terrible oaths."

I shall refer again later in this book to the affinity between the Druses and Freemasons of the Grand Orient.

The Assassins

It will be seen that the Druses, distinguishing themselves from other Ismaili sects by their worship of Hakim, yet retaining genuine religious beliefs, had not carried on the atheistical tradition of Abdullah ibn Maymūn and of the Grand Lodge of Cairo. But this tradition was to find in 1090 an exponent in the Persian Hasan Saba, a native of Khorasan, the son of Ali, a strict Shiah, who, finding himself suspected of heretical ideas, ended by declaring himself a Sunni. Hasan, brought up in this atmosphere of duplicity, was therefore well fitted to play the Machiavellian rôle of an Ismaili Dai.

Von Hammer regards Hasan as a mighty genius, one of a

splendid triad, of which the two others were his schoolfellows the poet Omar Khayyám and Nizam ul Mulk, Grand Vizier under the Seljuk Sultan, Malik Shah. Hasan, having through the protection of Nizam ul Mulk secured titles and revenues and finally risen to office at the Court of the Sultan, attempted to supplant his benefactor and eventually retired in disgrace, vowing vengeance against the Sultan and vizier. At this juncture he encountered several Ismailis, one of whom, a Dai named Mumin, finally converted him to the principles of his sect, and Hasan, declaring himself now to be a convinced adherent of the Fatimite Khalifas, journed to Cairo, where he was received with honour by the Dar ul Hikmat and also by the Khalifa Mustansir, to whom he became counsellor. But his intrigues once more involving him in disgrace, he fled to Aleppo and laid the foundations of his new sect. After enlisting proselytes in Bagdad, Ispahan, Khusistan, and Damaghan, he succeeded in obtaining by strategy the fortress of Alamut in Persia on the Caspian Sea, where he completed the plans for his great secret society which was to become for ever infamous under the name of the Hashishiyīn, or *Assassins.*

Under the pretence of belief in the doctrines of Islam and also of adherence to the Ismaili line of succession from the Prophet, Hasan Saba now set out to pave his way to power, and in order to achieve this end adopted the same method as Abdullah ibn Maymūn. But the terrible efficiency of Hasan's society consisted in the fact that a system of physical force was now organized in a manner undreamt of by his predecessor. As von Hammer has observed in an admirable passage:

Opinions are powerless, so long as they only confuse the brain, without arming the hand. Scepticism and free-thinking, as long as they occupied only the minds of the indolent and philosophical, have caused the ruin of no throne, for which purpose religious and political fanaticism are the strongest levers in the hands of nations. It is nothing to the ambitious man what people believe, but it is everything to know how he may turn them for the execution of his projects.[1]

Thus, as in the case of the French Revolution, "whose first movers," von Hammer also observes, "were the tools or leaders of secret societies," it was not mere theory but the method of enlisting numerous dupes and placing weapons in their hands that brought about the "Terror" of the Assassins

[1] Von Hammer, *The History of the Assassins*, pp. 45, 46.

46 SECRET SOCIETIES

six centuries before that of their spiritual descendants, the Jacobins of 1793.

Taking as his groundwork the organization of the Grand Lodge of Cairo, Hasan reduced the nine degrees to their original number of seven, but these now received a definite nomenclature, and included not only real initiates but active agents.

Descending downwards, the degrees of the Assassins were thus as follows: first, the Grand Master, known as the Shaikh-al-Jabal or "Old Man of the Mountain"—owing to the fact that the Order always possessed itself of castles in mountainous regions; second, the Dail Kebir or Grand Priors; third, the fully initiated Dais, religious nuncios and political emissaries; fourth, the Rafiqs or associates, in training for the higher degrees; fifth, the Fadais or "devoted," who undertook to deliver the secret blow on which their superiors had decided; sixth, the Lasiqs, or law brothers; and lastly the "common people," who were to be simply blind instruments. If the equivalents to the words "Dai," "Rafiqs," and "Fadais" given by von Hammer and Dr. Bussell as "Master Masons," "Fellow Crafts," and "Entered Apprentices" are accepted, an interesting analogy with the degrees of Freemasonry is provided.

Designs against religion were, of course, not admitted by the Order; "strict uniformity to Islam was demanded from all the lower rank of uninitiated, but the *adept* was taught to see through the deception of 'faith and works.' He believed in nothing and recognized that all acts or means were indifferent and the (secular) end alone to be considered."[1]

Thus the final object was domination by a few men consumed with the lust of power "under the cloak of religion and piety," and the method by which this was to be established was the wholesale assassination of those who opposed them.

In order to stimulate the energy of the Fadais, who were required to carry out these crimes, the superiors of the Order had recourse to an ingenious system of delusion. Throughout the territory occupied by the Assassins were exquisite gardens with fruit trees, bowers of roses, and sparkling streams. Here were arranged luxurious resting-places with Persian carpets and soft divans, around which hovered black-eyed "houris" bearing wine in gold and silver drinking-vessels, whilst soft music mingled with the murmuring water and the song of

[1] Dr. F. W. Bussell, *Religious Thought and Heresy in the Middle Ages,* p. 368.

birds. The young man whom the Assassins desired to train for a career of crime was introduced to the Grand Master of the Order and intoxicated with haschisch—hence the name " Hashishiyīn " applied to the sect, from which the word assassin is derived. Under the brief spell of unconsciousness induced by this seductive drug the prospective Fadai was then carried into the garden, where on awaking he believed himself to be in Paradise. After enjoying all its delights he was given a fresh dose of the opiate, and, once more unconscious, was transported back to the presence of the Grand Master, who assured him that he had never left his side but had merely experienced a foretaste of the Paradise that awaited him if he obeyed the orders of his chiefs. The neophyte, thus spurred on by the belief that he was carrying out the commands of the Prophet, who would reward him with eternal bliss, eagerly entered into the schemes laid down for him and devoted his life to murder. Thus by the lure of Paradise the Assassins enlisted instruments for their criminal work and established a system of organized murder on a basis of religious fervour. " ' Nothing is true and all is allowed ' was the ground of their secret doctrine, which, however, being imparted but to few and concealed under the veil of the most austere religionism and piety, restrained the mind under the yoke of blind obedience."[1] To the outside world all this remained a profound mystery; fidelity to Islam was proclaimed as the fundamental doctrine of the sect, and when the envoy of Sultan Sajar was sent to collect information on the religious beliefs of the Order he was met with the assurance: " We believe in the unity of God, and consider that only as true wisdom which accords with His word and the commands of the prophet."

Von Hammer, answering the possible contention that, as in the case of the Templars and the Bavarian Illuminati, these methods of deception might be declared a calumny on the Order, points out that in the case of the Assassins no possible doubt existed, for their secret doctrines were eventually revealed by the leaders themselves, first by Hasan II, the third successor of Hasan Saba, and later by Jalal-ud-din Hasan, who publicly anathematized the founders of the sect and ordered the burning of the books that contained their designs against religion—a proceeding which, however, appears to have been a strategical manœuvre for restoring confidence

[1] Von Hammer, op. cit., p. 55.

in the Order and enabling him to continue the work of sub-version and crime. A veritable Reign of Terror was thus established throughout the East; the Rafiqs and Fadais " spread themselves in troops over the whole of Asia and darkened the face of the earth "; and " in the annals of the Assassins is found the chronological enumeration of celebrated men of all nations who have fallen the victims of the Ismailis, to the joy of their murderers and the sorrow of the world."[1]

Inevitably this long and systematic indulgence in blood-lust recoiled on the heads of the leaders, and the Assassins, like the Terrorists of France, ended by turning on each other. The Old Man of the Mountain himself was murdered by his brother-in-law and his son Mohammed; Mohammed, in his turn, whilst " aiming at the life of his son Jalal-ud-din, was anticipated by him with poison, which murder was again avenged by poison," so that from " Hasan the Illuminator " down to the last of his line the Grand Masters fell by the hands of their next-of-kin, and " poison and the dagger prepared the grave which the Order had opened for so many."[2] Finally in 1250 the conquering hordes of the Mongol Mangu Khan swept away the dynasty of the Assassins.

But, although as reigning powers the Assassins and Fati-mites ceased to exist, the sects from which they derived have continued up to the present day; still every year at the celebration of the Moharram the Shiahs beat their breasts and besprinkle themselves with blood, calling aloud on the martyred heroes Hasan and Husain; the Druses of the Lebanon still await the return of Hakim, and in that inscrutable East, the cradle of all the mysteries, the profoundest European adept of secret society intrigue may find himself outdistanced by pastmasters in the art in which he believed himself proficient.

The sect of Hasan Saba was the supreme model on which all systems of organized murder working through fanaticism, such as the Carbonari and the Irish Republican Brotherhood, were based, and the signs, the symbols, the initiations, of the Grand Lodge of Cairo formed the groundwork for the great secret societies of Europe.

How came this system to be transported to the West? By what channel did the ideas of these succeeding Eastern sects penetrate to the Christian world? In order to answer this question we must turn to the history of the Crusades.

---

[1] Von Hammer, op. cit., pp. 83, 89.   [2] Ibid., p. 164.

3

THE TEMPLARS

IN the year 1118—nineteen years after the first crusade had ended with the defeat of the Moslems, the capture of Antioch and Jerusalem, and the instalment of Godefroi de Bouillon as king of the latter city—a band of nine French *gentilshommes,* led by Hugues de Payens and Godefroi de Saint-Omer, formed themselves into an Order for the protection of pilgrims to the Holy Sepulchre. Baldwin II, who at this moment succeeded to the throne of Jerusalem, presented them with a house near the site of the Temple of Solomon—hence the name of Knights Templar under which they were to become famous. In 1128 the Order was sanctioned by the Council of Troyes and by the Pope, and a rule was drawn up by St. Bernard under which the Knights Templar were bound by the vows of poverty, chastity, and obedience.

But although the Templars distinguished themselves by many deeds of valour, the regulation that they were to live solely on alms led to donations so enormous that, abandoning their vow of poverty, they spread themselves over Europe, and by the end of the twelfth century had become a rich and powerful body. The motto that the Order had inscribed upon its banner, " *Non nobis, Domine, sed nomini tuo da gloriam,*" was like-wise forgotten, for, their faith waxing cold, they gave them-selves up to pride and ostentation. Thus, as an eighteenth-century masonic writer has expressed it:

The war, which for the greater number of warriors of good faith proved the source of weariness, of losses and misfortunes, became for them (the Templars) only the opportunity for booty and aggrandize-ment, and if they distinguished themselves by a few brilliant actions, their motive soon ceased to be a matter of doubt when they were seen to enrich themselves even with the spoils of the confederates, to increase their credit by the extent of the new possessions they had acquired, to carry arrogance to the point of rivalling crowned princes in pomp and grandeur, to refuse their aid against the enemies of the faith, as the history of Saladin testifies, and finally to ally themselves with that horrible and sanguinary prince named the Old Man of the Mountain, Prince of the Assassins.[1]

The truth of the last accusation is, however, open to question. For a time, at any rate, the Templars had been at war with the Assassins. When in 1152 the Assassins murdered Raymond, Comte de Tripoli, the Templars entered their territory and forced them to sign a treaty by which they were to pay a yearly tribute of 12,000 gold pieces in expiation of the crime. Some years later the Old Man of the Mountain sent an ambassador to Amaury, King of Jerusalem, to tell him privately that if the Templars would forgo the payment of this tribute he and his followers would embrace the Christian faith. Amaury accepted, offering at the same time to compensate the Templars, but some of the Knights assassinated the ambassador before he could return to his master. When asked for reparations the Grand Master threw the blame on an evil one-eyed Knight named Gautier de Maisnil.[2]

It is evident, therefore, that the relations between the Templars and the Assassins were at first far from amicable; nevertheless, it appears probable that later on an understanding was brought about between them. Both on this charge and on that of treachery towards the Christian armies, Dr. Bussell's impartial view of the question may be quoted:

When in 1149 the Emperor Conrad III failed before Damascus, the Templars were believed to have a secret understanding with the garrison of that city; . . . in 1154 they were said to have sold, for 60,000 gold pieces, a prince of Egypt who had wished to become a Christian; he was taken home to suffer certain death at the hands of his fanatical family. In 1166 Amaury, King of Jerusalem, hanged twelve members of the Order for betraying a fortress to Nureddin.

And Dr. Bussell goes on to say that it cannot be disputed that they had " long and important dealings " with the Assassins " and were therefore suspected (not unfairly) of imbibing their precepts and following their principles."[3]

By the end of the thirteenth century the Templars had become suspect, not only in the eyes of the clergy, but of the general public. "Amongst the common people," one of their latest apologists admits, "vague rumours circulated. They

[1] *Développement des abus introduits dans la Franc-maçonnerie*, p. 56 (1780).
[2] Jules Loiseleur, *La doctrine secrète des Templiers*, p. 89.
[3] Dr. F. W. Bussell, D.D., *Religious Thought and Heresy in the Middle Ages*, pp. 796, 797 note.

talked of the covetousness and want of scruple of the Knights, of their passion for aggrandizement and their rapacity. Their haughty insolence was proverbial. Drinking habits were attributed to them; the saying was already in use ' to drink like a Templar.' The old German word *Tempelhaus* indicated a house of ill-fame."[1]

The same rumours had reached Clement V even before his accession to the papal throne in 1305,[2] and in this same year he summoned the Grand Master of the Order, Jacques du Molay, to return to France from the island of Cyprus, where he was assembling fresh forces to avenge the recent reverses of the Christian armies.

Du Molay arrived in France with sixty other Knights Templar and 150,000 gold florins, as well as a large quantity of silver that the Order had amassed in the East.[3]

The Pope now set himself to make enquiries concerning the charges of " unspeakable apostasy against God, detestable idolatry, execrable vice, and many heresies " that had been " secretly intimated " to him. But, to quote his own words:

Because it did not seem likely nor credible that men of such religion who were believed often to shed their blood and frequently expose their persons to the peril of death for Christ's name, and who showed such great and many signs of devotion both in divine offices as well as in fasts, as in other devotional observances, should be so forgetful of their salvation as to do these things, we were unwilling . . . to give ear to this kind of insinuation . . ,. (*hujusmodi insinuacioni ac delacioni ipsorum . . . aurem noluimus inclinare*).[4]

The King of France, Philippe le Bel, who had hitherto been the friend of the Templars, now became alarmed and urged the Pope to take action against them; but before the Pope was able to find out more about the matter, the King took the law into his own hands and had all the Templars in France arrested on October 13, 1307. The following charges were

[1] G. Mollat, *Les Papes d'Avignon*, p. 233 (1912).
[2] Michelet, *Procès des Templiers*, I. 2 (1841). This work largely consists of the publication in Latin of the Papal *bulls* and trials of the Templars before the Papal Commission in Paris contained in the original document once preserved at *Notre Dame*. Michelet says that another copy was sent to the Pope and kept under the triple key of the Vatican. Mr. E. J. Castle, K.C., however, says that he has enquired about the whereabouts of this copy and it is no longer in the Vatican (*Proceedings against the Templars in France and in England for Heresy*, republished from *Ars Quatuor Coronatorum*, Vol. XX. Part III. p. 1).
[3] M. Raynouard, *Monuments historiques relatifs à la condamnation des Chevaliers du Temple et de l'abolition de leur Ordre*, p. 17 (1813).
[4] Michelet, op. cit. I. 2 (1841).

then brought against them by the Inquisitor for France before whom they were examined:

1. The ceremony of initiation into their Order was accompanied by insults to the Cross, the denial of Christ, and gross obscenities.

2. The adoration of an idol which was said to be the image of the true God.

3. The omission of the words of consecration at Mass.

4. The right that the lay chiefs arrogated to themselves of giving absolution.

5. The authorization of unnatural vice.

To all these infamies a great number of the Knights, including Jacques du Molay, confessed in almost precisely the same terms; at their admission into the Order, they said, they had been shown the cross on which was the figure of Christ, and had been asked whether they believed in Him; when they answered yes, they were told in some cases that this was wrong (*dixit sibi quod male credebat*),[1] because He was not God, He was a false prophet (*quia falsus propheta erat, nec erat Deus*).[2] Some added that they were then shown an idol or a bearded head which they were told to worship[3]; one added that this was of such " a terrible aspect that it seemed to him to be the face of some devil, called in French *un maufé*, and that whenever he saw it he was so overcome with fear that he could hardly look at it without fear and trembling."[4] All who confessed declared that they had been ordered to spit on the crucifix, and very many that they had received the injunction to commit obscenities and to practise unnatural vice. Some said that on their refusal to carry out these orders they had been threatened with imprisonment, even perpetual imprisonment; a few said they had actually been incarcerated[5]; one declared that he had been terrorized, seized by the throat, and threatened with death.[6]

Since, however, a number of these confessions were made

---

[1] Michelet, *Procès des Templiers*, II. 333.

[2] Ibid., pp. 295, 333.

[3] Ibid., pp. 290, 299, 300.

[4] " Dixit per juramentum suum quod ita est terribilis figure et aspectus quod videbatur sibi quod esset figura cujusdam demonis, dicendo gallice *d'un maufé*, et quod quocienscumque videbat ipsum tantus timor eum invadebat, quod vix poterat illud respicere nisi cum maximo timore et tremore." —Ibid., p. 364.

[5] Ibid., pp. 284, 338. " Ipse minabatur sibi quod nisi faceret, ipse poneret-eum in carcere perpetuo."—Ibid., p. 307.

[6] " Et fuit territus plus quam unquam fuit in vita sua: et statim unus eorum accepit eum per gutur, dicens quod oportebat quod hoc faceret, vel moreretur."—Ibid., p. 296.

under torture, it is more important to consider the evidence provided by the trial of the Knights at the hands of the Pope, where this method was not employed.

Now, at the time the Templars were arrested, Clement V, deeply resenting the King's interference with an Order which existed entirely under papal jurisdiction, wrote in the strongest terms of remonstrance to Philippe le Bel urging their release, and even after their trial, neither the confessions of the Knights nor the angry expostulations of the King could persuade him to believe in their guilt.[1] But as the scandal concerning the Templars was increasing, he consented to receive in private audience " a certain Knight of the Order, of great nobility and held by the said Order in no slight esteem," who testified to the abominations that took place on the reception of the Brethren, the spitting on the cross, and other things which were not lawful nor, humanly speaking, decent.[2]

The Pope then decided to hold an examination of seventy-two French Knights at Poictiers in order to discover whether the confessions made by them before the Inquisitor at Paris could be substantiated, and at this examination, conducted without torture or pressure of any kind in the presence of the Pope himself, the witnesses declared on oath that they would tell " the full and pure truth." They then made confessions which were committed to writing in their presence, and these being afterwards read aloud to them, they expressly and willingly approved them (*perseverantes in illis eas expresse et sponte, prout recitate fuerunt approbarunt*).[3]

Besides this, an examination of the Grand Master, Jacques du Molay, and the Preceptors of the Order was held in the presence of " three Cardinals and four public notaries and many other good men." These witnesses, says the official report, " having sworn with their hands on the Gospel of God " (*ad sancta dei evangelia ab iis corporaliter tacta*) that—

they would on all the aforesaid things speak the pure and full truth, they, separately, freely, and spontaneously, without any coercion and fear, deposed and confessed among other things, the denial of Christ and spitting upon the cross when they were received into the Order of the Temple. And some of them (deposed and confessed) that under the same form, namely, with denial of Christ and spitting on the cross, they had received many Brothers

---

[1] Mollat, op. cit., p. 241.
[2] *Procès des Templiers*, I. 3: Mr. E. J. Castle, op. cit. Part III. p. 3. (It should be noted that Mr. Castle's paper is strongly in favour of the Templars.)
[3] Ibid., I. 4.

into the Order. Some of them too confessed certain other horrible and disgusting things on which we are silent. . . . Besides this, they said and confessed that those things which are contained in the confessions and depositions of heretical depravity which they made lately before the Inquisitor (of Paris) were true.

Their confessions, being again committed to writing, were approved by the witnesses, who then with bended knees and many tears asked for and obtained absolution.[1]

The Pope, however, still refused to take action against the whole Order merely because the Master and Brethren around him had "gravely sinned," and it was decided to hold a papal commission in Paris. The first sitting took place in November 1309, when the Grand Master and 231 Knights were summoned before the pontifical commissioners. "This enquiry," says Michelet, "was conducted slowly, with much consideration and gentleness (*avec beaucoup de ménagement et de douceur*) by high ecclesiastical dignitaries, an archbishop, several bishops, etc."[2] But although a number of the Knights, including the Grand Master, now retracted their admissions, some damning confessions were again forthcoming.

It is impossible within the scope of this book to follow the many trials of the Templars that took place in different countries—in Italy, at Ravenna, Pisa, Bologna, and Florence, where torture was not employed and blasphemies were admitted,[3] or in Germany, where torture was employed but no confessions were made and a verdict was given in favour of the Order. A few details concerning the trial in England may, however, be of interest.

It has generally been held that torture was not applied in England owing to the humanity of Edward II, who at first absolutely refused to listen to any accusations against the Order.[4] On December 10, 1307, he had written to the Pope in these terms:

And because the said Master or Brethren constant in the purity of the Catholic faith have been frequently commended by us, and by all our kingdom, both in their life and morals, we are unable to believe in suspicious stories of this kind until we know with greater certainty about these things.

We, therefore, pity from our souls the suffering and losses of the

[1] *Procès des Templiers*, I. 5.
[2] Michelet in Preface to Vol. I. of *Procès des Templiers*.
[3] Jules Loiseleur, *La Doctrine Secrète des Templiers*, p. 40 (1872).
[4] Ibid., p. 16.

Sd. Master and brethren, which they suffer in consequence of such infamy, and we supplicate most affectionately your Sanctity if it please you, that considering with favour suited to the good character of the Master and brethren, you may deem fit to meet with more indulgence the detractions, calumnies and charges by certain envious and evil disposed persons, who endeavour to turn their good deeds into works of perverseness opposed to divine teaching; until the said charges attributed to them shall have been brought legally before you or your representatives here and more fully proved.[1]

Edward II also wrote in the same terms to the Kings of Portugal, Castile, Aragon, and Sicily. But two years later, after Clement V had himself heard the confessions of the Order, and a Papal Bull had been issued declaring that " the unspeakable wickednesses and abominable crimes of notorious heresy " had now " come to the knowledge of almost everyone," Edward II was persuaded to arrest the Templars and order their examination. According to Mr. Castle, whose interesting treatise we quote here, the King would not allow torture to be employed, with the result that the Knights denied all charges; but later, it is said, he allowed himself to be overpersuaded, and "torture appears to have been applied on one or two occasions,"[2] with the result that three Knights confessed to all and were given absolution.[3] At Southwark, however, " a considerable number of brethren " admitted that " they had been strongly accused of the crimes of negation and spitting, they did not say they were guilty but that they could not purge themselves . . . and therefore they abjured these and all other heresies."[4] Evidence was also given against the Order by outside witnesses, and the same stories of intimidation at the ceremony of reception were told.[5] At any rate, the result of the investigation was not altogether satisfactory, and the Templars were

[1] *Proceedings against the Templars in France and England for Heresy*, by E. J. Castle, Part I. p. 16, quoting Rymer, Vol. III. p. 37.
[2] Ibid., Part II. p. 1.
[3] Ibid., Part II. pp. 25–7.
[4] Ibid., Part II. p. 30.
[5] " Another witness of the Minor Friars told the Commissioners he had heard from Brother Robert of Tukenham that a Templar had a son who saw through a partition that they asked one professing if he believed in the Crucified, showing him the figure, whom they killed upon his refusing to deny Him, but the boy, some time after, being asked if he wished to be a Templar said no, because he had seen this thing done. Saying this, he was killed by his father. . . . The twenty-third witness, a Knight, said that his uncle entered the Order healthy and joyfully, with his birds and dogs, and the third day following he was dead, and he suspected it was on account of the crimes he had heard of them, and that the cause of his death was he would not consent to the evil deeds perpetrated by other brethren."— Ibid., Part II. p. 13.

finally suppressed in England as elsewhere by the Council of Vienne in 1312.

In France more rigorous measures were adopted and fifty-four Knights who had retracted their confessions were burnt at the stake as " relapsed heretics " on May 12, 1310. Four years later, on March 14, 1314, the Grand Master, Jacques du Molay, suffered the same fate.

Now, however much we must execrate the barbarity of this sentence—as also the cruelties that had preceded it—this is no reason why we should admit the claim of the Order to noble martyrdom put forward by the historians who have espoused their cause. The character of the Templars is not rehabilitated by condemning the conduct of the King and Pope. Yet this is the line of argument usually adopted by the defenders of the Order. Thus the two main contentions on which they base their defence are, firstly, that the confessions of the Knights were made under torture, therefore they must be regarded as null and void; and, secondly, that the whole affair was a plot concerted between the King and Pope in order to obtain possession of the Templars' riches. Let us examine these contentions in turn.

In the first place, as we have seen, all confessions were not made under torture. No one, as far as I am aware, disputes Michelet's assertion that the enquiry before the Papal Commission in Paris, at which a number of Knights adhered to the statements they had made to the Pope, was conducted without pressure of any kind. But further, the fact that confessions are made under torture does not necessarily invalidate them as evidence. Guy Fawkes also confessed under torture, yet it is never suggested that the whole story of the Gunpowder Plot was a myth. Torture, however much we may condemn it, has frequently proved the only method for overcoming the intimidation exercised over the mind of a conspirator; a man bound by the terrible obligations of a confederacy and fearing the vengeance of his fellow-conspirators will not readily yield to persuasion, but only to force. If, then, some of the Templars were terrorized by torture, or even by the fear of torture, it must not be forgotten that terrorism was exercised by both sides. Few will deny that the Knights were bound by oaths of secrecy, so that on one hand they were threatened with the vengeance of the Order if they betrayed its secrets, and on the other faced with torture if they refused to confess. Thus they found themselves between the devil and the deep sea. It was therefore not a case of a mild and unoffending Order meeting

with brutal treatment at the hands of authority, but of the
victims of a terrible autocracy being delivered into the hands
of another autocracy.

Moreover, do the confessions of the Knights appear to be
the outcome of pure imagination such as men under the
influence of torture might devise? It is certainly difficult to
believe that the accounts of the ceremony of initiation given in
detail by men in different countries, all closely resembling each
other, yet related in different phraseology, could be pure inventions. Had the victims been driven to invent they would
surely have contradicted each other, have cried out in their
agony that all kinds of wild and fantastic rites had taken place
in order to satisfy the demands of their interlocutors. But no,
each appears to be describing the same ceremony more or less
completely, with characteristic touches that indicate the
personality of the speaker, and in the main all the stories
tally.

The further contention that the case against the Templars
was manufactured by the King and Pope with a view to obtaining their wealth is entirely disproved by facts. The latest
French historian of mediæval France, whilst expressing disbelief
in the guilt of the Templars, characterizes this counter-
accusation as " puerile." " Philippe le Bel," writes M. Funck-
Brentano, " has never been understood; from the beginning
people have not been just to him. This young prince was one
of the greatest kings and the noblest characters that have
appeared in history."[1]

Without carrying appreciation so far, one must nevertheless
accord to M. Funck-Brentano's statement of facts the attention
it merits. Philippe has been blamed for debasing the coin of
the realm; in reality he merely ordered it to be mixed with
alloy as a necessary measure after the war with England,[2] precisely as own coinage was debased in consequence of the recent
war. This was done quite openly and the coinage was restored
at the earliest opportunity. Intensely national, his policy of
attacking the Lombards, exiling the Jews, and suppressing the
Templars, however regrettable the methods by which it was
carried out, resulted in immense benefits to France; M. Funck-
Brentano has graphically described the prosperity of the whole
country during the early fourteenth century—the increase of
population, flourishing agriculture and industry. " In Provence

---

[1] F. Funck-Brentano, *Le Moyen Age*, p. 396 (1922).
[2] Ibid., p. 384.

and Languedoc one meets swineherds who have vineyards; simple cowherds who have town houses."[1]

The attitude of Philippe le Bel towards the Templars must be viewed in this light—ruthless suppression of any body of people who interfered with the prosperity of France. His action was not that of arbitrary authority; he " proceeded," says M. Funck-Brentano, " by means of an appeal to the people. In his name Nogaret (the Chancellor) spoke to the Parisians in the garden of the Palace (October 13, 1307). Popular assemblies were convoked all over France ";[2] " the Parliament of Tours, with hardly a dissentient vote, declared the Templars worthy of death. The University of Paris gave the weight of their judgement as to the fullness and authenticity of the confessions."[3] Even assuming that these bodies were actuated by the same servility as that which has been attributed to the Pope, how are we to explain the fact that the trial of the Order aroused no opposition among the far from docile people of Paris? If the Templars had indeed, as they professed, been leading noble and upright lives, devoting themselves to the care of the poor, one might surely expect their arrest to be followed by popular risings. But there appears to have been no sign of this.

As to the Pope, we have already seen that from the outset he had shown himself extremely reluctant to condemn the Order, and no satisfactory explanation is given of his change of attitude except that he wished to please the King. As far as his own interests were concerned, it is obvious that he could have nothing to gain by publishing to the world a scandal that must inevitably bring opprobrium on the Church. His lamentations to this effect in the famous Bull[4] clearly show that he recognized this danger and therefore desired at all costs to clear the accused Knights, if evidence could be obtained in their favour. It was only when the Templars made damning admissions in his presence that he was obliged to abandon their defence.[5] Yet we are told that he did this out of base compliance with the wishes of Philippe le Bel.

Philippe le Bell is thus represented as the arch-villain of the

[1] F. Funck Brentano, op. cit., p. 396.
[2] Ibid., p. 387.
[3] Dean Milman, *History of Latin Christianity*, VII. 213.
[4] E. J. Castle, op. cit., Part I. p. 22.
[5] Thus even M. Mollat admits: " En tout cas leurs dépositions, défavorables à l'Ordre, l'impressionnèrent si vivement que, par une série de graves mesures, il abandonna une à une toutes ses oppositions."—*Les Papes d'Avignon*, p. 242.

whole piece, through seven long years hounding down a blameless Order—from whom up to the very moment of their arrest he had repeatedly received loans of money—solely with the object of appropriating their wealth. Yet after all we find that the property of the Templars was not appropriated by the King, but was given by him to the Knights of St. John of Jerusalem!

What was the fate of the Templars' goods? Philippe le Bel decided that they should be handed over to the Hospitallers. Clement V states that the Orders given by the King on this subject were executed. Even the domain of the Temple in Paris . . . up to the eve of the Revolution was the property of the Knights of St. John of Jerusalem. The royal treasury kept for itself certain sums for the costs of the trial. These had been immense.[1]

These facts in no way daunt the antagonists of Philippe, who we are now assured—again without any proof whatever—was overruled by the Pope in this matter. But setting all morality aside, as a mere question of policy, is it likely that the King would have deprived himself of his most valuable financial supporters and gone to the immense trouble of bringing them to trial without first assuring himself that he would benefit by the affair? Would he, in other words, have killed the goose that laid the golden eggs without any guarantee that the body of the goose would remain in his possession? Again, if, as we are told, the Pope suppressed the Order so as to please the King, why should he have thwarted him over the whole purpose the King had in view? Might we not expect indignant remonstrances from Philippe at thus being baulked of the booty he had toiled so long to gain? But, on the contrary, we find him completely in agreement with the Pope on this subject. In November 1309 Clement V distinctly stated that " Philippe the Illustrious, King of France," to whom the facts concerning the Templars had been told, was " not prompted by avarice since he desired to keep or appropriate for himself no part of the property of the Templars, but liberally and devotedly left them to us and the Church to be administered," etc.[2]

Thus the whole theory concerning the object for which the Templars were suppressed falls to the ground—a theory which on examination is seen to be built up entirely on the plan of imputing motives without any justification in facts. The

[1] F. Funck-Brentano, op. cit., p. 392.
[2] E. J. Castle, *Proceedings against the Templars*, A.Q.C., Vol. XX. Part III. p. 3.

King acted from cupidity, the Pope from servility, and the Templars confessed from fear of torture—on these pure hypotheses defenders of the Order base their arguments.

The truth is, far more probably, that if the King had any additional reason for suppressing the Templars it was not envy of their wealth but fear of the immense power their wealth conferred; the Order dared even to defy the King and to refuse to pay taxes. The Temple in fact constituted an *imperium in imperio* that threatened not only the royal authority but the whole social system.[1] An important light is thrown on the situation by M. Funck-Brentano in this passage:

> As the Templars had houses in all countries, they practised the financial operations of the international banks of our times; they were acquainted with letters of change, orders payable at sight, they instituted dividends and annuities on deposited capital, advanced funds, lent on credit, controlled private accounts, undertook to raise taxes for the lay and ecclesiastical seigneurs.[2]

Through their proficiency in these matters—acquired very possibly from the Jews of Alexandria whom they must have met in the East—the Templars had become the " international financiers " and " international capitalists " of their day; had they not been suppressed, all the evils now denounced by Socialists as peculiar to the system they describe as " Capitalism "—trusts, monopolies, and " corners "—would in all probability have been inaugurated during the course of the fourteenth century in a far worse form than at the present day, since no legislation existed to protect the community at large. The feudal system, as Marx and Engels perceived, was the principal obstacle to exploitation by a financial autocracy.[3]

Moreover, it is by no means improbable that this order of things would have been brought about by the violent overthrow of the French monarchy—indeed, of all monarchies; the Templars, " those terrible conspirators," says Eliphas Lévi, " threatened the whole world with an immense revolution."[4]

[1] Even Raynouard, the apologist of the Templars (op. cit., p. 19), admits that, if less unjust and violent measures had been adopted, the interest of the State and the safety of the throne might have justified the abolition of the Order.
[2] Funck-Brentano, op. cit., p. 386.
[3] " The bourgeoisie, whenever it has conquered power, has destroyed all feudal, patriarchal, and idyllic relations. It has pitilessly torn asunder all the many-coloured feudal bonds which united men to their ' natural superiors,' and has left no tie twixt man and man but naked self-interest and callous cash payment."—*The Communist Manifesto.*
[4] Eliphas Lévi, *Histoire de la Magie*, p. 273.

Here perhaps we may find the reason why this band of dissolute and rapacious nobles has enlisted the passionate sympathy of democratic writers. For it will be noticed that these same writers who attribute the King's condemnation of the Order to envy of their wealth never apply this argument to the demagogues of the eighteenth century and suggest that their accusations against the nobles of France were inspired by cupidity, nor would they ever admit that any such motive may enter into the diatribes against private owners of wealth to-day. The Templars thus remain the only body of capitalists, with the exception of the Jews, to be not only pardoned for their riches but exalted as noble victims of prejudice and envy. Is it merely because the Templars were the enemies of monarchy? Or is it that the world revolution, whilst attacking private owners of property, has never been opposed to International Finance, particularly when combined with anti-Christian tendencies?

It is the continued defence of the Templars which, to the present writer, appears the most convincing evidence against them. For even if one believes them innocent of the crimes laid to their charge, how is it possible to admire them in their later stages? The fact that cannot be denied is that they were false to their obligations; that they took the vow of poverty and then grew not only rich but arrogant; that they took the vow of chastity and became notoriously immoral.[1] Are all these things then condoned because the Templars formed a link in the chain of world revolution?

At this distance of time the guilt or innocence of the Templars will probably never be conclusively established either way; on the mass of conflicting evidence bequeathed to us by history no one can pronounce a final judgement.

Without attempting to digmatize on the question, I would suggest that the real truth may be that the Knights were both innocent and guilty, that is to say, that a certain number were initiated into the secret doctrine of the Order whilst the majority remained throughout in ignorance. Thus according to the evidence of Stephen de Stapelbrugge, an English Knight, "there were two modes of reception, one lawful and good and the other contrary to the Faith."[2] This would account for the fact that some of the accused declined to confess even under the greatest pressure. These may really have known nothing of the real doctrines of the Order,

[1] E. J. Castle, op. cit., A.Q.C., Vol. XX. Part I. p. 11.
[2] Ibid., Part II. p. 24.

which were confided orally only to those whom the superiors regarded as unlikely to be revolted by them. Such have always been the methods of secret societies, from the Ismailis onward.

This theory of a double doctrine is put forward by Loiseleur, who observes:

> If we consult the statutes of the Order of the Temple as they have come down to us, we shall certainly discover there is nothing that justifies the strange and abominable practices revealed at the Inquiry. But . . . besides the public rule, had not the Order another one, whether traditional or written, authorizing or even prescribing these practices—a secret rule, revealed only to the initiates?[1]

Eliphas Lévi also exonerates the majority of the Templars from complicity in either anti-monarchical or anti-religious designs:

> These tendencies were enveloped in profound mystery and the Order made an outward profession of the most perfect orthodoxy. The Chiefs alone knew whither they were going; the rest followed unsuspectingly.[2]

What, then, was the Templar heresy? On this point we find a variety of opinions. According to Wilcke, Ranke, and Weber it was " the unitarian deism of Islam "[3]; Lecouteulx de Canteleu thinks, however, it was derived from heretical Islamic sources, and relates that whilst in Palestine, one of the Knights, Guillaume de Montbard, was initiated by the Old Man of the Mountain in a cave of Mount Lebanon.[4] That a certain resemblance existed between the Templars and the Assassins has been indicatd by von Hammer,[5] and further emphasized by the Freemason Clavel:

> Oriental historians show us, at different periods, the Order of the Templars maintaining intimate relations with that of the Assassins, and they insist on the affinity that existed between the two associations. They remark that they had adopted the same colours, white and red; that they had the same organization, the same hierarchy of degrees, those of fedavi, refik, and dai in one corresponding to those of novice, professed, and knight in the other; that both

[1] Loiseleur, op. cit., pp. 20, 21.
[2] Histoire de la Magie, p. 277.
[3] Dr. F. W. Bussell, Religious Thought and Heresy in the Middle Ages, p. 803.
[4] Les Sectes et Sociétés Secrètes, p. 85.
[5] History of the Assassins, p. 80.

conspired for the ruin of the religions they professed in public, and
that finally both possessed numerous castles, the former in Asia,
the latter in Europe.[1]

But in spite of these outward resemblances it does not appear
from the confessions of the Knights that the secret doctrine
of the Templars was that of the Assassins or of any Ismaili
sect by which, in accordance with orthodox Islamism, Jesus
was openly held up as a prophet, although, secretly, indifference to all religion was inculcated. The Templars, as far as
can be discovered, were anti-Christian deists; Loiseleur considers that their ideas were derived from Gnostic or Manichean
dualists—Cathari, Paulicians, or more particularly Bogomils,
of which a brief account must be given here.

The *Paulicians,* who flourished about the seventh century
A.D., bore a resemblance to the Cainites and Ophites in their
detestation of the Demiurgus and in the corruption of their
morals. Later, in the ninth century, the *Bogomils,* whose
name signifies in Slavonic "friends of God" and who had
migrated from Northern Syria and Mesopotamia to the Balkan
Peninsula, particularly Thrace, appeared as a further development of Manichean dualism. Their doctrine may be summarized thus:

God, the Supreme Father, has two sons, the elder Satanael,
the younger Jesus. To Satanael, who sat on the right hand
of God, belonged the right of governing the celestial world,
but, filled with pride, he rebelled against his Father and fell
from Heaven. Then, aided by the companions of his fall, he
created the visible world, image of the celestial, having like
the other its sun, moon, and stars, and last he created man
and the serpent which became his minister. Later Christ
came to earth in order to show men the way to Heaven, but
His death was ineffectual, for even by descending into Hell
He could not wrest the power from Satanael, i.e. Satan.

This belief in the impotence of Christ and the necessity
therefore for placating Satan, not only "the Prince of this
world," but its creator, led to the further doctrine that Satan,
being all-powerful, should be adored. Nicetas Choniates, a
Byzantine historian of the twelfth century, described the followers of this cult as "Satanists," because "considering Satan
powerful they worshipped him lest he might do them harm";
subsequently they were known as Luciferians, their doctrine
(as stated by Neuss and Vitoduranus) being that Lucifer was

[1] F. T. B. Clevel, *Histoire Pittoresque de la Franc-Maçonnerie*, p. 356 (1843).

unjustly driven out of Heaven, that one day he will ascend there again and be restored to his former glory and power in the celestial world.

The Bogomils and Luciferians were thus closely akin, but whilst the former divided their worship between God and His two sons, the latter worshipped Lucifer only, regarding the material world as his work and holding that by indulging the flesh they were propitiating their Demon-Creator. It was said that a black cat, the symbol of Satan, figured in their ceremonies as an object of worship, also that at their horrible nocturnal orgies sacrifices of children were made and their blood used for making the Eucharistic bread of the sect.[1]

> Thus the Templars recognize at the same time a good god, incommunicable to man and consequently without symbolic representation, and a bad god, to whom they give the features of an idol of fearful aspect.[2]

Their most fervent worship was addressed to this god of evil, who alone could enrich them. " They said with the Luciferians: ' The elder son of God, Satanael or Lucifer alone has a right to the homage of mortals; Jesus his younger brother does not deserve this honour.' "[3]

Although we shall not find these ideas so clearly defined in the confessions of the Knights, some colour is lent to this theory by those who related that the reason given to them for not believing in Christ was " that He was nothing, He was a false prophet and of no value, and that they should believe in the Higher God of Heaven who could save them."[4] According to Loiseleur, the idol they were taught to worship, the bearded head known to history as Baphomet, represented " the inferior god, organizer and dominator of the material world, author of good and evil here below, him by whom evil was introduced into creation."[5]

The etymology of the word Baphomet is difficult to discover; Raynouard says it originated with two witnesses heard at

---

[1] Loiseleur, op. cit., p. 66.
[2] Ibid., p. 143.
[3] Ibid., p. 141.
[4] " Dixit sibi quod non crederet in eum, quia nichil erat, et quod erat quidam falsus propheta, et nichil valebat; immo crederet in Deum Celi superiorem, qui poterat salvare."—Michelet, Procès des Templiers, II. 404. Cf. ibid., p. 384: " Quidem falsus propheta est; credas solummodo in Deum Celi, et non in istum."
[5] Loiseleur, op. cit., p. 37.

Carcassonne who spoke of " Figura Baffometi," and suggests
that it was a corruption of " Mohammed," whom the Inquisitors wished to make the Knights confess they were taught
to adore.[1]   But this surmise with regard to the intentions of
the Inquisitors seems highly improbable, since they must have
been well aware that, as Wilcke points out, the Moslems forbid
all idols.[2]   For this reason Wilcke concludes that the Moham-
medanism of the Templars was combined with Cabalism and
that their idol was in reality the *macroprosopos*, or head of
the Ancient of Ancients, represented as an old man with a
long beard, or sometimes as three heads in one, which has
already been referred to under the name of the Long Face
in the first chapter of this book—a theory which would agree
with Eliphas Lévi's assertion that the Templars were " initiated
into the mysterious doctrines of the Cabala."[3]   But Lévi goes
on to define this teaching under the name of Johannism.
It is here that we reach a further theory with regard to the
secret doctrine of the Templars—the most important of all,
since it emanates from masonic and neo-Templar sources thus
effectually disposing of the contention that the charge brought
against the Order of apostasy from the Catholic faith is solely
the invention of Catholic writers.

In 1842 the Freemason Ragon related that the Templars
learnt from the " initiates of the East " a certain Judaic doctrine
which was attributed to St. John the Apostle; therefore " they
renounced the religion of St. Peter " and became Johannites.[4]
Eliphas Lévi expresses the same opinion.

Now, these statements are apparently founded on a legend
which was first published early in the nineteenth century, when
an association calling itself the *Ordre du Temple* and claiming
direct descent from the original Templar Order published two
works, the *Manuel des Chevaliers de l'Ordre du Temple* in
1811, and the *Lévitikon* in 1831, together with a version of the
Gospel of St. John differing from the Vulgate.   These books,
which appear to have been printed only for private circulation
amongst the members and are now extremely rare, relate that
the Order of the Temple had never ceased to exist since the

---

[1] Raynouard, op. cit., p. 301.
[2] Wilhelm Ferdinand Wilcke, *Geschichte des Tempelherrenordens*, II. 302–12,
(1827).
[3] Eliphas Lévi, *Histoire de la Magie*, p. 273.
[4] J. M. Ragon, *Cours Philosophique et Interprétatif des Initiations anciennes
et modernes*, édition sacrée à l'usage des Loges et des Maçons SEULEMENT
(5,842), p. 37.   In a footnote on the same page Ragon, however, refers to
John the Baptist in this connexion.

days of Jacques du Molay, who appointed Jacques de
Larménie his successor in office, and from that time onwards
a line of Grand Masters had succeeded each other without a
break up to the end of the eighteenth century, when it ceased
for a brief period but was reinstituted under a new Grand
Master, Fabré Palaprat, in 1804. Besides publishing the list
of all Grand Masters, known as the " Charter of Larmenius,"
said to have been preserved in the secret archives of the
Temple, these works also reproduce another document drawn
from the same repository describing the origins of the Order.
This manuscript, written in Greek on parchment, dated 1154,
purports to be partly taken from a fifth-century MS. and relates
that Hugues de Payens, first Grand Master of the Templars,
was initiated in 1118—that is to say, in the year the Order
was founded—into the religious doctrine of " the Primitive
Christian Church" by its Sovereign Pontiff and Patriarch,
Theoclet, sixtieth in direct succession from St. John the
Apostle. The history of the Primitive Church is then given
as follows:

Moses was initiated in Egypt. Profoundly versed in the physical,
theological, and metaphysical mysteries of the priests, he knew how
to profit by these so as to surmount the power of the Mages and
deliver his companions. Aaron, his brother, and the chiefs of the
Hebrews became the depositaries of his doctrine. . . .
The Son of God afterwards appeared on the scene of the world. . . .
He was brought up at the school of Alexandria. . . . Imbued with
a spirit wholly divine, endowed with the most astounding qualities
(dispositions), he was able to reach all the degrees of Egyptian
initiation. On his return to Jerusalem, he presented himself before
the chiefs of the Synagogue. . . . Jesus Christ, directing the fruit of his
lofty meditations towards universal civilization and the happiness
of the world, rent the veil which concealed the truth from the
peoples. He preached the love of God, the love of one's neighbour,
and equality before the common Father of all men. . . .
Jesus conferred evangelical initiation on his apostles and disciples.
He transmitted his spirit to them, divided them into several orders
after the practice of John, the beloved disciple, the apostle of
fraternal love, whom he had instituted Sovereign Pontiff and
Patriarch. . . .

Here we have the whole Cabalistic legend of a secret doctrine
descending from Moses, of Christ as an Egyptian initiate and
founder of a secret order—a theory, of course, absolutely
destructive of belief in His divinity. The legend of the *Ordre
du Temple* goes on to say:

Up to about the year 1118 (i.e. the year the Order of the Temple was founded) the mysteries and the hierarchic Order of the initiation of Egypt, transmitted to the Jews by Moses, then to the Christians by J.C., were religiously preserved by the successors of St. John the Apostle. These mysteries and initiations, regenerated by the evangelical initiation (or baptism), were a sacred trust which the simplicity of the primitive and unchanging morality of the *Brothers of the East* had preserved from all adulteration. . . .

The Christians, persecuted by the infidels, appreciating the courage and piety of these brave crusaders, who, with the sword in one hand and the cross in the other, flew to the defence of the holy places, and, above all, doing striking justice to the virtues and the ardent charity of Hugues de Payens, held it their duty to confide to hands so pure the treasures of knowledge acquired throughout so many centuries, sanctified by the cross, the dogma and the morality of the Man-God. Hugues was invested with the Apostolic Patriarchal power and placed in the legitimate order of the successors of St. John the apostle or the evangelist.

Such is the origin of the foundation of the Order of the Temple and of the fusion in this Order of the different kinds of initiation of the Christians of the East designated under the title of Primitive Christians or Johannites.

It will be seen at once that all this story is subtly subversive of true Christianity, and that the appellation of Christians applied to the Johannites is an imposture. Indeed Fabré Palaprat, Grand Master of the *Ordre du Temple* in 1804, who in his book on the Templars repeats the story contained in the *Lévitikon and the Manuel des Chevaliers du Temple,* whilst making the same profession of " primitive Christian " doctrines descending from St. John through Theoclet and Hugues de Payens to the Order over which he presides, goes on to say that the secret doctrine of the Templars " was essentially contrary to the canons of the Church of Rome and that it is principally to this fact that one must attribute the persecution of which history has preserved the memory."[1] The belief of the Primitive Christians, and consequently that the Templars, with regard to the miracles of Christ is that He " did or may have done extraordinary or miraculous things," and that since " God can do things incomprehensible to human intelligence," the Primitive Church venerates " all the acts of Christ as they are described in the Gospel, whether it considers them as acts of human science or whether as acts of divine power."[2] Belief in the divinity of Christ is thus left an open question,

---

[1] J. B. Fabré Palaprat, *Recherches historiques sur les Templiers*, p. 31 (1835).
[2] Ibid., p. 37.

and the same attitude is maintained towards the Resurrection, of which the story is omitted in the Gospel of St. John possessed by the Order. Fabré Palaprat further admits that the gravest accusations brought against the Templars were founded on facts which he attempts to explain away in the following manner:

The Templars having in 1307 carefully abstracted all the manuscripts composing the secret archives of the Order from the search made by authority, and these authentic manuscripts having been preciously preserved since that period, we have to-day the certainty that the Knights endured a great number of religious and moral trials before reaching the different degrees of initiation: thus, for example, the recipient might receive the injunction under pain of death to trample on the crucifix or to worship an idol, but if he yielded to the terror which they sought to inspire in him he was declared unworthy of being admitted to the higher grades of the Order. One can imagine in this way how beings, too feeble or too immoral to endure the trials of initiation, may have accused the Templars of giving themselves up to infamous practices and of having superstitious beliefs.

It is certainly not surprising that an Order which gave such injunctions as these, for whatever purpose, should have become the object of suspicion.

Eliphas Lévi, who, like Ragon, accepts the statements of the *Ordre du Temple* concerning the " Johannite " origin of the Templars' secret doctrine, is, however, not deceived by these professions of Christianity, and boldly asserts that the Sovereign Pontiff Theoclet initiated Hugues de Payens "into the mysteries and hopes of his pretended Church, he lured him by the ideas of sacerdotal sovereignty and supreme royalty, he indicated him finally as his successor. So the Order of the Knights of the Temple was stained from its origin with schism and conspiracy against Kings."[1] Further, Lévi relates that the real story told to initiates concerning Christ was no other than the infamous *Toledot Yeshu* described in the first chapter of this book, and which the Johannites dared to attribute to St. John.[2] This would accord with the confession of the Catalonian Knight Templar, Galcerandus de Teus, who stated that the form of absolution in the Order was: " I pray God that He may pardon your sins as He pardoned St. Mary Magdalene and the thief on the cross "; but the witness went on to explain:

[1] Eliphas Lévi, *Histoire de la Magie*, p. 277.
[2] Eliphas Lévi, *La Science des Esprits*, pp. 26–9, 40, 41.

By the thief of which the head of the Chapter speaks, is meant, according to our statutes, that Jesus or Christ who was crucified by the Jews because he was not God, and yet he said he was God and the King of the Jews, which was an outrage to the true God who is in Heaven. When Jesus, a few moments before his death, had his side pierced by the lance of Longinus, he repented of having called himself God and King of the Jews and he asked pardon of the true God; then the true God pardoned him. It is thus that we apply to the crucified Christ these words: "as God pardoned the thief on the cross."[1]

Raynouard, who quotes this deposition, stigmatizes it as "singular and extravagant"; M. Matter agrees that it is doubt-less extravagant, but that "it merits attention. There was a whole system there, which was not the invention of Galcerant."[2] Eliphas Lévi provides the clue to that system and to the reason why Christ was described as a thief, by indicating the Cabalistic legend wherein He was described as having *stolen* the sacred Name from the Holy of Holies. Elsewhere he explains that the Johannites "made themselves out to be the only people initiated into the true mysteries of the religion of the Saviour. They professed to know the real history of Jesus Christ, and by adopting part of Jewish traditions and the stories of the Talmud, they made out that the facts related in the Gospels "— that is to say, the Gospels accepted by the orthodox Church— "were only allegories of which St. John gives the key."[3]

But it is time to pass from legend to facts. For the whole story of the initiation of the Templars by the "Johannites" rests principally on the documents produced by the Ordre du Temple in 1811. According to the Abbés Grégoire and Münter the authenticity and antiquity of these documents are beyond dispute. Grégoire, referring to the parchment manuscript of the *Lévitikon* and Gospel of St. John, says that "Hellenists versed in paleography believe this manuscript to be of the thirteenth century, others declare it to be earlier and to go back to the eleventh century."[4] Matter, on the other hand, quoting Münter's opinion that the manuscripts in the archives of the modern Templars date from the thirteenth century, observes that this is all a tissue of errors and that the critics, including the learned Professor Thilo of Halle, have recognized that the manuscript in question, far from belonging to the thirteenth century, dates from the beginning of the eighteenth.

[1] Raynouard, op. cit., p. 281.
[2] Matter, *Histoire du Gnosticisme*, III. 330.
[3] Eliphas Lévi, *Histoire de la Magie*, p. 275.
[4] M. Grégoire, *Histoire des Sectes religieuses*, II. 407 (1828).

From the arrangement of the chapters of the Gospel, M. Matter arrives at the conclusion that it was intended to accompany the ceremonies of some masonic or secret society.[1] We shall return to this possibility in a later chapter.

The antiquity of the manuscript containing the history of the Templars thus remains an open question on which no one can pronounce an opinion without having seen the original. In order, then, to judge of the probability of the story that this manuscript contained it is necessary to consult the facts of history and to discover what proof can be found that any such sect as the Johannites existed at the time of the Crusades or earlier. Certainly none is known to have been called by this name or by one resembling it before 1622, when some Portuguese monks reported the existence of a sect whom they described as " Christians of St. John " inhabiting the banks of the Euphrates. The appellation appears, however, to have been wrongly applied by the monks, for the sectarians in question, variously known as the Mandæans, Mandaites, Sabians, Nazoreans, etc., called themselves Mandaï Iyahi, that is to say, the disciples, or rather the wise men, of John, the word *mandaï* being derived from the Chaldean word *manda,* corresponding to the Greek word γνῶσις , or wisdom.[2] The multiplicity of names given to the Mandæans arises apparently from the fact that in their dealings with other communities they took the name of Sabians, whilst they called the wise and learned amongst themselves Nazoreans.[3] The sect formerly inhabited the banks of the Jordan, but was driven out by the Moslems, who forced them to retire to Mesopotamia and Babylonia, where they particularly affected the neighbourhood of rivers in order to be able to carry out their peculiar baptismal rites.[4]

There can be no doubt that the doctrines of the Mandæans do resemble the description of the Johannite heresy as given by Eliphas Lévi, though not by the *Ordre du Temple,* in that the Mandæans professed to be the disciples of St. John—the Baptist, however, not the Apostle—but were at the same time the enemies of Jesus Christ. According to the Mandæans' *Book of John* (Sidra d'Yahya), Yahya, that is to say, St. John, baptized myriads of men during forty years in the Jordan. By a mistake—or in response to a written mandate from heaven

[1] Matter, *Histoire du Gnosticisme,* III. 323.
[2] Ibid., III. p. 120.
[3] *Jewish Encyclopædia,* article on Mandæans.
[4] Grégoire, op. cit., IV. 241.

saying, " Yahya, baptize the liar in the Jordan "—he baptized the false prophet Yishu Meshiha (the Messiah Jesus), son of the devil Ruha Kadishta.[1] The same idea is found in another book of the sect, called .he " Book of Adam," which represents Jesus as the perverter of St. John's doctrine and the disseminator of iniquity and perfidy throughout the world.[2] The resemblance between all this and the legends of the Talmud, the Cabala, and the Toledot Yeshu is at once apparent; moreover, the Mandæans claim for the " Book of Adam " the same origin as the Jews claimed for the Cabala, namely, that it was delivered to Adam by God through the hands of the angel Razael.[3] This book, known to scholars as the *Codex Nasaræus*, is described by Münter as " a sort of mosaic without order, without method, where one finds mentioned Noah, Abraham, Moses, Solomon, the Temple of Jerusalem, St. John the Baptist, Jesus Christ, the Christians, and Mohammed." M. Matter, whilst denying any proof of the Templar succession from the Mandæans, nevertheless gives good reason for believing that the sect itself existed from the first centuries of the Christian era and that its books dated from the eighth century[4]; further that these Mandæans or Nazoreans—not to be confounded with the pre-Christian Nazarites or Christian Nazarenes—were Jews who revered St. John the Baptist as the prophet of ancient Mosaism, but regarded Jesus Christ as a false Messiah sent by the powers of darkness.[5] Modern Jewish opinion confirms this affirmation of Judaic inspiration and agrees with Matter in describing the Mandæans as Gnostics: " Their sacred books are in an Aramaic dialect, which has close affinities with that of the Talmud of Babylon." The Jewish influence is distinctly visible in the Mandæan religion. " It is essentially of the type of ancient Gnosticism, traces of which are found in the Talmud, the Midrash, and in a modified form the later Cabala."[6]

[1] *Jewish Encyclopædia*, and Hastings' *Encyclopædia of Religion and Ethics*, article on Mandæans.
[2] *Codex Nasaræus*, Liber Adam appellatus, trans. from the Syriac into Latin by Matth. Norberg (1815), Vol. I. 109: " Sed, Johanne hac ætate Hierosolymæ nato, Jordanumque deinceps legente, et baptismum peragente, veniet Jeschu Messias, summisse se gerens, ut baptismo Johannis baptizetur, et Johannis per sapientiam sapiat. Pervertet vero doctrinam Johannis, et mutato Jordani baptismo, perversisque justitiæ dictis, iniquitatem et perfidiam per mundum disseminabit."
[3] Article on the *Codex Nasaræus* by Silvestre de Sacy in the *Journal des Savants* for November 1819, p. 651; cf. passage in the Zohar, section Bereschith, folio 55.
[4] Matter, op. cit., III. 119, 120. De Sacy (op. cit., p. 654) also attributes the *Codex Nasaræus* to the eighth century.
[5] Matter, op. cit., III. 118.
[6] *Jewish Encyclopædia*, article on Mandæans.

It may then be regarded as certain that a sect existed long before the time of the Crusades corresponding to the description of the Johannites given by Eliphas Lévi in that it was Cabalistic, anti-Christian, yet professedly founded on the doctrines of one of the St. Johns. Whether it was by this sect that the Templars were indoctrinated must remain an open question. M. Matter objects that the evidence lacking to such a conclusion lies in the fact that the Templars expressed no particular reverence for St. John; but Loiseleur asserts that the Templars did prefer the Gospel of St. John to that of the other evangelists, and that modern masonic lodges claiming descent from the Templars possess a special version of this Gospel said to have been copied from the original on Mount Athos.[1] It is also said that "Baphomets" were preserved in the masonic lodges of Hungary, where a debased form of Masonry, known as Johannite Masonry, survives to this day. If the Templar heresy was that of the Johannites, the head in question might possibly represent that of John the Baptist, which would accord with the theory that the word Baphomet was derived from Greek words signifying baptism of wisdom. This would, moreover, not be incompatible with Loiseleur's theory of an affinity between the Templars and the Bogomils, for the Bogomils also possessed their own version of the Gospel of St. John, which they placed on the heads of their neophytes during the ceremony of initiation,[2] giving as the reason for the peculiar veneration they professed for its author that they regarded St. John as the servant of the Jewish God Satanael.[3] Eliphas Lévi even goes so far as to accuse the Templars of following the occult practices of the Luciferians, who carried the doctrines of the Bogomils to the point of paying homage to the powers of darkness:

Let us declare for the edification of the vulgar . . . and for the greater glory of the Church which has persecuted the Templars, burned the magicians and excommunicated the Free-Masons, etc., let us say boldly and loudly, that all the initiates of the occult sciences . . . have adored, do and will always adore that which is signified by this frightful symbol [the Sabbatic goat].[4] Yes, in our

[1] Loiseleur, op. cit., p. 52.
[2] Ibid., p. 51; Matter, op. cit., III. 305.
[3] Hastings' *Encyclopædia*, article on Bogomils.
[4] The Sabbatic goat is clearly of Jewish origin. Thus the Zohar relates that "Tradition teaches us that when the Israelites evoked evil spirits, these appeared to them under the form of he-goats and made known to them all that they wished to learn."—Section Ahre Moth, folio 70a (de Pauly, V. 191).

profound conviction, the Grand Masters of the Order of the Templars adored Baphomet and caused him to be adored by their initiates.[1]

It will be seen, then, that the accusation of heresy brought against the Templars does not emanate solely from the Catholic Church, but also from the secret societies. Even our Freemasons, who, for reasons I shall show later, have generally defended the Order, are now willing to admit that there was a very real case against them. Thus Dr. Ranking, who has devoted many years of study to the question, has arrived at the conclusion that Johannism is the real clue to the Templar heresy. In a very interesting paper published in the masonic journal *Ars Quatuor Coronatorum*, he observes that " the record of the Templars in Palestine is one long tale of intrigue and treachery on the part of the Order," and finally:

That from the very commencement of Christianity there has been transmitted through the centuries a body of doctrine incompatible with Christianity in the various official Churches. . . .

That the bodies teaching these doctrines professed to do so on the authority of St. John, to whom, as they claimed, the true secrets had been committed by the Founder of Christianity.

That during the Middle Ages the main support of the Gnostic bodies and the main repository of this knowledge was the Society of the Templars.[2]

What is the explanation of this choice of St. John for the propagation of anti-Christian doctrines which we shall find continuing up to the present day? What else than the method of perversion which in its extreme form becomes Satanism, and consists in always selecting the most sacred things for the purpose of desecration? Precisely then because the Gospel of St. John is the one of all the four which most insists on the divinity of Christ, the occult anti-Christian sects have habitually made it the basis of their rites.

---

[1] Eliphas Lévi, *Dogme et Rituel de la Haute Magie*, II. 209.
[2] *Some Notes on various Gnostic Sects and their Possible Influence on Freemasonry*, by D. F. Ranking, reprinted from *A.Q.C.*, Vol. XXIV. pp. 27, 28 (1911).

4

THREE CENTURIES OF OCCULTISM

It has been shown in the foregoing chapters that from very early times occult sects had existed for two purposes—esoteric and political. Whilst the Manicheans, the early Ismailis, the Bogomils, and the Luciferians had concerned themselves mainly with religious or esoteric doctrines, the later Ismailis, the Fatimites, the Karmathites, and Templars had combined secrecy and occult rites with the political aim of domination. We shall find this double tradition running through all the secret society movement up to the present day.

The Dualist doctrines attributed to the Templars were not, however, confined to this Order in Europe, but had been, as we have seen, those professed by the Bogomils and also by the Cathari, who spread westwards from Bulgaria and Bosnia to France. It was owing to their sojourn in Bulgaria that the Cathari gained the popular nickname of "Bulgars" or "Bourgres," signifying those addicted to unnatural vice. One section of the Cathari in the South of France became known after 1180 as the Albigenses, thus called from the town of Albi, although their headquarters were really in Toulouse. Christians only in name, they adhered in secret to the Gnostic and Manichean doctrines of the earlier Cathari, which they would appear to have combined with Johannism, since, like this Eastern sect, they claimed to possess their own Gospel of St. John.[1]

Although not strictly a secret society, the Albigenses were divided after the secret society system into initiates and semi-initiates. The former, few in number, known as the *Perfecti,* led in appearance an austere life, refraining from

---

[1] "Their meetings were held in the most convenient spot, often on mountains or in valleys; the only essentials were a table, a white cloth, and a copy of the Gospel of St. John, that is, their own version of it."—Dr. Ranking, op. cit., p. 15 (*A.Q.C.*, Vol. XXIV.). Cf. Gabriele Rossetti, *The Anti-Papal Spirit,* I. 230, where it is said "the sacred books, and especially that of St. John, were wrested by this sect into strange and perverted meanings."

meat and professing abhorrence of oaths or of lying. The
mystery in which they enveloped themselves won for them
the adoring reverence of the *Credentes,* who formed the great
majority of the sect and gave themselves up to every vice, to
usury, brigandage, and perjury, and whilst describing marriage
as prostitution, condoning incest and all forms of licence.[1] The
Credentes, who were probably not fully initiated into the
Dualist doctrines of their superiors, looked to them for
salvation through the laying-on of hands according to the
system of the Manicheans.

It was amongst the nobles of Languedoc that the Albigenses
found their principal support. This " Judæa of France," as it
has been called, was peopled by a medley of mixed races,
Iberian, Gallic, Roman, and Semitic.[2] The nobles, very different
from the "ignorant and pious chivalry of the North," had
lost all respect for their traditions. "There were few who
in going back did not encounter some Saracen or Jewish grand-
mother in their genealogy."[3] Moreover, many had brought
back to Europe the laxity of morals they had contracted during
the Crusades. The Comte de Comminges practised polygamy,
and, according to ecclesiastical chronicles, Raymond VI, Comte
de Toulouse, one of the most ardent of the Albigense *Credentes,*
had his harem.[4] The Albigensian movement has been falsely
represented as a protest merely against the tyranny of the
Church of Rome; in reality it was a rising against the fundamental doctrines of Christianity—more than this, against all
principles of religion and morality. For whilst some of the
sect openly declared that the Jewish law was preferable to that
of the Christians,[5] to others the God of the Old Testament
was as abhorrent as the "false Christ" who suffered at
Golgotha; the old hatred of the Gnostics and Manicheans for
the demiurgus lived again in these rebels against the social
order. Forerunners of the seventeenth-century Libertines and
eighteenth-century Illuminati, the Albigense nobles, under the
pretext of fighting the priesthood, strove to throw off all the
restraints the Church imposed.

Inevitably the disorders that took place throughout the

[1] Michelet, *Histoire de France,* III. 18, 19 (1879 edition).
[2] Michelet, op. cit., p. 10. "L'élément sémitique, juif et arabe, était
fort en Languedoc." Cf. A. E. Waite, *The Secret Tradition in Freemasonry,*
I. 118: "The South of France was a centre from which went forth much
of the base occultism of Jewry as well as its theosophical dreams."
[3] Michelet, op. cit., p. 12.
[4] Ibid., p. 15.
[5] Graetz, *History of the Jews,* III. 517.

South of France led to reprisals, and the Albigenses were suppressed with all the cruelty of the age—a fact which has afforded historians the opportunity to exalt them as noble martyrs, victims of ecclesiastical despotism. But again, as in the case of the Templars, the fact that they were persecuted does not prove them innocent of the crimes laid to their charge.

At the beginning of the fourteenth century another development of Dualism, far more horrible than the Manichean heresy of the Albigenses, began to make itself felt. This was the cult of Satanism, or black magic. The subject is one that must be approached with extreme caution, owing to the fact that on one hand much that has been written about it is the result of mediæval superstition, which sees in every departure from the Roman Catholic Faith the direct intervention of the Evil One, whilst on the other hand the conspiracy of history, which denies *in toto* the existence of the Occult Power, discredits all revelations on this question, from whatever source they emanate, as the outcome of hysterical imagination.[1] This is rendered all the easier since the subject by its amazing extravagance lends itself to ridicule.

It is, however, idle to deny that the cult of evil has always existed; the invocation of the powers of darkness was practised in the earliest days of the human race and, after the Christian era, found its expression, as we have seen, in the Cainites, the Euchites, and the Luciferians. These are not surmises, but actual facts of history. Towards the end of the twelfth century Luciferianism spread eastwards through Styria, the Tyrol, and Bohemia, even as far as Brandenburg; by the beginning of the thirteenth century it had invaded western Germany, and in the fourteenth century reached its zenith in that country, as also in Italy and France. The cult had now reached a further stage in its development, and it was not the mere propitiation of Satanael as the prince of this world practised by the Luciferians, but actual Satanism—the love of evil for the sake of evil—which formed the doctrine of the sect known in Italy

[1] Thus Hastings' *Encyclopædia of Religion and Ethics* omits all reference to Satanism before 1880 and observes: " The evidence of the existence of either Satanists or Palladists consists entirely of the writings of a group of men in Paris." It then proceeds to devote five columns out of the six and a half which compose the article to describing the works of two notorious romancers, Léo Taxil and Bataille. There is not a word of real information to be found here.

as *la vecchia religione* or the "old religion." Sorcery was adopted as a profession, and witches, not, as is popularly supposed, sporadic growths, were trained in schools of magic to practise their art. These facts should be remembered when the Church is blamed for the violence it displayed against witchcraft—it was not individuals, but a system which it set out to destroy.

The essence of Satanism is desecration. In the ceremonies for infernal evocation described by Eliphas Lévi we read: "It is requisite to profane the ceremonies of the religion one belongs to and to trample its holiest symbols under foot."[1] This practice found a climax in desecrating the Holy Sacrament. The consecrated wafer was given as food to mice, toads, and pigs, or defiled in unspeakable ways. A revolting description of the Black Mass may be found in Huysmans's book *Là-bas*. It is unnecessary to transcribe the loathsome details here. Suffice it, then, to show that this cult had a very real existence, and if any further doubt remains on the matter, the life of Gilles de Rais supplies documentary evidence of the visible results of black magic in the Middle Ages.

Gilles de Rais was born at Machecoul in Brittany about the year 1404. The first period of his life was glorious; the companion and guide of Jeanne d'Arc, he became Maréchal of France and distinguished himself by many deeds of valour. But after dissipating his immense fortune, largely on Church ceremonies carried out with the wildest extravagance, he was led to study alchemy, partly by curiosity and partly as a means for restoring his shattered fortunes. Hearing that Germany and Italy were the countries where alchemy flourished, he enlisted Italians in his service and was gradually drawn into the further region of magic. According to Huysmans, Gilles de Rais had remained until this moment a Christian mystic under the influence of Jeanne d'Arc, but after her death— possibly in despair—he offered himself to the powers of darkness. Evokers of Satan now flocked to him from every side, amongst them Prelati, an Italian, by no means the old and wrinkled sorcerer of tradition, but a young and attractive man of charming manners. For it was from Italy that came the most skilful adepts in the art of alchemy, astrology, magic, and infernal evocation, who spread themselves over Europe, particularly France. Under the influence of these initiators Gilles de Rais signed a letter to the devil in a meadow near

[1] Précis of Eliphas Lévi's writings by Arthur E. Waite, *The Mysteries of Magic*, p. 215.

Machecoul asking him for "knowledge, power, and riches," and offering in exchange anything that might be asked of him with the exception of his life or his soul. But in spite of this appeal and of a pact signed with the blood of the writer, no Satanic apparitions were forthcoming.

It was then that, becoming still more desperate, Gilles de Rais had recourse to the abominations for which his name has remained infamous—still more frightful invocations, loathsome debaucheries, perverted vice in every form, Sadic cruelties, horrible sacrifices, and, finally, holocausts of little boys and girls collected by his agents in the surrounding country and put to death with the most inhuman tortures. During the years 1432-40 literally hundreds of children disappeared. Many of the names of the unhappy little victims were preserved in the records of the period. Gilles de Rais met with a well-deserved end: in 1440 he was hanged and burnt. So far he does not appear to have found a panegyrist to place him in the ranks of noble martyrs.

It will, of course, be urged that the crimes here described were those of a criminal lunatic and not to be attributed to any occult cause; the answer to this is that Gilles was not an isolated unit, but one of a group of occultists who cannot all have been mad. Moreover, it was only after his invocation of the Evil One that he developed these monstrous proclivities. So also his eighteenth-century replica, the Marquis de Sade, combined with his abominations an impassioned hatred of the Christian religion.

What is the explanation of this craze for magic in Western Europe? Deschamps points to the Cabala, "that science of demoniacal arts, of which the Jews were the initiators," and undoubtedly in any comprehensive review of the question the influence of the Jewish Cabalists cannot be ignored. In Spain, Portugal, Provence, and Italy the Jews by the fifteenth century had become a power; as early as 1450 they had penetrated into the intellectual circles of Florence, and it was also in Italy that, a century later, the modern Cabalistic school was inaugurated by Isaac Luria (1533-72), whose doctrines were organized into a practical system by the Hasidim of Eastern Europe for the writing of amulets, the conjuration of devils, mystical jugglery with numbers and letters, etc.[1] Italy in the fifteenth century was thus a centre from which Cabalistic influences radiated, and it may be that the Italians who

---

[1] *Jewish Encyclopædia,* article on Cabala.

indoctrinated Gilles de Rais had drawn their inspiration from
this source. Indeed Eliphas Lévi, who certainly cannot be
accused of " Anti-Semitism," declares that " the Jews, the most
faithful trustees of the secret of the Cabala, were almost always
the reat masters of magic in the Middle Ages,"[1] and suggests
that Gilles de Rais took his monstrous recipes for using the
blood of murdered children " from some of those old Hebrew
grimoires (books on magic), which, if they had been known,
would have sufficed to hold up the Jews to the execration of
the whole earth."[2] Voltaire, in his *Henriade,* likewise attributes
the magical blood-rites practised in the sixteenth century to
Jewish inspiration:

> Dans l'ombre de la nuit, sous une voûte obscure,
> Le silence conduit leur assemblée impure.
> A la pâle lueur d'un magique flambeau
> S'élève un vil autel dressé sur un tombeau.
> C'est là que des deux rois on plaça les images,
> Objets de leur terreur, objets de leurs outrages.
> Leurs sacrilèges mains ont mêlé sur l'autel
> A des noms infernaux le nom de l'Éternel.
> Sur ces murs ténébreux des lances sont rangées,
> Dans des vases de sang leurs pointes sont plongées;
> Appareil menaçant de leur mystère affreux.
> Le prêtre de ce temple est un de ces Hébreux
> Qui, proscrits sur la terre et citoyens du monde,
> Portent de mers en mers leur misère profonde,
> Et, d'un antique ramas de superstitions,
> Ont rempli dès longtemps toutes les nations, etc.

Voltaire adds in a footnote: " It was ordinarily Jews that were
made use of for magical operations. This ancient superstition comes from the secrets of the Cabala, of which the Jews
called themselves the sole depositaries. Catherine de Medicis,
the Maréchal d'Ancre, and many others employed Jews for
these spells."

This charge of black magic recurs all through the history of
Europe from the earliest times. The Jews are accused of
poisoning wells, of practising ritual murder, of using stolen
church property for purposes of desecration, etc. No doubt
there enters into all this a great amount of exaggeration,
inspired by popular prejudice and mediæval superstition. Yet,
whilst condemning the persecution to which the Jews were

---

[1] *Dogme et Rituel de la Haute Magie,* II. 220 (1861). It is curious to notice
that Sir James Frazer, in his vast compendium on magic, *The Golden Bough,*
never once refers to any of the higher adepts—Jews, Rosicrucians, Satanists,
etc., or to the Cabala as a source of inspiration. The whole subject is treated
as if the cult of magic were the spontaneous outcome of primitive or peasant
mentality.

[2] *Histoire de la Magie,* p. 289.

subjected on this account, it must be admitted that they laid themselves open to suspicion by their real addiction to magical arts. If ignorant superstition is found on the side of the persecutors, still more amazing superstition is found on the side of the persecuted. Demonology in Europe was in fact essentially a Jewish science, for although a belief in evil spirits existed from the earliest times and has always continued to exist amongst primitive races, and also amongst the ignorant classes in civilized countries, it was mainly through the Jews that these dark superstitions were imported to the West, where they persisted not merely amongst the lower strata of the Jewish population, but formed an essential part of Jewish tradition. Thus the Talmud says:

If the eye could perceive the demons that people the universe, existence would be impossible. The demons are more numerous than we are: they surround us on all sides like trenches dug round vineyards. Every one of us has a thousand on his left hand and ten thousand on his right. The discomfort endured by those who attend rabbinical conferences . . . comes from the demons mingling with men in these circumstances. Besides, the fatigue one feels in one's knees in walking comes from the demons that one knocks up against at every step. If the clothing of the Rabbis wears out so quickly, it is again because the demons rub up against them. Whoever wants to convince himself of their presence has only to surround his bed with sifted cinders and the next morning he will see the imprints of cocks' feet.[1]

The same treatise goes on to give directions for seeing demons by burning portions of a black cat and placing the ashes in one's eye: "then at once one perceives the demons." The Talmud also explains that devils particularly inhabit the water-spouts on houses and are fond of drinking out of water-jugs, therefore it is advisable to pour a little water out of a jug before drinking, so as to get rid of the unclean part.[2]

These ideas received a fresh impetus from the publication of the Zohar, which, a Jewish writer tells us, "from the

---

[1] Talmud, treatise Berakhoth, folio 6. The Talmud also gives directions on the manner of guarding against occult powers and the onslaught of disease. The tract Pesachim declares that he who stands naked before a candle is liable to be seized with epilepsy. The same tract also states that "a man should not go out alone on the night following the fourth day or on the night following the Sabbath, because an evil spirit, called Agrath, the daughter of Ma'hlath, together with one hundred and eighty thousand other evil spirits, go forth into the world and have the right to injure anyone they should chance to meet."

[2] Talmud, treatise Hullin, folios 143, 144.

fourteenth century held almost unbroken sway over the minds of the majority of the Jews. In it the Talmudic legends concerning the existence and activity of the *shedhim* (demons) are repeated and amplified, and a hierarchy of demons was established corresponding to the heavenly hierarchy. . . . Manasseh [ben Israel]'s *Nishmat Hayim* is full of information concerning belief in demons. . . . Even the scholarly and learned Rabbis of the seventeenth century clung to the belief."[1]

Here, then, it is not a case of ignorant peasants evolving fantastic visions from their own scared imaginations, but of the Rabbis, the acknowledged leaders of a race claiming civilized traditions and a high order of intelligence, deliberately inculcating in their disciples the perpetual fear of demoniacal influences. How much of this fear communicated itself to the Gentile population? It is at any rate a curious coincidence to notice the resemblances between so-called popular superstitions and the writings of the Rabbis. For example, the vile confessions made both by Scotch and French peasant women accused of witchcraft concerning the nocturnal visits paid them by male devils[2] find an exact counterpart in passages of the Cabala, where it is said that " the demons are both male and female, and they also endeavour to consort with human beings —a conception from which arises the belief in *incubi* and *succubæ*."[3] Thus, on Jewish authority, we learn the Judaic origin of this strange delusion.

It is clearly to the same source that we may trace the magical formulæ for the healing of diseases current at the same period. From the earliest times the Jews had specialized in medicine, and many royal personages insisted on employing Jewish doctors,[4] some of whom may have acquired medical knowledge of a high order. The Jewish writer Margoliouth dwells on this fact with some complacency, and goes on to contrast the

---

[1] Hastings' *Encyclopædia of Religion and Ethics,* article on Jewish Magic by M. Gaster.

[2] Margaret Alice Murray, *The Witch Cult in Western Europe,* and Jules Garinet, *Histoire de la Magie en France,* p. 163 (1818).

[3] Hastings' *Encyclopædia,* article on Jewish Magic by M. Gaster. See the Zohar, treatise Bereschith, folio 54b, where it is said that all men are visited in their sleep by female devils. " These demons never appear under any other form but that of human beings, but they have no hair on their heads. . . . In the same way as to men, male devils appear in dreams to women, with whom they have intercourse."

[4] The Rev. Moses Margoliouth, *The History of the Jews in Great Britain,* I. 82. The same author relates further on (p. 304) that Queen Elizabeth's Hebrew physician Rodrigo Lopez was accused of trying to poison her and died a victim of persecution.

scientific methods of the Hebrew doctors with the quackeries of the monks:

> In spite of the reports circulated by the monks, that the Jews were sorcerers (in consequence of their superior medical skill), Christian patients would frequent the houses of the Jewish physicians in preference to the monasteries, where cures were pretended to have been effected by some extraordinary relics, such as the nails of St. Augustine, the extremity of St. Peter's second toe, . . . etc. It need hardly be added that the cures effected by the Jewish physicians were more numerous than those by the monkish impostors.[1]

Yet in reality the grotesque remedies which Margoliouth attributes to Christian superstition appear to have been partly derived from Jewish sources. The author of a further article on Magic in Hastings' *Encyclopædia* goes on to say that the magical formulæ handed down in Latin in ancient medical writings and used by the monks were mainly of Eastern origin, derived from Babylonish, Egyptian, and Jewish magic. The monks therefore " played merely an intermediate rôle."[2] Indeed, if we turn to the Talmud we shall find cures recommended no less absurd than those which Margoliouth derides. For example:

> The eggs of a grasshopper as a remedy for toothache, the tooth of a fox as a remedy for sleep, viz. the tooth of a live fox to prevent sleep and of a dead one to cause sleep, the nail from the gallows where a man was hanged, as a remedy for swelling.[3]

A strongly " pro-Semite " writer quotes a number of Jewish medical writings of the eighteenth century, republished as late as the end of the nineteenth, which show the persistence of these magical formulæ amongst the Jews. Most of these are too loathsome to transcribe; but some of the more innocuous are as follows: " For epilepsy kill a cock and let it putrefy." " In order to protect yourself from all evils, gird yourself with the rope with which a criminal has been hung." Blood of different kinds also plays an important part: " Fox's blood and wolf's blood are good for stone in the bladder, ram's blood for colic, weasel blood for scrofula," etc.—these to be externally applied.[4]

---

[1] The Rev. Moses Margoliouth, *The History of the Jews in Great Britain*, I. 83.
[2] Hastings' *Encyclopædia*, article on Teutonic Magic by F. Hälsig.
[3] Talmud, tract Sabbath.
[4] Hermann L. Strack, *The Jews and Human Sacrifice*, Eng. trans., pp. 140, 141 (1900).

But to return to Satanism. Whoever were the secret inspirers of magical and diabolical practices during the fourteenth to the eighteenth centuries, the evidence of the existence of Satanism during this long period is overwhelming and rests on the actual facts of history. Details quite as extravagant and revolting as those contained in the works of Eliphas Lévi[1] or in Huysmans's *Là-bas* are given in documentary form by Margaret Alice Murray in her singularly passionless work relating principally to the witches of Scotland.[2]

The cult of evil is a reality—by whatever means we may seek to explain it. Eliphas Lévi, whilst denying the existence of Satan " as a superior personality and power," admits this fundamental truth: " Evil exists; it is impossible to doubt it. We can do good or evil. There are beings who knowingly and voluntarily do evil."[3] There are also beings who love evil. Lévi has admirably described the spirit that animates such beings in his definition of black magic:

Black magic is really but a combination of sacrileges and murders graduated with a view to the permanent perversion of the human will and the realization in a living man of the monstrous phantom of the fiend. It is, therefore, properly speaking, the religion of the devil, the worship of darkness, the hatred of goodness exaggerated to the point of paroxysm; it is the incarnation of death and the permanent creation of hell.[4]

The Middle Ages, which depicted the devil fleeing from holy water, were not perhaps quite so benighted as our superior modern culture has led us to suppose. For that " hatred of goodness exaggerated to the point of paroxysm," that impulse to desecrate and defile which forms the basis of black magic and has manifested itself in successive phases of the world-revolution, springs from fear. So by their very hatred the powers of darkness proclaim the existence of the powers of light and their own impotence. In the cry of the demoniac: "What have we to do with Thee, Jesus of Nazareth? art Thou come to destroy us? I know Thee who Thou art, the

[1] See pages 215 and 216 of *The Mysteries of Magic*, by A. E. Waite.
[2] See also A. S. Turberville, *Mediæval Heresy and the Inquisition*, pp. 111–12 (1920), ending with the words: " The voluminous records of the holy tribunal, the learned treatises of its members, are the great repositories of the true and indisputable facts concerning the abominable heresies of sorcery and witchcraft."
[3] *Histoire de la Magie*, p. 15.
[4] *The Mysteries of Magic*, p. 221.

Holy One of God," do we not hear the unwilling tribute of the vanquished to the victor in the mighty conflict between good and evil?

THE ROSICRUCIANS

In dealing with the question of Magic it is necessary to realize that although to the world in general the word is synonymous with necromancy, it does not bear this significance in the language of occultism, particularly the occultism of the sixteenth and seventeenth centuries. Magic at this date was a term employed to cover many branches of investigation which Robert Fludd, the English Rosicrucian, classified under various headings, of which the first three are as follows: (1) "*Natural Magic*, . . . that most occult and secret department of physics by which the mystical properties of natural substances are extracted"; (2) *Mathematical Magic*, which enables adepts in the art to "construct marvellous machines by means of their geometrical knowledge"; whilst (3) *Venefic Magic* "is familiar with potions, philtres, and with various preparations of poisons."[1]

It is obvious that all these have now passed into the realms of science and are no longer regarded as magical arts; but the further categories enumerated by Fludd and comprised under the general heading of *Necromantic Magic* retain the popular sense of the term. These are described as (1) *Goetic*, which consists in "diabolical commerce with unclean spirits, in rites of criminal curiosity, in illicit songs and invocations, and in the evocation of the souls of the dead"; (2) *Maleficent*, which is the adjuration of the devils by the virtue of Divine Names; and (3) *Theurgic*, purporting "to be governed by good angels and the Divine Will, but its wonders are most frequently performed by evil spirits, who assume the names of God and of the angels." (4) "The last species of magic is the *Thaumaturgic*, begetting illusory phenomena; by this art the Magi produced their phantoms and other marvels." To this list might be added *Celestial Magic*, or knowledge dealing with the influence of the heavenly bodies, on which astrology is based.

The forms of magic dealt with in the preceding part of this chapter belong therefore to the second half of these categories, that is to say, to Necromantic Magic. But at the same period another movement was gradually taking shape which concerned itself with the first category enumerated above, that is to say, the secret properties of natural substances.

[1] A. E. Waite, *The Real History of the Rosicrucians*, p. 293.

A man whose methods appear to have approached to the modern conception of scientific research was Theophrastus Bombastus von Hohenheim, commonly known as Paracelsus, the son of a German doctor, born about 1493, who during his travels in the East is said to have acquired a knowledge of some secret doctrine which he afterwards elaborated into a system for the healing of diseases. Although his ideas were thus doubtless drawn from some of the same sources as those from which the Jewish Cabala descended, Paracelsus does not appear to have been a Cabalist, but a scientist of no mean order, and, as an isolated thinker, apparently connected with no secret association, does not enter further into the scope of this work.

Paracelsus must therefore not be identified with the school of so-called " Christian Cabalists," who, from Raymond Lulli, the " doctor illuminatus " of the thirteenth century, onward, drew their inspiration from the Cabala of the Jews. This is not to say that the influence under which they fell was wholly pernicious, for, just as certain Jews appear to have acquired some real medical skill, so also they appear to have possessed some real knowledge of natural science, inherited perhaps from the ancient traditions of the East or derived from the writings of Hippocrates, Galen, and other of the great Greek physicians and as yet unknown to Europe. Thus Eliphas Lévi relates that the Rabbi Jechiel, a Cabalistic Jew protected by St. Louis, possessed the secret of ever-burning lamps,[1] claimed later by the Rosicrucians, which suggests the possibility that some kind of luminous gas or electric light may have been known to the Jews. In alchemy they were the acknowledged leaders; the most noted alchemist of the fourteenth century, Nicholas Flamel, discovered the secret of the art from the book of " Abraham the Jew, Prince, Priest, Levite, Astrologer, and Philosopher," and this actual book is said to have passed later into the possession of Cardinal Richelieu.[2]

It was likewise from a Florentine Jew, Alemanus or Datylus, that Pico della Mirandola, the fifteenth-century mystic, received instructions in the Cabala[3] and imagined that he had discovered in it the doctrines of Christianity. This delighted Pope Sixtus IV, who thereupon ordered Cabalistic writings to be translated into Latin for the use of divinity students. At the same time the Cabala was introduced into

[1] *Histoire de la Magie*, p. 266.
[2] John Yarker, *The Arcane Schools*, p. 205.
[3] Drach (*De l'Harmonie entre l'Église et la Synagogue*, II. p. 30) says that Pico della Mirandola paid a Jew 7,000 ducats for the Cabalistic MSS. from which he drew his thesis.

Germany by Reuchlin, who had learnt Hebrew from the Rabbi Jacob b. Jechiel Loans, court physician to Frederick III, and in 1494 published a Cabalistic treatise *De Verbo Mirifico,* showing that all wisdom and true philosophy are derived from the Hebrews. Considerable alarm appears, however, to have been created by the spread of Rabbinical literature, and in 1509 a Jew converted to Christianity, named Pfefferkorn, persuaded the Emperor Maximilian I to burn all Jewish books except the Old Testament. Reuchlin, consulted on this matter, advised only the destruction of the Toledot Yeshu and of the Sepher Nizzachon by the Rabbi Lipmann, because these works " were full of blasphemies against Christ and against the Christian religion," but urged the preservation of the rest. In this defence of Jewish literature he was supported by the Duke of Bavaria, who appointed him professor at Ingoldstadt, but was strongly condemned by the Dominicans of Cologne. In reply to their attacks Reuchlin launched his defence *De Arte Cabalistica,* glorifying the Cabala, of which the " central doctrine for him was the Messianology around which all its other doctrines grouped themselves."[1] His whole philosophical system, as he himself admitted, was in fact entirely Cabalistic, and his views were shared by his contemporary Cornelius Agrippa of Nettesheim. As a result of these teachings a craze for Cabalism spread amongst Christian prelates, statesmen, and warriors, and a number of Christian thinkers took up the doctrines of the Cabala and " essayed to work them over in their own way." Athanasius Kircher and Knorr, Baron von Rosenroth, author of the *Kabbala Denudata,* in the course of the seventeenth century " endeavoured to spread the Cabala among the Christians by translating Cabalistic works which they regarded as most ancient wisdom." " Most of them," the *Jewish Encyclopædia* goes on to observe derisively, " held the absurd idea that the Cabala contained proofs of the truth of Christianity. . . . Much that appears Christian [in the Cabala] is, in fact, nothing but the logical development of certain ancient esoteric doctrines."[2]

The Rosicrucians appear to have been the outcome both of this Cabalistic movement and of the teachings of Paracelsus. The earliest intimation of their existence was given in a series of pamphlets which appeared at the beginning of the seventeenth century. The first of these, entitled the *Fama Fraternitatis; or a Discovery of the Fraternity of the most Laudable*

[1] *Jewish Encyclopædia,* articles on Cabala and Reuchlin.
[2] Ibid., article on Cabala.

Order of the Rosy Cross, was published at Cassel in 1614 and the *Confessio Fraternitatis* early in the following year. These contain what may be described as the " Grand Legend " of Rosicrucianism, which has been repeated with slight variations up to the present day. Briefly, this story is as follows[1]:

" The most godly and highly-illuminated Father, our brother C.R.," that is to say, Christian Rosenkreutz, " a German, the chief and original of our Fraternity," was born in 1378, and some sixteen years later travelled to the East with a Brother P.A.L., who had determined to go to the Holy Land. On reaching Cyprus, Brother P.A.L. died and " so never came to Jerusalem." Brother C.R., however, having become acquainted with certain Wise Men of " Damasco in Arabia," and beheld what great wonders they wrought, went on alone to Damasco. Here the Wise Men received him, and he then set himself to study Physick and Mathematics and to translate the Book M into Latin. After three years he went to Egypt, whence he journeyed on to Fez, where " he did get acquaintance with those who are called the Elementary inhabitants, who revealed to him many of their secrets. . . . Of those of Fez he often did confess that their Magia was not altogether pure and also that their Cabala was defiled with their religion, but notwithstanding he knew how to make good use of the same." After two years Brother C.R. departed the city Fez and sailed away with many costly things into Spain, where he conferred with the learned men and being " ready bountifully to impart all his arts and secrets " showed them amongst other things how " there might be a society in Europe which might have gold, silver, and precious stones sufficient for them to bestow on kings for their necessary uses and lawful purposes. . . ."

Christian Rosenkreutz then returned to Germany, where " there is nowadays no want of learned men, Magicians, Cabalists, Physicians, and Philosophers." Here he " builded himself a fitting and neat habitation in which he ruminated his voyage and philosophy and reduced them together in a true memorial." At the end of five years' meditation there " came again into his mind the wished-for Reformation: accordingly he chose " some few adjoyned with him," the Brethren G.V., I.A., and I.O.—the last of whom " was very expert and well learned in Cabala as his book H witnesseth "—to form a circle

[1] The following résumé is taken from the recent reprint of the *Fama* and *Confessio* brought out by the " Societas Rosicruciana in Anglia," and printed by W. J. Parrett (Margate, 1923). The story, which, owing to the extraordinary confusion of the text, is difficult to resume as a coherent narrative is given in the *Fama*; the dates are given in the *Confessio*.

of initiates. "After this manner began the Fraternity of the Rosy Cross." Five other Brethren were afterwards added, all Germans except I.A., and these eight constituted his new building called Sancti Spiritus. The following agreement was then drawn up:

First, that none of them should profess any other thing than to cure the sick, and that gratis.

Second, none of the posterity should be constrained to wear one certain kind of habit, but therein to follow the custom of the country.

Third, that every year, upon the day C., they should meet together at the house Sancti Spiritus, or write the cause of his absence.

Fourth, every Brother should look about for a worthy person who, after his decease, might succeed him.

Fifth, the word C.R. should be their seal, mark, and character.

Sixth, the Fraternity should remain secret one hundred years.

Finally Brother C.R. died, but where and when, or in what country he was buried, remained a secret. The date, however, is generally given as 1484 In 1604 the Brethren who then constituted the inner circle of the Order discovered a door on which was written in large letters

Post 120 Annos Patebo.

On opening the door a vault was disclosed to view, where beneath a brass tablet the body of Christian Rosenkreutz was found, "whole and unconsumed," with all his "ornaments and attires," and holding in his hand the parchment " I " which " next unto the Bible is our greatest treasure," whilst beside him lay a number of books, amongst others the *Vocabulario* of Paracelsus, who, however, the *Fama* observes, earlier " was none of our Fraternity."[1]

The Brethren now knew that after a time there would be " a general reformation both of divine and human things." While declaring their belief in the Christian faith, the *Fama* goes on to explain that:

Our Philosophy is not a new invention, but as Adam after his fall hath received it and as Moses and Solomon used it, . . . wherein Plato, Aristotle, Pythagoras, and others did hit the mark and wherein Enoch, Abraham, Moses, Solomon, did excel, but especially wherewith that wonderful Book the Bible agreeth.

[1] Incidentally Paracelsus was not born until 1493, that is to say nine years after Christian Rosenkreutz is supposed to have died.

It will be seen that, according to this Manifesto, Rosicrucian-ism was a combination of the ancient secret tradition handed down from the patriarchs through the philosophers of Greece and of the first Cabala of the Jews.

The " Grand Legend " of Rosicrucianism rests, however, on no historical evidence; there is, in fact, not the least reason to suppose that any such person as Christian Rosenkreutz ever existed. The Illuminatus von Knigge in the eighteenth century asserted that:

It is now recognized amongst enlightened men that no real Rosicrucians have existed, but that the whole of what is contained in the *Fama* and the *Universal Reformation of the World* [another Rosicrucian pamphlet which appeared in the same year] was only a subtle allegory of Valentine Andrea, of which afterwards partly deceivers (such as the Jesuits) and partly visionaries made use in order to realize this dream.[1]

What, then, was the origin of the name Rose-Cross? According to one Rosicrucian tradition, the word " Rose " does not derive from the flower depicted on the Rosicrucian cross, but from the Latin word *ros,* signifying " dew," which was sup-posed to be the most powerful solvent of gold, whilst *crux,* the cross, was the chemical hieroglyphic for " light."[2] It is said that the Rosicrucians interpreted the initials on the cross INRI by the sentence " Igne Nitrum Roris Invenitur."[3] Supposing this derivation to be correct, it would be interesting to know whether any connexion could be traced between the first appearance of the word Rosie Cross in the *Fama Fraterni-tatis* at the date of 1614 and the cabalistic treatise of the celebrated Rabbi of Prague, Shabbethai Sheftel Horowitz, entitled *Shefa Tal,* that is to say, " The Effusion of Dew," which appeared in 1612.[4] Although this book has often been reprinted, no copy is to be found in the British Museum, so I am unable to pursue this line of enquiry further. A simpler explanation may be that the Rosy Cross derived from the Red Cross of the Templars. Mirabeau, who as a Freemason and an Illuminatus was in a position to discover many facts about the secret societies of Germany during his stay in the country, definitely asserts that " the Rose Croix Masons of the

[1] *Nachtrag von weitern Originalschriften des Illuminatenordens,* Part II. p. 148 (Munich, 1787).
[2] Mackey, *Lexicon of Freemasonry,* p. 265.
[3] Ibid., p. 150.
[4] *Jewish Encyclopædia,* article on Shabbethai Horowitz.

seventeenth century were only the ancient Order of the Templars secretly perpetuated."[1]

Lecouteulx de Canteleu is more explicit:

> In France the Knights (Templar) who left the Order, henceforth hidden, and so to speak unknown, formed the Order of the Flaming Star and of the Rose-Croix, which in the fifteenth century spread itself in Bohemia and Silesia. Every Grand officer of these Orders had all his life to wear the Red Cross and to repeat every day the prayer of St. Bernard.[2]

Eckert states that the ritual, symbols, and names of the Rose-Croix were borrowed from the Templars, and that the Order was divided into seven degrees, according to the seven days of creation, at the same time signifying that their " principal aim was that of the mysterious, the investigation of Being and of the forces of nature."[3]

The Rosicrucian Kenneth Mackenzie, in his *Masonic Cyclopædia,* appears to suggest the same possibility of Templar origin. Under the heading of Rosicrucians he refers enigmatically to an invisible fraternity that has existed from very ancient times, as early as the days of the Crusades, " bound by solemn obligations of impenetrable secrecy," and joining together in work for humanity and to " glorify the good." At various periods of history this body has emerged into a sort of temporary light; but its true name has never transpired and is only known to the innermost adepts and rulers of the society." " The Rosicrucians of the sixteenth century finally disappeared and re-entered this invisible fraternity "—from which they had presumably emerged. Whether any such body really existed or whether the above account is simply an attempt at mystification devised to excite curiosity, the incredulous may question. The writer here observes that it would be indiscreet to say more, but elsewhere he throws out a hint that may have some bearing on the matter, for in his article on the Templars he says that after the suppression of the Order it was revived in a more secret form and subsists to the present day. This would exactly accord with Mirabeau's statement that the Rosicrucians were only the Order of the Templars secretly perpetuated. Moreover, as we shall see later, according to a legend preserved by the Royal Order of Scotland, the degree of the Rosy Cross had been instituted by that Order in conjunction with the

---

[1] Mirabeau, *Histoire de la Monarchie Prussienne,* V. 76.
[2] Lecouteulx de Canteleu, *Les Sectes et Sociétés Secrètes,* p. 97.
[3] Eckert, *La Franc-Maçonnerie dans sa véritable signification,* II. 48.

Templars in 1314, and it would certainly be a remarkable coincidence that a man bearing the name of Rosenkreutz should happen to have inaugurated a society, founded, like the Templars, on Eastern secret doctrines during the course of the same century, without any connexion existing between the two.

I would suggest, then, that Christian Rosenkreutz was a purely mythical personage, and that the whole legend concerning his travels was invented to disguise the real sources whence the Rosicrucians derived their system, which would appear to have been a compound of ancient esoteric doctrines, of Arabian and Syrian magic, and of Jewish Cabalism, partly inherited from the Templars but reinforced by direct contact with Cabalistic Jews in Germany. The Rose-Croix, says Mirabeau, " were a mystical, Cabalistic, theological, and magical sect," and Rosicrucianism thus became in the seventeenth century the generic title by which everything of the nature of Cabalism, Theosophy, Alchemy, Astrology, and Mysticism was designated. For this reason it has been said that they cannot be regarded as the descendants of the Templars. Mr. Waite, in referring to " the alleged connexion between the Templars and the Brethren of the Rosy Cross," observes:

> The Templars were not alchemists, they had no scientific pretensions, and their secret, so far as it can be ascertained, was a religious secret of an anti-Christian kind. The Rosicrucians, on the other hand, were pre-eminently a learned society and they were also a Christian sect.[1]

The fact that the Templars do not appear to have practised alchemy is beside the point; it is not pretended that the Rosicrucians followed the Templars in every particular, but that they were the inheritors of a secret tradition passed on to them by the earlier Order. Moreover, that they were a learned society, or even a society at all, is not at all certain, for they would appear to have possessed no organization like the Templars or the Freemasons, but to have consisted rather of isolated occultists bound together by some tie of secret knowledge concerning natural phenomena. This secrecy was no doubt necessary at a period when scientific research was liable to be regarded as sorcery, but whether the Rosicrucians really accomplished anything is extremely doubtful. They are said to have been alchemists; but did they ever succeed in transmuting metals? They are described as learned, yet do the pamphlets emanating from the Fraternity betray any

[1] A. E. Waite, *The Real History of the Rosicrucians*, p. 216.

proof of superior knowledge? "The Chymical Marriage of Christian Rosenkreutz," which appeared in 1616, certainly appears to be the purest nonsense—magical imaginings of the most puerile kind; and Mr. Waite himself observes that the publication of the *Fama* and the *Confessio Fraternitatis* will not add new lustre to the Rosicrucian reputations:

> We are accustomed to regard the adepts of the Rosy Cross as beings of sublime elevation and preternatural physical powers, masters of Nature, monarchs of the intellectual world. . . . But here in their own acknowledged manifestos they avow themselves a mere theosophical offshoot of the Lutheran heresy, acknowledging the spiritual supremacy of a temporal prince, and calling the Pope anti-Christ. . . . We find them intemperate in their language, rabid in their religious prejudices, and instead of towering giant-like above the intellectual average of their age, we see them buffeted by the same passions and identified with all opinions of the men by whom they were environed. The voice which addresses us behind the mystical mask of the Rose-Croix does not come from an intellectual throne. . . .

So much for the Rosicrucians as a " learned society."

What, then, of their claim to be a Christian body? The Rosicrucian student of the Cabala, Julius Sperber, in his *Echo of the Divinely Illuminated Fraternity of the Admirable Order of the R.C.* (1615), has indicated the place assigned to Christ by the Rosicrucians. In De Quincey's words:

> Having maintained the probability of the Rosicrucian pretensions on the ground that such *magnalia Dei* had from the creation downwards been confided to the keeping of a few individuals—agreeably to which he affirms that Adam was the first Rosicrucian of the Old Testament and Simeon the last—he goes on to ask whether the Gospel put an end to the secret tradition? By no means, he answers: Christ established a new "college of magic" among His disciples, and the greater mysteries were revealed to St. John and St. Paul.

John Yarker, quoting this passage, adds: "This, Brother Findel points out, was a claim of the Carpocratian Gnostics"; it was also, as we have seen, a part of the Johannite tradition which is said to have been imparted to the Templars. We shall find the same idea of Christ as an "initiate" running all through the secret societies up to the present day.

These doctrines not unnaturally brought on the Rosicrucians the suspicion of being an anti-Christian body. The writer of a contemporary pamphlet published in 1624, declares that "this fraternity is a stratagem of the Jews and Cabalistic

Hebrews, in whose philosophy, says Pic de la Mirandole, all things are . . . as if hidden in the majesty of truth or as . . . in very sacred Mysteries."[1]

Another work, *Examination of the Unknown and Novel Cabala of the Brethren of the Rose-Cross,* agrees with the assertion that the chief of this " execrable college is Satan, that its first rule is denial of God, blasphemy against the most simple and undivided Trinity, trampling on the mysteries of the redemption, spitting in the face of the mother of God and of all the saints." The sect is further accused of compacts with the devil, sacrifices of children, of cherishing toads, making poisonous powders, dancing with fiends, etc.

Now, although all this would appear to be quite incompatible with the character of the Rosicrucians as far as it is known, we have already seen that the practices here described were by no means imaginary; in this same seventeenth century, when the fame of the Rosicrucians was first noised abroad, black magic was still, as in the days of Gilles de Rais, a horrible reality, not only in France but in England, Scotland, and Germany, where sorcerers of both sexes were continually put to death.[2] However much we may deplore the methods employed against these people or question the supernatural origin of their cult, it would be idle to deny that the cult itself existed.

Moreover, towards the end of the century it assumed in France a very tangible form in the series of mysterious dramas known as the " Affaire des Poisons," of which the first act took place in 1666, when the celebrated Marquise de Brinvilliers embarked on her amazing career of crime in collaboration with her lover Sainte-Croix. This extraordinary woman, who for ten years made a hobby of trying the effects of various slow poisons on her nearest relations, thereby causing the death of her father and brothers, might appear to have been merely an isolated criminal of the abnormal type but for the sequel to her exploits in the epidemic of poisoning which followed and during twenty years kept Paris in a state of terror. The investigations of the police finally led to the discovery of a whole band of magicians and alchemists—" a vast ramification of malefactors

---

[1] " *Traicté des Athéistes, Déistes, Illuminez d'Espagne et Nouveaux Prétendus Invisibles, dits de la Confrairie de la Croix-Rosaire, élevez depuis quelques années dans le Christianisme,*" forming the second part of the " *Histoire Générale de Progrès et Décadence de l'Héréie Moderne—A la suite du Premier*" de M. Florimond de Raemond, Conseiller du Roy, etc.

[2] See G. M. Trevelyan, *England under the Stuarts,* pp. 32, 33, and James Howell, *Familiar Letters* (edition of 1753), pp. 49, 435. James Holwell was clerk to the Privy Council of Charles I.

covering all France "—who specialized in the art of poisoning without fear of detection.

Concerning all these sorcerers, alchemists, compounders of magical powders and philtres, frightful rumours circulated, " pacts with the devil were talked of, sacrifices of new-born babies, incantations, sacrilegious Masses and other practices as disquieting as they were lugubrious."[1] Even the King's mistress, Madame de Montespan, is said to have had recourse to black Masses in order to retain the royal favour through the agency of the celebrated sorceress La Voisin, with whom she was later implicated in an accusation of having attempted the life of the King.

All the extraordinary details of these events have recently been described in the book of Madame Latour, where the intimate connexion between the poisoners and the magicians is shown. In the opinion of contemporaries, these were not isolated individuals:

> Their methods were too certain, their execution of crime too skilful and too easy for them not to have belonged, either directly or indirectly, to a whole organization of criminals who prepared the way, and studied the method of giving to crime the appearance of illness, of forming, in a word, a school.[2]

The author of the work here quoted draws an interesting parallel between this organization and the modern traffic in cocaine, and goes on to describe the three degrees into which it was divided: firstly, the Heads, cultivated and intelligent men, who understood chemistry, physics, and nearly all useful sciences, " invisible counsellors but supreme, without whom the sorcerers and diviners would have been powerless "; secondly, the visible magicians employing mysterious processes, complicated rites and terrifying ceremonies; and thirdly, the crowd of nobles and plebeians who flocked to the doors of the sorcerers and filled their pockets in return for magic potions, philtres, and, in certain cases, insidious poisons. Thus La Voisin must be placed in the second category; " in spite of her luxury, her profits, and her fame," she " is only a subaltern agent in this vast organization of criminals. She depends entirely for her great enterprises on the intellectual chiefs of the corporation. . . ."[3]

---

[1] Th.-Louis Latour, *Princesses, Dames et Adventurières du Règne de Louis XIV*, p. 278 (Eugène Figuière, Paris, 1923).
[2] Ibid., p. 297.
[3] Ibid., p. 306.

Who were these intellectual chiefs? The man who first
initiated Madame de Brinvilliers' lover Sainte-Croix into the
art of poisoning was an Italian named Exili or Eggidi; but the
real initiate from whom Eggidi and another Italian poisoner
had learnt their secrets is said to have been Glaser, variously
described as a German or a Swiss chemist, who followed the
principles of Paracelsus and occupied the post of physician to
the King and the Duc d'Orléans.[1] This man, about whose
history little is known, might thus have been a kind of Rosicrucian. For since, as has been said, the intellectual chiefs
from whom the poisoners derived their inspiration were men
versed in chemistry, in science, in physics, and the treatment
of diseases, and since, further, they included alchemists and
people professing to be in possession of the Philosopher's Stone,
their resemblance with the Rosicrucians is at once apparent.
Indeed, in turning back to the branches of magic enumerated
by the Rosicrucian Robert Fludd, we find not only Natural
Magic, " that most occult and secret department of physics
by which the mystical properties of natural substances are
extracted," but also Venefic Magic, which " is familiar with
potions, philtres, and with various preparations of poisons."

The art of poisoning was therefore known to the Rosicrucians,
and, although there is no reason to suppose it was ever practised
by the heads of the Fraternity, it is possible that the inspirers
of the poisoners may have been perverted Rosicrucians, that
is to say, students of those portions of the Cabala relating to
magic both of the necromantic and venefic varieties, who turned
the scientific knowledge which the Fraternity of the Rosy Cross
used for healing to a precisely opposite and deadly purpose.
This would explain the fact that contemporaries like the author
of the *Examination of the Unknown and Novel Cabala of the
Brethren of the Rose-Cross* should identify these brethren with
the magicians and believe them to be guilty of practices deriving from the same source as Rosicrucian knowledge—the Cabala
of the Jews. Their modern admirers would, of course, declare
that they were the poles asunder, the difference being between
white and black magic. Huysmans, however, scoffs at this
distinction and says the use of the term " white magic " was
a ruse of the Rose-Croix.

But of the real doctrines of the Rosicrucians no one can speak
with certainty. The whole story of the Fraternity is wrapped
in mystery. Mystery was avowedly the essence of their

[1] *Œuvres complètes de Voltaire*, Vol. XXI. p. 129 (1785 edition); *Biographie
Michaud*, article on Glaser.

system; their identity, their aims, their doctrines, are said to have been kept a profound secret from the world. Indeed it is said that no real Rosicrucian ever allowed himself to be known as such. As a result of this systematic method of concealment, sceptics on the one hand have declared the Rosicrucians to have been charlatans and impostors or have denied their very existence, whilst on the other hand romancers have exalted them as depositaries of supernatural wisdom. The question is further obscured by the fact that most accounts of the Fraternity—as, for example, those of Eliphas Lévi, Hargrave Jennings, Kenneth Mackenzie, Mr. A. E. Waite, Dr. Wynn Westcott, and Mr. Cadbury Jones—are the work of men claiming or believing themselves to be initiated into Rosicrucianism or other occult systems of a kindred nature and as such in possession of peculiar and exclusive knowledge. This pretension may at once be dismissed as an absurdity; nothing is easier than for anyone to make a compound out of Jewish Cabalism and Eastern theosophy and to label it Rosicrucianism, but no proof whatever exists of any affiliation between the self-styled Rosicrucians of to-day and the seventeenth-century " Brothers of the Rosy Cross."[1]

In spite of Mr. Waite's claim, " The Real History of the Rosicrucians " still remains to be written, at any rate in the English language. The book he has published under this name is merely a superficial study of the question largely composed of reprints of Rosicrucian pamphlets accessible to any student. Mr. Wigston and Mrs. Pott merely echo Mr. Waite. Thus everything that has been published hitherto consists in the repetition of Rosicrucian legends or in unsubstantiated theorizings on their doctrines. What we need are facts. We want to know who were the early Rosicrucians, when the Fraternity originated, and what were its real aims. These researches must be made, not by an occultist weaving his own theories into the subject, but by a historian free from any prejudices for or against the Order, capable of weighing evidence and bringing a judicial mind to bear on the material to be found in the libraries of the Continent—notably the Bibliothèque de l'Arsenal in Paris. Such a work would be a valuable contribution to the history of secret societies in our country.

But if the Continental Brethren of the Rose-Croix form but a

---

[1] This assertion finds confirmation in the *Encyclopædia Britannica*, article on the Rosicrucians, which states: " In no sense are modern Rosicrucians derived from the Fraternity of the seventeenth century."

shadowy group of " Invisibles " whose identity yet remains a mystery, the English adepts of the Order stand forth in the light of day as philosophers well known to their age and country. That Francis Bacon was initiated into Rosicrucianism is now recognized by Freemasons, but a more definite link with the Rosicrucians of the Continent was Robert Fludd, who after travelling for six years in France, Germany, Italy, and Spain—where he formed connexions with Jewish Cabalists[1]— was visited by the German Jew Rosicrucian Michel Maier— doctor to the Emperor Rudolf—by whom he appears to have been initiated into further mysteries.

In 1616 Fludd published his *Tractatus Apologeticus,* defending the Rosicrucians against the charges of " detestable magic and diabolical superstition " brought against them by Libavius. Twelve years later Fludd was attacked by Father Mersenne, to whom a reply was made " by Fludd or a friend of Fludd's " containing a further defence of the Order. " The Book," says Mr. Waite, " treats of the noble art of magic, the foundation and nature of the Cabala, the essence of veritable alchemy, and of the Causa Fratrum Rosae Crucis. It identifies the palace or home of the Rosicrucians with the Scriptural House of Wisdom."

In further works by English writers the Eastern origin of the Fraternity is insisted on. Thus Thomas Vaughan, known as Eugenius Philalethes, writing in praise of the Rosicrucians in 1652, says that " their knowledge at first was not purchased by their own disquisitions, for they received it from the Arabians, amongst whom it remained as the monument and legacy of the Children of the East. Nor is this at all improbable, for the Eastern countries have been always famous for magical and secret societies."

Another apologist of the Rosicrucians, John Heydon, who travelled in Egypt, Persia, and Arabia, is described by a contemporary as having been in " many strange places among the Rosie Crucians and at their castles, holy houses, temples, sepulchres, sacrifices." Heydon himself, whilst declaring that he is not a Rosicrucian, says that he knows members of the Fraternity and its secrets, that they are sons of Moses, and that " this Rosie Crucian Physick or Medicine, I happily and unexpectedly alight upon in Arabia." These references to castles, temples, sacrifices, encountered in Egypt, Persia, and Arabia inevitably recall memories of both Templars and

---

[1] *Jewish Encyclopædia,* article on the Cabala.

Ismailis. Is there no connexion between " the Invisible Mountains of the Brethren " referred to elsewhere by Heydon and the Mountains of the Assassins and the Freemasons? between the Scriptural " House of Wisdom " and the Dar-ul-Hikmat or Grand Lodge of Cairo, the model for Western masonic lodges?

It is as the precursors of the crisis which arose in 1717 that the English Rosicrucians of the seventeenth century are of supreme importance. No longer need we concern ourselves with shadowy Brethren laying dubious claim to supernatural wisdom, but with a concrete association of professed Initiates proclaiming their existence to the world under the name of Freemasonry.

5

ORIGINS OF FREEMASONRY

"THE origin of Freemasonry," says a masonic writer of the
eighteenth century, "is known to Freemasons alone."[1]
If this was once the case, it is so no longer, for, although
the question would certainly appear to be one on which the
initiated should be most qualified to speak, the fact is that no
official theory on the origin of Freemasonry exists; the great
mass of the Freemasons do *not* know or care to know anything
about the history of their Order, whilst Masonic authorities are
entirely disagreed on the matter. Dr. Mackey admits that " the
origin and source whence first sprang the institution of
Freemasonry has given rise to more difference of opinion and
discussion among masonic scholars than any other topic in
the literature of the institution."[2] Nor is this ignorance
maintained merely in books for the general public, since in
those specially addressed to the Craft and at discussions in
lodges the same diversity of opinion prevails, and no decisive
conclusions appear to be reached. Thus Mr. Albert Churchward, a Freemason of the thirtieth degree, who deplores the
small amount of interest taken in this matter by Masons in
general, observes:

Hitherto 'there have been so many contradictory opinions and
theories in the attempt to supply the origin and the reason whence,
where, and why the Brotherhood of Freemasonry came into
existence, and all the "different parts" and various rituals of the
"different degrees." All that has been written on this has hitherto
been *theories*, without any facts for their fundation.[3]

In the absence, therefore, of any origin universally recognized
by the Craft, it is surely open to the lay mind to speculate on

[1] *A Free Mason's Answer to the Suspected Author of a Pamphlet entitled
"Jachin and Boaz," or an Authentic Key to Freemasonry*, p. 10 (1762).
[2] Quoted by R. F. Gould, *History of Freemasonry*, I. 5, 6.
[3] *Signs and Symbols of Primordial Man*, p. 1 (1910).

the matter and to draw conclusions from history as to which of the many explanations put forward seems to supply the key to the mystery.

According to the *Royal Masonic Cyclopædia,* no less than twelve theories have been advanced as to the origins of the Order, namely, that Masonry derived:

" (1) From the patriarchs. (2) From the mysteries of the pagans. (3) From the construction of Solomon's Temple. (4) From the Crusades. (5) From the Knights Templar. (6) From the Roman Collegia of Artificers. (7) From the operative masons of the Middle Ages. (8) From the Rosicrucians of the sixteenth century. (9) From Oliver Cromwell. (10) From Prince Charles Stuart for political purposes. (11) From Sir Christopher Wren, at the building of St. Paul's. (12) From Dr. Desaguliers and his friends in 1717."

This enumeration is, however, misleading, for it implies that in *one* of these various theories the true origin of Freemasonry may be found. In reality modern Freemasonry is a dual system, a blend of two distinct traditions—of operative masonry, that is to say the actual art of building, and of speculative theory on the great truths of life and death. As a well-known Freemason, the Count Goblet d'Alviella, has expressed it: " Speculative Masonry " (that is to say, the dual system we now know as Freemasonry) " is the legitimate offspring of a fruitful union between the professional guild of mediæval Masons and of a secret group of philosophical Adepts, the first having furnished the form and the second the spirit."[1]   In studying the origins of the present system we have therefore (1) to examine separately the history of each of these two traditions, and (2) to discover their point of junction.

OPERATIVE MASONRY

Beginning with the first of these two traditions, we find that guilds of working masons existed in very ancient times. Without going back as far as ancient Egypt or Greece, which would be beyond the scope of the present work, the course of these associations may be traced throughout the history of Western Europe from the beginning of the Christian era. According to certain masonic writers, the Druids originally came from Egypt and brought with them traditions relating to the art of building. The *Culdees,* who later on established schools and colleges in this country for the teaching of arts,

[1] *Ars Quatuor Coronatorum,* XXXII. Part I. p. 47.

sciences, and handicrafts, are said to have derived from the Druids.

But a more probable source of inspiration in the art of building are the Romans, who established the famous collegia of architects referred to in the list of alternative theories given in the *Masonic Cyclopædia*. Advocates of the Roman Collegia origin of Freemasonry might be right as far as operative masonry is concerned, for it is to the period following on the Roman occupation of Britain that our masonic guilds can with the greatest degree of certainty be traced. Owing to the importance the art of building now acquired it is said that many distinguished men, such as St. Alban, King Alfred, King Edwin, and King Athelstan, were numbered amongst its patrons,[1] so that in time the guilds came to occupy the position of privileged bodies and were known as " free corporations "; further that York was the first masonic centre in England, largely under the control of the Culdees, who at the same period exercised much influence over the Masonic Collegia in Scotland, at Kilwinning, Melrose, and Aberdeen.[2]

But it must be remembered that all this is speculation. No documentary evidence has ever been produced to prove the existence of masonic guilds before the famous York charter of A.D. 926, and even the date of this document is doubtful. Only with the period of Gothic architecture do we reach firm ground. That guilds of working masons known in France as " Compagnonnages " and in Germany as " Steinmetzen " did then form close corporations and possibly possess secrets connected with their profession is more than probable. That, in consequence of their skill in building the magnificent cathedrals of this period, they now came to occupy a privileged position seems fairly certain.

The Abbé Grandidier, writing from Strasbourg in 1778, traces the whole system of Freemasonry from these German guilds: " This much-vaunted Society of Freemasons is nothing but a servile imitation of an ancient and useful *confrèrie* of real masons whose headquarters was formerly at Strasbourg and of which the constitution was confirmed by the Emperor Maximilian in 1498."[3]

As far as it is possible to discover from the scanty documentary evidence the fourteenth, fifteenth, and sixteenth

---

[1] Preston's *Illustrations of Masonry*, pp. 143, 147, 153 (1804).
[2] John Yarker, *The Arcane Schools*, pp. 269, 327, 329.
[3] Published in the *Essai sur la Secte des Illuminés* by the Marquis de Luchet, p. 236 (1792 edition).

centuries provide, the same privileges appear to have been accorded to the guilds of working masons in England and Scotland, which, although presided over by powerful nobles and apparently on occasion admitting members from outside the Craft, remained essentially operative bodies. Nevertheless we find the assemblies of Masons suppressed by Act of Parliament in the beginning of the reign of Henry VI, and later on an armed force sent by Queen Elizabeth to break up the Annual Grand Lodge at York. It is possible that the fraternity merely by the secrecy with which it was surrounded excited the suspicions of authority, for nothing could be more law-abiding than its published statutes. Masons were to be " true men to God and the Holy Church," also to the masters that they served. They were to be honest in their manner of life and " to do no villainy whereby the Craft or the Science may be slandered."[1]

Yet the seventeenth-century writer Plot, in his *Natural History of Staffordshire*, expresses some suspicion with regard to the secrets of Freemasonry. That these could not be merely trade secrets relating to the art of building, but that already some speculative element had been introduced to the lodges, seems the more probable from the fact that by the middle of the seventeenth century not only noble patrons headed the Craft, but ordinary gentlemen entirely unconnected with building were received into the fraternity. The well-known entry in the diary of Elias Ashmole under the date of October 16, 1646, clearly proves this fact: " I was made a Freemason at Warrington in Lancashire with Col. Henry Mainwaring of Karticham [?] in Cheshire. The names of those that were then of the Lodge, Mr. Rich. Penket, Warden, Mr. James Collier, Mr. Rich. Sankey, Henry Littler, John Ellam, Rich. Ellam and Hugh Brewer."[2] " It is now ascertained," says Yarker, " that the majority of the members present were not operative masons."[3]

Again, in 1682 Ashmole relates that he attended a meeting held at Mason Hall in London, where with a number of other

---

[1] Brother Chalmers Paton, *The Origin of Freemasonry: the 1717 Theory Exploded*, quoting ancient charges preserved in a MS. in possession of the Lodge of Antiquity in London, written in the reign of James II, but "supposed to be really of much more ancient date."

[2] *Ars Quatuor Coronatorum*, XXV. p. 240, paper by J. E. S. Tuckett on *Dr. Rawlinson and the Masonic Entries in Elias Ashmole's Diary*, with facsimile of entry in Diary which is preserved in the Bodleian Library (Ashmole MS. 1136, fol. 19).

[3] Yarker, *The Arcane Schools*, p. 383.

ORIGINS OF FREEMASONRY 103

gentlemen he was admitted into "the Fellowship of the Free-masons," that is to say, into the second degree. We have then clear proof that already in the seventeenth century Freemasonry had ceased to be an association composed exclusively of men concerned with building, although eminent architects ranked high in the Order; Inigo Jones is said to have been Grand Master under James I, and Sir Christopher Wren to have occupied the same position from about 1685 to 1702. But it was not until 1703 that the Lodge of St. Paul in London officially announced "that the privileges of Masonry should no longer be restricted to operative Masons, but extended to men of various professions, provided they were regularly approved and initiated into the Order."[1]

This was followed in 1717 by the great *coup d'état* when Grand Lodge was founded, and Speculative Masonry, which we now know as Freemasonry, was established on a settled basis with a ritual, rules, and constitution drawn up in due form. It is at this important date that the official history of Freemasonry begins.

But before pursuing the course of the Order through what is known as the "Grand Lodge Era," it is necessary to go back and enquire into the origins of the philosophy that was now combined with the system of operative masonry. This is the point on which opinions are divided and to which the various theories summarized in the *Masonic Cyclopædia* relate. Let us examine each of these in turn.

SPECULATIVE MASONRY

According to certain sceptics concerning the mysteries of Freemasonry, the system inaugurated in 1717 had no existence before that date, but "was devised, promulgated, and palmed upon the world by Dr. Desaguliers, Dr. Anderson, and others, who then founded the Grand Lodge of England." Mr. Paton, in an admirable little pamphlet,[2] has shown the futility of this contention and also the injustice of representing the founders of Grand Lodge as perpetrating so gross a deception.

This 1717 theory ascribes to men of the highest character the invention of a system of mere imposture. . . . It was brought forward with pretensions which its framers knew to be false pretensions of high antiquity; whereas . . . it had newly been invented in their

---

[1] Preston's *Illustrations of Masonry*, p. 208 (1804).
[2] *The Origins of Freemasonry: the 1717 Theory Exploded.*

studies. Is this likely? Or is it reasonable to ascribe such conduct to honourable men, without even assigning a probable motive for it?

We have indeed only to study masonic ritual—which is open to everyone to read—in order to arrive at the same conclusion, that there could be no motive for this imposture, and further that these two clergymen cannot be supposed to have evolved the whole thing out of their heads. Obviously some movement of a kindred nature must have led up to this crisis. And since Elias Ashmole's diary clearly proves that a ceremony of masonic initiation had existed in the preceding century, it is surely only reasonable to conclude that Drs. Anderson and Desaguliers revised but did not originate the ritual and constitutions drawn up by them.

Now, although the ritual of Freemasonry is couched in modern and by no means classical English, the ideas running through it certainly bear traces of extreme antiquity. The central idea of Freemasonry concerning a loss which has befallen man and the hope of its ultimate recovery is in fact no other than the ancient secret tradition described in the first chapter of this book. Certain masonic writers indeed ascribe to Free-masonry precisely the same genealogy as that of the early Cabala, declaring that it descended from Adam and the first patriarchs of the human race, and thence through groups of Wise Men amongst the Egyptians, Chaldeans, Persians, and Greeks.[1] Mr. Albert Churchward insists particularly on the Egyptian origin of the speculative element in Freemasonry: " Brother Gould and other Freemasons will never understand the meaning and origin of our sacred tenets till they have studied and unlocked the mysteries of the past." This study will then reveal the fact that " the Druids, the Gymnosophists of India, the Magi of Persia, and the Chaldeans of Assyria had all the same religious rites and ceremonies as practised by their priests who were initiated to their Order, and that these were solemnly sworn to keep the doctrines a profound secret from the rest of mankind. All these flowed from one source—Egypt."[2]

Mr. Churchward further quotes the speech of the Rev. Dr. William Dodd at the opening of a masonic temple in 1794, who traced Freemasonry from " the first astronomers on the plains of Chaldea, the wise and mystic kings and

[1] The Rev. G. Oliver, *The Historical Landmarks of Freemasonry*, pp. 55, 57, 62, 318 (1845).
[2] *Signs and Symbols of Primordial Man*, p. 185 (1910).

priests of Egypt, the sages of Greece and philosophers of Rome,"
etc.[1]

But how did these traditions descend to the masons of the
West? According to a large body of masonic opinion in this
country which recognizes only a single source of inspiration
to the system we now know as Freemasonry, the speculative as
well as the operative traditions of the Order descended from
the building guilds and were imported to England by means
of the Roman Collegia. Mr. Churchward, however, strongly
dissents from this view:

> In the new and revised edition of the Perfect Ceremonies,
> according to our E. working, a theory is given that Freemasonry
> originated from certain guilds of workmen which are well known
> in history as the "Roman College of Artificers." There is no
> foundation of fact for such a theory. Freemasonry is now, and al-
> ways was, an Eschatology, as may be proved by the whole of our
> signs, symbols, and words, and our rituals.[2]

But what Mr. Churchward fails to explain is how this
eschatology reached the working masons; moreover why, if as
he asserts, it derived from Egypt, Assyria, India, and Persia,
Freemasonry no longer bears the stamp of these countries.
For although vestiges of Sabeism may be found in the decora-
tion of the lodges, and brief references to the mysteries of
Egypt and Phœnicia, to the secret teaching of Pythagoras, to
Euclid, and to Plato in the Ritual and instructions of the Craft
degrees—nevertheless the form in which the ancient tradition
is clothed, the phraseology and pass-words employed, are
neither Egyptian, Chaldean, Greek, nor Persian, but Judaic.
Thus although some portion of the ancient secret tradition
may have penetrated to Great Britain through the Druids or
the Romans—versed in the lore of Greece and Egypt—another
channel for its introduction was clearly the Cabala of the
Jews. Certain masonic writers recognize this double tradition,
the one descending from Egypt, Chaldea, and Greece, the other
from the Israelites, and assert that it is from the latter

---

[1] *Signs and Symbols of Primordial Man,* p. 8 (1910).

[2] Ibid., p. 7. The German Freemason Findel disagrees with both the
Roman Collegia and the Egypt theory, and, like the Abbé Grandidier, indicates the *Steinmetzen* of the fifteenth century as the real progenitors of the
Order: "All attempts to trace the history of Freemasonry farther back
than the Middle Ages have been . . . failures, and placing the origin of
the Fraternity in the mysteries of Egypt . . . must be rejected as a wild
and untenable hypothesis."—*History of Freemasonry* (Eng. trans.), p. 25.

source their system is derived.[1] For after tracing its origin from Adam, Noah, Enoch, and Abraham, they proceed to show its line of descent through Moses, David, and Solomon[2] —descent from Solomon is in fact officially recognized by the Craft and forms a part of the instructions to candidates for initiation into the first degree. But, as we have already seen, this is the precise genealogy attributed to the Cabala by the Jews. Moreover, modern Freemasonry is entirely built up on the Solomonic, or rather the Hiramic legend. For the sake of readers unfamiliar with the ritual of Freemasonry a brief *résumé* of this " Grand Legend " must be given here.

Solomon, when building the Temple, employed the services of a certain artificer in brass, named Hiram, the son of a widow of the tribe of Naphthali, who was sent to him by Hiram, King of Tyre. So much we know from the Book of Kings, but the masonic legend goes on to relate that Hiram, the widow's son, referred to as Hiram Abiff, and described as the master-builder, met with an untimely end. For the purpose of preserving order the masons working on the Temple were divided into three classes, Entered Apprentices, Fellow Crafts, and Master Masons, the first two distinguished by different pass-words and grips and paid at different rates of wages, the last consisting only of three persons—Solomon himself, Hiram King of Tyre, who had provided him with wood and precious stones, and Hiram Abiff. Now, before the completion of the Temple fifteen of the Fellow Crafts conspired together to find out the secrets of the Master Masons and resolved to waylay Hiram Abiff at the door of the Temple.

At the last moment twelve of the fifteen drew back, but the remaining three carried out the fell design, and after threatening Hiram in vain in order to obtain the secrets, killed him with three blows on the head, delivered by each in turn. They then conveyed the body away and buried it on Mount Moriah in Jerusalem. Solomon, informed of the disappearance

[1] Dr. Oliver and Dr. Mackey thus refer to true and spurious Masonry, the former descending from Noah, through Shem, Abraham, Isaac, Jacob, and Moses to Solomon—hence the appellation of Noachites sometimes applied to Freemasons—the latter from Cain and the Gymnosophists of India to Egypt and Greece. They add that a union between the two took place at the time of the building of the Temple of Solomon through Hiram Abiff, who was a member of both, being by birth a Jew and artificer of Tyre, and from this union Freemasonry descends. According to Mackey, therefore, Jewish Masonry is the true form.—*A Lexicon of Freemasonry*, pp. 323–5; Oliver's *Historical Landmarks of Freemasonry*, I. 60.
[2] Rev. G. Oliver, *The Historical Landmarks of Freemasonry*, pp. 55, 57 (1845).

of the master-builder, sent out fifteen Fellow Crafts to seek for him; five of these, having arrived at the mountain, noticed a place where the earth had been disturbed and there discovered the body of Hiram. Leaving a branch of acacia to mark the spot, they returned with their story to Solomon, who ordered them to go and exhume the body—an order that was immediately carried out.

The murder and exhumation, or "raising," of Hiram, accompanied by extraordinary lamentations, form the climax of Craft Masonry; and when it is remembered that in all probability no such tragedy ever took place, that possibly no one known as Hiram Abiff ever existed,[1] the whole story can only be regarded as the survival of some ancient cult relating not to an actual event, but to an esoteric doctrine. A legend and a ceremony of this kind is indeed to be found in many earlier mythologies; the story of the murder of Hiram had been foreshadowed by the Egyptian legend of the murder of Osiris and the quest for his body by Isis, whilst the lamentations around the tomb of Hiram had a counterpart in the mourning ceremonies for Osiris and Adonis—both, like Hiram, subsequently "raised"—and later on in that which took place around the catafalque of Manes, who, like Hiram, was barbarously put to death and is said to have been known to the Manicheans as "the son of the widow." But in the form given to it by Freemasonry the legend is purely Judaic, and would therefore appear to have derived from the Judaic version of the ancient tradition. The pillars of the Temple, Jachin and Boaz, which play so important a part in Craft Masonry, are symbols which occur in the Jewish Cabala, where they are described as two of the ten Sephiroths.[2] A writer of the eighteenth century, referring to "fyve curiosities" he has discovered in Scotland, describes one as—

The Mason word, which tho' some make a Misterie of it, I will not conceal a little of what I know. It is lyke a Rabbinical Tradition in way of Comment on Jachin and Boaz, the Two Pillars erected in Solomon's Temple with ane Addition delyvered from Hand to Hand, by which they know and become familiar one with another.[3]

This is precisely the system by which the Cabala was handed down amongst the Jews. The *Jewish Encyclopædia* lends

[1] *The Jewish Encyclopædia* (article on Freemasonry) characterizes the name Hiram Abifi as a misunderstanding of 2 Chron. ii. 13.

[2] Clavel, *Histoire pittoresque de la Franc-Maçonnerie*, p. 340; Matter, *Histoire du Gnosticisme*, I. 145.

[3] *Quoted in A.Q.C.*, XXXII. Part I. p. 36.

colour to the theory of Cabalistic transmission by suggesting that the story of Hiram "may possibly trace back to the Rabbinic legend concerning the Temple of Solomon," that "while all the workmen were killed so that they should not build another temple devoted to idolatry, Hiram himself was raised to Heaven like Enoch."[1]

How did this Rabbinic legend find its way into Freemasonry? Advocates of the Roman Collegia theory explain it in the following manner.

After the building of the Temple of Solomon the masons who had been engaged in the work were dispersed and a number made their way to Europe, some to Marseilles, some perhaps to Rome, where they may have introduced Judaic legends to the Collegia, which then passed on to the Comacini Masters of the seventh century and from these to the mediæval working guilds of England, France, and Germany. It is said that during the Middle Ages a story concerning the Temple of Solomon was current amongst the *compagnonnages* of France. In one of these groups, known as "the children of Solomon," the legend of Hiram appears to have existed much in its present form; according to another group the victim of the murder was not Hiram Abiff, but one of his companions named Maître Jacques, who, whilst engaged with Hiram on the construction of the Temple, met his death at the hands of five wicked Fellow Crafts, instigated by a sixth, the Père Soubise.[2]

But the date at which this legend originated is unknown. Clavel thinks that the "Hebraic mysteries" existed as early as the Roman Collegia, which he describes as largely Judaized[3]; Yarker expresses precisely the opposite view: "It is not so difficult to connect Freemasonry with the Collegia; the difficulty lies in attributing Jewish traditions to the Collegia, and we say on the evidence of the oldest charges that such traditions had no existence in Saxon times."[4] Again: "So far as this country is concerned, we know nothing from documents of a Masonry dating from Solomon's Temple until after the Crusades, when the constitution believed to have been sanctioned by King Athelstan gradually underwent a change."[5] In a discussion which took place recently at the.

---

[1] Article on Freemasonry, giving reference to Pesik, R.V. 25a (ed. Friedmann).
[2] Clavel, op. cit., 364, 365; Lecouteulx de Canteleu, *Les Sectes et Sociétés Secrètes*, p. 120.
[3] Clavel, op. cit., p. 82.
[4] Yarker, *The Arcane Schools*, p. 257.   [5] Ibid., p. 242.

Quatuor Coronati Lodge the Hiramic legend could only be traced back—and then without absolute certainty—to the fourteenth century, which would coincide with the date indicated by Yarker.[1]

Up to this period the lore of the masonic guilds appears to have contained only the exoteric doctrines of Egypt and Greece —which may have reached them through the Roman Collegia, whilst the traditions of Masonry are traced from Adam, Jabal, Tubal Cain, from Nimrod and the Tower of Babel, with Hermes and Pythagoras as their more immediate progenitors.[2] These doctrines were evidently in the main geometrical or technical, and in no sense Cabalistic. There is therefore some justification for Eckert's statement that " the Judeo-Christian mysteries were not yet introduced into the masonic corporations; nowhere can we find the least trace of them. Nowhere do we find any classification, not even that of masters, fellow-crafts, and apprentices. We observe no symbol of the Temple of Solomon; all their symbolism relates to masonic labours and to a few philosophical maxims of morality."[3] The date at which Eckert, like Yarker, places the introduction of these Judaic elements is the time of the Crusades.

But whilst recognizing that modern Craft Masonry is largely founded on the Cabala, it is necessary to distinguish between the different Cabalas. For by this date no less than three Cabalas appear to have existed: firstly, the ancient secret tradition of the patriarchs handed down from the Egyptians through the Greeks and Romans, and possibly through the Roman Collegia to the Craft Masons of Britain; secondly, the Jewish version of this tradition, the first Cabala of the Jews, in no way incompatible with Christianity, descending from Moses, David and Solomon to the Essenes and the more en-lightened Jews; and thirdly, the perverted Cabala, mingled by the Rabbis with magic, barbaric superstitions, and—after the death of Christ—with anti-Christian legends.

Whatever Cabalistic elements were introduced into Craft

---

[1] " According to Prof. Marks and Prof. Hayter Lewis, the story of Hiram Abiff is at least as old as the fourteenth century."—J. E. S. Tuckett in *The Origin of Additional Degrees, A.Q.C.,* XXXII. Part I. p. 14. It should be noted that no Mason who took part in the discussion brought evidence to show that it dated from before this period. Cf. *Freemasonry Before the Existence of Grand Lodges* (1923), by Wor. Bro. Lionel Vibert, I.C.S., p. 135, where it is suggested that the Hiramic legend dates from an incident in one of the French building guilds in 1401.

[2] Yarker, op. cit., p. 348; Eckert, op. cit., II. 36.

[3] Eckert, op. cit., II. 28.

Masonry at the time of the Crusades appear to have belonged to the second of these traditions, the unperverted Cabala of the Jews, known to the Essenes. There are, in fact, striking resemblances betwen Freemasonry and Essenism—degrees of initiation, oaths of secrecy, the wearing of the apron, and a certain masonic sign; whilst to the Sabeist traditions of the Essenes may perhaps be traced the solar and stellar symbolism of the lodges.[1] The Hiramic legend may have belonged to the same tradition.

THE TEMPLAR TRADITION

If then no documentary evidence can be brought forward to show that either the Solomonic legend or any traces of Judaic symbolism and traditions existed either in the monuments of the period or in the ritual of the masons before the fourteenth century, it is surely reasonable to recognize the plausibility of the contention put forward by a great number of masonic writers—particularly on the Continent—that the Judaic elements penetrated into Masonry by means of the Templars.[2] The Templars, as we have already seen, had taken their name from the Temple of Solomon in Jerusalem. What then more likely than that during the time they had lived there they had learnt the Rabbinical legends connected with the Temple? According to George Sand, who was deeply versed in the history of secret societies, the Hiramic legend was adopted by the Templars as symbolic of the destruction of their Order. " They wept over their impotence in the person of Hiram. The word lost and recovered is their empire. . . ."[3] The Freemason Ragon likewise declares that the catastrophe they lamented was the catastrophe that destroyed their Order.[4] Further, the Grand Master whose fate they deplored was Jacques du Molay. Here then we have two bodies in France at the same period, the Templars and the *compagnonnages*, both possessing a legend concerning the Temple of Solomon and both mourning a Maître Jacques who had been barbarously put to death. If we accept the

---

[1] " The Essenes, in common with other Syrian sects, possessed and adhered to the ' true principles ' of Freemasonry."—Bernard H. Springett, *Secret Sects of Syria and the Lebanon*, p. 91.

[2] " The esoteric doctrine of the Judeo-Christian mysteries evidently penetrated into the masonic guilds (ateliers) only with the entry of the Templars after the destruction of their Order."—Eckert, op. cit., II. 28.

[3] *La Comtesse de Rudolstadt*, II. 185.

[4] Ragon, *Cours philosophique des Initiations*, p. 34.

possibility that the Hiramic legend existed amongst the masons before the Crusades, how are we to explain this extraordinary coincidence? It is certainly easier to believe that the Judaic traditions were introduced to the masons by the Templars and grafted on to the ancient lore that the masonic guilds had inherited from the Roman Collegia.

That some connexion existed between the Templars and the working masons is indicated by the new influence that entered into building at this period. A modern Freemason comparing " the beautifully designed and deep-cut marks of the true Gothic period, say circa 1150-1350," with " the careless and roughly executed marks, many of them mere scratches, of later periods," points out that " the Knights Templars rose and fell with that wonderful development of architecture." The same writer goes on to show that some of the most important masonic symbols, the equilateral triangle and the Mason's square surmounting two pillars, came through from Gothic times.[1] Yarker asserts that the level, the flaming star, and the Tau cross which have since passed into the symbolism of Freemasonry may be traced to the Knights Templar, as also the five-pointed star in Salisbury Cathedral, the double triangle in Westminster Abbey, Jachin and Boaz, the circle and the pentagon in the masonry of the fourteenth century. Yarker cites later, in 1556, the eye and crescent moon, the three stars and the ladder of five steps, as further evidences of Templar influence.[2] " The Templars were large builders, and Jacques du Molay alleged the zeal of his Order in decorating churches in the process against him in 1310; hence the alleged connexion of Templary and Freemasonry is bound to have a substratum of truth."[3]

Moreover, according to a masonic tradition, an alliance definitely took place between the Templars and the masonic guilds at this period. During the proceedings taken against the Order of the Temple in France it is said that Pierre d'Aumont and seven other Knights escaped to Scotland in the guise of working masons and landed in the Island of Mull. On St. John's Day, 1307, they held their first chapter. Robert Bruce then took them under his protection, and seven years later they fought under his standard at Bannockburn against Edward II, who had suppressed their Order in England. After

[1] Mr. Sidney Klein in *Ars Quatuor Coronatorum*, XXXII. Part I. pp. 42, 43.
[2] John Yarker, *The Arcane Schools*, pp. 195, 318, 341, 342, 361.
[3] Ibid., p. 196.

this battle, which took place on St. John the Baptist's Day in summer (June 24), Robert Bruce is said to have instituted the Royal Order of H.R.M. (Heredom) and Knights of the R.S.Y.C.S. (Rosy Cross).[1] These two degrees now constitute the Royal Order of Scotland, and it seems not improbable that in reality they were brought to Scotland by the Templars. Thus, according to one of the early writers on Freemasonry, the degree of the Rose-Croix originated with the Templars in Palestine as early as 1188[2]; whilst the Eastern origin of the word Heredom, supposed to derive from a mythical mountain on an island south of the Hebrides[3] where the Culdees practised their rites, is indicated by another eighteenth-century writer, who traces it to a Jewish source.[4] In this same year of 1314 Robert Bruce is said to have united the Templars and the Royal Order of H.R.M. with the guilds of working masons, who had also fought in his army, at the famous Lodge of Kilwinning, founded in 1286,[5] which now added to its name that of Heredom and became the chief seat of the Order.[6] Scotland was essentially a home of operative masonry, and, in view of the Templar's prowess in the art of building, what more natural than that the two bodies should enter into an alliance? Already in England the Temple is said between 1155 and 1199 to have administered the Craft.[7] It is thus at Heredom of Kilwinning, " the Holy House of Masonry "—" Mother Kilwinning," as it is still known to Freemasons—that a speculative element of a fresh kind may

[1] Official history of the Order of Scotland quoted by Bro. Fred. H. Buckmaster in *The Royal Order of Scotland*, published at the offices of *The Freemason*, pp. 3, 5, 7; A. E. Waite, *Encyclopædia of Freemasonry*, II. 219; Yarker, *The Arcane Schools*, p. 330; Mackey, *Lexicon of Freemasonry*, p. 267.

[2] Baron Westerode in the *Acta Latomorum* (1784), quoted by Mackey, op. cit., p. 265. Mr. Bernard H. Springett also asserts that this degree originated in the East (*Secret Sects of Syria and the Lebanon*, p. 294).

[3] Chevalier de Bérage, *Les Plus Secrets Mystères des Hauts Grades de la Maçonnerie dévoilés, ou le vrai Rose Croix* (1768); Waite, *The Secret Tradition in Freemasonry*, I. 3.

[4] In 1784 some French Freemasons wrote to their English brethren saying: " It concerns us to know if there really exists in the island of Mull, formerly Melrose . . . in the North of Scotland, a Mount Heredom, or if it does not exist." In reply a leading Freemason, General Rainsford, referred them to the word אדני חד (Har Adonai), i.e. Mount of God (*Notes on the Rainsford Papers in A.Q.C.*, XXVI. 99). A more probable explanation appears, however, to be that Heredom is a corruption of the Hebrew word " Harodim," signifying princes or rulers.

[5] F. H. Buckmaster, *The Royal Order of Scotland*, p. 5. Lecouteulx de Canteleu says, however, that Kilwinning had been the great meeting-place of Masonry since 1150 (*Les Sectes et Sociétés Secrètes*, p. 104). Eckert, op. cit., II. 33.

[6] Mackey, *Lexicon of Freemasonry*, p. 267.

[7] Clavel, op. cit., p. 90; Eckert, op. cit., II. 27.

have found its way into the lodges. Is it not here, then, that we may see that "fruitful union between the professional guild of mediæval masons and a secret group of philosophical Adepts" alluded to by Count Goblet d'Aviella and described by Mr. Waite in the following words:

The mystery of the building guilds—whatever it may be held to have been—was that of a simple, unpolished, pious, and utilitarian device; and this daughter of Nature, in the absence of all intention on her own part, underwent, or was coerced into one of the strangest marriages which has been celebrated in occult history. It so happened that her particular form and figure lent itself to such a union, etc.[1]?

Mr. Waite with his usual vagueness does not explain when and where this marriage took place, but the account would certainly apply to the alliance between the Templars and Scottish guilds of working masons, which, as we have seen, is admitted by masonic authorities, and presents exactly the conditions described, the Templars being peculiarly fitted by their initiation into the legend concerning the building of the Temple of Solomon to co-operate with the masons, and the masons being prepared by their partial initiation into ancient mysteries to receive the fresh influx of Eastern tradition from the Templars.

A further indication of the Templar influence in Craft Masonry is the system of degrees and initiations. The names of Entered Apprentice, Fellow Craft, and Master Mason are said to have derived from Scotland,[2] and the analogy between these and the degrees of the Assassins has already been shown. Indeed, the resemblance between the outer organization of Freemasonry and the system of the Ismailis is shown by many writers. Thus Dr. Bussell observes: " No doubt together with some knowledge of geometry regarded as an esoteric trade secret, many symbols to-day current did pass down from very primitive times. But a more certain model was the Grand Lodge of the Ismailis in Cairo "—that is to say the Dar-ul-Hikmat.[3] Syed Ameer Ali also expresses the opinion that " Makrisi's account of the different degrees of initiation adopted in this lodge forms an invaluable record of Free-

---

[1] A. E. Waite, *The Secret Tradition in Freemasonry*, I. 8.
[2] " Our names of E.A., F.C., and M.M. were derived from Scotland."— *A.Q.C.*, XXXII. Part I. p. 40. Clavel, however, says that these existed in the Roman Collegia (*Histoire pittoresque*, p. 82).
[3] *Religious Thought and Heresy in the Middle Ages*, p. 372.

masonry. In fact, the lodge at Cairo became the model of all the Lodges created afterwards in Christendom."[1] Mr. Bernard Springett, a Freemason, quoting this passage, adds: "In this last assertion I am myself greatly in agreement."[2]

It is surely therefore legitimate to surmise that this system penetrated to Craft Masonry through the Templars, whose connexion with the Assassins—offshoot of the Dar-ul-Hikmat— was a matter of common knowledge.

The question of the Templar succession in Freemasonry forms perhaps the most controversial point in the whole history of the Roman Collegia theory, Continental Masons more generally accepting it, and even glorying in it.[3] Mackey, in his *Lexicon of Freemasonry,* thus sums up the matter:

The connexion between the Knights Templar and the Freemasons has been repeatedly asserted by the enemies of both institutions, and has often been admitted by their friends. Lawrie, on this subject, holds the following language: "We know that the Knights Templar not only possessed the mysteries but performed the ceremonies and inculcated the duties of Freemasons," and he attributes the dissolution of the Order to the discovery of their being Freemasons and their assembling in secret to practise the rites of the Order.[4]

This explains why Freemasons have always shown indulgence to the Templars.

It was above all Freemasonry [says Findel], which—because it falsely held itself to be a daughter of Templarism—took the greatest pains to represent the Order of the Templars as innocent and therefore free from all mystery. For this purpose not only legends and unhistorical facts were brought forward, but manœuvres were also resorted to in order to suppress the truth. The masonic reverers of the Temple Order bought up the whole edition of the *Actes du Procès* of Moldenhawer, because this showed the guilt of the Order; only a few copies reached the booksellers. . . . Already several decades before . . . the Freemasons in their unhistorical efforts had been guilty of real forgery. Dupuy had published his *History of the Trial of the Templars* as early as 1654 in Paris, for which he had made use of the original of the *Actes du Procès,* according to which the guilt of the Order leaves no room for doubt. . . . But when

---

[1] *The Spirit of Islam,* p. 337.
[2] *Secret Sects of Syria and the Lebanon,* p. 181 (1922).
[3] See, for example, Bouillet's *Dictionnaire Universel d'Histoire et de Géographie* (1860), article on Templars: "Les Francs-Maçons prétendent se rattacher à cette secte."
Lexicon of Freemasonry, p. 185.

in the middle of the eighteenth century several branches of Free-masonry wished to recall the Templar Order into being, the work of Dupuy was naturally very displeasing. It had already been current amongst the public for a hundred years, so it could no longer be bought; therefore they falsified it.[1]

Accordingly in 1751 a reprint of Dupuy's work appeared with the addition of a number of notes and remarks and mutilated in such a way as to prove not the guilt but the innocence of the Templars.

Now, although British Masonry has played no part in these intrigues, the question of the Templar succession has been very inadequately dealt with by the masonic writers of our country. As a rule they have adopted one of two courses—either they have persistently denied connexion with the Templars or they have represented them as a blameless and cruelly maligned Order. But in reality neither of these expedients is necessary to save the honour of British Masonry, for not even the bitterest enemy of Masonry has ever suggested that British masons have adopted any portion of the Templar heresy. The Knights who fled to Scotland may have been perfectly innocent of the charges brought against their Order; indeed, there is good reason to believe this was the case. Thus the *Manuel des Chevaliers de l'Ordre du Temple* relates the incident in the following manner:

After the death of Jacques du Molay, some Scottish Templars having become apostates, at the instigation of Robert Bruce ranged themselves under the banners of a new Order[2] instituted by this prince and in which the receptions were based on those of the Order of the Temple. It is there that we must seek the origin of Scottish Masonry and even that of the other masonic rites. The Scottish Templars were excommunicated in 1324 by Larmenius, who declared them to be *Templi desertores* and the Knights of St. John of Jerusalem, *Dominiorum Militiæ spoliatores*, placed for ever outside the pale of the Temple: *Extra girum Templi, nunc et in futurum, volo, dico et jubeo.* A similar anathema has since been launched by several Grand Masters against Templars who were rebellious to legitimate authority. From the schism that was intro-duced into Scotland a number of sects took birth.[3]

[1] *Findel, Geschichte der Freimaurerei*, II. 156, 157 (1892 edition). Dr. Bussell (op. cit., p. 804), referring to Dupuy's work, also observes: "An editor of a later edition (Brussels, 1751) undoubtedly was a Freemason who tried to clear the indictment and affiliate to the condemned Order the new and rapidly increasing brotherhood of speculative deism."
[2] The Royal Order of Scotland.
[3] *Manuel des Chevaliers de l'Ordre du Temple*, p. 10 (1825 edition).

This account forms a complete exoneration of the Scottish Templars; as apostates from the bogus Christian Church and the doctrines of Johannism they showed themselves loyal to the true Church and to the Christian faith as formulated in the published statutes of their Order. What they appear, then, to have introduced to Masonry was their manner of reception, that is to say their outer forms and organization, and possibly certain Eastern esoteric doctrines and Judaic legends concerning the building of the Temple of Solomon in no way incompatible with the teaching of Christianity.

It will be noticed, moreover, that in the ban passed by the *Ordre du Temple* on the Scottish Templars the Knights of St. John of Jerusalem are also included. This is a further tribute to the orthodoxy of the Scottish Knights. For to the Knights of St. John of Jerusalem—to whom the Templar property was given—no suspicion of heresy had ever attached. After the suppression of the Order of the Temple in 1312 a number of the Knights joined themselves to the Knights of St. John of Jerusalem, by whom the Templar system appears to have been purged of its heretical elements. As we shall see later, the same process is said to have been carried out by the Royal Order of Scotland, All this suggests that the Templars had imported a secret doctrine from the East which was capable either of a Christian or an anti-Christian interpretation, that through their connexion with the Royal Order of Scotland and the Knights of St. John of Jerusalem this Christian interpretation was preserved, and finally that it was this pure doctrine which passed into Freemasonry. According to early masonic authorities, the adoption of the two St. Johns as the patron saints of Masonry arose, not from Johannism, but from the alliance between the Templars and the Knights of St. John of Jerusalem.[1]

It is important to remember that the theory of the Templar connexion with Freemasonry was held by the Continental Freemasons of the eighteenth century, who, living at the time the Order was reconstituted on its present basis, were clearly in a better position to know its origins than we who are separated from that date by a distance of two hundred years. But since their testimony first comes to light at the period of the upper degrees, in which the Templar influence is more clearly visible than in Craft Masonry, it must be reserved for a later chapter. Before passing on to this further stage in the

[1] Oration of Chevalier Ramsay (1737); Baron Tschoudy, *L'Étoile Flamboyante*, I. 20 (1766).

history of the Craft, it is necessary to consider one more link in the chain of the masonic tradition—the " Holy Vehm."

THE VEHMGERICHTS[1]

These dread tribunals, said to have been established by Charlemagne in 772[2] in Westphalia, had for their avowed object the establishment of law and order amidst the unsettled and even anarchic conditions that then reigned in Germany. But by degrees the power arrogated to itself by the " Holy Vehm " became so formidable that succeeding emperors were unable to control its workings and found themselves forced to become initiates from motives of self-protection. During the twelfth century the Vehmgerichts, by their continual executions, had created a veritable " Red Terror," so that the East of Germany was known as the Red Land. In 1371, says Lecouteulx de Canteleu, a fresh impetus was given to the " Holy Vehm " by a number of the Knights Templar who, on the dissolution of their Order, had found their way to Germany and now sought admission to the Secret Tribunals.[3] How much of Templar lore passed into the hand of the Vehmgerichts it is impossible to know, but there is certainly a resemblance between the methods of initiation and intimidation employed by the Vehms and those described by certain of the Templars, still more between the ceremony of the Vehms and the ritual of Freemasonry.

Thus the members of the Vehms, known as the *Wissende* (or Enlightened), were divided into three degrees of initiation: the Free Judges, the veritable Free Judges, and the Holy Judges of the Secret Tribunal. The candidate for initiation was led blindfold before the dread Tribunal, presided over by a *Stuhlherr* (or master of the chair) or his substitute, a *Freigraf*, with a sword and branch of willow at his side. The initiate was then bound by a terrible oath not to reveal the secrets of the " Holy Vehm," to warn no one of danger threatening them by its decrees, to denounce anyone, whether father, mother, brother, sister, friend, or relation, if such a one had been condemned by the Tribunal. After this he was given the password and grip by which the confederates recognized each other. In the event of his turning traitor or revealing the secrets confided

---

[1] The description of the Vehmic Tribunals that follows here is largely taken from Lombard de Langres, *Les Sociétés Secrètes en Allemagne* (1819), quoting original documents preserved at Dortmund.
[2] Clavel derides this early origin and says it was the *Francs-juges* themselves who claimed Charlemagne as their founder (*Histoire pittoresque*, p. 357).
[3] Lecouteulx de Canteleu, *Les Sectes et Sociétés Secrètes*, p. 100.

to him his eyes were bandaged, his hands tied behind his back, and his tongue was torn out through the back of his neck, after which he was hanged by the feet till he was dead, with the solemn imprecation that his body should be given as a prey to the birds of the air.

It is difficult to believe that the points of resemblance with modern masonic ritual[1] which may here be discerned can be a mere matter of coincidence, yet it would be equally unreasonable to trace the origins of Freemasonry to the Vehmgerichts. Clearly both derived from a common source, either the old pagan traditions on which the early Vehms were founded or the system of the Templars. The latter seems the more probable for two reasons: firstly, on account of the resemblance between the methods of the Vehmgerichts and the Assassins, which would be explained if the Templars formed the connecting link; and secondly, the fact that in contemporary documents the members of the Secret Tribunals were frequently referred to under the name of Rose-Croix.[2]   Now, since, as we have seen, the degree of the Rosy Cross is said to have been brought to Europe by the Templars, this would account for the persistence of the name in the Vehmgerichts as well as in the Rosicrucians of the seventeenth century, who are said to have continued the Templar tradition. Thus Templarism and Rosicrucianism appear to have been always closely connected, a fact which is not surprising since both derive from a common source—the traditions of the near East.

This brings us to an alternative theory concerning the channel through which Eastern doctrines, and particularly Cabalism, found their way into Freemasonry. For it must be admitted that one obstacle to the complete acceptance of the theory of the Templar succession exists, namely, that although the Judaic element cannot be traced further back than the Crusades, neither can it with certainty be pronounced to have come into existence during the three centuries that followed after. Indeed, before the publication of Anderson's "Constitutions" in 1723 there is no definite evidence that the Solomonic legend had been incorporated into the ritual of British Masonry. So although the possession of the legend by the *compagnonnages*

[1] According to Walter Scott's account of the Vehmgerichts in *Anne of Geierstein,* the initiate was warned that the secrets confided to him were " neither to be spoken aloud nor whispered, to be told in words or written in characters, to be carved or to be painted, or to be otherwise communicated, either directly or by parable and emblem." This formula, if accurate, would establish a further point of resemblance.

[2] Lombard de Langres, *Les Sociétés Secrètes en Allemagne,* p. 241 (1819); Lecouteulx de Canteleu, *Les Sectes et Sociétés Secrètes,* p. 99.

of the Middle Ages would tend to prove its antiquity, there is always the possibility that it was introduced by some later body of adepts than the Templars. According to the partisans of a further theory, these adepts were the Rosicrucians.

ROSICRUCIAN ORIGIN

One of the earliest and most eminent precursors of Freemasonry is said to have been Francis Bacon. As we have already seen, Bacon is recognized to have been a Rosicrucian, and that the secret philosophical doctrine he professed was closely akin to Freemasonry is clearly apparent in his *New Atlantis*. The reference to the " Wise Men of the Society of Solomon's House " cannot be a mere coincidence. The choice of Atlantis—the legendary island supposed to have been submerged by the Atlantic Ocean in the remote past—would suggest that Bacon had some knowledge of a secret tradition descending from the earliest patriarchs of the human race, whom, like the modern writer Le Plongeon, he imagined to have inhabited the Western hemisphere and to have been the predecessors of the Egyptian initiates. Le Plongeon, however, places this early seat of the mysteries still further West than the Atlantic Ocean, in the region of Mayax and Yucatan.[1]

Bacon further relates that this tradition was preserved in its pure form by certain of the Jews, who, whilst accepting the Cabala, rejected its anti-Christian tendencies. Thus in this island of Bensalem there are Jews " of a far differing disposition from the Jews in other parts. For whereas they hate the name of Christ, and have a secret inbred rancour against the people amongst whom they live; these contrariwise give unto our Saviour many high attributes," but at the same time they believe " that Moses by a secret Cabala ordained the laws of Bensalem which they now use, and that when the Messiah should come and sit on His throne at Jerusalem, the King of Bensalem should sit at His feet, whereas other kings should keep at a great distance." This passage is of particular interest as showing that Bacon recognized the divergence between the ancient secret tradition descending from Moses and the perverted Jewish Cabala of the Rabbis, and that he was perfectly aware of the tendency even among the best of Jews to turn the former to the advantage of the Messianic dreams.

Mrs. Pott, who in her *Francis Bacon and his Secret Society* sets out to prove that Bacon was the founder of Rosicrucianism

[1] A. le Plongeon, *Sacred Mysteries among the Mayas and the Quichas* (1886).

and Freemasonry, ignores all the previous history of the secret tradition. Bacon was not the originator but the inheritor of the ideas on which both these societies were founded. And the further contention that Bacon was at the same time the author of the greatest dramas in the English language and of *The Chymical Marriage of Christian Rosengreutz* is manifestly absurd. Nevertheless, Bacon's influence amongst the Rosicrucians is apparent; Heydon's *Voyage to the Land of the Rosicrucians* is in fact a mere plagiarism of Bacon's *New Atlantis*.

Mrs. Pott seems to imagine that by proclaiming Bacon to have been the founder or even a member of the Order of Freemasonry she is revealing a great masonic secret which Freemasons have conspired to keep dark. But why should the Craft desire to disown so illustrious a progenitor or seek to conceal his connexion with the Order if any such existed? Findel, indeed, frankly admits that the *New Atlantis* contained unmistakable allusions to Freemasonry and that Bacon contributed to its final transformation.[1] This was doubtless brought about largely by the English Rosicrucians who followed after. To suggest then that Freemasonry originated with the Rosicrucians is to ignore the previous history of the secret tradition. Rosicrucianism was not the beginning but a link in the long chain connecting Freemasonry with far earlier secret associations. The resemblance betwen the two Orders admits of no denial. Thus Yarker writes: "The symbolic tracing of the Rosicrucians was a Square Temple approached by seven steps . . . here also we find the two pillars of Hermes, the five-pointed star, sun and moon, compasses, square and triangle." Yarker further observes that "even Wren was more or less a student of Hermeticism, and if we had a full list of Freemasons and Rosicrucians we should probably be surprised at the numbers who belonged to both systems."[2]

Professor Bühle emphatically states that "Freemasonry is neither more nor less than Rosicrucianism as modified by those who transplanted it into England." Chambers, who published his famous *Cyclopædia* in 1728, observes: "Some who are no friends to Freemasonry, make the present flourishing society of Freemasons a branch of *Rosicrucians,* or rather the Rosicrucians themselves under a new name or relation, viz. as retainers to building. And it is certain there are some Freemasons who have all the characters of Rosicrucians."

[1] Findel, *History of Freemasonry* (Eng. trans., 1866), pp. 131, 132.
[2] John Yarker, *The Arcane Schools*, p. 216, 431.

The connexion between Freemasonry and Rosicrucianism is, however, a question hardly less controversial than that of the connexion between Freemasonry and Templarism.

Dr. Mackey violently disputes the theory. " The Rosicrucians," he writes, " as this brief history indicates, had no connexion whatever with the masonic fraternity. Notwithstanding this fact, Barruel, the most malignant of our revilers, with a characteristic spirit of misrepresentation, attempted to identify the two institutions."[1] But the aforesaid " brief history " indicates nothing of the kind, and the reference to Barruel as a malignant reviler for suggesting a connexion, which, as we have seen, many Freemasons admit, shows on which side this " spirit of misrepresentation " exists. It is interesting, however, to note that in the eyes of certain masonic writers connexion with the Rosicrucians is regarded as highly discreditable; the fraternity would thus appear to have been less blameless than we have been taught to believe. Mr. Waite is equally concerned with proving that there " is no traceable connexion between Masonry and Rosicrucianism," and he goes on to explain that Freemasonry was never a learned society, that it never laid claim to " any transcendental secrets of alchemy and magic, or to any skill in medicine," etc.[2]

The truth may lie between the opposing contentions of Prof. Bühle and his two masonic antagonists. The Freemasons were clearly, for the reasons given by Mr. Waite, not a mere continuation of the Rosicrucians, but more likely borrowed from the Rosicrucians a part of their system and symbols which they adapted to their own purpose. Moreover, the incontrovertible fact is that in the list of English Freemasons and Rosicrucians we find men who belonged to both Orders and amongst these two who contributed largely to the constitutions of English Freemasonry.

The first of these is Robert Fludd, whom Mr. Waite describes as " the central figure of Rosicrucian literature, . . . an intellectual giant, . . . a man of immense erudition, of exalted mind, and, to judge by his writings, of extreme personal sanctity. Ennemoser describes him as one of the most distinguished disciples of Paracelsus. . . ."[3] Yarker adds this clue: " In 1630 we find Fludd, the chief of the Rosicrucians, using architectural language, and there is proof that his Society was divided into degrees, and from the fact

---

[1] *Lexicon of Freemasonry*, p. 298.
[2] Waite, *The Real History of the Rosicrucians*, p. 403.
[3] Ibid., p. 283.

that the Masons' Company of London had a copy of the Masonic Charges ' presented by Mr. fflood ' we may suppose that he was a Freemason before 1620."[1]

A still more important link is Elias Ashmole, the antiquary, astrologer, and alchemist, founder of the Ashmolean Museum at Oxford, who was born in 1617. An avowed Rosicrucian, and as we have seen, also a Freemason, Ashmole displayed great energy in reconstituting the Craft; he is said to have perfected its organization, to have added to it further mystic symbols, and according to Ragon, it was he who drew up the ritual of the existing three Craft degrees—Entered Apprentice, Fellow-Craft, and Master Mason—which was adopted by Grand Lodge in 1717. Whence did these fresh inspirations come but from the Rosicrucians? For, as Ragon also informs us, in the year that Ashmole was received into Freemasonry the Rosicrucians held their meeting in the same room at Mason Hall![2]

How, then, can it be said that there was "no traceable connexion between Freemasonry and Rosicrucianism? and why should it be the part of a "malignant reviler" to connect them? It is not suggested that Rosicrucians, such as Fludd or Ashmole, imported any magical elements into Freemasonry, but simply the system and symbols of the Rose-Croix with a certain degree of esoteric learning. That Rosicrucianism forms an important link in the chain of the secret tradition is therefore undeniable.

THE SEVENTEENTH-CENTURY RABBIS

There is, however, a third channel through which the Judaic legends of Freemasonry may have penetrated to the Craft, namely, the Rabbis of the seventeenth century. The Jewish writer Bernard Lazare has declared that "there were Jews around the cradle of Freemasonry,"[3] and if this statement is applied to the period preceding the institution of Grand Lodge in 1717 it certainly finds confirmation in fact. Thus it is said

[1] Yarker, *The Arcane Schools,* p. 430.

[2] "Yarker pronounces Elias Ashmole to have been circa 1686 ' the leading spirit, both in Craft Masonry and in Rosicrucianism,' and is of opinion that his diary establishes the fact ' that both societies fell into decay together in 1682.' He adds: ' It is evident therefore that the Rosicrucians . . . found the operative Guild conveniently ready to their hand, and grafted upon it their own mysteries . . . also, from this time Rosicrucianism disappears, and Freemasonry springs into life with all the possessions of the former.' "—*Speculative Freemasonry, an Historical Lecture,* delivered March 31, 1883, p. 9; quoted by Gould, *History of Freemasonry,* II. 138.

[3] *L'Antisémitisme,* p. 339.

that in the preceding century the coat-of-arms now used by Grand Lodge had been designed by an Amsterdam Jew, Jacob Jehuda Leon Templo, colleague of Cromwell's friend the Cabalist, Manasseh ben Israel.[1] To quote Jewish authority on this question, Mr. Lucien Wolf writes that Templo " had a monomania for . . . everything relating to the Temple of Solomon and the Tabernacle of the Wilderness. He constructed gigantic models of both these edifices."[2] These he exhibited in London, which he visited in 1675 and earlier, and it seems not unreasonable to conclude that this may have provided a fresh source of inspiration to the Freemasons who framed the masonic ritual some forty years later. At any rate, the masonic coat-of-arms still used by Grand Lodge of England is undoubtedly of Jewish design.

"This coat," says Mr. Lucien Wolf, " is entirely composed of Jewish symbols," and is " an attempt to display heraldically the various forms of the Cherubim pictured to us in the second vision of Ezekiel—an Ox, a Man, a Lion, and an Eagle—and thus belongs to the highest and most mystical domain of Hebrew symbolism."[3]

In other words, this vision, known to the Jews as the " Mercaba,"[4] belongs to the Cabala, where a particular interpretation is placed on each figure so as to provide an esoteric meaning not perceptible to the uninitiated.[5] The masonic coat-of-arms is thus entirely Cabalistic; as is also the seal on the diplomas of Craft Masonry, where another Cabalistic figure, that of a man and woman combined, is reproduced.[6]

Of the Jewish influence in Masonry after 1717 I shall speak later.

To sum up, then, the origins of the system we now know as Freemasonry are not to be found in one source alone. The twelve alternative sources enumerated in the *Masonic Cyclopædia* and quoted at the beginning of this chapter may all have contributed to its formation. Thus Operative Masonry may have

[1] *Jewish Encyclopædia,* articles on Leon and Manasseh ben Israel.
[2] Article on " Anglo-Jewish Coats-of-arms " by Lucien Wolf in *Transactions of the Jewish Historical Society,* Vol. II. p. 157.
[3] *Transactions of the Jewish Historical Society of England,* Vol. II. p. 156. A picture of Templo forms the frontispiece of this volume, and a reproduction of the coat-of-arms of Grand Lodge is given opposite to p. 156.
[4] Zohar, section Jethro, folio 70b (de Pauly's trans., Vol. III. 311).
[5] The Cabalistic interpretation of the Mercaba will be found in the Zohar, section Bereschith, folio 18b (de Pauly's trans., Vol. I. p. 115).
[6] " By figure of a man is always meant that of the male and female together."—Ibid., p. 116.

descended from the Roman Collegia and through the operative masons of the Middle Ages, whilst Speculative Masonry may have derived from the patriarchs and the mysteries of the pagans.   But the source of inspiration which admits of no denial is the Jewish Cabala.   Whether this penetrated to our country through the Roman Collegia, the *compagnonnages,* the Templars, the Rosicrucians, or through the Jews of the seventeenth and eighteenth centuries, whose activities behind the scenes of Freemasonry we shall see later, is a matter of speculation.   The fact remains that when the ritual and constitutions of Masonry were drawn up in 1717, although certain fragments of the ancient Egyptian and Pythagorean doctrines were retained, the Judaic version of the secret tradition was the one selected by the founders of Grand Lodge on which to build up their system.

6

THE GRAND LODGE ERA

WHATEVER were the origins of the Order we now know as Freemasonry, it is clear that during the century preceding its reorganization under Grand Lodge of London the secret system of binding men together for a common purpose, based on Eastern esoteric doctrines, had been anticipated by the Rosicrucians. Was this secret system employed, however by any other body of men? It is certainly easy to imagine how in this momentous seventeenth century, when men of all opinions were coalescing against opposing forces—Lutherans combining against the Papacy, Catholics rallying their forces against invading Protestantism, Republicans plotting in favour of Cromwell, Royalists in their turn plotting to restore the Stuarts, finally Royalists plotting against each other on behalf of rival dynasties—an organization of this kind, enabling one to work secretly for a cause and to set invisibly vast numbers of human beings in motion, might prove invaluable to any party.

Thus, according to certain masonic writers on the Continent, the system used by the Rosicrucians in their fight against " Popery " was also employed by the Jesuits for a directly opposite purpose. In the manuscripts of the Prince of Hesse published by Lecouteulx de Canteleu it is declared that in 1714 the Jesuits used the mysteries of the Rose-Croix. Mirabeau also relates that " the Jesuits profited by the internal troubles of the reign of Charles I to possess themselves of the symbols, the allegories, and the carpets (tapis) of the Rose-Croix masons, who were only the ancient order of the Templars secretly perpetuated. It may be seen by means of what imperceptible innovations they succeeded in substituting their catechism to the instruction of the Templars."[1]

Other Continental writers again assert that Cromwell, the arch-opponent of the Catholic Church, was " a higher initiate

---

[1] *Histoire de la Monarchie Prussienne*, VI. 76.

of masonic mysteries," and used the system for his own eleva-
tion to power[1]; further, that he found himself outdistanced
by the Levellers; that this sect, whose name certainly suggests
masonic inspiration, adopted for its symbols the square and
compass,[2] and in its claim of real equality threatened the
supremacy of the usurper. Finally, Elias Ashmole, the
Rosicrucian Royalist, is said to have turned the masonic system
against Cromwell, so that towards the end of the seventeenth
century the Order rallied to the Stuart cause.[3]

But all this is pure speculation resting on no basis of known
facts. The accusation that the Jesuits used the system of the
Rose-Croix as a cover to political intrigues is referred to by
the Rosicrucian Eliphas Lévi as the outcome of ignorance,
which "refutes itself." It is significant to notice that it
emanates mainly from Germany and from the Illuminati; the
Prince of Hesse was a member of the *Stricte Observance* and
Mirabeau an Illuminatus at the time he wrote the passage
quoted above. That in the seventeenth century certain
Jesuits played the part of political intriguers I suppose their
warmest friends will hardly deny, but that they employed any
secret or masonic system seems to me perfectly incapable of
proof. I shall return to this point later, however, in connexion
with the Illuminati.

As to Cromwell, the only circumstance that lends any colour
to the possibility of his connexion with Freemasonry is his
known friendship for Manasseh ben Israel, the colleague of
the Rabbi Templo who designed the coat-of-arms later
adopted by Grand Lodge. If, therefore, the Jews of Amsterdam were a source of inspiration to the Freemasons of the
seventeenth century, it is not impossible that Cromwell may
have been the channel through which this influence first
penetrated.

In the matter of the Stuarts we are, however, on firm
ground with regard to Freemasonry. That the lodges at the
end of the seventeenth century were Royalist is certain, and
there seems good reason to believe that, when the revolution
of 1688 divided the Royalist cause, the Jacobites who fled to
France with James II took Freemasonry with them.[4] With

---

[1] Lecouteulx de Canteleu, op. cit., p. 105.
[2] Ibid., p. 106; Lombard de Langres, *Les Sociétés Secrètes en Allemagne*, p. 67.
[3] Monsignor George F. Dillon, *The War of Anti-Christ with the Church and Christian Civilization*, p. 24 (1885).
[4] Brother Chalmers I. Paton, *The Origin of Freemasonry: the 1717 Theory Exploded*, p. 34.

the help of the French they established lodges in which, it is said, masonic rites and symbols were used to promote the cause of the Stuarts. Thus the land of promise signified Great Britain, Jerusalem stood for London, and the murder of Hiram represented the execution of Charles I.[1]

Meanwhile Freemasonry in England did not continue to adhere to the Stuart cause as it had done under the ægis of Elias Ashmole, and by 1717 is said to have become Hanoverian.

From this important date the official history of the present system may be said to begin; hitherto everything rests on stray documents, of which the authenticity is frequently doubtful, and which provide no continuous history of the Order. In 1717 for the first time Freemasonry was established on a settled basis and in the process underwent a fundamental change. So far it would seem to have retained an operative element, but in the transformation that now took place this was entirely eliminated, and the whole Order was transformed into a middle- and upper-class speculative body. This *coup d'état*, already suggested in 1703, took place in 1716, when four London lodges of Freemasons met together at the Apple Tree Tavern in Charles Street, Covent Garden, " and having put into the chair the oldest Master Mason (now the Master of a lodge), they constituted themselves a Grand Lodge, *pro tempore,* in due form." On St. John the Baptist's Day, June 24 of the next year, the annual assembly and banquet were held at the Goose and Gridiron in St. Paul's Churchyard, when Mr. Antony Sayer was elected Grand Master and invested with all the badges of office.[2]

It is evident from the above account that already in 1717 the speculative elements must have predominated in the lodges, otherwise we might expect to find the operative masons taking some part in these proceedings and expressing their opinion as to whether their association should pass under the control of men entirely unconnected with the Craft. But no, the leaders of the new movement all appear to have belonged to the middle class, nor from this moment do either masons or architects seem to have played any prominent part in Freemasonry.

But the point that official history does not attempt to

---

[1] Lecouteulx de Canteleu, op. cit., p. 107; Robison's *Proofs of a Conspiracy,* p. 27; Dillon, op. cit., p. 24; Mackey, *Lexicon of Freemasonry,* p. 148.
[2] Preston's *Illustrations of Masonry,* p. 209 (1804); Anderson's *New Book of Constitutions* (1738).

elucidate is the reason for this decision.   Why should the Freemasons of London—whether they were at this date a speculative or only a semi-speculative association—have suddenly recognized the necessity of establishing a Grand Lodge and drawing up a ritual and " Constitution "?   It is evident, then, that some circumstances must have arisen which led them to take this important step.   I would suggest that the following may be the solution to the problem.

Freemasonry, as we have seen, was a system that could be employed in any cause and had now come to be used by intriguers of every kind—and not only by intriguers, but by merely convivial bodies, " jolly Brotherhoods of the Bottle," who modelled themselves on masonic associations.[1]   But the honest citizens of London who met and feasted at the Goose and Gridiron were clearly not intriguers, they were neither Royalist nor Republican plotters, neither Catholic nor Lutheran fanatics, neither alchemists nor magicians, nor can it be supposed that they were simply revellers.   If they were political, they were certainly not supporters of the Stuarts; on the contrary, they were generally reported to have been Hanoverian in their sympathies, indeed Dr. Bussell goes so far as to say that Grand Lodge was instituted to support the Hanoverian dynasty.[2]   It would be perhaps nearer the truth to conclude that if they were Hanoverian it was because they were constitutional, and the Hanoverian dynasty having now been established they wished to avoid further changes.   In a word, then, they were simply men of peace, anxious to put an end to dissensions, who, seeing the system of Masonry utilized for the purpose of promoting discord, determined to wrest it from the hands of political intriguers and restore it to its original character of brotherhood, though not of brotherhood between working masons only, but between men drawn from all classes and professions.   By founding a Grand Lodge in London and drawing up a ritual and " Constitutions," they hoped to prevent the perversion of their signs and symbols and to establish the Order on a settled basis.

According to Nicolai this pacific purpose had already animated English Freemasons under the Grand Mastership of

[1] *Ars Quatuor Coronatorum*, XXV. p. 31.   See account of some of these convivial masonic societies in this paper entitled " An Apollinaric Summons."
[2] *Religious Thought and Heresy in the Middle Ages*, p. 373.   A " Past Grand Master," in an article entitled " The Crisis in Freemasonry," in the *English Review* for August 1922, takes the same view.   " It is true . . . that the Craft Lodges in England were originally Hanoverian clubs, as the Scottish lodges were Jacobite clubs."

Sir Christopher Wren: " Its principal object from this period was to moderate the religious hatreds so terrible in England during the reign of James II and to try and establish some kind of concord or fraternity, by weakening as far as possible the antagonisms arising from the differences of religions, ranks, and interests." An eighteenth-century manuscript of the Prince of Hesse quoted by Lecouteulx de Canteleu expresses the view that in 1717 " *the mysteries of Freemasonry were reformed and purified in England of all political tendencies.*"

In the matter of religion, Craft Masonry adopted an equally non-sectarian attitude. The first " Constitutions " of the Order, drawn up by Dr. Anderson in 1723, contain the following paragraph:

CONCERNING GOD AND RELIGION

A Mason is obliged, by his tenure, to obey the moral Law; and if he rightly understands the Art, he will never be a stupid Atheist, nor an irreligious Libertine. But though in ancient Times Masons were charged in every Country to be of the Religion of that Country or Nation, whatever it was, yet, 'tis now thought more expedient only to oblige them to that Religion in which all men agree, leaving their particular Opinions to themselves; that is to be good Men and true, or Men of Honour and Honesty, by whatever Denominations or Persuasions they may be distinguish'd; whereby Masonry becomes the Centre of Union and the Means of Conciliating true Friendship among Persons that must have remained at a perpetual Distance.

The phrase " that Religion in which all men agree " has been censured by Catholic writers as advocating a universal religion in the place of Christianity. But this by no means follows. The idea is surely that Masons should be men adhering to that law of right and wrong common to all religious faiths. Craft Masonry may thus be described as Deist in character, but not in the accepted sense of the word which implies the rejection of Christian doctrines. If Freemasonry had been Deist in this sense might we not expect to find some connexion between the founders of Grand Lodge and the school of Deists—Toland, Bolingbroke, Woolston, Hume, and others—which flourished precisely at this period? Might not some analogy be detected between the organization of the Order and the Sodalities described in Toland's *Pantheisticon,* published in 1720? But of this I can find no trace whatever. The principal founders of Grand Lodge were, as we have seen, clergymen, both engaged in preaching Christian doctrines at their respective churches.[1] It is surely therefore reasonable to conclude that Freemasonry at the time of its reorganization in 1717 was Deistic only in so far that it invited men to meet together on the common ground of a belief in God. Moreover, some of the early English rituals contain distinctly Christian elements. Thus both in *Jachin and Boaz* (1762) and *Hiram or the Grand Master Key to the Door of both Antient and Modern Freemasonry by a Member of the Royal Arch* (1766) we find prayers in the lodges concluding with the name of Christ. These passages were replaced much later by purely Deistic formulas under the Grand Mastership of the free-thinking Duke of Sussex in 1813.

But in spite of its innocuous character, Freemasonry, merely by reason of its secrecy, soon began to excite alarm in the public mind. As early as 1724 a work entitled *The Grand Mystery of the Freemasons Discovered* had provoked an angry remonstrance from the Craft[2]; and when the French edict against the Order was passed, a letter signed " Jachin " appeared in *The Gentleman's Magazine* declaring the " Freemasons who have lately been suppressed not only in France but in Holland " to be " a dangerous Race of Men ":

No Government ought to suffer such clandestine Assemblies where Plots against the State may be carried on, under the Pretence of Brotherly Love and good Fellowship.

The writer, evidently unaware of possible Templar traditions, goes on to observe that the sentinel placed at the door of the lodge with a drawn sword in his hand " is not the only mark of their being a military Order "; and suggests that the title of Grand Master is taken in imitation of the Knights of Malta. " Jachin," moreover, scents a Popish plot:

They not only admit Turks, Jews, Infidels, but even Jacobites, non-jurors and Papists themselves . . . how can we be sure that

---

[1] Dr. Anderson, a native of Aberdeen and at this period minister of the Presbyterian Church in Swallow Street, and Dr. Desaguliers, of French Protestant descent, who had taken holy orders in England and in this same year of 1717 lectured before George I, who rewarded him with a benefice in Norfolk (*Dictionary of National Biography*, articles on James Anderson and John Theophilus Desaguliers).

[2] *The Free Mason's Vindication, being an answer to a scandalous libel entitled* (sic) *The Grand Mystery of the Free Masons discover'd*, etc. (Dublin, 1725). It is curious that this reply is to be found in the British Museum (Press mark 8145, h. 1. 44), but not the book itself. Yet Mr. Waite thinks it sufficiently important to include in a " Chronology of the Order," in his *Encyclopædia of Freemasonry*, I. 335.

those Persons who are known to be well affected, are let into all their Mysteries? They make no scruple to acknowledge that there is a Distinction between Prentices and Master Masons and who knows whether they may not have an higher Order of Cabalists, who keep the Grand Secret of all entirely to themselves?[1]

Later on in France, the Abbé Pérau published his satires on Freemasonry, *Le Secret des Francs-Maçons* (1742), *L'Ordre des Francs-Maçons trahi et le Secret des Mopses révélé* (1745), and *Les Francs-Maçons écrasés* (1746)[2] and in about 1761 another English writer said to be a Mason brought down a torrent of invective on his head by the publication of the ritual of the Craft Degrees under the name of *Jachin and Boaz*.[3]

It must be admitted that from all this controversy no party emerges in' a very charitable light, Catholics and Protestants alike indulging in sarcasms and reckless accusations against Freemasonry, the Freemasons retorting with far from brotherly forbearance.[4] But, again, one must remember that all these men were of their age—an age which seen through the eyes of. Hogarth would certainly not appear to have been distinguished for delicacy. It should be noted, however, when one reads in masonic works of the " persecutions " to which Freemasonry has been subjected, that aggression was not confined only to the one side in the conflict; moreover, that the Freemasons at this

---

[1] *Gentleman's Magazine* for April 1737.

[2] Dates given in *A.Q.C.*, XXXII. Part I. pp. 11, 12, and Deschamps, *Les Sociétés Secrètes et la Société*, III. 29. The writer of the paper in *A.Q.C.* appears not to recognize the authorship of the second work *L'Ordre des Francs-Maçons trahi;* but on p. xxix of this book the signature of Abbé Pérau appears in the masonic cypher of the period derived from the masonic word LUX. This cypher is, of course, now well known. It will be found on p. 73 of Clavel's *Histoire pittoresque*.

[3] The British Museum possesses no earlier edition of this work than that of 1797, but the first edition must have appeared at least thirty-five years earlier, as *A Free Mason's Answer to the suspected Author of . . . Jachin and Boaz*, of which a copy may be found in the British Museum (Press mark 112, d. 41), is dated 1762. This book bears on the title-page the following quotation from Shakespeare:
    " Oh, that Heaven would put in every honest Hand a Whip
        to lash the Rascal naked through the World."

[4] The author of *Jachin and Boaz* says in the 1797 edition that in reply to this work he has received " several anonymous Letters, containing the lowest Abuse and scurrilous Invectives; nay some have proceeded so far as to threaten his Person. He requests the Favour of all enraged Brethren, who shall chuse to display their Talents for the future, that they will be so kind as to pay the Postage of their Letters for there can be no Reason why he should put up with their ill Treatment and pay the Piper into the Bargain. Surely there must be something in this Book very extraordinary; a something they cannot digest, thus to excite the Wrath and Ire of these hot-brained Mason-bit Gentry." One letter he has received calls him " a Scandalous Stinking Pow Catt (sic)."

period were divided amongst themselves and expressed with regard to opposing groups much the same suspicions that non-Masons expressed with regard to the Order as a whole. For the years following after the suppression of Masonry in France were marked by the most important development in the history of the modern Order—the inauguration of the Additional Degrees.

THE ADDITIONAL DEGREES

The origin and inspiration of the additional degrees has provoked hardly less controversy in masonic circles than the origin of Masonry itself. It should be explained that Craft Masonry, or Blue Masonry—that is to say, the first three degrees of Entered Apprentice, Fellow Craft, and Master Mason of which I have attempted to trace the history—were the only degrees recognized by Grand Lodge at the time of its foundation in 1717 and still form the basis of all forms of modern Masonry. On this foundation were erected, somewhere between 1740 and 1743, the degree of the Royal Arch and the first of the series of upper degrees now known as the Scottish Rite or as the Ancient and Accepted Rite. The acceptance or rejection of this superstructure has always formed a subject of violent controversy between Masons, one body affirming that Craft Masonry is the only true and genuine Masonry, the other declaring that the real object of Masonry is only to be found in the higher degrees. It was this controversy, centring round the Royal Arch degree, that about the middle of the eighteenth century split Masonry into opposing camps of Ancients and Moderns, the Ancients declaring that the R.A. was "the Root, Heart, and Marrow of Freemasonry,"[1] the Moderns rejecting it. Although worked by the Ancients from 1756 onwards, this degree was definitely repudiated by Grand Lodge in 1792,[2] and only in 1813 was officially received into English Freemasonry.

The R.A. degree, which is said nevertheless to be contained in embryo in the 1723 Book of Constitutions,[3] is purely Judaic—a glorification of Israel and commemorating the building of the second Temple. That it was derived from the Jewish Cabala seems probable, and Yarker, commenting on the

---

[1] *A.Q.C.*, XXXII. Part I. p. 34.
[2] Ibid.
[3] Ibid., p. 15. Mackey also thinks that R.A. was introduced in 1740, but that before that date it formed part of the Master's degree (*Lexicon of Freemasonry*, p. 299).

phrase in the *Gentleman's Magazine* quoted above—" Who knows whether they (the Freemasons) have not a higher order of Cabalists, who keep the Grand Secret of all entirely to themselves "—observes: " It looks very like an intimation of the Royal Arch degree, [1] and elsewhere he states that " the Royal Arch degree, when it had the Three Veils, must have been the work, even if by instruction, of a Cabalistic Jew about 1740, and from this time we may expect to find a secret tradition grafted upon Anderson's system."[2]

Precisely in this same year of 1740 Mr. Waite says that " an itinerant pedlar of the Royal Arch degree is said to have propagated it in Ireland, claiming that it was practised at York and London,"[3] and in 1744 a certain Dr. Dassigny wrote that the minds of the Dublin brethren had been lately disturbed about Royal Arch Masonry owing to the activities in Dublin of " a number of traders or hucksters in pretended Masonry," whom the writer connects with " Italians " or the " Italic Order."

A Freemason quoting this passage in a recent discussion on the upper degrees expresses the opinion that these hucksters were " Jacobite emissaries disguised under the form of a pretended Masonry," and that " by Italians and Italian Order he intends a reference to the Court of King James III, i.e. the Old Pretender at Rome, and to the Ecossais (Italic) Order of Masonry."[4] It is much more likely that he had referred to another source of masonic instruction in Italy which I shall indicate in a later chapter.

But precisely at the moment when it is suggested that the Jacobites were intriguing to introduce the Royal Arch degree into Masonry they are also said to have been engaged in elaborating the " Scottish Rite." Let us examine this contention.

FREEMASONRY IN FRANCE

The foundation of Grand Lodge in London had been followed by the inauguration of Masonic Lodges on the Continent—in 1721 at Mons, in 1725 in Paris, in 1728 at Madrid, in 1731 at The Hague, in 1733 at Hamburg, etc. Several of

---

[1] Yarker, *The Arcane Schools,* p. 437.
[2] Review by Yarker of Mr. A. E. Waite's book *The Secret Tradition in Freemasonry* in *The Equinox,* Vol. I. No. 7, p. 414.
[3] *Encyclopædia of Freemasonry,* II. 56.
[4] *A.Q.C.,* Vol. XXXII, Part I. p. 23.

these received their warrant from the Grand Lodge of England. But this was not the case with the Grand Lodge of Paris, which did not receive a warrant till 1743.

The men who founded this lodge, far from being non-political, were Jacobite leaders engaged in active schemes for the restoration of the Stuart dynasty. The leader of the group, Charles Radcliffe, had been imprisoned with his brother, the ill-fated Lord Derwentwater who was executed on Tower Hill in 1716. Charles had succeeded in escaping from Newgate and made his way to France, where he assumed the title of Lord Derwentwater, although the Earldom had ceased to exist under the bill of attainder against his brother.[1] It was this Lord Derwentwater—afterwards executed for taking part in the 1745 rebellion—who with several other Jacobites is said to have founded the Grand Lodge of Paris in 1725, and himself to have become Grand Master.

The Jacobite character of the Paris lodge is not a matter of dispute. Mr. Gould relates that "the colleagues of Lord Derwentwater are stated to have been a Chevalier Maskeline, a Squire Heguerty, and others, all partisans of the Stuarts."[2] But he goes on to contest the theory that they used Freemasonry in the Stuart cause, which he regards as amounting to a charge of bad faith. This is surely unreasonable. The founders of Grand Lodge in Paris did not derive from Grand Lodge in London, from which they held no warrant,[3] but, as we have seen, took their Freemasonry with them to France before Grand Lodge of London was instituted; they were therefore in no way bound by its regulations. And until the Constitutions of Anderson were published in 1723 no rule had been laid down that the Lodges should be non-political. In the old days Freemasonry had always been Royalist, as we see from the ancient charges that members should be "true liegemen of the King"; and if the adherents of James Edward saw in him their rightful sovereign, they may have conceived that they

[1] Correspondence on Lord Derwentwater in *Morning Post* for September 15, 1922. Mr. Waite (*The Secret Tradition in Freemasonry*, I. 113) wrongly gives the name of Lord Derwentwater as John Radcliffe and in his *Encyclopædia of Freemasonry* as James Radcliffe. But James was the name of the third Earl, beheaded in 1716.

[2] Gould, op. cit. III. 138. "The founders were all of them Britons."—*A.Q.C.*, XXXII. Part I. p. 6.

[3] "If we turn to our English engraved lists we find that whatever Lodge (or Lodges) may have existed in Paris in 1725 must have been unchartered, for the first French Lodge on our roll is on the list for 1730-32. . . . It would appear probable . . . that Derwentwater's Lodge . . . was an informal Lodge and did not petition for a warrant till 1732."—Gould, *History of Freemasonry*, III. 138.

were using Freemasonry for a lawful purpose in adapting it to his cause. So although we may applaud the decision of the London Freemasons to purge Freemasonry of political tendencies and transform it into a harmonious system of brotherhood, we cannot accuse the Jacobites in France of bad faith in not conforming to a decision in which they had taken no part and in establishing lodges on their own lines.

Unfortunately, however, as too frequently happens when men form secret confederacies for a wholly honourable purpose, their ranks were penetrated by confederates of another kind. It has been said in an earlier chapter that, according to the documents produced by the *Ordre du Temple* in the early part of the nineteenth century, the Templars had never ceased to exist in spite of their official suppression in 1312, and that a line of Grand Masters had succeeded each other in unbroken succession from Jacques du Molay to the Duc de Cossé-Brissac, who was killed in 1792. The Grand Master appointed in 1705 is stated to have been Philippe, Duc d'Orléans, later the Regent. Mr. Waite has expressed the opinion that all this was an invention of the late eighteenth century, and that the Charter of Larmenius was fabricated at this date though not published until 1811 by the revived *Ordre du Temple* under the Grand Master, Fabré Palaprat. But evidence points to a contrary conclusion. M. Matter, who, as we have seen, disbelieves the story of the *Ordre du Temple* and the authenticity of the Charter of Larmenius in so far as it professes to be a genuine fourteenth-century document, nevertheless asserts that the *savants* who have examined it declare it to date from the early part of the eighteenth century, at which period Matter believes the Gospel of St. John used by the Order to have been arranged so as " to accompany the ceremonies of some masonic or secret society." Now, it was about 1740 that a revival of Templarism took place in France and Germany; we cannot therefore doubt that if Matter is right in this hypothesis, the secret society in question was that of the Templars, whether they existed as lineal descendants of the twelfth-century Order or merely as a revival of that Order. The existence of the German Templars at this date under the name of the *Stricte Observance* (which we shall deal with in a further chapter) is indeed a fact disputed by no one; but that there was also an *Ordre du Temple* in France at the very beginning of the eighteenth century must be regarded as highly probable. Dr. Mackey, John Yarker, and Lecouteulx de Canteleu (who, owing to his possession of

Templar documents, had exclusive sources of information) all declare this to have been the case and accept the Charter of Larmenius as authentic. " It is quite certain," says Yarker, " that there was at this period in France an *Ordre du Temple,* with a charter from John Mark Larmenius, who claimed appointment from Jacques du Molay. Philippe of Orléans accepted the Grand Mastership in 1705 and signed the Statutes."[1]

Without, however, necessarily accepting the Charter of Larmenius as authentic let us examine the probability of this assertion with regard to the Duc d'Orléans.

Amongst the Jacobites supporting Lord Derwentwater at the Grand Lodge of Paris was a certain Andrew Michael Ramsay, known as Chevalier Ramsay, who was born at Ayr near the famous Lodge of Kilwinning, where the Templars are said to have formed their alliance with the masons in 1314. In 1710 Ramsay was converted to the Roman Catholic faith by Fénelon and in 1724 became tutor to the sons of the Pretender at Rome. Mr. Gould has related that during his stay in France, Ramsay had formed a friendship with the Regent, Philippe, Duc d'Orléans, who was Grand Master of the *Ordre de Saint-Lazare,* instituted during the Crusades as a body of Hospitallers devoting themselves to the care of the lepers and which in 1608 had been joined to the *Ordre du Mont-Carmel.* It seems probable from all accounts that Ramsay was a Chevalier of this Order, but he cannot have been admitted into it by the Duc d'Orléans, for the Grand Master of the Ordre de Saint-Lazare was not the Duc d'Orléans but the Marquis de Dangeau, who, on his death in 1720, was succeeded by the son of the Regent, the Duc de Chartres.[2] If, then, Ramsay was admitted to any Order by the Regent, it was surely the *Ordre du Temple,* of which the Regent is said to have been the Grand Master at this date.

Now, the infamous character of the Duc d'Orléans is a matter of common knowledge; moreover, during the Regency—that period of impiety and moral dissolution hitherto unparalleled in the history of France—the chief of council was the Duc de Bourbon, who later placed his mistress the Marquise de Prie and the financier Paris Duverney at the head of affairs, thus creating a scandal of such magnitude that he was exiled

---

[1] John Yarker, *The Arcane Schools,* p. 462.
[2] Gautier de Sibert, *Histoire des Ordres Royaux, Hospitaliers-Militaires de Notre-Dame du Carmel et de Saint-Lazare de Jérusalem,* Vol. II. p. 193 (Paris, 1772).

in 1726 through the influence of Cardinal Fleury. This Duc de Bourbon in 1737 is said to have become Grand Master of the Temple. " It was thus," observes de Canteleu, " that these two Grand Masters of the Temple degraded the royal authority and ceaselessly increased hatred against the government."

It would therefore seem strange that a man so upright as Ramsay appears to have been, who had moreover but recently been converted to the Catholic Church, should have formed a friendship with the dissolute Regent of France, unless there had been some bond between them. But here we have a possible explanation—Templarism. Doubtless during Ramsay's youth at Kilwinning many Templar traditions had come to his knowledge, and if in France he found himself befriended by the Grand Master himself, what wonder that he should have entered into an alliance which resulted in his admission to an Order he had been accustomed to revere and which, moreover, was represented to him as the *fons et origo* of the masonic brotherhood to which he also belonged? It is thus that we find Ramsay in the very year that the Duc de Bourbon is said to have been made Grand Master of the Temple artlessly writing to Cardinal Fleury asking him to extend his protection to the society of Freemasons in Paris and enclosing a copy of the speech which he was to deliver on the following day, March 21, 1737. It is in this famous oration that for the first time we find Freemasonry traced to the Crusades:

At the time of the Crusades in Palestine many princes, lords, and citizens associated themselves, and vowed to restore the Temple of the Christians in the Holy Land, and to employ themselves in bringing back their architecture to its first institution. They agreed upon several ancient signs and symbolic words drawn from the well of religion in order to recognize themselves amongst the heathens and Saracens. These signs and words were only communicated to those who promised solemnly, and even sometimes at the foot of the altar, never to reveal them. This sacred promise was therefore not an execrable oath, as it has been called, but a respectable bond to unite Christians of all nationalities into one confraternity. Some time afterwards our Order formed an intimate union with the Knights of St. John of Jerusalem. From that time our Lodges took the name of Lodges of St. John.[1]

[1] This oration has been published several times and has been variously attributed to Ramsay and the Duc d'Antin. The author of a paper in *A.Q.C.*, XXXII. Part I., says on p. 7: "Whether Ramsay delivered his speech or not is doubtful, but it is certain that he wrote it. It was printed in an obscure and obscene Paris paper called the *Almanach des Cocus* for 1741 and is there said to have been ' pronounced ' by ' Monsieur de R—Grand Orateur de l'Ordre.' It was again printed in 1742 by Bro. De la Tierce in his *Histoire, Obligations et Statuts, etc.*, . . . and De la Tierce says that it was

This speech of Ramsay's has raised a storm of controversy amongst Freemasons because it contains a very decided hint of a connexion between Templarism and Freemasonry. Mr. Tuckett, in the paper referred to above, points out that only the Knights of St. John of Jerusalem are here mentioned,[1] but Ramsay distinctly speaks of "our Order" forming a union with the Knights of St. John of Jerusalem, and we know that the Templars did eventually form such a union. The fact that Ramsay does not mention the Templars by name admits of a very plausible explanation. It must be remembered that, as Mr. Gould has shown, a copy of the oration was enclosed by Ramsay in his letter to Cardinal Fleury appealing for royal protection to be extended to Freemasonry; it is therefore hardly likely that he would have proclaimed a connexion between the Order he was anxious to present in the most favourable light and one which had formerly been suppressed by King and Pope. Moreover, if the Charter of Larmenius is to be believed, the newly elected Grand Master of the Temple was the Duc de Bourbon, who had already incurred the Cardinal's displeasure. Obviously, therefore, Templar influence was kept in the background. This is not to imply bad faith on the part of Ramsay, who doubtless held the Order of Templars to be wholly praiseworthy; but he could not expect the King or Cardinal to share his view, and therefore held it more prudent to refer to the progenitors of Freemasonry under the vague description of a crusading body. Ramsay's well-meant effort met, however, with no success. Whether on account of this unlucky reference by which the Cardinal may have detected Templar influence or for some other reason, the appeal for royal protection was not only refused, but the new Order, which hitherto Catholics had been allowed to enter, was now prohibited by Royal edict. In the following year, 1738, the Pope, Clement XII, issued a bull, *In Eminenti*,

---

'prononcé par le Grand Maître des Francs-Maçons de France' in the year 1740. . . . A. G. Jouast (*Histoire du G.O.*, 1865) says the Oration was delivered at the Installation of the Duc d'Antin as G.M. on 24th June, 1738, and the same authority states that it was first printed at the Hague in 1738, bound up with some poems attributed to Voltaire, and some licentious tales by Piron. . . . Bro. Gould remarks: ' If such a work really existed at that date, it was probably the original of the "*Lettre philosophique par M. de V——, avec plusieurs pièces galantes,*" London, 1757.' " Mr. Gould has, however, provided very good evidence that Ramsay was the author of the oration by Daruty's discovery of the letter to Cardinal Fleury, which together with the oration itself (translated from De la Tierce's version) he reproduces in his *History of Freemasonry*, Vol. III. p. 84.

[1] *A.Q.C., XXII.* Part I. p. 10.

banning Freemasonry and excommunicating Catholics who took part in it.

But this prohibition appears to have been without effect, for Freemasonry not only prospered but soon began to manufacture new degrees. And in the masonic literature of the following thirty years the Templar tradition becomes still more clearly apparent. Thus the Chevalier de Bérage in a well-known pamphlet, of which the first edition is said to have appeared in 1747,[1] gives the following account of the origins of Freemasonry:

This Order was instituted by Godefroi de Bouillon in Palestine in 1330,[2] after the decadence of the Christian armies, and was only communicated to the French Masons some time after and to a very small number, as a reward for the obliging services they rendered to several of our English and Scottish Knights, from whom true Masonry is taken. Their Metropolitan Lodge is situated on the Mountain of Heredom where the first Lodge was held in Europe and which exists in all its splendour. The General Council is still held there and it is the seal of the Sovereign Grand Master in office. This mountain is situated between the West and North of Scotland at sixty miles from Edinburgh.

Apart from the historical confusion of the first sentence, this passage is of interest as evidence that the theory of a connexion between certain crusading Knights and the Lodge of Heredom of Kilwinning was current as early as 1747. The Baron Tschoudy in his *Etoile Flamboyante,* which appeared in 1766, says that the crusading origin of Freemasonry is the one officially taught in the lodges, where candidates for initiation are told that several Knights who had set forth to rescue the holy places of Palestine from the Saracens " formed an association under the name of Free Masons, thus indicating that their principal desire was the reconstruction of the Temple of Solomon," that, further, they adopted certain signs, grips, and passwords as a defence against the Saracens, and finally that " our Society . . . fraternized on the footing of an Order with the Knights of St. John of Jerusalem, from which it is apparent that the Freemasons borrowed the custom of

[1] *Les plus secrets mystères des Hauts Grades de la Maçonnerie dévoilés, ou le vrai Rose-Croix.* À Jerusalem. M.DCC.LXVII. (*A.Q.C.,* Vol. XXXII. Part I. p. 13, refers, however, to an edition of 1747).
[2] As Godefroi de Bouillon died in 1100, I conclude his name to have been introduced here in error by de Bérage or the date of 1330 to have been a misprint.

regarding St. John as the patron of the whole Order in general."[1]
After the crusades " the Masons kept their rites and methods
and in this way perpetuated the royal art by establishing
lodges, first in England, then in Scotland," etc.[2]

In this account, therefore, Freemasonry is represented as
having been instituted for the defence of Christian doctrines.
De Bérage expresses the same view and explains that the object
of these Crusaders in thus binding themselves together was to
protect their lives against the Saracens by enveloping their
sacred doctrines in a veil of mystery. For this purpose they
made use of Jewish symbolism, which they invested with a
Christian meaning. Thus the Temple of Solomon was used to
denote the Church of Christ, the bough of acacia signified the
Cross, the square and the compass the union between the Old
and New Testaments, etc. So " the mysteries of Masonry were
in their principle, and are still, nothing else than those of the
Christian religion."[3]

Baron Tschoudy, however, declares that all this stops short
of the truth, that Freemasonry originated long before the
Crusades in Palestine, and that the real " ancestors, fathers,
authors of the Masons, those illustrious men of whom I will
not say the date nor betray the secret," were a " disciplined
body " whom Tschoudy describes by the name of " the Knights
of the Aurora and Palestine." After " the almost total
destruction of the Jewish people " these " Knights " had always
hoped to regain possession of the domains of their fathers and
to rebuild the Temple, and they carefully preserved their
" regulations and particular liturgy," together with a " sublime
treatise " which was the object of their continual study and of
their philosophical speculations. Tschoudy further relates that
they were students of the " occult sciences," of which alchemy
formed a part, and that they had " abjured the principles of the

[1] Dr. Mackey confirms this assertion, *Lexicon of Freemasonry*, p. 304.
[2] *Etoile Flamboyante*, I. pp. 18-20.
[3] The same theory that Freemasonry originated in Palestine as a system
of protection for the Christian faith is given almost verbatim in the instructions to the candidate for initiation into the degree of " Prince of the Royal
Secret " published in *Monitor of Freemasonry* (Chicago, 1860), where it is
added that " the brethren assembled round the tomb of Hiram, is a representation of the disciples lamenting the death of Christ on the Cross."
Weishaupt, founder of the eighteenth-century Illuminati, also showed—
although in a spirit of mockery—how easily the legend of Hiram could be
interpreted in this manner, and suggested that at the periods when the Christians were persecuted they enveloped their doctrines in secrecy and symbolism.
" That was necessary in times and places where the Christians lived amongst
the heathens, for example in the East at the time of the Crusades."—*Nachtrag
zur Originalschriften*, Part II. p. 123.

Jewish religion in order to follow the lights of the Christian faith." At the time of the Crusades the Knights of Palestine came out from the desert of the Thebaïd, where they had remained hidden, and joined to themselves some of the crusaders who had remained in Jerusalem. Declaring that they were the descendants of the masons who had worked on the Temple of Solomon, they professed to concern themselves with "speculative architecure," which served to disguise a more glorious point of view. From this time they took the name of Free Masons, presented themselves under this title to the crusading armies and assembled under their banners.[1]

It would of course be absurd to regard any of the foregoing accounts as historical facts; the important point is that they tend to prove the fallacy of supposing that the Johannite-Templar theory originated with the revived *Ordre du Temple,* since one corresponding to it so closely was current in the middle of the preceding century. It is true that in these earlier accounts the actual words "Johannite" and "Templar" do not occur, but the resemblance between the sect of Jews professing the Christian faith but possessing a "particular liturgy" and a "sublime treatise"—apparently some early form of the Cabala—dealing with occult science, and the Mandæans or Johannites with their Cabalistic "Book of Adam," their Book of John, and their ritual, is at once apparent. Further, the allusions to the connexion between the Knights who had been indoctrinated in the Holy Land and the Scottish lodges coincides exactly with the Templar tradition, published not only by the *Ordre du Temple* but handed down in the Royal Order of Scotland.

From all this the following facts stand out: (1) that whilst British Craft Masonry traced its origin to the operative guilds of masons, the Freemasons of France from 1737 onwards placed the origin of the Order in crusading chivalry; (2) that it was amongst these Freemasons that the upper degrees known as the Scottish Rite arose; and (3) that, as we shall now see, these degrees clearly suggest Templar inspiration.

The earliest form of the upper degrees appears to have been the one given by de Bérage, as follows:

1. Parfait Maçon Élu.
2. Élu de Perignan.
3. Élu des Quinze.
4. Petit Architecte.

---

[1] *Étoile Flamboyante,* pp. 24-9.

5. Grand Architecte.
6. Chevalier de l'Épée et de Rose-Croix.
7. Noachite ou Chevalier Prussien.

The first of these to make its appearance is believed to have been the one here assigned to the sixth place. This degree known in modern Masonry as " Prince of the Rose-Croix of Heredom or Knight of the Pelican and Eagle " became the eighteenth and the most important degree in what was later called the Scottish Rite, or at the present time in England the Ancient and Accepted Rite.

Why was this Rite called Scottish? " It cannot be too strongly insisted on," says Mr. Gould, " that all Scottish Masonry has nothing whatever to do with the Grand Lodge of Scotland, nor, with one possible exception—that of the Royal Order of Scotland—did it ever originate in that country."[1] But in the case of the Rose-Croix degree there is surely some justification for the term in legend, if not in proven fact, for, as we have already seen, according to the tradition of the Royal Order of Scotland this degree had been contained in it since the fourteenth century, when the degrees of H.R.M. (Heredom) and R.S.Y.C.S. (Rosy Cross) are said to have been instituted by Robert Bruce in collaboration with the Templars after the battle of Bannockburn. Dr. Mackey is one of the few Masons who admit this probable affiliation, and in referring to the tradition of the Royal Order of Scotland observes: " From that Order it seems to us by no means improbable that the present degree of Rose-Croix de Heredom may have taken its origin."[2]

But the Rose-Croix degree, like the Templar tradition from which it appears to have descended, is capable of a dual interpretation, or rather of a multiple interpretation, for no degree in Masonry has been subject to so many variations. That on the Continent it had descended through the Rosicrucians in an alchemical form seems more than probable. It would .certainly be difficult to believe that a degree of R.S.Y.C.S. was imported from the East and incorporated in the Royal Order of Scotland in 1314; that by a mere coincidence a man named Christian Rosenkreutz was— according to the Rosicrucian legend—born in the same century and transmitted a secret doctrine he had discovered in the East to the seventeenth-century Brethren of the Rosy Cross;

---

[1] Gould, *History of Freemasonry*, III. 92.
[2] Mackey's *Lexicon of Freemasonry*, p. 267.

and finally, that a degree of the Rose-Croix was founded in circ. 1741 without any connexion existing between these succeeding movements.   Even if we deny direct affiliation, we must surely admit a common source of inspiration producing, if not a continuation, at any rate a periodic revival of the same ideas.   Dr. Oliver indeed admits affiliation between the seventeenth-century fraternity and the eighteenth-century degree, and after pointing out that the first indication of the Rose-Croix degree appears in the *Fama Fraternitatis* in 1613, goes on to say:

> It was known much sooner, although not probably as a degree in Masonry, for it existed as a cabalistic science from the earliest times in Egypt, Greece, and Rome, as well as amongst the Jews and Moors in times more recent, and in our own country the names of Roger Bacon, Fludd, Ashmole, and many others are found in its list of adepts.[1]

Dr. Mackey, quoting this passage, observes that " Oliver confounds the masonic Rose-Croix with the alchemical Rosicrucians," and proceeds to give an account of the Rose-Croix degree as worked in England and America, which he truly describes as " in the strictest sense a Christian degree."[2]   But the point Dr. Mackey overlooks is that this is only one version of the degree, which, as we shall see later, has been and still is worked in a very different manner on the Continent.

It is, however, certain that the version of the Rose-Croix degree first adopted by the Freemasons of France in about 1741 was not only so Christian but so Catholic in character as to have given rise to the belief that it was devised by the Jesuits in order to counteract the attacks of which Catholicism was the object.[3]   In a paper on the Additional Degrees Mr. J. S. Tuckett writes:

> There is undeniable evidence that in their *earliest forms* the Ecossais or Scots Degrees were Roman Catholic; I have a MS. Ritual in French of what I believe to be the *original* Chev. de l'Aigle or S.·.P.·.D.·.R.·.C.·. (Souverain Prince de Rose-Croix) and in it the New Law is declared to be " la foy Catholique," and the Baron Tschoudy in his *L'Etoile Flamboyante* of 1766 describes the same Degree as " le Catholicisme mis en grade " (Vol. I. p. 114).   I suggest that Ecossais or Scots Masonry was intended to be a Roman Catholic

---

[1] Oliver's *Landmarks of Freemasonry*, II. 81, note 35.
[2] *Lexicon of Freemasonry*, p. 270.
[3] Clavel, *Histoire pittoresque de la Franc-Maçonnerie*, p. 166.

as well as a Stuart form of Freemasonry, in which none but those devoted to both Restorations were to be admitted.[1]

But is it necessary to read this political intention into the degree? If the tradition of the Royal Order of Scotland is to be believed, the idea of the Rose-Croix degree was far older than the Stuart cause, and dated back to Bannockburn, when the degree of Heredom with which it was coupled was instituted in order " to correct the errors and reform the abuses which had crept in among the three degrees of St. John's Masonry," and to provide a " Christianized form of the Third Degree," " purified of the dross of paganism and even of Judaism."[2] Whether the antiquity attributed to these degrees can be proved or not, it certainly appears probable that the legend of the Royal Order of Scotland had some foundation in fact, and therefore that the ideas embodied in the eighteenth-century Rose-Croix degree may have been drawn from the store of that Order and brought by the Jacobites to France. At the same time there is no evidence in support of the statement made by certain Continental writers that Ramsay actually instituted this or any of the upper degrees. On the contrary, in his Oration he expressly states that Freemasonry is composed of the Craft degrees only :

We have amongst us three kinds of brothers: Novices or Apprentices, Fellows or Professed Brothers, Masters or Perfected Brethren. To the first are explained the moral virtues; to the second the heroic virtues; to the last the Christian virtues. . . .

It might be said then that the Rose-Croix degree was here foreshadowed in the Masters' degree, in that the latter definitely inculcated Christianity. This would be perfectly in accord with Ramsay's point of view as set forth in his account of his conversion by Fénelon. When he first met the Archbishop of Cambrai in 1710, Ramsay relates that he had lost faith in all Christian sects and had resolved to " take refuge in a wise Deism limited to respect for the Divinity and for the immutable ideas of pure virtue," but that his conversation with Fénelon led him to accept the Catholic faith. And he goes on to show that " Monsieur de Cambrai turned Atheists into Deists, Deists into Christians, and Christians into Catholics by a sequence of ideas full of enlightenment and feeling."[3]

---

[1] A.Q.C., XXXII. Part I. p. 17.
[2] The Royal Order of Scotland, by Bro. Fred. H. Buckmaster, p. 3.
[3] Histoire de la Vie et des Ouvrages de Messire François de Salignac de la Mothe-Fénelon, archevêque de Cambrai, pp. 105, 149 (1727).

Might not this be the process which Ramsay aimed at introducing into Freemasonry—the process which in fact does form part of the masonic system in England to-day, where the Atheist must become, at least by profession, a Deist before he can be admitted to the Craft Degrees, whilst the Rose-Croix degree is reserved solely for those who profess the Christian faith?   Such was undoubtedly the idea of the men who introduced the Rose-Croix degree into France; and Ragon, who gives an account of this " Ancien Rose-Croix Francais "— which is almost identical with the degree now worked in England, but long since abandoned in France—objects to it on the very score of its Christian character.[1]

In this respect the Rose-Croix amongst all the upper degrees introduced to France in the middle of the eighteenth century stands alone, and it alone can with any probability be attributed to Scottish Jacobite inspiration.   It was not, in fact, until three or four years after Lord Derwentwater or his mysterious successor Lord Harnouester[2] had resigned the Grand Master-ship in favour of the Duc d'Antin in 1738 that the additional degrees were first heard of, and it was not until eight years after the Stuart cause had received its death-blow at Culloden, that is to say, in 1754, that the Rite of Perfection in which the so-called Scots Degrees were incorporated was drawn up in the following form:

RITE OF PERFECTION

1. Entered Apprentice.
2. Fellow Craft.
3. Master Mason.
4. Secret Master.
5. Perfect Master.
6. Intimate Secretary.
7. Intendant of the Buildings.
8. Provost and Judge.
9. Elect of Nine.
10. Elect of Fifteen.
11. Chief of the Twelve Tribes.
12. Grand Master Architect.
13. Knight of the Ninth Arch.

---

[1] J. M. Ragon, *Ordre Chapitral, Nouveau Grade de Rose-Croix*, p. 35.
[2] The identity of Lord Harnouester has remained a mystery. It has been suggested that Harnouester is only a French attempt to spell Derwent-water, and therefore that the two Grand Masters referred to were one and the same person.

14. Ancient Grand Elect.
15. Knight of the Sword.
16. Prince of Jerusalem.
17. Knight of the East and West.
18. Rose-Croix Knight.
19. Grand Pontiff.
20. Grand Patriarch.
21. Grand Master of the Key of Masonry.
22. Prince of Libanus or Knight of the Royal Axe.
23. Sovereign Prince Adept.
24. Commander of the Black and White Eagle.
25. Commander of the Royal Secret.[1]

We have only to glance at the nomenclature of the last twenty-two of these degrees to see that on the basis of mere operative Masonry there has been built up a system composed of two elements: crusading chivalry and Judaic tradition. What else is this but Templarism? Even Mr. Gould, usually so reticent on Templar influence, admits it at this period:

In France . . . some of the Scots lodges would appear to have very early manufactured new degrees, connecting these very distinguished Scots Masons with the Knights Templar, and thus given rise to the subsequent flood of Templarism. The earliest of all are supposed to have been the Masons of Lyons who invented the Kadosch degree, representing the vengeance of the Templars, in 1741. From that time new rites multiplied in France and Germany, but all those of French origin contain Knightly, and almost all, Templar grades. In every case the connecting link was composed of one or more Scots degrees.[2]

The name Kadosch here mentioned is a Hebrew word signifying " holy " or " consecrated," which in the Cabala is found in conjunction with the Tetragrammaton.[3] The degree is said to have developed from that of Grand Elect,[4] one of the three " degrees of vengeance " celebrating with sanguin-

---

[1] In 1786 the seventh and eighth degrees were transposed, the eleventh became Sublime Knight Elect, the twentieth Grand Master of all Symbolic, the twenty-first Noachite or Prussian Knight, the twenty-third Chief of the Tabernacle, the twenty-fourth Prince of the Tabernacle, the twenty-fifth Knight of the Brazen Serpent. The thirteenth is now known as the Royal Arch of Enoch and must not be confounded with the Royal Arch, which is the complement of the third degree. The fourteenth is now the Scotch Knight of Perfection, the fifteenth Knight of the Sword or of the East, and the twentieth is Venerable Grand Master.

[2] *History of Freemasonry*, III. 93. Thory gives the date of the Kadosch degree as 1743, which seems correct.

[3] Zohar, section Bereschith, folio 18b.

[4] *A.Q.C.*, XXVI: " Templar Legends in Freemasonry."

ary realism the avenging of the murder of Hiram. But in its final form of Knight Kadosch—later to become the thirtieth degree of the "Ancient and Accepted Scottish Rite"—the Hiramic legend was changed into the history of the Templars with Jacques du Molay as the victim.[1] So the reprobation of attack on authority personified by the master-builder becomes approbation of attack on authority in the person of the King of France.

The introduction of the upper degrees with their political and, later on, anti-Christian tendencies thus marked a complete departure from the fundamental principle of Freemasonry that "nothing concerning the religion or government shall ever be spoken of in the lodge." For this reason they have been assailed not only by anti-masonic writers but by Freemasons themselves.[2] To represent Barruel and Robison as the enemies of Freemasonry is therefore absolutely false; neither of these men denounced Craft Masonry as practised in England, but only the superstructure erected on the Continent. Barruel indeed incurs the reproaches of Mounier for his championship of English Freemasons:

He vaunts their respect for religious opinion and for authority. When he speaks of Freemasons in general they are impious, rebellious successors of the Templars and Albigenses, but *all those of England are innocent*. More than this, all the Entered Apprentices, Fellow Crafts, and Master Masons in all parts of the world are innocent; there are only guilty ones in the higher degrees, which are not essential to the institution and are sought by a small number of people.[3]

[1] "This degree is intimately connected with the ancient order of the Knights Templars, a history of whose destruction, by the united efforts of Philip, King of France, and Pope Clement V, forms a part of the instructions given to the candidate. The dress of the Knights is black, as an emblem of mourning for the extinction of the Knights Templars, and the death of Jacques du Molay, their last Grand Master. . . ."—Mackey, *Lexicon of Freemasonry*, p. 172.

[2] Mr. J. E. S. Tuckett, in the paper before mentioned, quotes the Articles of Union of 1813, in which it is said that "pure ancient Masonry consists of three degrees and no more," and goes on to observe that: "According to this view those other Degrees (which for convenience may be called Additional Degrees) are not real Masonry at all, but an extraneous and spontaneous growth springing up around the 'Craft' proper, later in date, and mostly foreign, i.e. non-British in origin, and the existence of *any* such degrees is by some writers condemned as a contamination of the 'pure ancient Freemasonry' of our forefathers."—*A.Q.C.*, XXXII. Part I. p. 5.

[3] J. J. Mounier, *De l'Influence attribuée aux Philosophes, aux Francs-Maçons et aux Illuminés sur la Révolution Française*, p. 148 (1822). See also letter from the Duke of Northumberland at Alnwick to General Rainsford dated January 19, 1799, defending Barruel from the charge of attacking Masonry and pointing out that he only indicated the upper degrees, *A.Q.C.*, XXVI, p. 112.

In this opinion of Barruel's a great number of Masonic writers concur—Clavel, Ragon, Rebold, Thory, Findel, and others too numerous to mention; all indicate Craft Masonry as the only true kind and the upper degrees as constituting a danger to the Order. Rebold, who gives a list of these writers, quotes a masonic publication, authorized by the Grand Orient and the Supreme Council of France, in which it is said that " from all these rites there result the most foolish conceptions, . . . the most absurd legends, . . . the most extravagant systems, the most immoral principles, and those the most dangerous for the peace and preservation of States," and that therefore except the first three degrees of Masonry, which are really ancient and universal, everything is " chimera, extravagance, futility, and lies."[1] Did Barruel and Robison ever use stronger language than this?

To attribute the perversion of Masonry to Jacobite influence would be absurd. How could it be supposed that either Ramsay or Lord Derwentwater (who died as a devout Catholic on the scaffold in 1746) could have been concerned in an attempt to undermine the Catholic faith or the monarchy of France? I would suggest, then, that the term " Scots Masonry " became simply a veil for Templarism—Templarism, moreover, of a very different kind to that from which the original degree of the Rose-Croix was derived. It was this so-called Scots Masonry that, after the resignation of Lord Derwentwater, " boldly came forward and claimed to be not merely a part of Masonry but the real Masonry, possessed of superior knowledge and entitled to greater privileges and the right to rule over the ordinary, i.e. Craft Masonry."[2] The Grand Lodge of France seems, however, to have realized the danger of submitting to the domination of the Templar element, and on the death of the Duc d'Antin and his replacement by the Comte de Clermont in 1743, signified its adherence to English Craft Masonry by proclaiming itself Grande Loge *Anglaise* de France and reissued the " Constitutions " of Anderson, first published in 1723, with the injunction that the Scots Masters should be placed on the same level as the simple Apprentices and Fellow Crafts and allowed to wear no badges of distinction.[3]

Grand Lodge of England appears to have been reassured by

[1] Em. Rebold, *Histoire des Trois Grandes Loges de Francs-Maçons en France*, pp. 9, 10 (1864).
[2] *A.Q.C.*, XXXII. Part I. 21.
[3] *A.Q.C.*, XXXII. Part I. 22. It is curious that in this discussion by members of the Quatuor Coronati Lodge the influence of the Templars, which provides the only key to the situation, is almost entirely ignored.

THE GRAND LODGE ERA

this proclamation as to the character of French Freemasonry, for now, in 1743, it at last delivered a warrant to Grand Lodge of France. Yet in reality it was from this moment that French Freemasonry degenerated the most rapidly. The Order was soon invaded by intriguers. This was rendered all the easier by the apathy of the Comte de Clermont, appointed Grand Master in 1743, who seems to have taken little interest in the Order and employed a substitute in the person of a dancing master named Lacorne, a man of low character through whose influence the lodges fell into a state of anarchy. Freemasonry was thus divided into warring factions: Lacorne and the crowd of low-class supporters who had followed him into the lodges founded a Grand Lodge of their own (Grande Loge Lacorne), and in 1756 the original Freemasons again attempted to make Craft Masonry the national Masonry of France by deleting the word " Anglaise " from the appellation of Grand Lodge, and renaming it " Grand Loge Nationale de France." But many lodges still continue to work the additional degrees.

The rivalry between the two groups became so violent that in 1767 the government intervened and closed down Grand Lodge.

The Templar group had, however, formed two separate associations, the " Knights of the East " (1756) and the " Council of the Emperors of the East and West " (1758). In 1761 a Jew named Stephen Morin was sent to America by the " Emperors " armed with a warrant from the Duc de Clermont and Grand Lodge of Paris and bearing the sonorous title of " Grand Elect Perfect and Sublime Master," with orders to establish a Lodge in that country. In 1766 he was accused in Grand Lodge of " propagating strange and monstrous doctrines " and his patent of Grand Inspector was withdrawn.[1] Morin, however, had succeeded in establishing the Rite of Perfection. Sixteen Inspectors, nearly all Jews, were now appointed. These included Isaac Iong, Isaac de Costa, Moses Hayes, B. Spitser, Moses Cohen, Abraham Jacobs, and Hyman Long.

Meanwhile in France the closing of Grand Lodge had not prevented meetings of Lacorne's group, which, on the death of the Duc de Clermont in 1772, instituted the " Grand Orient " with the Duc de Chartres—the future " Philippe Égalité "— as Grand Master. The Grand Orient then invited the Grande Loge to revoke the decree of expulsion and unite with it, and this offer being accepted, the revolutionary party inevitably

[1] Yarker, *The Arcane Schools*, pp. 479-82.

carried all before it, and the Duc de Chartres was declared Grand Master of all the councils, chapters, and Scotch lodges of France.[1]   In 1782 the "Council of Emperors" and the "Knights of the East" combined to form the "Grand Chapitre Général de France," which in 1786 joined up with the Grand Orient.   The victory of the revolutionary party was then complete.

It is necessary to enter into all these tedious details in order to understand the nature of the factions grouped together under the banner of Masonry at this period. The Martinist Papus attributes the revolutionary influences that now prevailed in the lodges to their invasion by the Templars, and goes on to explain that this was owing to a change that had taken place in the *Ordre du Temple*. Under the Grand Mastership of the Regent and his successor the Duc de Bourbon, the revolutionary elements amongst the Templars had had full play, but from 1741 onwards the Grand Masters of the Order were supporters of the monarchy. When the Revolution came, the Duc de Cossé-Brissac, who had been Grand Master since 1776, perished amongst the defenders of the throne. It was thus that by the middle of the century the Order of the Temple ceased to be a revolutionary force, and the discontented elements it had contained, no longer able to find in it a refuge, threw themselves into Freemasonry, and entering the higher degrees turned them to their subversive purpose. According to Papus, Lacorne was a member of the Templar group, and the dissensions that took place were principally a fight between the ex-Templars and the genuine Freemasons which ended in the triumph of the former:

Victorious rebels thus founded the Grand Orient of France. So a contemporary Mason is able to write: "It is not excessive to say that the masonic revolution of 1773 was the prelude and the precursor of the Revolution of 1789." What must be well observed is the secret action of the Brothers of the Templar Rite. It is they who are the real fomentors of revolution, the others are only docile agents.[2]

But all this attributes the baneful influence of Templarism to the French Templars alone, and the existence of such a body

[1] Mackey, *Lexicon of Freemasonry*, p. 119.

[2] *Martines de Pasqually;* par Papus, président du Suprême Conseil de l'Ordre Martiniste, p. 144 (1895). Papus is the pseudonym of Dr. Gerard Encausse.

rests on no absolutely certain evidence. What is certain and admits of no denial on the part of any historian, is the inauguration of a Templar Order in Germany at the very moment when the so-called Scottish degrees were introduced into French Masonry. We shall now return to 1738 and follow events that were taking place at this important moment beyond the Rhine.

7

GERMAN TEMPLARISM AND FRENCH ILLUMINISM

THE year after Ramsay's oration—that is to say in 1738—Frederick, Crown Prince of Prussia, the future Frederick the Great, who for two years had been carrying on a correspondence with Voltaire, suddenly evinced a curiosity to know the secrets of Freemasonry which he had hitherto derided as " Kinderspiel," and accordingly went through a hasty initiation during the night of August 14-15, whilst passing through Brunswick.[1]

The ceremony took place not at a masonic lodge, but at a hotel, in the presence of a deputation summoned by the Graf von Lippe-Bückeburg from Grand Lodge of Hamburg for the occasion. It is evident that something of an unusual kind must have occurred to necessitate these speedy and makeshift arrangements. Carlyle, in his account of the episode, endeavours to pass it off as a "very trifling circumstance "—a reason the more for regarding it as of the highest importance since we know now from facts that have recently come to light how carefully Carlyle was spoon-fed by Potsdam whilst writing his book on Frederick the Great.[2]

But let us follow Frederick's masonic career. In June 1740, after his accession to the throne, his interest in Masonry had clearly not waned, for we find him presiding over a lodge at Charlottenburg, where he received into the Order two of his brothers, his brother-in-law, and Duke Frederick William of Holstein-Beck. At his desire the Baron de Bielfeld and his privy councillor Jordan founded a lodge at Berlin, the " Three Globes," which by 1746 had no less than fourteen lodges under its jurisdiction.

In this same year of 1740 Voltaire, in response to urgent

---

[1] Gould, *History of Freemasonry*, III. 241.
[2] See the very important article on this question that appeared in *The National Review* for February 1923, showing that Carlyle was assisted gratuitously throughout his work by a German Jew named Joseph Neuberg and was supplied with information and finally decorated by the Prussian Government.

invitations, paid his first visit to Frederick the Great in Germany. Voltaire is usually said not to have yet become a Mason, and the date of his initiation is supposed to have been 1778, when he was received into the *Loge des Neuf Sœurs* in Paris. But this by no means precludes the possibility that he had belonged to another masonic Order at an earlier date. At any rate, Voltaire's visit to Germany was followed by two remarkable events in the masonic world of France. The first of these was the institution of the additional degrees; the second—perhaps not wholly unconnected with the first—was the arrival in Paris of a masonic delegate from Germany named von Marschall, who brought with him instructions for a new or rather a revived Order of Templarism, in which he attempted to interest Prince Charles Edward and his followers.

Von Marschall was followed about two years later by Baron von Hunt, who had been initiated in 1741 into the three degrees of Craft Masonry in Germany and now came to consecrate a lodge in Paris. According to von Hundt's own account, he was then received into the Order of the Temple by an unknown Knight of the Red Plume, in the presence of Lord Kilmarnock,[1] and was presented as a distinguished Brother to Prince Charles Edward, whom he imagined to be Grand Master of the Order.[2] But all this was afterwards shown to be a pure frabrication, for Prince Charles Edward dened all knowledge of the affair, and von Hundt himself admitted later that he did not know the name of the lodge or chapter in which he was received, but that he was directed from " a hidden centre " and by Unknown Superiors, whose identity he was bound not to reveal.[3] In reality it appears that von Hundt's account was exactly the opposite of the truth,[4] and that it was von Hundt who, seconding von Marschall's effort, tried to enrol Prince Charles Edward in the new German Order by assuring him that he could raise powerful support for the Stuart cause under the cover of reorganizing the Templar Order, of which he claimed to possess the true secrets handed down from the Knights of the fourteenth century. By way of further rehabilitating the Order, von

[1] Executed in 1746 as a partisan of the Stuarts.
[2] Gould, op. cit., Vol. III. pp. 101, 110; *A.Q.C.*, Vol. XXXII. Part I. p. 31.
[3] A. E. Waite, *The Secret Tradition in Freemasonry*, I. 296, 370, 415.
[4] Clavel (*Histoire pittoresque de la Franc-Maçonnerie*, p. 185) says it was afterwards discovered that " the Pretender, far from having made de Hundt a Templar, on the contrary was made a Templar by him." But other authorities deny that Prince Charles Edward was initiated even into Freemasonry.

Hundt declared that all the accusations brought against it by Philippe le Bel and the Pope were based on false charges manufactured by two recreant Knights named Noffodei and Florian as a revenge for having been deprived of their commands by the Order in consequence of certain crimes they had committed.[1] According to Lecouteulx de Canteleu, von Hundt eventually succeeded—after the defeat of Culloden—in persuading Prince Charles Edward to enter his Order. But this is extremely doubtful. At any rate, when in 1751 von Hundt officially founded his new Templar Order under the name of the *Stricte Observance,* the unfortunate Charles Edward played no part at all in the scheme. As Mr. Gould has truly observed, " no trace of Jacobite intrigues ever blended with the teaching of the *Stricte Observance.*"[2]

The *Order of the Stricte Observance* was in reality a purely German association composed of men drawn entirely from the intellectual and aristocratic classes, and, in imitation of the chivalric Orders of the past, known to each other under knightly titles. Thus Prince Charles of Hesse became Eques a Leone Resurgente, Duke Ferdinand of Brunswick Eques a Victoria, the Prussian minister von Bischoffswerder Eques a Grypho, Baron de Wächter Eques a Ceraso, Christian Bode (Councillor of Legation in Saxe-Gotha) Eques a Lilio Convallium, von Haugwitz (Cabinet Minister of Frederick the Great) Eques a Monte Sancto, etc.

But according to the declarations of the Order the official leaders, Knights of the Moon, the Star, the Golden Sun, or of the Sacred Mountain, were simply figure-heads; the real leaders, known as the " Unknown Superiors," remained in the background, unadorned by titles of chivalry but exercising supreme jurisdiction over the Order. The system had been foreshadowed by the " Invisibles " of seventeenth-century Rosicrucianism; but now, instead of an intangible group whose very existence was only known vaguely to the world, there appeared in the light of day a powerful organization led apparently by men of influence and position yet secretly directed by hidden chiefs.[3] Mirabeau has described the advent of these mysterious directors in the following passage:

[1] Lecouteulx de Canteleu, *Les Sectes et Sociétés Secrètes,* p. 242; Clavel, op. cit., p. 184.
[2] Gould, op. cit., III. 100.
[3] Ibid., III. 99, 103; Waite, *Secret Tradition in Freemasonry,* I. 289: "The Rite of the Stricte Observance was the first masonic system which claimed to derive its authority from Unknown Superiors, irresponsible themselves but claiming absolute jurisdiction and obedience without question."

In about 1756 there appeared, as if they had come out of the ground, men sent, they said, by unknown superiors, and armed with powers to reform the order [of Freemasonry] and re-establish it in its ancient purity. One of these missionaries, named Johnston, came to Weimar and Jena, where he established himself. He was received in the best way in the world by the brothers [Freemasons], who were lured by the hope of great secrets, of important discoveries which were never made known to them.[1]

Now, in the manuscripts of the Prince of Hesse published by Lecouteulx de Canteleu it is said that this man Johnston, or rather Johnson, who proclaimed himself to be " Grand Prior of the Order," was a Jew named Leicht or Leucht.[2] Gould says that his real name was either Leucht or Becker, but that he professed to be an Englishman, although unable to speak the English language, hence his assumption of the name Johnson.[3] Mr. Gould has described Johnson as a " consummate rogue and an unmitigated vagabond . . . of almost repulsive demeanour and of no education, but gifted with boundless impudence and low cunning." Indeed, von Hundt himself, after enlisting Johnson's services, found him too dangerous and declared him to be an adventurer. Johnson was thereupon arrested by von Hundt's friend the councillor von Pritsch, and thrown into the castle of Wartburg, where sudden death ended his career.

It is, however, improbable that Mirabeau could be right in indicating Johnson as one of the " Unknown Superiors," who were doubtless men of vaster conceptions than this adventurer appears to have been. Moreover, the manner of his end clearly proves that he occupied a subordinate position in the *Stricte Observance*.

Here, then, we have a very curious sequence of events which it may be well to recapitulate briefly in order to appreciate their full significance:

1737. Oration of Chevalier Ramsay indicating Templar origin of Freemasonry, but making no mention of upper degrees.

1738. Duc d'Antin becomes Grand Master of French Freemasonry in the place of Lord " Harnouester."

---

[1] *Histoire de la Monarchie Prussienne*, V. 61 (1788).
[2] *Les Sectes et Sociétés Secrètes*, p. 246.
[3] Gould, op. cit., III. 102. Waite (*Encyclopædia of Freemasonry*, II. 23) says Johnson was "in reality named Leucht, an Englishman by his claim—who did not know English and is believed to have been a Jew."

1738.   Frederick, Crown Prince of Prussia, initiated into Masonry at Brunswick.

1740.   Voltaire pays his first visit to Frederick, now King.

1741.   Baron von Marschall arrives in Paris with a plan for reviving the Templar Order.

Templar degrees first heard of in France under name of " Scots Masonry."

1743.   Arrival in France of Baron von Hundt with fresh plans for reviving the Templar Order.

Degree of Knight Kadosch celebrating vengeance of Templars said to have been instituted at Lyons.

1750.   Voltaire goes to spend three years with Frederick.

1751.   Templar Order of the Stricte Observance founded by von Hundt.

1754.   Rite of Perfection (early form of Scottish Rite) founded in France.

1761.   Frederick acknowledged head of Scottish Rite.

   „   Morin sent to found Rite of Perfection in America.

1762.   Grand Masonic Constitutions ratified in Berlin.[1]

It will be seen then that what Mr. Gould describes as " the flood of Templarism," which both he and Mr. Tuckett attribute to the so-called Scots Masons,[2] corresponds precisely with the decline of Jacobite and the rise of German influence. Would it not therefore appear probable that, except in the case of the Rose-Croix degree, the authors of the upper degrees were not Scotsmen nor Jacobites, that Scots Masonry was a term used to cover not merely Templarism but more especially German Templarism, and that the real author and inspirer of the movement was Frederick the Great? No, it is significant to find that in the history of the *Ordre du Temple,* published at the beginning of the nineteenth century, Frederick the Great is cited as one of the most distinguished members of this Order in the past,[3] and the Abbé Grégoire adds that he was " consecrated " at Remersberg (Rheinsberg?) in 1738, that is to say in the same year that he was initiated into Masonry at Brunswick.[4]   There is therefore a definite reason for connecting Frederick with Templarism at this date.

[1] Mackey, op. cit., p. 331.
[2] Gould, *History of Freemasonry,* III. 93; *A.Q.C.,* XXXII. Part I. p. 24.
[3] *Lévitikon,* p. 8 (1831); Fabré Palaprat, *Recherches historiques sur les Templiers,* p. 28 (1835).
[4] M. Grégoire, *Histoire des Sectes Religieuses,* II. 401.   Findel says that very soon after Frederick's return home from Brunswick " a lodge was secretly organized in the castle of Rheinsberg " (*History of Freemasonry,* Eng. trans., p. 252).   This lodge would appear then to have been a Templar, not a Masonic Lodge.

I would suggest, then, that the truth about the Templar succession may be found in one of the two following theories:

1. That the documents produced by the *Ordre du Temple* in the nineteenth century, including the Charter of Larmenius, were genuine; that the Order had never ceased to exist since the days of the Crusades; that the Templar heresy was Johannism, but that this was not held by the Templars who escaped to Scotland; that the Rose-Croix degree in its purely Christian form was introduced by the Scottish Templars to Scotland and four hundred years later brought by Ramsay to France; that the Master of the Temple at this date was the Regent, Philippe Duc d'Orléans, as stated in the Charter of Larmenius. Finally, that after this, fresh Templar degrees were introduced from Germany by von Hundt, acting on behalf of Frederick the Great.

2. That the documents produced by the *Ordre du Temple* in the nineteenth century were, as M. Matter declares, early eighteenth-century fabrications; that although, in view of the tradition preserved in the Royal Order of Scotland, there appears to be good reason to believe the story of the Scottish Templars and the origin of the Rose-Croix degree, the rest of the history of the Templars, including the Charter of Larmenius, was an invention of the " Concealed Superiors " of the *Stricte Observance* in Germany, and that the most important of these " Concealed Superiors " were Frederick the Great and Voltaire.

I shall not attempt to decide which of these two theories is correct; all that I do maintain is that in either case the preponderating rôle in Templarism at this crisis was played by Frederick the Great, probably with the co-operation of Voltaire, who in his *Essai sur les Mœurs* championed the cause of the Templars. Let us follow the reasons for arriving at this conclusion.

Ramsay's oration in 1737 connecting Freemasonry with the Templars may well have come to the ears of Frederick and suggested to him the idea of using Masonry as a cover for his intrigues—hence his hasty initiation at Brunswick. But in order to acquire influence in a secret society it is always necessary to establish a claim to superior knowledge, and Templarism seemed to provide a fruitful source of inspiration. For this purpose new light must be thrown on the Order. Now, there was probably no one better qualified than Voltaire, with his knowledge of the ancient and mediæval world and hatred of the Catholic Church, to undertake the construction of a historical romance subversive of the Catholic faith—hence the urgent summons to the philosopher to visit Frederick. We can imagine Voltaire delving amongst the records of the past in order to reconstruct the Templar heresy. This was clearly Gnostic, and the Mandæans or Christians of St. John may well have appeared to present the required characteristics. If it could be shown that here in Johannism true " primitive Christianity " was to be found, what a blow for the " infâme "! A skilful forger could easily be found to fabricate the documents said to have been preserved in the secret archives of the Order. Further we find von Marschall arriving in the following year in France to reorganize the Templars, and von Hundt later claiming to be in possession of the true secrets of the Order handed down from the fourteenth century. That some documents bearing on this question were either discovered or fabricated under the direction of Frederick the Great seems the more probable from the existence of a masonic tradition to this effect. Thus Dr. Oliver quotes a Report of the Grand Inspectors-General in the nineteenth century stating that:

> During the Crusades, at which 27,000 Masons were present, some masonic MSS. of great importance were discovered among the descendants of the ancient Jews, and that other valuable documents were found at different periods down to the year of Light 5557 (i.e. 1553), at which time a record came to light in Syrian characters, relating to the most remote antiquity, and from which it would appear that the world is many thousand years older than given by the Mosaic account. Few of these characters were translated till the reign of our illustrious and most enlightened Brother Frederick II, King of Prussia, whose well-known zeal for the Craft was the cause of so much improvement in the Society over which he condescended to preside.[1]

I suggest, then, that the documents here referred to and containing the secrets claimed by von Hundt may have been the ones afterwards published by the *Ordre du Temple* in the nineteenth century, and that if unauthentic they were the work of Voltaire, aided probably by a Jew capable of forging Syriac manuscripts. That Johnson was the Jew in question seems probable, since Findel definitely asserts that the history of the continuation of the Order of Knights Templar was his work.[2] Frederick, as we know, was in the habit of employing Jews to carry out shady transactions, and he may well have used Johnson to forge documents as he used Ephraim to coin

[1] Oliver, *Historical Landmarks in Freemasonry*, II. 110.
[2] Findel, *History of Freemasonry* (Eng. trans.), p. 290.

false money for him. It would be further quite in keeping
with his policy to get rid of the man as soon as he had served
his purpose, lest he should betray his secrets.

At any rate, whatever were the methods employed by
Frederick the Great for obtaining control over Masonry, the
fruitful results of that "very trifling circumstance," his
initiation at Brunswick, become more and more apparent as
the century advances. Thus when in 1786 the Rite of Perfection was reorganized and rechristened the "Ancient and
Accepted Scottish Rite"—always the same Scottish cover for
Prussianism!—it is said to have been Frederick who conducted
operations, drew up the new Constitutions of the Order, and
rearranged the degrees so as to bring the total number up to
thirty-three,[1] as follows:

26. Prince of Mercy.
27. Sovereign Commander of the Temple.
28. Knight of the Sun.
29. Grand Scotch Knight of St. Andrew.
30. Grand Elect Knight of Kadosch.
31. Grand Inspector Inquisitor Commander.
32. Sublime Prince of the Royal Secret.
33. Sovereign Grand Inspector-General.

In the last four degrees Frederick the Great and Prussia
play an important part; in the thirtieth degree of Knight
Kadosch, largely modelled on the Vehmgerichts, the Knights
wear Teutonic crosses, the throne is surmounted by the double-
headed eagle of Prussia, and the President, who is called Thrice
Puissant Grand Master, represents Frederick himself; in the
thirty-second degree of Sublime Prince of the Royal Secret,
Frederick is described as the head of Continental Freemasonry;
in the thirty-third degree of Sovereign Grand Inspector-
General the jewel is again the double-headed eagle, and the
Sovereign Grand Commander is Frederick, who at the time
this degree was instituted figured with Philippe, Duc d'Orléans,

[1] On this point see *inter alia* Mackey, *Lexicon of Freemasonry*, pp. 91, 328.
In England and in the Grand Orient of France most of the upper degrees
have fallen into disuse, and this rite, known in England as the Ancient and
Accepted Rite and in France as the Scottish Rite, consists of five degrees
only in addition to the three Craft degrees (known as Blue Masonry), which
form the basis of all masonic rites. These five degrees are the eighteenth
Rose-Croix, the thirtieth Knight Kadosch, and the thirty-first to the thirty-
third. The English Freemason, on being admitted to the upper degrees,
therefore advances at one bound from the third degree of Master Mason to
the eighteenth degree of Rose-Croix, which thus forms the first of the upper
degrees. The intermediate degrees are, however, still worked in America.

160 SECRET SOCIETIES

Grand Master of the Grand Orient, as his lieutenant. The most important of these innovations was the thirty-second degree, which was in reality a system rather than a degree for bringing together the Masons of all countries under one head—hence the immense power acquired by Frederick. By 1786 French Masonry was thus entirely Prussianized and Frederick had indeed become the idol of Masonry everywhere. Yet probably no one ever despised Freemasonry more profoundly. As the American Mason Albert Pike shrewdly observed:

> There is no doubt that Frederick came to the conclusion that the great pretensions of Masonry in the blue degrees were merely imaginary and deceptive. He ridiculed the Order, and thought its ceremonies mere child's play; and some of his sayings to that effect have been preserved. It does not at all follow that he might not at a later day have found it politic to put himself at the head of an Order that had become a power. . . .[1]

It is not without significance to find that in the year following the official foundation of the Stricte Observance, that is to say in 1752, Lord Holdernesse, in a letter to the British Ambassador in Paris, Lord Albemarle, headed " Very secret," speaks of " the influence which the King of Prussia has of late obtained over all the French Councils "; and a few weeks later Lord Albemarle refers to " the great influence of the Prussian Court over the French Councils by which they are so blinded as not to be able to judge for themselves."[2]

But it is time to turn to another sphere of activity which Masonry opened out to the ambitions of Frederick.

The making of the Encyclopédie, which even those writers the most sceptical with regard to secret influences behind the revolutionary movement admit to have contributed towards the final cataclysm, is a question on which official history has thrown but little light. According to the authorized version of the story—as related, for example, in Lord Morley's work on the Encyclopædists—the plan of translating Ephraim Chambers's Cyclopædia, which had appeared in 1728, was suggested to Diderot " some fifteen years later " by a French bookseller named Le Breton. Diderot's " fertile and energetic intelligence transformed the scheme. . . . It was resolved to

---

[1] Scottish Rite of Freemasonry: the Constitutions and Regulations of 1762, by Albert Pike, Sovereign Grand Commander of the Supreme Council of the Thirty-third Degree for the Southern Jurisdiction of the United States, p. 138 (A.M. 5632).
[2] R.O. State Papers, Foreign, France, Vol. 243, Jan. 2 and Feb. 19, 1752.

make Chambers's work a mere starting-point for a new enterprise of far wider scope." We then go on to read of the
financial difficulties that now beset the publisher, of the
embarrassment of Diderot, who "felt himself unequal to the
task of arranging and supervising every department of a new
book that was to include the whole circle of the sciences," of
the fortunate enlisting of d'Alembert as a collaborator, and
later of men belonging to all kinds of professions, "all united
in a work that was as useful as it was laborious, without any
view of interest . . . without any common understanding and
agreement," further, of the cruel persecutions encountered at
the hands of the Jesuits, "who had expected at least to have
control of the articles on theology," and finally of the tyrannical
suppression of the great work on account of the anti-Christian
tendencies these same articles displayed.[1]

Now for a further light on the matter.

In the famous speech of the Chevalier Ramsay already
quoted, which was delivered at Grand Lodge of Paris in 1737,
the following passage occurs:

The fourth quality required in our Order is the taste for useful
sciences and the liberal arts. Thus, the Order exacts of each of
you to contribute, by his protection, liberality, or labour, to a
vast work for which no academy can suffice, because all these
societies being composed of a very small number of men, their
work cannot embrace an object so extended. All the Grand
Masters in Germany, England, Italy, and elsewhere exhort all the
learned men and all the artisans of the Fraternity to unite to furnish
the materials for a Universal Dictionary of all the liberal arts and
useful sciences; excepting only theology and politics. The work
has already been commenced in London, and by means of the
unions of our brothers it may be carried to a conclusion in a few
years.[2]

So after all it was no enterprising bookseller, no brilliantly
inspired philosopher, who conceived the idea of the *Encyclopédie*, but a powerful international organization able to employ
the services of more men than all the academies could

[1] John Morley, *Diderot and the Encyclopædists*, Vol. I. pp. 123-47 (1886).
[2] Gould, op. cit., III. 87. Mr. Gould naïvely adds in a footnote to this
passage: "The proposed Dictionary is a curious crux—is it possible that the
Royal Society may have formed some such idea?" The beginning already
made in London was of course the *Cyclopædia* of Chambers, published in
1728, and Chambers, who in the following year was made a Fellow of the
Royal Society, if not himself a Mason numbered many prominent Masons
amongst his friends, including the globe-maker Senex to whom he had been
apprenticed and who published Anderson's *Constitutions* in 1723. (See *A.Q.C.*,
XXXII. Part I. p. 18.)

supply, which devised the scheme at least six years before the date at which it is said to have occurred to Diderot. Thus the whole story as usually told to us would appear to be a complete fabrication—struggling publishers, toiling *littérateurs* carrying out their superhuman task as " independent men of letters " without the patronage of the great—which Lord Morley points out as " one of the most important facts in the history of the Encyclopædia "—writers of all kinds bound together by no " common understanding or agreement," are all seen in reality to have been closely associated as " artisans of the Fraternity " carrying out the orders of their superiors.

The *Encyclopédie* was therefore essentially a Masonic publication, and Papus, whilst erroneously attributing the famous oration and consequently the plan of the *Encyclopédie* to the inspiration of the Duc d'Antin, emphasizes the importance of this fact. Thus, he writes:

The Revolution manifests itself by two stages:

1st. *Intellectual revolution,* by the publication of the *Encyclopédie,* due to French Freemasonry under the high inspiration of the Duc d'Antin.

2nd. *Occult revolution* in the Lodges, due in great part to the members of the Templar Rite and executed by a group of expelled Freemasons afterwards amnestied.[1]

The masonic authorship of the *Encyclopédie* and the consequent dissemination of revolutionary doctrines has remained no matter of doubt to the Freemasons of France; on the contrary, they glory in the fact. At the congress of the Grand Orient in 1904 the Freemason Bonnet declared:

In the eighteenth century the glorious line of Encyclopædists formed in our temples a fervent audience which was then alone in invoking the radiant device as yet unknown to the crowd: " Liberty, Equality, Fraternity." The revolutionary seed quickly germinated amidst this *élite*. Our illustrious Freemasons d'Alembert, Diderot, Helvetius, d'Holbach, Voltaire, Condorcet, completed the evolution of minds and prepared the new era. And, when the Bastille fell, Freemasonry had the supreme honour of giving to humanity the charter (i.e. the Declaration of the Rights of Man) which it had elaborated with devotion. (*Applause*.)

This charter, the orator went on to say, was the work of the Freemason Lafayette, and was adopted by the Constituent Assembly, of which more than 300 members were Freemasons.

[1] Papus, *Martines de Pasqually,* p. 146 (1895).

But in using the lodges to sow the seeds of revolution, the Encyclopædists betrayed not only the cause of monarchy but of Masonry as well. It will be noticed that, in conformity with true masonic principles, Ramsay in his oration expressly stated that the encyclopædia was to concern itself with the liberal arts and sciences[1] and that theology and politics were to be excluded from the contemplated scheme. How, then, did it come to pass that these were eventually the two subjects to which the Encyclopædists devoted the greatest attention, so that their work became principally an attack on Church and monarchy? If Papus was right in attributing this revolutionary tendency to the *Encyclopédie* from the time of the famous oration, then Ramsay could only be set down as the profoundest hypocrite or as the mouthpiece of hypocrites professing intentions the very reverse of their real designs. A far more probable explanation seems to be that during the interval between Ramsay's speech and the date when the *Encyclopédie* was begun in earnest, the scheme underwent a change. It will be noticed that the year of 1746, when Diderot and d'Alembert are said to have embarked on their task, coincided with the decadence of French Freemasonry under the Comte de Clermont and the invasion of the lodges by the subversive elements; thus the project propounded with the best intentions by the Freemasons of 1737 was filched by their revolutionary successors and turned to a diametrically opposite purpose.

But it is not to the dancing-master Lacorne and his middle-class following that we can attribute the efficiency with which not only the *Encyclopédie* but a host of minor revolutionary publications were circulated all over France. Frederick the Great had seen his opportunity. If I am right in my surmise that Ramsay's speech had reached the ears of Frederick, the prospect of the *Encyclopédie* contained therein may well have appeared to him a magnificent method for obtaining a footing in the intellectual circles of France; hence then, doubtless, an additional reason for his hasty initiation into Masonry, his summons to Voltaire, and his subsequent overtures to Diderot and d'Alembert, who, by the time the first volume of the *Encyclopédie* appeared in 1751, had both been made members of the Royal Academy of Prussia. In the following year Frederick offered d'Alembert the presidency of the

---

[1] Evidently a reference to the seven liberal arts and sciences enumerated in the Fellow Craft's degree—Grammar, Rhetoric, Logic, Arithmetic, Geometry, Music, and Astronomy.

Academy in place of Maupertuis, an offer which was refused; but in 1755 and again in 1763 d'Alembert visited Frederick in Germany and received his pension regularly from Berlin. It is therefore not surprising that when the *Encyclopédie* had reached the letter P, it included, in an unsigned article on Prussia, a panegyric on the virtues and the talents of the illustrious monarch who presided over the destinies of that favoured country.

The art of Frederick the Great, as of his successors on the throne of the Hohenzollerns, was to make use of every movement that could further the design of Prussian supremacy. He used the Freemasons as he used the philosophers and as he used the Jews, to carry out his great scheme—the destruction of the French monarchy and of the alliance between France and Austria. Whilst through his representatives at the Court of France he was able to create discord between Versailles and Vienna and bring discredit on Marie Antoinette, through his allies in the masonic lodges and in the secret societies he was able to reach the people of France. The gold and the printing presses of Frederick the Great were added to those of the Orléanistes for the circulation of seditious literature throughout the provinces.[1]

So as the century advanced the association founded by Royalists and Catholics was turned into an engine of destruction by revolutionary intriguers; the rites and symbols were gradually perverted to an end directly opposed to that for which they had been instituted, and the two degrees of Rose-Croix and Knight Kadosch came to symbolize respectively war on religion and war on the monarchy of France.

It is no orthodox Catholic but an occultist and Rosicrucian who thus describes the rôle of Masonry in the Revolution:

Masonry has not only been profaned but it has been served as a cover and pretext for the plots of anarchy, by the occult influence of the avengers of Jacques du Molay and the continuers of the schismatic work of the Temple. Instead of avenging the death of Hiram, they have avenged his assassins. The anarchists have taken the plumb-line, the square, and the mallet and have written on them liberty, equality, fraternity. That is to say,

[1] In 1767 Voltaire writes to Frederick asking him to have certain books printed in Berlin and circulated in Europe " at a low price which will facilitate the sales." To this Frederick replies: " You can make use of my printers according to your desires," etc. (letter of May 5, 1767). I have referred elsewhere to the libels against Marie Antoinette circulated by Frederick's agents in France. See my *French Revolution*, pp. 27, 183.

liberty for envyings, equality in degradation, fraternity for destruction. Those are the men whom the Church has justly condemned
and that she will always condemn.[1]

But it is time to turn to another masonic power which
meanwhile had entered the lists, the Martinistes or French
Illuminés.

FRENCH ILLUMINISM

Whilst Frederick the Great, the Freemasons, the Encyclopædists, and the Orléanistes were working on the material
plane to undermine the Church and monarchy in France,
another cult had arisen which by the middle of the century
succeeded in insinuating itself into the lodges. This was a
recrudescence of the old craze for occultism, which now spread
like wildfire all over Europe from Bordeaux to St. Petersburg.
During the reign of Anna of Courland (1730-40) the Russian
Court was permeated with superstition, and professional
magicians and charlatans of every kind were encouraged.
The upper classes of Germany in the eighteenth century proved
equally susceptible to the attractions of the supernatural, and
princes desirous of long life or greater power eagerly pursued
the quest of the Philosopher's Stone, the " Elixir of Life,"
and evoked spirits under the direction of occultists in their
service.

In France occultism, reduced to a system, adopted the outer
forms of Masonry as a cover to the propagation of its doctrines.
It was in 1754 that Martines de Pasqually (or Paschalis), a
Rose-Croix Mason,[2] founded his Order of Élus Cohens (Elected
Priests), known later as the *Martinistes* or the French *Illuminés*.
Although brought up in the Christian faith, Pasqually has been
frequently described as a Jew. The Baron de Gleichen, himself a Martiniste and a member of the Amis Réunis,[3] throws an
interesting light on the matter in this passage: " Pasqualis
was originally Spanish, perhaps of the Jewish race, since his

---

[1] Eliphas Lévi, *Histoire de la Magie*, p. 407. The rôle of Freemasonry
in preparing the Revolution habitually denied by the conspiracy of history
is nevertheless clearly recognized in masonic circles—applauded by those
of France, deplored by those of England and America. An American manual
in my possession contains the following passage: " The Masons . . . (it is
now well settled by history) *originated the Revolution* with the infamous
Duke of Orleans at their head."—*A Ritual and Illustrations of Freemasonry*,
p. 31 note.

[2] Papus, *Martines de Pasqually*, p. 150.

[3] Benjamin Fabre, *Eques a Capite Galeato*, p. 88.

disciples inherited from him a large number of Jewish manuscripts."[1]

It was " this Cabalistic sect,"[2] the Martinistes, which now became the third great masonic power in France.

The rite of the Martinistes was broadly divided into two classes, in the first of which was represented the fall of man and in the second his final restoration—a further variation on the masonic theme of a loss and a recovery. After the first three Craft degrees came the Cohen degrees of the same— Apprentice Cohen, Fellow Craft Cohen, and Master Cohen— then those of Grand Architect, Grand Elect of Zerubbabel or Knight of the East; but above these were concealed degrees leading up to the Rose-Croix, which formed the capstone of the edifice.[3] Pasqually first established his rite at Marseilles, Toulouse, and Bordeaux, then in Paris, and before long Martiniste lodges spread all over France with the centre at Lyons under the direction of Willermoz, a prosperous merchant living there. From this moment other occult Orders sprang up in all directions. In 1760 Dom Pernetti founded his sect of " Illuminés d'Avignon " in that city, declaring himself a high initiate of Freemasonry and teaching the doctrines of Swedenborg. Later a certain Chastanier founded the "Illuminés Théosophes," a modified version of Pernetti's rite; and in 1783 the Marquis de Thomé started a purified variety of Swedenborgianism under the name of " Rite of Swedenborg."

Beneath all these occult sects one common source of inspiration is to be found—the perverted and magical Cabala of the Jews, that conglomeration of wild theosophical imaginings and barbaric superstitions founded on ancient pagan cults and added to throughout seventeen centuries by succeeding generations of Jewish occultists.[4] This influence is particularly to be detected in the various forms of the Rose-Croix degree, which in nearly all these associations forms the highest and most secret degree. The ritual of " the eminent Order of the Knights of the Black Eagle or Sovereigns of the Rose-Croix," a secret and unpublished document of the eighteenth century, which differs entirely from the published rituals, explains that no one can attain to knowledge of the higher sciences without the " Clavicules de Salomon," of which the

[1] *Souvenirs du Baron de Gleichen*, p. 151.
[2] Henri Martin, *Histoire de France*, XVI. 529.
[3] Heckethorn, *Secret Societies*, I. 218; Waite, *Secret Tradition*, II. 155, 156.
[4] "The ceremonial magic of Pasqually followed that type which I connect with the debased Kabbalism of Jewry."—A. E. Waite, *The Secret Tradition in Freemasonry*, II. 175.

real secrets were never committed to print and which is said
to contain the whole of Cabalistic science.[1] The catechism of
this same degree deals mainly with the transmutation of metals,
the Philosopher's Stone, etc.

In the Rite of Perfection as worked in France and America
this Cabalistic influence is shown in those degrees known under
the name of the " Ineffable Degrees," derived from the Jewish
belief in the mystery that surrounds the Ineffable Name of
God.   According to the custom of the Jews, the sacred name
Jehovah or Jah-ve, composed of the four letters yod, he, vau,
he, which formed the Tetragrammaton, was never to be pronounced by the profane, who were obliged to substitute for it
the word " Adonai."   The Tetragrammaton might only be
uttered once a year on the Day of Atonement by the High
Priest in the Holy of Holies amid the sound of trumpets and
cymbals, which prevented the people from hearing it.   It is
said that in consequence of the people thus refraining from its
utterance, the true pronunciation of the name was at last lost.
The Jews further believed that the Tetragrammaton was
possessed of unbounded powers.   " He who pronounces it
shakes heaven and earth and inspires the very angels with
astonishment and terror."[2]   The Ineffable Name thus conferred miraculous gifts; it was engraved on the rod of Moses
and enabled him to perform wonders, just as, according to the
Toledot Yeshu, it conferred the same powers on Christ.

This superstition was clearly a part of Rosicrucian tradition,
for the symbol of the Tetragrammaton within a triangle,
adopted by the masonic lodges, figures in Fludd's Cabalistic
system.[3]   In the " Ineffable degrees " it was invested with all
the mystic awe by which it is surrounded in Jewish theology,
and, according to early American working: " Brothers and
Companions of these degrees received the name of God as it
was revealed to Enoch and were sworn to pronounce it but
once in their lives."

In the alchemical version of the Rose-Croix degree referred
to above the Ineffable Name is actually invested with magical

---

[1] An eighteenth-century manuscript of *Les vrais clavicules du roi Salomon,*
translated from the Hebrew, was sold in Paris in 1921.
[2] Mackey, *Lexicon of Freemasonry,* p. 156.
[3] A. E. Waite, *The Doctrine and Literature of the Kabbalah,* p. 369. Ragon
elsewhere gives an account of the philosophical degree of the Rose-Croix,
in which the sacred formula I.N.R.I., which plays an important part in
the Christian form of this degree, is interpreted to mean Igne Natura Reno-
vatur Integra—Nature is renewed by fire.—*Nouveau Grade de Rose Croix,*
p. 69.   Mackey gives this as an alternative interpretation of the Rosicrucians.
—*Lexicon of Freemasonry,* p. 150.

powers as in the Jewish Cabala. Ragon, after describing the
Jewish ceremony when the word Jehovah was pronounced by
the High Priest in the Holy of Holies, goes on to say that
" Schem-hamm-phorasch," another term for the Tetragrammaton, forms the sacred word of a Scotch degree, and that this
belief in its mystic properties " will be found at the head of
the instructions for the third degree of the Knight of the Black
Eagle, called Rose-Croix," thus:

Q. What is the most powerful name of God on the pentaculum?
A. Adonai.
Q. What is its power?
A. To move the Universe.

That one of the Knights who had the good fortune to pronounce
it cabalistically would have at his disposal the powers that inhabit
the four elements and the celestial spirits, and would possess all
the virtues possible to man.[1]

That this form of the Rose-Croix was of purely Jewish origin
is thus clearly evident. In the address to the candidate for
initiation into the Rose-Croix degree at the Lodge of the
" Contrat Social " it is stated:

This degree, which includes an Order of Perfect Masons, was
brought to light by Brother R., who took it from the Kabbalistic
treasure of the Doctor and Rabbi Néamuth, chief of the synagogue
of Leyden in Holland, who had preserved its precious secrets and
its costume, both of which we shall see in the same order in which
he placed them in his mysterious Talmud.[2]

Now, we know that in the eighteenth century a society of
Rosicrucian magicians had been instituted in Florence which
was believed to date back to the fifteenth century and to have
been partly, if not wholly composed of Orientals, as we shall
see in the next chapter; but it seems probable that this sect,
whilst secretly inspiring the Rose-Croix masons, was itself either
nameless or concealed under a disguise. Thus in 1782 an
English Freemason writes: " I have found some rather curious
MSS. in Algiers in Hebrew relating to the society of the
Rosicrucians, which exists at present under another name with
the same forms. I hope, moreover to be admitted to their
knowledge."[3]

[1] Ragon, *Maçonnerie Occulte*, p. 91.
[2] Gustave Bord, *La Franc-Maçonnerie en Francs, des Origines à* 1815,
p. 212 (1908).
[3] Letter from General Rainsford of October 1782, quoted in *Transactions
of the Jewish Historical Society*, Vol. VIII. p. 125.

It has frequently been argued that Jews can have played no part in Freemasonry at this period since they themselves were not admitted to the lodges. But this is by no means certain; in the article from *The Gentleman's Magazine* already quoted it is stated that Jews are admitted; de Luchet further quotes the instance of David Moses Hertz received in a London lodge in 1787; and the author of *Les Franc-Maçons écrasés*, published in 1746, states that he has seen three Jews received into a lodge at Amsterdam. In the "Melchisedeck Lodges" of the Continent non-Christians were openly admitted, and here again the Rose-Croix degree occupies the most important place. The highest degrees of this rite were the Initiated Brothers of Asia, the Masters of the Wise, and the Royal Priests, otherwise known as the degree of Melchisedeck or the true Brothers of the Rose-Croix.

This Order, usually described as the *Asiatic Brethren,* of which the centre was in Vienna and the leader a certain Baron von Eckhoffen, is said to have been a continuation of the "Brothers of the Golden and Rosy Cross," a revival of the seventeenth-century Rosicrucians organized in 1710 by a Saxon priest, Samuel Richter, known as Sincerus Renatus. The real origins of the Asiatic Brethren are, however, obscure and little literature on the subject is to be found in this country.[1] Their further title of "the Knights and Brethren of St. John the Evangelist" suggests Johannite inspiration and was clearly an imposture, since they included Jews, Turks, Persians, and Armenians. De Luchet, who as a contemporary was in a position to acquire first-hand information, thus describes the organization of the Order, which, it will be seen, was entirely Judaic. "The superior direction is called the small and constant Sanhedrim of Europe. The names of those employed by which they conceal themselves from their inferiors are Hebrew. The signs of the third principal degree (i.e. the Rose-Croix) are Urim and Thummim. . . . The Order

---

[1] De Luchet (*Essai sur la Secte des Illuminés,* p. 212) refers to the following works in connexion with the Order:
1. *Nouvelles authentiques des Chevaliers et Frères Initiés d'Asie.*
2. *Reçoit-on, peut-on recevoir les Juifs parmi les Franc-Maçons?*
3. *Nouvelles authentiques de l'Asie,* by Frederick de Bascamp, nommé Lazapolski (1787).
Wolfstieg, in his *Bibliographie der Freimaurischer Literatur,* Vol. II. p. 283, gives Friedrich Münter as the author of the first of the above, and also mentions amongst others a work by Gustave Brabée, *Die Asiatischen Brüder in Berlin und Wien.* But none of these are to be found in the British Museum, nor is the book of Rolling (published in 1787), which gives away the secrets of the sect.

has the true secrets and the explanations, moral and physical, of the hierogyphics of the very venerable Order of Freemasonry."[1] The initiate had to swear absolute submission and unswerving obedience to the laws of the Order and to follow its laws implicitly to the end of his life, without asking by whom they were given or whence they came.

"Who," asks de Luchet, "gave to the Order these so-called secrets? That is the great and insidious question for the secret societies. But the Initiate who remains, and must remain eternally in the Order, never finds this out, he dare not even ask it, he must promise never to ask it. In this way those who participate in the secrets of the Order remain the Masters."

Again, as in the *Stricte Observance,* the same system of "Concealed Superiors"—the same blind obedience to unknown directors!

Under the guidance of these various sects of Illuminés a wave of occultism swept over France, and lodges everywhere became centres of instruction on the Cabala, magic, divination, alchemy, and theosophy[2]; masonic rites degenerated into ceremonies for the evocation of spirits—women, who were now admitted to these assemblies, screamed, fainted, fell into convulsions, and lent themselves to experiments of the most horrible kind.[3]

By means of these occult practices the *Illuminés* in time became the third great masonic power in France, and the rival Orders perceived the expediency of joining forces. Accordingly in 1771 an amalgamation of all the masonic groups was effected at the new lodge of the *Amis Réunis.*

The founder of this lodge was Savalette de Langes, Keeper of the Royal Treasury, Grand Officer of the Grand Orient, and a high initiate of Masonry—"versed in all mysteries, in all the lodges, and in all the plots." In order to unite them he made his lodge a mixture of all sophistic, Martiniste, and masonic systems, "and as a bait to the aristocracy organized balls and concerts at which the adepts, male and female, danced and feasted, or sang of the beauties of their liberty

[1] Books in Wolfstieg's list refer to the Order as " the only true and genuine Freemasonry " (die einzige wahre und echte Freimaurerei).

[2] Clavel, *Histoire pittoresque,* etc., p. 167.

[3] The Baron de Gleichen, in describing the "Convulsionists," says that young women allowed themselves to be crucified, sometimes head downwards, at these meetings of the fanatics. He himself saw one nailed to the floor and her tongue cut with a razor. (*Souvenirs du Baron de Gleichen,* p. 185.)

and equality, little knowing that above them was a secret committee which was arranging to extend this equality beyond the lodge to rank and fortune, to castles and to cottages, to marquesses and bourgeois " alike.[1]

A further development of the Amis Réunis was the Rite of the *Philalèthes*, compounded by Savalette de Langes in 1773 out of Swedenborgian, Martiniste, and Rosicrucian mysteries, into which the higher initiates of the Amis Réunis—Court de Gebelin, the Prince de Hesse, Condorcet, the Vicomte de Tavannes, Willermoz, and others—were initiated. A modified form of this rite was instituted at Narbonne in 1780 under the name of " Free and Accepted Masons du Rit Primitif," the English nomenclature being adopted (according to Clavel) in order to make it appear that the rite emanated from England. In reality its founder, the Marquis de Chefdebien d'Armisson, a member of the Grand Orient and of the Amis Réunis, drew his inspiration from certain German Freemasons with whom he maintained throughout close relations and who were presumably members of the Stricte Observance, since Chefdebien was a member of this Order, in which he bore the title of " Eques a Capite Galeato." The correspondence that passed between Chefdebien and Salvalette de Langes, recently discovered and published in France, is one of the most illuminating records of the masonic ramifications in existence before the Revolution ever brought to light.[2] To judge by the tone of these letters, the leaders of the Rit Primitif would appear to have been law-abiding and loyal gentlemen devoted to the Catholic religion, yet in their passion for new forms of Masonry and thirst for occult lore ready to associate themselves with every kind of adventurer and charlatan who might be able to initiate them into further mysteries. In the curious notes drawn up by Savalette for the guidance of the Marquis de Chefdebien we catch a glimpse of the power behind the philosophers of the *salons* and the aristocratic adepts of the lodges— the professional magicians and men of mystery; and behind

---

[1] Barruel, *Mémoires sur le Jacobinisme*, IV. 263.
[2] *Franciscus, Eques a Capite Galeato*, published by Benjamin Fabre with preface by Copin Albancelli. A paper on this book appears in *Ars Quatuor Coronatorum*, Vol. XXX. Part II. The author, Mr. J. E. S. Tuckett, describes it as a book of extraordinary interest to Freemasons. Without sharing Mr. Tuckett's admiration for the members of the Rit Primitif, I agree with him that M. Fabre attributes to them too much guile and fails to substantiate his charge of revolutionary designs. They appear to have been the perfectly honourable · dupes of subtler brains. Incidentally Mr. Tuckett erroneously gives the real name of " Eques a Capite Galeato " as Chefdebien d'Armand; it should be d'Armisson.

these again the concealed directors of the secret societies, the *real initiates.*

THE MAGICIANS

The part played by magicians during the period preceding the French Revolution is of course a matter of common knowledge and has never been disputed by official history. But like the schools of philosophers this sudden crop of magicians is always represented as a sporadic growth called into being by the idle and curious society of the day. The important point to realize is that just as the philosophers were all Freemasons, the principal magicians were not only Freemasons but members of occult secret societies. It is therefore not as isolated charlatans but as agents of some hidden power that we must regard the men whom we will now pass in a rapid survey.

One of the first to appear in the field was Schroepfer, a coffee-house keeper of Leipzig, who declared that no one could be a true Freemason without practising magic. Accordingly he proclaimed himself the " reformer of Freemasonry," and set up a lodge in his own house with a rite based on the Rose-Croix degree for the purpose of evoking spirits. The meetings took place at dead of night, when by means of carefully arranged lights, magic mirrors, and possibly of electricity, Schroepfer contrived to produce apparitions which his disciples—under the influence of strong punch—took to be visitors from the other world.[1] In the end Schroepfer, driven crazy by his own incantations, blew out his brains in a garden near Leipzig.

According to Lecouteulx de Canteleu, it was Schroepfer who indoctrinated the famous " Comte de Saint-Germain "— " The Master " of our modern co-masonic lodges. The identity of this mysterious personage has never been established[2]; by some contemporaries he was said to be a natural son of the King of Portugal, by others the son of a Jew and a Polish Princess. The Duc de Choiseul on being asked whether he knew the origin of Saint-Germain replied: " No doubt we know it, he is the son of a Portuguese Jew who exploits

[1] De Luchet, *Essai sur la Secte des Illuminés*, p. 208. Gould, op. cit., III. 116.
[2] It is amusing to note that Mr. Waite confuses him with the rightful bearer of the name, Claude Louis, Comte de Saint-Germain, Minister of War under Louis XVI, for in *The Secret Tradition in Freemasonry*, Vol. II., a picture of the real Count is appended to a description of the adventurer.

the credulity of the town and Court."[1] In 1780 a rumour went
round that his father was a Jew of Bordeaux, but according to
the *Souvenirs of the Marquise de Créquy* the Baron de Breteuil
discovered from the archives of his Ministry that the pretended Comte de Saint-Germain was the son of a Jewish doctor
of Strasburg, that his real name was Daniel Wolf, and that he
was born in 1704.[2] The general opinion thus appears to have
been in favour of his Jewish ancestry.

Saint-German seems first to have been heard of in Germany
about 1740, where his marvellous powers attracted the attention of the Maréchal de Belle-Isle, who, always the ready dupe
of charlatans, brought him back with him to the Court of
France, where he speedily gained the favour of Madame de
Pompadour. The Marquise before long presented him to the
King, who granted him an apartment at Chambord and,
enchanted by his brilliant wit, frequently spent long evenings
in conversation with him in the rooms of Madame de Pompadour. Meanwhile his invention of flat-bottomed boats for
the invasion of England raised him still higher in the estima-
tion of the Maréchal de Belle-Isle. In 1761 we hear of him as
living in great splendour in Holland and giving out that he
had reached the age of seventy-four, though appearing to be
only fifty; if this were so, he must have been ninety-seven at
the time of his death in 1784 at Schleswig. But this feat of
longevity is far from satisfying his modern admirers, who
declare that Saint-Germain did not die in 1784, but is still
alive to-day in some corner of Eastern Europe. This is in
accordance with the theory, said to have been circulated by
Saint-Germain himself, that by the eighteenth century he had
passed through several incarnations and that the last one had
continued for 1,500 years. Barruel, however, explains that
Saint-Germain in thus referring to his age spoke in masonic
language, in which a man who has taken the first degree is
said to be three years old, after the second five, or the third
seven, so that by means of the huge increase the higher degrees
conferred it might be quite possible for an exalted adept to
attain the age of 1,500.

Saint-Germain has been represented by modern writers—
not only those who compose his following—as a person of

---

[1] *Biographie Michaud*, article on Saint-Germain.
[2] *Souvenirs de la Marquise de Créquy*, III. 65. Francois Bournand (*Histoire de la Franc-Maçonnerie*, p. 106) confirms this story: "The man who
called himself the Comte de Saint-Germain was in reality only the son of
an Alsatian Jew named Wolf."

extraordinary attainments, a sort of super-man towering over the minor magicians of his day. Contemporaries, however, take him less seriously and represent him rather as an expert charlatan whom the wits of the *salons* made the butt of pleasantries. His principal importance to the subject of this book consists, however, in his influence on the secret societies. According to the *Mémoires authentiques pour servir à l'histoire du Comte de Cagliostro,* Saint-Germain was the " Grand Master of Freemasonry,"[1] and it was he who initiated Cagliostro into the mysteries of Egyptian masonry.

Joseph Balsamo, born in 1743, who assumed the name of Comte de Cagliostro, as a magician far eclipsed his master. Like Saint-Germain, he was generally reputed to be a Jew— the son of Pietro Balsamo, a Sicilian tradesman of Jewish origin[2]—and he made no secret of his arden admiration for the Jewish race. After the death of his parents he escaped from the monastery in which he had been placed at Palermo and joined himself to a man known as Altotas, said to have been an Armenian, with whom he travelled to Greece and Egypt.[3] Cagliostro's travels later took him to Poland and Germany, where he was initiated into Freemasonry,[4] and finally to France; but it was in England that he himself declared that he elaborated his famous " Egyptian Rite," which he founded officially in 1782. According to his own account, this rite was derived from a manuscript by a certain George Cofton—whose identity has never been discovered—which he bought by chance in London.[5] Yarker, however, expresses the opinion that " the rite of Cagliostro was clearly that of Pasqually,"', and that if he acquired it from a manuscript in London it would indicate that Pasquilly had disciples in that city. A far more probable explanation is that Cagliostro derived his Egyptian masonry from the same source as that on which Pasqually had drawn for his Order of Martinistes, namely the Cabala, and that it was not from a single manuscript but from an eminent Jewish Cabalist in London that he took his instructions. Who this may have been we shall soon see. At any rate, in a contemporary account of Cagliostro we find him described as " a doctor initiated into Cabalistic

[1] *Nouvelle Biographie Générale,* article on Saint-Germain.
[2] Frederick Bülau, *Geheime Geschichten und räthselhafte Menschen,* I. 311 (1850); Eckert, *La Franc-Maçonnerie dans sa véritable signification,* II. 80, quoting Lening's *Encyclopédie des Franc-Maçons.*
[3] Lecouteulx de Canteleu, op. cit., pp. 171, 172.
[4] Clavel, *Histoire pittoresque,* p. 175.
[5] Ibid., p. 175.

art " and a Rose-Croix; but after founding his own rite he
acquired the name of Grand Copht, that is to say, Supreme
Head of Egyptian Masonry, a new branch that he wished to
graft on to old European Freemasonry.[1] We shall return to
his further masonic adventures later.

In a superior category to Saint-German and Cagliostro was
the famous Swabian doctor Mesmer, who has given his name
to an important branch of natural science. In about 1780
Mesmer announced his great discovery of " animal magnetism,
the principle of life in all organized beings, the soul of all that
breathes." But if to-day Mesmerism has come to be regarded
as almost synonymous with hypnotism and in no way a branch
of occultism, Mesmer himself—stirring the fluid in his magic
bucket, around which his disciples wept, slept, fell into trances
or convulsions, raved or prophesied[2]—earned not unnaturally
the reputation of a charlatan. The Freemasons, eager to discover the secret of the magic bucket, hastened to enrol him
in their Order, and Mesmer was received into the Primitive
Rite of Free and Accepted Masons in 1785.[3]

Space forbids a description of the minor magicians who
flourished at this period—of *Schroeder,* founder in 1776 of a
chapter of " True and Ancient Rose-Croix Masons," practising
certain magical, theosophical, and alchemical degrees; of
Gassner, worker of miracles in the neighbourhood of Ratis-
bonne; of " the Jew Leon," one of a band of charlatans who
made large sums of money with magic mirrors in which the
imaginative were able to see their absent friends, and who
was finally banished from France by the police,—all these and
many others exploited the credulity and curiosity of the upper
classes both in France and Germany between the years of
1740 and 1790. De Luchet, writing before the French Revolution, describes the part played in their mysteries by the soul
of a Cabalistic Jew named Gablidone who had lived before
Christ, and who predicted that " in the year 1800 there will
be, on our globe, a very remarkable revolution, and there will
be no other religion but that of the patriarchs."[4]

How are we to account for this extraordinary wave of
Cabalism in Western Europe? By whom was it inspired?
If, as Jewish writers assure us, neither Martines Pasqually,
Saint-Germain, Cagliostro, nor any of the visible occultists

[1] Figuier, *Histoire du Merveilleux,* IV. 9-11 (1860).
[2] Mounier, *De l'influence attribuée,* etc., p. 140.
[3] Benjamin Fabre, *Franciscus eques a Capite Galeato,* p. 24.
[4] De Luchet, *Essai sur la Secte des Illuminés* (1792 edition), p. 234.

or magicians were Jews, the problem only becomes the more insoluble. We cannot believe that Sanhedrims, Hebrew hieroglyphics, the contemplation of the Tetragrammaton, and other Cabalistic rites originated in the brains of French and German aristocrats, philosophers, and Freemasons. Let us turn, then, to events taking place at this moment in the world of Jewry and see whether these may provide some clue.

8

THE JEWISH CABALISTS

IT has been shown in the preceding chapters that the Jewish Cabala played an important part in the occult and anti-Christian sects from the very beginning of the Christian era. The time has now come to enquire what part Jewish influence played meanwhile in revolutions. Merely to ask the question is to bring on oneself the accusation of " anti-Semitism," yet the Jewish writer Bernard Lazare has shown the falseness of this charge:

> This [he writes] is what must separate the impartial historian from anti-Semitism. The anti-Semite says: "The Jew is the preparer, the machinator, the chief engineer of revolutions"; the impartial historian confines himself to studying the part which the Jew, considering his spirit, his character, the nature of his philosophy, and his religion, may have taken in revolutionary processes and movements.[1]

Lazare himself expresses the opinion, however, that—

> The complaint of the anti-Semites seems to be founded: the Jew has the revolutionary spirit; consciously or not he is an agent of revolution. Yet the complaint complicates itself, for anti-Semitism accuses the Jews of being the cause of revolutions. Let us examine what this accusation is worth. . . .[2]

In the light of our present knowledge it would certainly be absurd to ascribe to the Jews the authorship of the conspiracy of Catiline or of the Gracchi, the rising of Jack Straw and Wat Tyler, Jack Cade's rebellion, the *jacqueries* of France, or the Peasants' Wars in Germany, although historical research may lead in time to the discovery of certain occult influences —not necessarily Jewish—behind the European insurrections here referred to. Moreover, apart from grievances or other

---

[1] *L'Antisémitisme*, p. 335.
[2] Ibid., p. 328.

causes of rebellion, the revolutionary spirit has always existed independently of the Jews. In all times and in all countries there have been men born to make trouble as the sparks fly upward.

Nevertheless, in modern revolutions the part played by the Jews cannot be ignored, and the influence they have exercised will be seen on examination to have been twofold—financial and occult. Throughout the Middle Ages it is as sorcerers and usurers that they incur the reproaches of the Christian world, and it is still in the same rôle, under the more modern terms of magicians and loan-mongers, that we detect their presence behind the scenes of revolution from the seventeenth century onward. Wherever money was to be made out of social or political upheavals, wealthy Jews have been found to back the winning side; and wherever the Christian races have turned against their own institutions, Jewish Rabbis, philosophers, professors, and occultists have lent them their support. It was not then necessarily that Jews created these movements, but they knew how to make use of them for their own ends.

It is thus that in the Great Rebellion we find them not amongst the Ironsides of Cromwell or the members of his State Council, but furnishing money and information to the insurgents, acting as army contractors, loan-mongers, and super-spies—or to use the more euphonious term of Mr. Lucien Wolf, as " political intelligencers " of extraordinary efficiency. Thus Mr. Lucien Wolf, in referring to Carvajal, " the great Jew of the Commonwealth," explains that " the wide ramifications of his commercial transactions and his relations with other Crypto-Jews all over the world placed him in an unrivalled position to obtain news of the enemies of the Commonwealth."[1]

It is obvious that a " secret service " of this kind rendered the Jews a formidable hidden power, the more so since their very existence was frequently unknown to the rest of the population around them. This precaution was necessary because Jews were not supposed to exist at that date in England. In 1290 Edward I had expelled them all, and for three and a half centuries they had remained in exile; the Crypto-Jews

[1] Article by Mr. Lucien Wolf, " The First English Jew," in *Transactions of the Jewish Historical Society of England,* Vol. II. p. 18. On this question see also the pamphlets by Mr. Lucien Wolf: *Crypto-Jews under the Commonwealth* (1894), Cromwell's *Jewish Intelligencers* (1891), and *Manasseh ben Israel's Mission to Oliver Cromwell* (1901), also articles on Cromwell, Carvajal, and Manasseh ben Israel in the *Jewish Encyclopædia.*

or Marranos who had come over from Spain contrived, however, to remain in the country by skilfully taking the colour of their surroundings. Mr. Wolf goes on to observe that Jewish services were regularly held in the secret Synagogue, but " in public Carvajal and his friends followed the practice of the secret Jews in Spain and Portugal, passing as Roman Catholics and regularly attending mass in the Spanish Ambassador's chapel."[1] But when war between England and Spain rendered this expedient inadvisable, the Marranos threw off the disguise of Christianity and proclaimed themselves followers of the Jewish faith.

Now, just at this period the Messianic era was generally believed by the Jews to be approaching, and it appears to have occurred to them that Cromwell might be fitted to the part. Consequently emissaries were despatched to search the archives of Cambridge in order to discover whether the Protector could possibly be of Jewish descent.[2] This quest proving fruitless, the Cabalist Rabbi of Amsterdam, Manasseh ben Israel,[3] addressed a petition to Cromwell for the readmission of the Jews to England, in which he adroitly insisted on the retribution that overtakes those who afflict the people of Israel and the rewards that await those who " cherish " them. These arguments were not without effect on Cromwell, who entertained the same superstition, and although he is said to have declined the Jews' offer to buy St. Paul's Cathedral and the Bodleian Library because he considered the £500,000 they offered inadequate,[4] he exerted every effort to obtain their readmission to the country. In this he encountered violent opposition, and it seems that Jews were not permitted to return in large numbers, or at any rate to enjoy full rights and privileges, until after the accession of Charles II, who in his turn had enlisted their financial aid.[5] Later, in 1688, the

[1] Lucien Wolf, " The First English Jew," in *Transactions of the Jewish Historical Society of England*, II. 20.

[2] Tovey, *Anglia Judaica*, p. 275.

[3] The *Jewish Encyclopædia*, in its article on Manasseh ben Israel, says: " He was full of cabalistic opinions, though he was careful not to expound them in those of his works that were written in modern languages and intended to be read by Gentiles." In its article on " Magic " the *Jewish Encyclopædia* refers to the " Nishmat Hayyim," a work by Manasseh ben Israel which " is filled with superstition and magic " and adds that " many Christian scholars were deluded."

[4] Tovey, *Anglia Judaica*, p. 259; Margoliouth, *History of the Jews in England*, II. 3.

[5] Mirabeau (*Sur la Réforme politique des Juifs*, 1787) thinks they may not have been allowed to return unconditionally until 1664. It was certainly at this date that they were formally granted free permission to live in England and practice their religion (Margoliouth, op. cit., II. 26).

Jews of Amsterdam helped with their credit the expedition of William of Orange against James II; the former in return brought many Jews with him to England. So a Jewish writer is able to boast that "a Monarch reigned who was indebted to Hebrew gold for his royal diadem."[1]

In all this it is impossible to follow any consecutive political plan; the rôle of the Jews seems to have been to support no cause consistently but to obtain a footing in every camp, to back any venture that offered a chance of profit. Yet mingled with these material designs were still their ancient Messianic dreams. It is curious to note that the same Messianic idea pervaded the Levellers, the rebels of the Commonwealth; such phrases as " Let Israel go free," " Israel's restoration is now beginning," recur frequently in the literature of the sect. Gerard Winstanley, one of the two principal leaders, addressed an epistle to " the Twelve Tribes of Israel that are circumcised in heart and scattered through all the Nations of the Earth," and promised them " David their King that they have been waiting for." The other leader of the movement, by name Everard, in fact declared, when summoned before the Lord Fairfax at Whitehall, that " he was of the race of the Jews."[2] It is true that the Levellers were by profession Christian, but after the manner of the Bavarian Illuminati and of the Christian Socialists two centuries later, claiming Christ as the author of their Communistic and equalitarian doctrines: " For Jesus Christ, the Saviour of all Men, is the greatest, first, and truest Leveller that ever was spoken of in the world." The Levellers are said to have derived originally from the German Anabaptists; but Claudio Jannet, quoting German authorities, shows that there were Jews amongst the Anabaptists. " They were carried away by their hatred of the name of Christian and imagined that their dreams of the restoration of the kingdom of Israel would be realized amidst the conflagration."[3] Whether this was so or not, it is clear that by the middle of the seventeenth century the mystical ideas of Judaism had penetrated into all parts of Europe. Was there then some Cabalistic centre from which they radiated? Let us turn our eyes eastward and we shall see.

Since the sixteenth century the great mass of Jewry had settled in Poland, and a succession of miracle-workers known

---

[1] Margoliouth, op. cit., II. 43.
[2] *The Digger Movement in the Days of the Commonwealth*, by Lewis H. Berens, pp. 36, 74, 76, 98, 141 (1906).
[3] Claudio Jannet, *Les Précurseurs de la Franc-Maçonnerie*, p. 47 (1187).

by the name of Zaddikim or Ba'al Shems had arisen. The latter word, which signifies " Master of the Name," originated with the German Polish Jews and was derived from the Cabalistic belief in the miraculous use of the sacred name of Jehovah, known as the Tetragrammaton.

According to Cabalistic traditions, certain Jews of peculiar sanctity or knowledge were able with impunity to make use of the Divine Name. A Ba'al Shem was therefore one who had acquired this power and employed it in writing amulets, invoking spirits, and prescribing cures for various diseases. Poland and particularly Podolia—which had not yet been ceded to Russia—became thus a centre of Cabalism where a series of extraordinary movements of a mystical kind followed each other. In 1666, when the Messianic era was still believed to be approaching, the whole Jewish world was convulsed by the sudden appearance of Shabbethai Zebi, the son of a poulterer in Smyrna named Mordecai, who proclaimed himself the promised Messiah and rallied to his support a huge following not only amongst the Jews of Palestine, Egypt, and Eastern Europe, but even the hard-headed Jews of the Continental bourses.[1] Samuel Pepys in his Diary refers to the bets made amongst the Jews in London on the chances of " a certain person now in Smyrna " being acclaimed King of the World and the true Messiah.[2]

Shabbethai, who was an expert Cabalist and had the temerity to utter the Ineffable Name Jehovah, was said to be possessed of marvellous powers, his skin exuded exquisite perfume, he indulged perpetually in sea-bathing and lived in a state of chronic ecstasy. The pretensions of Shabbethai, who took the title of " King of the Kings of the Earth," split Jewry in two; many Rabbis launched imprecations against him, and those who had believed in him were bitterly disillusioned when, challenged by the Sultan to prove his claim to be the Messiah by allowing poisoned arrows to be shot at him, he suddenly renounced the Jewish faith and proclaimed himself a Mohammedan. His conversion, however, appeared to be only partial, for " at times he would assume the rôle of a pious Mohammedan and revile Judaism; at others he would enter into relations with Jews as one of their own faith."[3] By this means he retained the allegiance both of Moslems and of Jews. But the Rabbis, alarmed for the cause of Judaism, succeeded in

---

[1] *Harmsworth Encyclopædia*, article on Jews.
[2] *Diary of Samuel Pepys*, date of February 19, 1666.
[3] *Jewish Encyclopædia*, article on Shabbethai Zebi B. Mordecai.

obtaining his incarceration by the Sultan in a castle near Belgrade, where he died of colic in 1676.[1]

This prosaic ending to the career of the Messiah did not, however, altogether extinguish the enthusiasm of his followers, and the Shabbethan movement continued into the next century. In Poland Cabalism broke out with renewed energy; fresh Zaddikim and Ba'al Shems arose, the most noted of these being Israel of Podolia, known as Ba'al Shem Tob, or by the initial letters of this name, Besht, who founded his sect of Hasidim in 1740.

Besht, whilst opposing bigoted Rabbinism and claiming the Zohar as his inspiration, did not, however, adhere strictly to the doctrine of the Cabala that the universe was an emanation of God, but evolved a form of Pantheism, declaring that the whole universe was God, that even evil exists in God since evil is not bad in itself but only in its relation to Man; sin therefore has no positive existence.[2] As a result the followers of Besht, calling themselves the " New Saints," and at his death numbering no less than 40,000, threw aside not only the precepts of the Talmud, but all the restraints of morality and even decency.[3]

Another Ba'al Shem of the same period was Heilprin, alias Joel Ben Uri of Satanov, who, like Israel of Podolia, professed to perform miracles by the use of the Divine Name and collected around him many pupils, who, on the death of their master, " formed a band of charlatans and shamelessly exploited the credulity of their contemporaries."[4]

But the most important of these Cabalistic groups was that of the Frankists, who were sometimes known as the Zoharists or the Illuminated,[5] from their adherence to the Zohar or book of Light, or in their birthplace Podolia as the Shabbethan Zebists, from their allegiance to the false Messiah of the preceding century—a heresy that had been " kept alive in secret circles which had something akin to a masonic organization."[6] The founder of this sect was Jacob Frank, a brandy distiller profoundly versed in the doctrines of the Cabala, who in 1755 collected around him a large following in Podolia and lived in a style of oriental magnificence, maintained by vast wealth

[1] Henry Hart Milman, *History of the Jews* (Everyman's Library), Vol. II. p. 445.

[2] *Jewish Encyclopædia*, article on Ba'al Shem Tob.

[3] Milman, op. cit., II. 446.

[4] *Jewish Encyclopædia*, article on Heilprin, Joel Ben Uri.

[5] Heckethorn, *Secret Societies*, I. 87.

[6] *Jewish Encyclopædia*, article on Jacob Frank.

of which no one ever discovered the source. The persecution to which he was subjected by the Rabbis led the Catholic clergy to champion his cause, whereupon Frank threw himself on the mercy of the Bishop of Kaminick, and publicly burnt the Talmud, declaring that he recognized only the Zohar, which, he alleged, admitted the doctrine of the Trinity. Thus the Zoharists "claimed that they regarded the Messiah-Deliverer as one of the three divinities, but failed to state that by the Messiah they meant Shabbethai Zebi."[1] The Bishop was apparently deceived by this manœuvre, and in 1759 the Zoharites declared themselves converted to Christianity, and were baptized, including Frank himself, who took the name of Joseph. " The insincerity of the Frankists soon became apparent, however, for they continued to inter-marry only among themselves and held Frank in reverence, calling him ' The Holy Master.' "[2] It soon became evident that, whilst openly embracing the Catholic faith, they had in reality retained their secret Judaism.[3] Moreover, it was discovered that Frank endeavoured to pass as a Mohammedan in Turkey; " he was therefore arrested in Warsaw and delivered to the Church tribunal on the charge of feigned conversion to Christianity and the spreading of a pernicious heresy."[4] Unlike his predecessor in apostasy, Shabbethai Zebi, Frank, however, came to no untimely end, but after his release from prison continued to prey on the credulity of Christians and frequently travelled to Vienna with his daughter, Eve, who succeeded in duping the pious Maria Theresa. But here also " the sectarian plans of Frank were found out,"[5] and he was obliged to leave Austria. Finally he settled at Offenbach and supported by liberal subsidies from the other Jews, he resumed his former splendour[6]

with a retinue of several hundred beautiful Jewish youth of both sexes; carts containing treasure were reported to be perpetually brought in to him, chiefly from Poland—he went out daily in great state to perform his devotions in the open field—he rode in a chariot drawn by noble horses; ten or twelve Hulans in red or green uniform, glittering with gold, by his side, with pikes in their hands and crests

[1] *Jewish Encyclopædia*, article on Jacob Frank.
[2] Ibid.
[3] Milman, op. cit., II. 447.
[4] *Jewish Encyclopædia*, article on Jacob Frank.
[5] Ibid.
[6] Ibid.: Heckethorn. *Secret Societies*, I. 87.

on their caps, eagles, or stags, or the sun and moon. . . . His followers believed him immortal, but in 1791 he died; his burial was as splendid as his mode of living—800 persons followed him to the grave.[1]

Now, it is impossible to study the careers of these magicians in Poland and Germany without being reminded of their counterparts in France. The family likeness between the "Baron von Offenbach," the "Comte de Saint-Germain" and the "Comte de Cagliostro" is at once apparent. All claimed to perform miracles, all lived with extraordinary magnificence on wealth derived from an unknown source, one was certainly a Jew, the other two were believed to be Jews, and all were known to be Cabalists. Moreover, all three spent many years in Germany, and it was whilst Frank was living as Baron von Offenbach close to Frankfurt that Cagliostro was received into the Order of the Stricte Observance in a subterranean chamber a few miles from that city. Earlier in his career he was known to have visited Poland, whence Frank derived. Are we to believe that all these men, so strangely alike in their careers, living at the same time and in the same places, were totally unconnected? It is a mere coincidence that this group of Jewish Cabalist miracle-workers should have existed in Germany and Poland at the precise moment that the Cabalist magicians sprang up in France? Is it again a coincidence that Martines Pasqually founded his "Kabbalistic sect" of Illuminés in 1754 and Jacob Frank his sect of Zoharites (or Illuminated) in 1755?

Moreover, when we know from purely Jewish sources that the Ba'al Shem Heilprin had many pupils "who formed a band of charlatans who shamelessly exploited the credulity of their contemporaries," that the Ba'al Shem Tob and Jacob Frank both had large followings, it is surely here that we may find the origin of those mysterious magicians who spread themselves over Europe at this date.

It will at once be asked: "But what proof is there that any one of these Ba'al Shems or Cabalists was connected with masonic or secret societies?" The answer is that the most important Ba'al Shem of the day, known as "the Chief of all the Jews," is shown by documentary evidence to have been

---

[1] Milman, op. cit., II. 448. Cf. description of pomp displayed by another member of the oppressed race named Fränkel, who appeared at a parade of Jewry at Prague in 1741 in a carriage drawn by six horses and surrounded by footmen and horseguards.—*Jewish Encyclopædia*, article on Fränkel, Simon Wolf.

an initiate of Freemasonry and in direct contact with the leaders of the secret societies. If then it is agreed that neither Saint-Germain nor Cagliostro can be proved to have been Jews, here we have a man concerned in the movement, more important than either, whose nationality admits of no doubt whatever.

This extraordinary personage, known as the " Ba'al Shem of London," was a Cabalistic Jew named Hayyim Samuel Jacob Falk, also called Dr. Falk, Falc, de Falk, or Falkon, born in 1708, probably in Podolia. The further fact that he was regarded by his fellow-Jews as an adherent of the Messiah Shabbethai Zebi clearly shows his connexion with the Podolian Zoharites. Falk was thus not an isolated phenomenon, but a member of one of the groups described in the foregoing pages. The following is a summary of the account given of the Ba'al Shem of London in the *Jewish Encyclopædia*:

Falk claimed to possess thaumaturgic powers and to be able to discover hidden treasure. Archenholz (*England und Italien,* I. 249) recounts certain marvels which he had seen performed by Falk in Brunswick and which he attributes to a special knowledge of chemistry. In Westphalia at one time Falk was sentenced to be burned as a sorcerer, but escaped to England. Here he was received with hospitality and rapidly gained fame as a Cabalist and worker of miracles. Many stories of his powers were current. He would cause a small taper to remain alight for weeks; an incantation would fill his cellar with coal; plate left with a pawnbroker would glide back into his house. When a fire threatened to destroy the Great Synagogue, he averted the disaster by writing four Hebrew letters on the pillars of the door.[1] [Obviously the Tetragrammaton.]

On his arrival in London in 1742 Falk appeared to be without means, but soon after he was seen to be in possession of considerable wealth, living in a comfortable house in Wellclose Square, where he had his private synagogue, whilst gold and silver plate adorned his table. His Journal, still preserved in the library of the United Synagogue, contains references to

[1] *Jewish Encyclopædia*, article on Falk, of whom a good portrait by Copley is given. On Falk see also *Ars Quatuor Coronatorum*, Vol. XXVI. Part I. pp. 98-105, and Vol. XXX. Part II; *Transactions of the Jewish Historical Society*, Vol. V. p. 148, article on " The Ba'al Shem of London," by the Rev. Dr. H. Adler, Chief Rabbi, and Vol. VIII, " Notes on some Contemporary References to Dr. Falk, the Ba'al Shem of London, in the Rainsford MSS. at the British Museum," by Gordon P. G. Hills. The following pages are taken entirely from these sources.

"mysterious journeyings" to and from Epping Forest, to meetings, a meeting-chamber in the forest, and chests of gold there buried. It was said that on one occasion when he was driving thither along Whitechapel Road, a back wheel of his carriage came off, which alarmed the coachman, but Falk ordered him to drive on and the wheel followed the carriage all the way to the forest.

The stories of Falk's miraculous powers are too numerous to relate here, but a letter written by an enthusiastic Jewish admirer, Sussman Shesnowzi, to his son in Poland will serve to show the reputation he enjoyed:

Hear, my beloved son, of the marvellous gifts entrusted to a son of man, who verily is not a man, a light of the captivity . . . a holy light, a saintly man . . . who dwells at present in the great city of London. Albeit I could not fully understand him on account of his volubility and his speaking as an inhabitant of Jerusalem. . . . His chamber is lighted by silver candlesticks on the walls, with a central eight-branched lamp made of pure silver of beaten work. And albeit it contained oil to burn a day and a night it remained enkindled for three weeks. On one occasion he abode in seclusion in his house for six weeks without meat and drink. When at the conclusion of this period ten persons were summoned to enter, they found him seated on a sort of throne, his head covered with a golden turban, a golden chain round his neck with a pendant silver star on which sacred names were inscribed. Verily this man stands alone in his generation by reason of his knowledge of holy mysteries. I cannot recount to you all the wonders he accomplishes. I am grateful, in that I am found worthy to be received among those who dwell within the shadow of his wisdom. . . . I know that many will believe my words, but others, who do not occupy themselves with mysteries, will laugh thereat. Therefore, my son, be very circumspect, and show this only to wise and discreet men. For here in London this matter has not been disclosed to anyone who does not belong to our Brotherhood.

The esteem in which Falk was held by the Jewish community, including the Chief Rabbi and the Rabbi of the new Synagogue, appears to have roused the resentment of his co-religionist Emden, who denounced him as a follower of the false Messiah and an exploiter of Christian credulity.

Falk [he wrote in a letter to Poland] had made his position by his pretence to be an adept in practical Cabala, by which means he professed to be able to discover hidden treasures; by his pretensions he had entrapped a wealthy captain whose fortune he had cheated him out of, so that he was reduced to depending on the

Rabbi's charity, and yet, despite this, wealthy Christians spend their money on him, whilst Falk spends his bounty on the men of his Brotherhood so that they may spread his fame.

In general Falk appears to have displayed extreme caution in his relations with Christian seekers after occult knowledge, for the *Jewish Encyclopædia* goes on to say: "Archenholz mentions a royal prince who applied to Falk in his quest for the philosopher's stone, but was denied admittance." Nevertheless Hayyum Azulai mentions (Ma'gal Tob, p. 13*b*):

That when in Paris in 1778 he was told by the Marchesa de Crona that the Ba'al Shem of London had taught her the Cabala. Falk seems also to have been on intimate terms with that strange adventurer Baron Theodor de Neuhoff. . . . Falk's principal friends were the London bankers Aaron Goldsmid and his son.[1] Pawnbroking and successful speculation enabled him to acquire a considerable fortune. He left large sums of money to charity, and the overseers of the United Synagogue in London still distribute annually certain payments left by him for the poor.

Nothing of all this would lead one to suppose that Falk could be regarded in the light of a black magician; it is therefore surprising to find Dr. Adler observing that a horrible account of a Jewish Cabalist in *The Gentleman's Magazine* for September 1762 "obviously refers to Dr. Falk, though his name is not mentioned."[2] This man is described as "a christened Jew and the biggest rogue and villain in all the world," who "had been imprisoned everywhere and banished out of all countries in Germany, and also sometimes publicly whipped, so that his back lost all the old skin, and became new again, and yet left never off from his villainies, but grew always worse." The writer goes on to relate that the Cabalist offered to teach him certain mysteries, but explained that before

---

[1] Falk does not appear to have brought good fortune to the Goldsmid family, for Margoliouth in a passage which evidently relates to Falk says that, according to Jewish legend, the suicide of Abraham Goldsmid and his brother was attributed to the following cause: "A Ba'al Shem, an operative Cabalist, in other words a thaumaturgos and prophet, used to live with the father of the Goldsmids. On his death-bed he summoned the patriarch Goldsmid, and delivered into his hands a box, which he strictly enjoined should not be opened till a certain period which the Ba'al Shem specified, and in case of disobedience a torrent of fearful calamities would overwhelm the Goldsmids. The patriarch's curiosity was not aroused for some time; but in a few years after the Ba'al Shem's death, Goldsmid, the aged, half sceptic, half curious, forced open the fatal box, and then the Goldsmids began to learn what it was to disbelieve the words of a Ba'al Shem."— Margoliouth, *History of the Jews*, II. 144.

[2] *Transactions of the Jewish Historical Society*, V. 162.

entering on any "experiments of the said godly mysteries, we must first avoid all churches and places of worshipping as unclean"; he then bound his initiate by a very strong oath and proceeded to tell him that he must steal a Hebrew Bible from a Protestant and also procure "one pound of blood out of the veins of an honest Protestant." The initiate thereupon robbed a Protestant of all his effects, but had himself bled of about three-quarters of a pound of blood, which he gave to the magician. He thus describes the ceremony that took place:

Then the next night about 11 o'clock, we both went into the garden of my own, and the cabalist put a cross, tainted with my blood, in each corner of the garden, and in the middle of the garden a threefold circle . . . in the first circle were written all the names of God in Hebrew; in the second all the names of the angels; and in the third the first chapter of the holy Gospel of St. John, and it was all written with my blood.

The cruelties then performed by the Cabalist on a he-goat are too loathsome to transcribe. The whole story, indeed, appears a farrago of nonsense and would not be worth quoting but for the fact that it appears to be taken seriously by Dr. Adler as a description of the great Ba'al Shem.

The death of Falk took place on April 17, 1782, and the epitaph on his grave in the cemetery at Globe Road, Mile End, "bears witness to his excellencies and orthodoxy": "Here is interred . . . the aged and honourable man, a great personage who came from the East, an accomplished sage, an adept in Cabbalah. . . . His name was known to the ends of the earth and distant isles," etc.

This then is surely the portrait of a most remarkable personage, a man known for his powers in England, France, and Germany, visited by a royal prince in search of the philosopher's stone, and acclaimed by one of his own race as standing alone in his generation by reason of his knowledge, yet whilst Saint-Germain and Cagliostro figure in every account of eighteenth-century magicians, it is only in exclusively Judaic or masonic works, not intended for the general public, that we shall find any reference to Falk. Have we not here striking evidence of the truth of M. André Baron's dictum: "Remember that the constant rule of the secret societies is that the real authors never show themselves"?

It will now be asked: what proof is there that Falk is

connected with any masonic or secret societies? True, in the accounts given by the *Jewish Encyclopædia,* the word Freemasonry is not once mentioned. But in the curious portrait of the great Ba'al Shem appended, we see him holding in his hand the pair of compasses, and before him, on the table at which he is seated, the double triangle or Seal of Solomon known amongst Jews as " the Shield of David," which forms an important emblem in Masonry.

Moreover, it is significant to find in the *Royal Masonic Encyclopædia* by the Rosicrucian Kenneth Mackenzie that a long and detailed article is devoted to Falk, though again without any reference to his connexion with Freemasonry. May we not conclude that in certain inner masonic circles the importance of Falk is recognized but must not be revealed to the uninitiated? Mr. Gordon Hills, in the above-quoted paper contributed to the *Ars Quatuor Coronatorum,* indulges in some innocent speculation as to the part Falk may have played in the masonic movement. " If," he observes, " Jewish Brethren did introduce Cabalistical learning into the so-called High Degrees, here we have one, who, if a Mason, would have been eminently qualified to do so."

Falk inded was far more than a Mason, he was a high initiate—the supreme oracle to which the secret societies applied for guidance. All this was disclosed a few years ago in the correspondence between Savalette de Langes and the Marquis de Chefdebien referred to in the previous chapter. Thus in the *dossiers* of the leading occultists supplied by Savalette we find the following note on the Ba'al Shem of London:

This Doctor Falk is known to many Germans. He is a very extraordinary man from every point of view. Some people believe him to be the Chief of all the Jews and attribute to purely political schemes all that is marvellous and singular in his life and conduct. He is referred to in a very curious manner, and as a Rose-Croix in the *Memoirs of the Chevalier de Rampsow* (i.e. Rentzov). He has had adventures with the Maréchal de Richelieu, great seeker of the Philosophers' Stone. He had a strange history with the Prince de Rohan Guéménée and the Chevalier de Luxembourg relating to Louis XV, whose death he foretold. He is almost inaccessible. In all the sects of savants in secret sciences he passes as a superior man. He is at present in England. The Baron de Gleichen can give good information about him. Try to get more at Frankfurt.[1]

[1] Benjamin Fabre, *Eques a Capite Galeato,* p. 84.

Again, in notes on other personages the name of Falk recurs with the same insistence on his importance as a high initiate:

Leman, pupil of Falk. . . .

The Baron de Gleichen . . . intimately connected with Wecter [Waechter] and Wakenfeldt. . . . He knows Falk. . . .

The Baron de Waldenfels . . . is, according to what I know from the Baron de Gleichen, the princes of Darmstadt, . . . and others, the most interesting man for you and me to know. If we made his acquaintance, he could give us the best information on all the most interesting objects of instruction. He knows Falk and Wecter.

Prince Louis d'Harmstadt . . . is also a member of the Amis Réunis, 12° and in charge of the Directories. He worked in his youth with a Jew whom he believes to be taught by Falk. . . .[1]

Here, then, behind the organization of the Stricte Observance, of the Amis Réunis, and the Philalèthes, we catch a glimpse at last of one of those *real initiates* whose identity has been so carefully kept dark. For Falk, as we see in these notes, was not an isolated sage; he had pupils, and to be one of these was to be admitted to the inner mysteries. Was Cagliostro one of these adepts? Is it here we may seek the explanation of the " Egyptian Rite " devised by him in London, and of his chance discovery on a bookstall in that city of a Cabalistic document by the mysterious " George Cofton," whose identity has never been revealed? I would suggest that the whole story of the bookstall was a fable and that it was not from any manuscript, but from Falk, that Cagliostro received his directions. Thus Cagliostro's rite was in reality concealed Cabalism.

That Falk was only one of several Concealed Superiors is further suggested by the intriguing correspondence of Savalette de Langes. " Schroeder," we read, " had for his master an old man of Suabia," by whom the Baron de Waechter was also said to have been instructed in Masonry, and to have become one of the most important initiates of Germany. Accordingly de Waechter was despatched by his Order to Florence in order to make enquiries on further secrets and on certain famous treasures about which Schroepfer, the Baron de Hundt, and others, had heard that Aprosi, the secretary of the Pretender, could give them information. Waechter, however, wrote to say that all they had been told on the latter point was fabulous, but that he had met in Florence certain " Brothers of the

---

[1] Benjamin Fabre, op. cit., pp. 88, 90, 98, 110.

Holy Land," who had initiated him into marvellous secrets; one in particular who is described as "a man who is not a European" had "perfectly instructed him." Moreover, de Waechter, who had set forth poor, returned loaded with riches attributed by his fellow-masons to the "Asiatic Brethren" he had frequented in Florence who possessed the art of making gold.[1] I would suggest then that these were the members of the "Italian Order" referred to by Mr. Tuckett, which, like Schroepfer and de Hundt, he imagined to have been connected with the Jacobites.

But all these secret sources of instruction are wrapped in mystery. Whilst Saint-Germain and Cagliostro—who is referred to in this correspondence in terms of light derision—emerge into the limelight, the real initiates remain concealed in the background. Falk "is almost inaccessible!" Yet one more almost forgotten document of the period may throw some light on the important part he played behind the scenes in Masonry.

It may be remembered that Archenholz had spoken of certain marvels he had seen performed by Falk in Brunswick. Now, in 1770 the German poet Gotthold Ephraim Lessing was made librarian to the Duke of Brunswick in that city. The fame of Falk may then have reached his ears. At any rate in 1771 Lessing, after having mocked at Freemasonry, was initiated in a masonic lodge at Hamburg, and in 1778 he published not only his famous masonic drama *Nathan der Weise,* in which the Jew of Jerusalem is shown in admirable contrast to the Christians and Mohammedans, but he also wrote five dialogues on Freemasonry which he dedicated to the Duke of Brunswick, Grand Master of all the German Lodges, and which he entitled "*Ernst und Falk: Gespräche fur Freimaurer.*"[2]

Lessing's friendship with Moses Mendelssohn has led to the popular theory, unsupported however by any real evidence, that the Jewish philosopher of Berlin provided the inspiration for the character of Nathan, but might it not equally have been provided by the miracle-worker of Brunswick? However, in the case of the dialogues less room is left for doubt. Falk is mentioned by name and represented as initiated into the highest mysteries of Freemasonry. This is of course not explained by Lessing's commentators, who give no clue to

[1] Clavel, *Histoire pittoresque,* pp. 188, 390; Robison's *Proofs of a Conspiracy,* p. 77.
[2] *The Royal Masonic Cyclopædia* describes both *Nathan der Weise* and *Ernst und Falk* as prominent works on Masonry.

his identity.[1] It is evident that Lessing committed an enormous blunder in thus letting so important a cat out of the
bag, for after the publication of the first three dialogues and
whilst the last two were circulating privately in manuscript
amongst the Freemasons, an order from the Duke of Brunswick
forbade their publication as dangerous. In spite of this prohibition, the rest of the series was printed, however without
Lessing's permission, in 1870 with a preface by an unknown
person describing himself as a non-mason.

The dialogues between Ernst and Falk throw a curious light
on the influences at work behind Freemasonry at this period
and gain immensely in interest when the identity of the two
men in question is understood. Thus Ernst, by whom Lessing
evidently represents himself, is at the beginning not a Freemason, and, whilst sitting with Falk in a wood, questions the
high initiate on the aims of the Order. Falk explains that
Freemasonry has always existed, but not under this name.
Its real purpose has never been revealed. On the surface it
appears to be a purely philanthropic association, but in reality
philanthropy forms no part of its scheme, its object being to
bring about a state of things which will render philanthropy
unnecessary. (*Was man gemeinlich gute Thaten zu nennen
pflegt entbehrlich zu machen.*) As an illustration Falk points
to an ant-heap at the foot of the tree beneath which the two
men are seated. " Why," he asks, " should not human beings
exist without government like the ants or bees?" Falk then
goes on to describe his idea of a Universal State, or rather a
federation of States, in which men will no longer be divided
by national, social, or religious prejudices, and where greater
equality will exist.

At the end of the third dialogue an interval occurs during
which Ernst goes away and becomes a Freemason, but on his
return expresses his disappointment to Falk at finding many
Freemasons engaged in such futilities as alchemy or the evocation of spirits. Others again seek to revive the * * *.
Falk replies that although the great secrets of Freemasonry
cannot be revealed by any man even if he wished it, one

---

[1] There is, however, the possibility that Lessing may have had in mind
another Falk living at the same period; this was " John Frederick Falk,
born at Hamburg of Jewish parents, reported to have been head of a Cabalistic
College in London and to have died about 1824 " (*Tranactions of the Jewish
Historical Society*, VIII. 128). But in view of the part which the correspondence of Savalette de Langes shows the Ba'al Shem of London to have
played in the background of Freemasonry, it seems more probable that he
was the Falk in question. At any rate, both were Jews and Cabalists.

thing, however, has been kept dark which should now be made public, and this is the relationship between the Freemasons and the * * *. "The * * * were in fact the Freemasons of their time." It seems probable from the context and from Falk's references to Sir Christopher Wren as the founder of the modern Order, that the asterisks denote the Rosicrucians.

The most interesting point of these dialogues is, however, the hint continually thrown out by Falk that there is something behind Freemasonry, something far older and far wider in its aims than the Order now known by this name—the modern Freemasons are for the most part only " playing at it." Thus, when Ernst complains that true equality has not been attained in the lodges since Jews are not admitted, Falk observes that he himself does not attend them, that true Freemasonry does not exist in outward forms—" A lodge bears the same relation to Freemasonry as a church to belief." In other words, the real initiates do not appear upon the scene. Here then we see the rôle of the " Concealed Superiors." What wonder that Lessing's dialogues were considered too dangerous for publication!

Moreover, in Falk's conception of the ideal social order and his indictment of what he calls " bourgeois society " we find the clue to movements of immense importance. Has not the system of the ant-heap or the beehive proved, as I have pointed out elsewhere, the model on which modern Anarchists, from Proudhon onwards, have formed their schemes for the reorganization of human life? Has not the idea of the " World State," " The Universal Republic " become the war-cry of the Internationalist Socialists, the Grand Orient Masons, the Theosophists, and the world-revolutionaries of our own day?

Was Falk, then, a revolutionary? This again will be disputed. Falk may have been a Cabalist, a Freemason, a high initiate, but what proof is there that he had any connexion with the leaders of the French Revolution? Let us turn again to the *Jewish Encyclopædia*:

Falk . . . is . . . believed to have given the Duc d'Orléans, to ensure his succession to the throne, a talisman consisting of a ring, which Philippe Egalité before mounting the scaffold is said to have sent to a Jewess, Juliet Goudchaux, who passed it on to his son, subsequently Louis Philippe.

The Baron de Gleichen, who " knew Falc," refers to a talisman of lapis-lazuli which the Duc d'Orléans had received in England from "the celebrated Falk Scheck, first Rabbi of the Jews," and says that a certain occultist, Madame de la Croix, imagined she had destroyed it by "the power of prayer." But the theory of its survival is further confirmed by the information supplied from Jewish sources to Mr. Gordon Hills, who states that Falk was "in touch with the French Court in the person of ' Prince Emanuel,'[1] whom he describes as a servant of the King of France," and adds that the talismanic ring which he gave to the Duc d'Orléans "is still in the possession of the family, having passed to King Louis Philippe and thence to the Comte de Paris."[2]

One fact, then, looms out of the darkness that envelops the secret power behind the Orléanist conspiracy, one fact of supreme importance, and based moreover on purely Jewish evidence: the Duke was in touch with Falk when in London and Falk supported his scheme of usurpation. Thus behind the arch-conspirator of the revolution stood "the Chief of all the Jews." Is it here perhaps, in Falk's "chests of gold," that we might find the source of some of those loans raised in London by the Duc d'Orléans to finance the riots of the Revolution, so absurdly described as "l'or de Pitt"?

The direct connexion between the attack on the French monarchy and Jewish circles in London is further shown by the curious sequel to the Gordon Riots. In 1780 the half-witted Lord George Gordon (as a Jewish writer describes him), the head of the so-called "Protestant" mob, marched on the House of Commons to protest against the bill for the relief of Roman Catholic disabilities and then proceeded to carry out his plan of burning down London. During the five days' rioting that ensued, property to the amount of £180,000 was destroyed. After this "the scion of the ducal house of Gordon proved the durability of his love for Protestantism by professing the Hebrew faith," and was received with the highest honours into the Synagogue. The same Jewish writer, who has described him earlier as half-witted, quotes this panegyric on

---

[1] Who can this have been?

[2] The Duchesse de Gontaut relates in her *Mémoires* that the Duc d'Orléans was one day driving through the forest of Fontainebleau when a man, half clothed and with a demented air, sprang towards the carriage, grimacing horribly. The Duke's suite, taking him for a madman, would have kept him at bay, but the Duke, at that moment awaking from sleep, unbuttoned his shirt and showed his assailant an iron ring suspended round his neck. At this sight the man took to his heels and disappeared into the wood. The mystery of this incident was never elucidated, and the Duke, when questioned on the matter, would offer no explanation. Could this ring have been Falk's talisman?

his orthodoxy: " He was very regular in his Jewish observances; every morning he was seen with the philacteries between
his eyes, and opposite his heart. . . . His Saturday's bread was
baked according to the manner of the Jews, his wine was
Jewish, his meat was Jewish, and he was the best Jew in the
congregation of Israel." And it was immediately after his
conversion to Judaism that he published in *The Public
Advertiser* the libel against Marie Antoinette which brought
about his imprisonment in Newgate.[1]

Now we know that Lord George Gordon met Cagliostro in
London in 1786.[2] Is it not probable that the author of the
scurrilous pamphlet and the magician concerned in the attack
on the Queen's honour through the Affair of the Necklace—
one a Jew by profession, the other said to be a Jew by race—
may have had some connexion with Philippe Egalité's Jewish
supporter, the miracle worker of Wellclose Square?

But already a vaster genius than Falk or Cagliostro, than
Pasqually or Savalette de Langes, had arisen, who, gathering
into his hands the threads of all the conspiracies, was able to
weave them together into a gigantic scheme for the destruction
of France and of the world.

[1] Margoliouth, op. cit., II. 121-4. See also *Life of Lord George Gordon* by
Robert Watson (1795), pp. 71, 72.
[2] Friedrich Bülau, *Geheime Geschichten und räthselhafte Menschen*, I. 325
(1850). *The Public Advertiser*, Aug. 22, 24, 1786.

9

THE BAVARIAN ILLUMINATI

THE question of the system to which I shall henceforth refer simply as Illuminism is of such immense importance to an understanding of the modern revolutionary movement that, although I have already described it in detail in *World Revolution,* it is necessary to devote a further chapter to it here in order to answer the objections made against my former account of the Order and also to show its connexion with earlier secret societies.

Now, the main contentions of those writers who, either consciously or unconsciously, attempt to mislead the public on the true nature and real existence of Illuminism are:

Firstly, that the case against Illuminism rests solely on the works of Robison, and of Barruel and later Catholic authorities.

Secondly, that all these writers misinterpreted or misquoted the Illuminati, who should be judged only by their own works.

Thirdly, that in reality the Illuminati were perfectly innocuous and even praiseworthy.

Fourthly, that they are of no importance, since they ceased to exist in 1786.

In the present chapter I propose therefore to answer all these contentions in turn and at the same time to make further examination into the origins of the Order.

ORIGINS OF THE ILLUMINATI

That Weishaupt was not the originator of the system he named Illuminism will be already apparent to every reader of the present work; it has needed, in fact, all the foregoing chapters to trace the source of Weishaupt's doctrines throughout the history of the world. From these it will be evident that men aiming at the overthrow of the existing social order and of all accepted religion had existed from the earliest times, and that in the Cainites, the Carpocratians, the Manichæns,

196

the Batinis, the Fatimites, and the Karmathites many of Weishaupt's ideas had already been foreshadowed. To the Manichæans, in fact, the word " Illuminati " may be traced— " gloriantur Manichæi se de caelo illuminatos."[1]

It is in the sect of Abdu'lah ibn Maymūn that we must seek the model for Weishaupt's system of organization. Thus de Sacy has described in the following words the manner of enlisting proselytes by the Ismailis:

> They proceeded to the admission and initiation of new proselytes only by degrees and with great reserve; for, as the sect had at the same time a political object and ambitions, its interest was above all to have a great number of partisans in all places and in all classes of society. It was necessary therefore to suit themselves to the character, the temperament, and the prejudices of the greater number; what one revealed to some would have revolted others and alienated for ever spirits less bold and consciences more easily alarmed.[2]

This passage exactly describes the methods laid down by Weishaupt for his " Insinuating Brothers "—the necessity of proceeding with caution in the enlisting of adepts, of not revealing to the novice doctrines that might be likely to revolt him, of " speaking sometimes in one way, sometimes in another, so that one's real purpose should remain impenetrable " to members of the inferior grades.

How did these Oriental methods penetrate to the Bavarian professor? According to certain writers, through the Jesuits. The fact that Weishaupt had been brought up by this Order has provided the enemies of the Jesuits with the argument that they were the secret inspirers of the Illuminati. Mr. Gould, indeed, has attributed most of the errors of the latter to this source; Weishaupt, he writes, incurred " the implacable enmity of the Jesuits, to whose intrigues he was incessantly exposed."[3] In reality precisely the opposite was the case, for, as we shall see, it was Weishaupt who perpetually intrigued against the Jesuits. That Weishaupt did, however, draw to a certain extent on Jesuit methods of training is recognized even by Barruel, himself a Jesuit, who, quoting Mirabeau, says that Weishaupt " admired above all those laws, that *régime* of the Jesuits, which, under one head, made men dispersed over

[1] Barruel, Vol. III. p. xi., quoting Gaultier.
[2] Silvestre de Sacy, " Mémoires sur la Dynastie des Assassins," in *Mémoires de l'Institut Royal de France*, Vol. IV. (1818).
[3] *History of Freemasonry*, III. 121.

the universe tend towards the same goal; he felt that one could imitate their methods whilst holding views diametrically opposed."[1] And again, on the evidence of Mirabeau, de Luchet, and von Knigge, Barruel says elsewhere: " It is here that Weishaupt appears specially to have wished to assimilate the régime of the sect to that of the religious orders and, above all, that of the Jesuits, by the total abandonment of their own will and judgement which he demands of his adepts. . . ." But Barruel goes on to show " the enormous difference that is to be found between religious obedience and Illuminist obedience." In every religious order men know that the voice of their conscience and of their God is even more to be obeyed than that of their superiors.

There is not a single one who, in the event that his superiors should order him to do things contrary to the duties of a Christian or of a good man, would not see an exception to be made to the obedience which he has sworn. This exception is often expressed and always clearly announced in all religious institutions; it is above all formal and positively repeated many times in that of the Jesuits. They are ordered to obey their superiors, but it is in the event that they see no sin in obeying, *ubi non cerneretur peccatum* (*Constitution des Jésuites,* part 3, chapter 1, parag. 2, vol. i., édition de Prague).[2]

Indeed, implicit obedience and the total surrender of one's own will and judgement forms the foundation of all military discipline; "theirs not to reason why, theirs not to make reply" is everywhere recognized as the duty of soldiers. The Jesuits being in a sense a military Order, acknowledging a General at their head, are bound by the same obligation. Weishaupt's system was something totally different. For whilst all soldiers and all Jesuits, when obeying their superiors, are well aware of the goal towards which they are tending, Weishaupt's followers were enlisted by the most subtle methods of deception and led on towards a goal entirely unknown to them. It is this that, as we shall see later, constitutes the whole difference between honest and dishonest secret societies. The fact is that the accusation of Jesuit intrigue behind secret societies has emanated principally from the secret societies themselves and would appear to have been a device adopted by them to cover their own tracks. No good evidence has ever been brought forward in support of their contention. The

[1] *Mémoires sur le Jacobinisme* (edition of 1819), Vol. III. p. 9.
[2] Ibid., III. 55, 56.

Jesuits, unlike the Templars and the Illuminati, were simply suppressed in 1773 without the formality of a trial, and were therefore never given the opportunity to answer the charges brought against them, nor, as in the case of these other Orders, were their secret statutes—if any such existed—brought to light. The only document ever produced in proof of these accusations was the " Monita Secreta,"; long since shown to be a forgery. At any rate, the correspondence of the Illuminati provides their best exoneration. The Marquis de Luchet, who was no friend of the Jesuits, shows the absurdity of confounding their aims with those of either the Freemasons or the Illuminati, and describes all three as animated by wholly different purposes.[1]

In all these questions it is necessary to seek a motive. I have no personal interest in defending the Jesuits, but I ask: what motive could the Jesuits have in forming or supporting a conspiracy directed against all thrones and altars? It has been answered me that the Jesuits at this period cared nothing for thrones and altars, but only for temporal power; yet— even accepting this unwarrantable hypothesis—how was this power to be exercised except through thrones and altars? Was it not through princes and the Church that the Jesuits had been able to bring their influence to bear on affairs of state? In an irreligious Republic, as events afterwards proved, the power of the whole clergy was bound to be destroyed. The truth is then, that, far from abetting the Illuminati, the Jesuits were their most formidable opponents, the only body of men sufficiently learned, astute, and well organized to outwit the schemes of Weishaupt. In suppressing the Jesuits it is possible that the Old Régime removed the only barrier capable of resisting the tide of revolution.

Weishaupt indeed, as we know, detested the Jesuits,[2] and took from them only certain methods of discipline, of ensuring obedience or of acquiring influence over the minds of his disciples; his aims were entirely different.

Where, then, did Weishaupt find his immediate inspiration? It is here that Barruel and Lecouteulx de Canteleu provide a clue not to be discovered in other sources. In 1771, they relate, a certain Jutland merchant named Kölmer, who had spent many years in Egypt, returned to Europe in search of converts to a secret doctrine founded on Manichæism that he

[1] *Essai sur la Secte des Illuminés*, pp. 28-39.
[2] "Our worst enemies the Jesuits."—Letter from Spartacus, *Original-schriften*, p. 306.

had learnt in the East. On his way to France he stopped at Malta, where he met Cagliostro and nearly brought about an insurrection amongst the people. Kölmer was therefore driven out of the island by the Knights of Malta and betook himself to Avignon and Lyons. Here he made a few disciples amongst the Illuminés and in the same year went on to Germany, where he encountered Weishaupt and initiated him into all the mysteries of his secret doctrine. According to Barruel, Weishaupt then spent five years thinking out his system, which he founded under the name of Illuminati on May 1, 1776, and assumed the "illuminated" name of "Spartacus."

Kölmer remains the most mysterious of all the mystery men of his day; at first sight one is inclined to wonder whether he may not have been another of the Cabalistic Jews acting as the secret inspirers of the magicians who appeared in the limelight. The name Kölmer might easily have been a corruption of the well-known Jewish name Calmer. Lecouteulx de Canteleu, however, suggests that Kölmer was identical with Altotas, described by Figuier as "this universal genius, almost divine, of whom Cagliostro has spoken to us with so much respect and admiration. This Altotas was not an imaginary personage. The Inquisition of Rome has collected many proofs of his existence without having been able to discover when it began or ended, for Altotas disappears, or rather vanishes like a meteor, which, according to the poetic fancy of romancers, would authorize us in declaring him immortal."[1] It is curious to notice that modern occultists, whilst attributing so much importance to Saint-Germain and the legend of his immortality, make no mention of Altotas, who appears to have been a great deal more remarkable. But, again, we must remember: "It is the unvarying rule of secret societies that the real authors never show themselves." If, then, Kölmer was the same person as Altotas, he would appear not to have been a Jew or a Cabalist, but an initiate of some Near Eastern secret society—possibly an Ismaili. Lecouteulx de Canteleu describes Altotas as an Armenian, and says that his system was derived from those of Egypt, Syria, and Persia. This would accord with Barruel's statement that Kölmer came from Egypt, and that his ideas were founded on Manichæism.

It would be necessary to set these statements aside as only

---

[1] Figuier, *Histoire de Merveilleux*, IV. 77.

the theories of Barruel or Lecouteulx, were it not that the
writings of the Illuminati betray the influence of some sect
akin to Manichæism. Thus " Spartacus " writes to " Cato "
that he is thinking of "warming up the old system of the
Ghebers and Parsees,"[1] and it will be remembered that the
Ghebers were one of the sects in which Dozy relates that
Abdullah ibn Maymūn found his true supporters. Later
Weishaupt goes on to explain that—

The allegory in which the Mysteries and Higher Grades must be
clothed is Fire Worship and the whole philosophy of Zoroaster or
of the old Parsees who nowadays only remain in India; therefore
in the further degrees the Order is called "Fire Worship" (Feuer-
dienst), the "Fire Order," or the "Persian Order"—that is, something magnificent beyond all expectation.[2]

At the same time the Persian calendar was adopted by the
Illuminati.[3]

It is evident that this pretence of Zoroastrianism was as
pure humbug as Weishaupt's later pretence of Christianity;
of the true doctrines of Zoroaster he shows no conception—
nor does he insist further on the point; but the above passage
would certainly lend colour to the theory that his system was
partly founded on Manichæism, that is to say, on perverted
Zoroastrianism, imparted to him by a man from the East,
and that the methods of the Batinis and Fatimites may have
been communicated to him through the same channel.
Hence the extraordinary resemblance between his plan of
organization and that of Abdullah ibn Maymūn, which consisted in political intriguing rather than in esoteric speculation.
Thus in Weishaupt's system the phraseology of Judaism, the
Cabalistic legends of Freemasonry, the mystical imaginings
of the Martinistes, play at first no part at all. For all forms
of "theosophy," occultism, spiritualism, and magic Weishaupt
expresses nothing but contempt, and the Rose-Croix masons
are bracketed with the Jesuits by the Illuminati as enemies
it is necessary to outwit at every turn.[4] Consequently no

[1] *Originalschriften des Illuminatenordens*, p. 230.
[2] Ibid., p. 331.
[3] In *World Revolution* I suggested a resemblance between the Jewish
calendar and that of the Illuminati. This was an error; the Jewish calendar
was adopted by the Scottish Rite, which, as we have seen, derived partly
from Judaic sources.
[4] Thus Zwack (alias Cato) writes: "We have not only hindered the
enlistings of the Rose-Croix but rendered their very name contemptible."—
Originalschriften, p. 8.

degree of Rose-Croix finds a place in Weishaupt's system, as in all the other masonic orders of the day which drew their influence from Eastern or Cabalistic sources.

It is true that " Mysteries " play a great part in the phrase-ology of the Order—" Greater and Lesser Mysteries," borrowed from ancient Egypt—whilst the higher initiates are decorated with such titles as " Epopte " and " Hierophant," taken from the Eleusinian Mysteries. Yet Weishaupt's own theories appear to bear no relation whatever to these ancient cults. On the contrary, the more we penetrate into his system, the more apparent it becomes that all the formulas he employs which derive from any religious source—whether Persian, Egyptian, or Christian—merely serve to disguise a purely material pur-pose, a plan for destroying the existing order of society. Thus all that was really ancient in Illuminism was the destructive spirit that animated it and also the method of organization it had imported from the East. Illuminism therefore marks an entirely new departure in the history of European secret societies. Weishaupt himself indicates this as one of the great secrets of the Order. " Above all," he writes to " Cato " (alias Zwack), " guard the origin and the novelty of ⊙ in the most careful way."[1] " The greatest mystery," he says again, " must be that the thing is new; the fewer who know this the better. . . . Not one of the Eichstadters knows this but would live or die for it that the thing is as old as Methuselah."[2]

This pretence of having discovered some fund of ancient wisdom is the invariable ruse of secret society adepts; the one thing never admitted is the identity of the individuals from whom one is receiving direction. Weishaupt himself declares that he has got it all out of books by means of arduous and unremitting labour. " What it costs me to read, study, think, write, cross out, and re-write! " he complains to Marius and Cato.[3] Thus, according to Weishaupt the whole system is the work of his own unaided genius, and the supreme direc-tion remains in his hands alone. Again and again he insists on this point in his correspondence.

If this were indeed the case, Weishaupt—in view of the efficiency achieved by the Order—must have been a genius of the first water, and it is difficult to understand why so remarkable a man should not have distinguished himself on

<hr>

[1] *Originalschriften*, p. 363. The word Illuminism is always represented by this symbol in the correspondence of the Illuminati.
[2] Ibid., p. 202.
[3] Ibid., p. 331.

other lines, but have remained almost unknown to posterity. It would therefore appear possible that Weishaupt, although undoubtedly a man of immense organizing capacity and endowed with extraordinary subtlety, was not in reality the sole author of Illuminism, but one of a group, which, recognizing his talents and the value of his untiring activity, placed the direction in his hands. Let us examine this hypothesis in the light of a document which was unknown to me when I wrote my former account of the Illuminati.

Barruel has pointed out that the great error of Robison was to describe Illuminism as arising out of Freemasonry, since Weishaupt did not become a Freemason until after he had founded his Order. It is true that Weishaupt was not officially received into Freemasonry until 1777, when he was initiated into the first degree at the Lodge " Theodore de Bon Conseil," at Munich. From this time we find him continually occupied in trying to discover more about the secrets of Freemasonry, whilst himself claiming superior knowledge.

But at the same time it is by no means certain that an inner circle of the Lodge Theodore may not have been first in the field and Weishaupt all the while an unconscious agent. A very curious light is thrown on this question by the *Mémoires* of Mirabeau.

Now, in *The French Revolution* and again in *World Revolution* I quoted the generally received opinion that Mirabeau, who was already a Freemason, was received into the Order of the Illuminati during his visit to Berlin in 1786. To this Mr. Waite replied: " All that is said about Mirabeau, his visit to Berlin, and his plot to ' illuminize ' French Freemasonry, may be disposed of in one sentence: there is no evidence to show that Mirabeau ever became a Mason. The province of Barruel was to colour everything. . . ."[1] Mr. Waite's statement may also be disposed of in one sentence: it is a pure invention. The province of Mr. Waite is to deny everything inconvenient to him. The evidence that Mirabeau was a Freemason does not rest on Barruel alone. M. Barthou, in his Life of Mirabeau, refers to it as a matter of common knowledge, and relates that a paper was found at Mirabeau's house describing a new Order to be grafted on Freemasonry. This document will be found in its entirety in the *Mémoires* of Mirabeau, where it is stated that:

Mirabeau had early entered an association of Freemasonry.

[1] A. E. Waite, " Freemasonry and the Jewish Peril," in *The Occult Review* for September 1920, p. 152.

This affiliation had accredited him to a Dutch lodge, and it seems that, either spontaneously or in response to a request, he thought of proposing an organization of which we possess the plan, written not by his hand . . . but by the hand of a copyist whom Mirabeau had attached to himself. . . . This work appears to have been that of Mirabeau; all his opinions, his principles, and his style will be found here.[1]

The same work goes on to print the document in full, which is headed: " Memoir concerning an intimate association to be established in the Order of Freemasonry so as to bring it back to its true principles and to make it really tend to the good of humanity, drawn up by the F. Mi——, at present named Arcesilas, in 1776."

As this Memoir is too long to reproduce in full here, M. Barthou's *résumé* will serve to give an idea of its contents[2]:

He [Mirabeau] was a Freemason from his youth. There was found amongst his papers, written by the hand of a copyist, an international organization of Freemasonry, which no doubt he dictated in Amsterdam. This project contains on the solidarity of men, on the benefits of instruction, and on the " correction of the system of governments and of legislations " views very superior to those of "The Essay on Despotism" (1772). The mind of Mirabeau had ripened. The duties he traces out for the " brothers of the higher grade " constitute even a whole plan of reforms which resemble very much in certain parts the work accomplished later by the Constituent [Assembly]: suppression of servitudes on the land and the rights of main morte, abolition of the corvées, of working guilds and of maîtrises [freedom of companies], of customs and excise duties, the diminution of taxation, liberty of religious opinions and of the press, the disappearance of special jurisdiction. In order to organize, to develop and arrive at his end, Mirabeau invokes the example of the Jesuits: "We have quite contrary views," he says, "that of enlightening men, of making them free and happy, but we must and we can do this by the same means, and who should prevent us doing for good what the Jesuits have done for evil?"[3]

---

[1] *Mémoires de Mirabeau écrits par lui-même, par son père, son oncle et son fils adoptif, et précédés d'une étude sur Mirabeau par Victor Hugo,* Vol. III. p. 47 (1834).

[2] I have expressly made use of M. Barthou's résumé instead of making one of my own, lest I should be said to have made judicious selections in order to suit the purpose of showing the resemblance between this Memoir and the passage from Mirabeau's other writings which follows. But M. Barthou's impartiality cannot be impugned, for he appears to know nothing about the Illuminati or Mirabeau's connexion with them, and regards the Memoir in question as solely the outcome of Mirabeau's mind which had " ripened " since 1772.

[3] F. Barthou, *Mirabeau,* p. 57.

Now in this Memoir Mirabeau makes no mention of Weis-haupt, but in his *Histoire de la Monarchie Prussienne* he gives a eulogistic account of the Bavarian Illuminati, referring to Weishaupt by name, and showing the Order to have arisen out of Freemasonry. It will be seen that this account corresponds point by point with the Memoir he had himself made out in 1776, that is to say, in the very year that Illuminism was founded:

The Lodge Theodore de Bon Conseil at Munich, where there were a few men with brains and hearts, was tired of being tossed about by the vain promises and quarrels of Masonry. The heads resolved to graft on to their branch another secret association to which they gave the name of the Order of the Illuminés. They modelled it on the Society of Jesus, whilst proposing to themselves views diametrically opposed.

Mirabeau then goes on to say that the great object of the Order was the amelioration of the present system of government and legislation, that one of its fundamental rules was to admit " no prince whatever his virtues,"[1] that it proposed to abolish—

The slavery of the peasants, the servitude of men to the soil, the rights of main morte and all the customs and privileges which abase humanity, the corvées under the condition of an equitable equivalent, all the corporations, all the maîtrises, all the burdens imposed on industry and commerce by customs, excise duties, and taxes . . . to procure a universal toleration for all religious opinions . . . to take away all the arms of superstition, to favour the liberty of the press, etc.[2]

From all this we see then that Mirabeau did not become an Illuminatus in 1786 as I had supposed before this document was known to me, but had been in the Order from the beginning apparently as one of its founders, first under the " Illuminated " name of Arcesilas and later under that of Leonidas. The Memoir found at his house was thus no other than the programme of the Illuminati evolved by him in collaboration with an inner ring of Freemasons belonging to the Lodge Theodore. The correspondence of the Illuminati in fact contains several references to an inner ring under the name of

[1] In the Memoir drawn up by Mirabeau quoted above we find this passage: " It must be a fundamental rule never to allow any prince to enter the association were he a god for virtue."—*Mémoires de Mirabeau*, III. 60.
[2] *Histoire de la Monarchie Prussienne*, V. 99.

" the secret chapter of the Lodge of St. Theodore," which, after his initiation into Masonry, Weishaupt indicates the necessity of bringing entirely under the control of Illuminism.   It is probable that Weishaupt was in touch with this secret chapter before his formal admission to the lodge.

Whether, then, the ideas of Illuminism arose in this secret chapter of the Lodge Theodore independently of Weishaupt, or whether they were imparted by Weishaupt to the Lodge Theodore after the directions had been given him by Kölmer, it is impossible to know; but in either case there would be some justification for Robison's assertion that Illuminism arose out of Freemasonry, or rather that it took birth amongst a group of Freemasons whose aims were not those of the Order in general.

What were these aims?   A plan of social and political " reform " which, as M. Barthou points out, much resembled the work accomplished later by the Constituent Assembly in France.   This admission is of great importance; in other words, the programme carried out by the Constituent Assembly in 1789 had been largely formulated in a lodge of German Freemasons who formed the nucleus of the Illuminati, in 1776. And yet we are told that Illuminism had no influence on the French Revolution!

It will be objected that the reforms here indicated were wholly admirable.   True, the abolition of the *corvée,* of *main morte,* and of servitudes were measures that met with the approval of all right-minded men, including the King of France himself.   But what of the abolition of the " working guilds " and " all the corporations," that is to say, the " trade unions " of the period, which was carried out by the infamous Loi Chapelier in 1791, a decree that is now generally recognized as one of the strangest anomalies of the Revolution?   Again, to whose interest was it to do away with the customs and excise duties of France?   To establish the absolute and unfettered liberty of the press and religious opinions?   The benefits these measures might be expected to confer on the French people were certainly problematical, but there could be no doubt of their utility to men who, like Frederick the Great, wished to ruin France and to break the Franco-Austrian alliance by the unrestricted circulation of libels against Marie Antoinette, who, like Mirabeau, hoped to bring about a revolution, or who, like Voltaire, wished to remove all obstacles to the spread of an anti-Christian propaganda.

It is therefore by no means impossible that Weishaupt was at first the agent of more experienced conspirators, whose purely political aims were disguised under a plan of social reform, and who saw in the Bavarian professor a clever organizer to be employed in carrying out their designs.

Whether this was so or not, the fact remains that from the time Weishaupt assumed control of the Order the plan of " social reform " described by Mirabeau vanishes entirely, for not a word do we find in the writings of the Illuminati about any pretended scheme for ameliorating the lot of the people, and Illuminism becomes simply a scheme of anarchic philosophy. The French historian Henri Martin has thus admirably summed up the system elaborated by " Spartacus ":

Weishaupt had made into an absolute theory the misanthropic gibes [*boutades*] of Rousseau at the invention of property and society, and without taking into account the statement so distinctly formulated by Rousseau on the impossibility of suppressing property and society once they had been established, he proposed as the end of Illuminism the abolition of property, social authority, of nationality, and the return of the human race to the happy state in which it formed only a single family without artificial needs, without useless sciences, every father being priest and magistrate. Priest of we know not what religion, for in spite of their frequent invocations of the God of Nature, many indications lead us to conclude that Weishaupt had, like Diderot and d'Holbach, no other God than Nature herself. From his doctrine would naturally follow the German ultra-Hegelianism and the system of anarchy recently developed in France, of which the physiognomy suggests a foreign origin.[1]

This summary of the aims of the Illuminati, which absolutely corroborates the view of Barruel and Robison, is confirmed in detail by the Socialist Freethinker of the nineteenth century Louis Blanc, who in his remarkable chapter on the " Révolutionnaires Mystiques " refers to Weishaupt as " One of the profoundest conspirators who have ever existed."[2] George Sand also, Socialist and *intime* of the Freemasons, wrote of " the European conspiracy of Illuminism " and the immense influence exercised by the secret societies of " mystic Germany." To say, then, that Barruel and Robison were alone in proclaiming the danger of Illuminism is simply a deliberate perversion of the truth, and it is difficult to understand why English Freemasons should have allowed themselves to be misled on this question.

[1] Henry Martin, *Histoire de France*, XVI. 533.
[2] Louis Blanc, *Histoire de la Révolution Française*, II. 84.

Thus the *Masonic Cyclopædia* observes that the Illuminati " were, as a rule, men of the strictest morality and humanity, and the ideas they sought to instil were those which have found universal acceptance in our own times." Preston, in his *Illustrations of Masonry*, also does his best to gloss over the faults of the Order, and even " the historian of Freemasonry " devotes to its founder this astounding apology. After describing Weishaupt as the victim of Jesuit intrigue, Mr. Gould goes on to say:

He conceived the idea of combating his foes with their own weapons, and forming a society of young men, enthusiastic in the cause of humanity, who should gradually be trained to work as one man to one end—the destruction of evil and the enhancement of good in this world. Unfortunately he had unconsciously imbibed that most pernicious doctrine that the end justifies the means, and his whole plan reveals the effects of his youthful teaching. . . . The man himself was without guile, ignorant of men, knowing them only by books, a learned professor, an enthusiast who took a wrong course in all innocence, and the faults of his head have been heavily visited upon his memory in spite of the rare qualities of his heart.[1]

One can only conclude that these extraordinary exonerations of an Order bitterly hostile to the true aims of Masonry proceed from ignorance of the real nature of Illuminism. In order to judge of this it is only necessary to consult the writings of the Illuminati themselves, which are contained in the following works:

1. *Einige Originalschriften des Illuminatenordens* (Munich, 1787).

2. *Nachtrag von weitern Originalschriften, etc.* (Munich, 1787).

3. *Die neuesten Arbeiten des Spartacus und Philo in dem Illuminaten-Orden* (Munich, 1794).

All these consist in the correspondence and papers of the Order which were seized by the Bavarian Government at the houses of two of the members, Zwack and Bassus, and published by order of the Elector. The authenticity of these documents has never been denied even by the Illuminati themselves; Weishaupt, in his published defence, endeavoured only to explain away the most incriminating passages. The publishers, moreover, were careful to state at the beginning of the first volume: " Those who might have any doubts on the authenticity of this collection may present themselves at the

[1] *History of Freemasonry,* III. 121.

Secret Archives here, where, on request, the original documents will be laid before them." This precaution rendered all dispute impossible.

Setting Barruel and Robison entirely aside, we shall now see from the evidence of their own writings, how far the Illuminati can be regarded as a praiseworthy and cruelly maligned Order. Let us begin with their attitude towards Freemasonry.

ILLUMINISM AND FREEMASONRY

From the moment of Weishaupt's admission into Freemasonry his whole conduct was a violation of the Masonic code. Instead of proceeding after the recognized manner by successive stages of initiation, he set himself to find out further secrets by underhand methods and then to turn them to the advantage of his own system. Thus about a year after his initiation he writes to Cato (alias Zwack): "I have succeeded in obtaining a profound glimpse into the secret of the Freemasons. I know their whole aim and shall impart it all at the right time in one of the higher degrees."[1]

Cato is then deputed to make further discoveries through an Italian Freemason, the Abbé Marotti, which he records triumphantly in his diary:

Interview with the Abbé Marotti on the question of Masonry, when he explained to me the whole secret, which is founded on old religion and Church history, and imparted to me all the higher degrees up to the Scottish. Informed Spartacus of this.[2]

Spartacus, however, unimpressed by this communication, replied drily:

Whether you know the aim of Masonry I doubt. I have myself included an insight into this structure in my plan, but reserved it for later degrees.[3]

Weishaupt then decides that all illuminated "Areopagites" shall take the first three degrees of Freemasonry[4]; but further:

That we shall have a masonic lodge of our own. That we shall regard this as our nursery garden. That to some of these Masons we shall not at once reveal that we have something more than the

---

[1] *Originalschriften*, p. 258.   [3] Ibid., p. 285.
[2] Ibid., p. 297.   [4] Ibid., p. 286.

Masons have. That at every opportunity we shall cover ourselves
with this [Masonry]. . . . All those who are not suited to the work
shall remain in the masonic Lodge and advance in that without
knowing anything of the further system.[1]

We shall find this plan of an inner secret circle concealed
within Freemasonry persisting up to our own day.

Weishaupt, however, admits himself puzzled with regard to
the past of Masonry, and urges " Porcius " to find out more on
this question from the Abbé Marotti:

See whether through him you can discover the real history, origin,
and the first founders of Masonry, for on this alone I am still
undecided.[2]

But it is in " Philo," the Baron von Knigge, a Freemason
and member of the Stricte Observance, in which he was known
as the Eques a Cygno, that Weishaupt finds his most efficient
investigator. Thus " Philo " writes to " Spartacus ":

I have now found in Cassel the best man, on whom I cannot
congratulate ourselves enough: he is Mauvillon, Grand Master of
one of the Royal York Lodges. So with him we have the whole
lodge in our hands. He has also got from there all their miserable
degrees [Er hat auch von dort aus alle ihre elenden Grade].[3]

No wonder that Weishaupt thereupon exclaims joyfully:
" Philo does more than we all expected, and he is the man who
alone will carry it all through."[4] Weishaupt then occupies
himself in trying to get a " Constitution " from London,
evidently without success, and also in wresting the Lodge
Theodore in Munich from the control of Berlin in order to
substitute his own domination, so that " the whole secret chapter
will be subjected to our ☉, leave everything to it, and await
further degrees from it alone."[5]

In all this Weishaupt shows himself not only an intriguer

---

[1] *Originalschriften*, p. 300. It seems that when a Freemason appeared likely
to fall in with the scheme of Illuminism, he was soon allowed to know of the
further system. Thus in the case of " Savioli " " Cato " writes: " Now that
he is a Mason I have put all about this ☉ before him, shown him what is
unimportant and at this opportunity taken up the general plan of our ☉,
and as this pleased him I said that such a thing really existed, whereat he
gave me his word that he would enter it."—*Originalschriften*, p. 289.

[2] Ibid., p. 303.
[3] Ibid., p. 361.
[4] Ibid., p. 363.
[5] Ibid., p. 360.

but a charlatan, inventing mysteries and degrees to impose on the credulity of his followers. "The mysteries, or so-called secret truths, are the finest of all," he writes to "Philipo Strozzi," "and give me much trouble."[1] So whilst heartily despising Freemasonry, theosophy, Rosicrucianism, and mysticism of every kind, his association with Philo leads him to perceive the utility of all these as a bait, and he allows Philo to draw up plans for a degree of Scottish Knight. But the result is pitiable, Philo's composition, a "semi-theosophical discourse and explanation of hieroglyphics" is characterized by Weishaupt as gibberish (kauderwelsche).[2]

Philo [he says again] is full of such follies, which betray his small mind. . . . On the Illuminatus Major follows the miserable degree of Scottish Knight entirely of his composition, and on the degree of Priest an equally miserable degree of Regent, . . . but I have already composed four more degrees compared to the worst of which the Priest's degree will be child's play, but I shall tell no one about it till I see how the thing goes. . . .[3]

The perfidy of the Illuminati with regard to the Freemasons is therefore apparent. Even Mounier, who set out to refute Barruel on the strength of the information supplied to him by the Illuminatus Bode, admits their duplicity in this respect.

Weishaupt [says Mounier] made the acquaintance of a Hanoverian, the Baron von Knigge, a famous intriguer, long practised in the charlatanism of lodges of Freemasons. On his advice new degrees were added to the old ones, and it was resolved to profit by Freemasonry whilst profoundly despising it. They decided that the degrees of Entered Apprentice, Fellow Craft, Master Mason, and Scotch Knight should be added to those of the Illuminati, and that they would boast of possessing exclusively the real secrets of the Freemasons and affirm that Illuminism was the real primitive Freemasonry.

"The papers of the Order seized in Bavaria and published," Mounier says again, show that "the Illuminati employed the forms of Freemasonry, but that they considered it in itself, apart from their own degrees, as a puerile absurdity and that they detested the Rose-Croix." Mounier, as a good disciple of Bode, takes much the same view and pities the naïveté of

---

[1] Originalschriften, p. 200.
[2] Nachtrag von . . . Originalschriften, I. 67.
[3] Ibid., p. 95.

the Freemasons, who, "like so many children, spend a great part of the time in their lodges playing at chapel."

Why in the face of all this should any British Masons take up the cudgels for the Illuminati and vilify Robison and Barruel for exposing them? The American Mackey, as a consistent Freemason, shows scant sympathy for this traitor in the masonic camp. "Weishaupt," he writes, "was a radical in politics and an infidel in religion, and he organized this association, not more for the purpose of aggrandizing himself, than of overturning Christianity and the institutions of society." And in a footnote he adds that Robison's *Proofs of a Conspiracy* "contain a very excellent exposition of the nature of this pseudo-masonic institution."[1]

The truth is that Weishaupt was one of the greatest enemies of British Freemasonry who ever lived, and genuine Freemasons will do themselves no good by defending him or his abominable system.

Let us now see how far, apart from their rôle in Masonry, the Illuminati can be regarded as noble idealists striving for the welfare of the human race.

IDEALISM OF THE ILLUMINATI

The line of defence adopted by the apologists of the Illuminati is always to quote the admirable principles professed by the Order, the "beautiful ideas" that run through their writings, and to show what excellent people were to be found amongst them.

Of course on their face value the Illuminati appear wholly admirable, of course there is nothing easier than to find innumerable passages in their writings breathing a spirit of the loftiest aspiration, and of course many excellent men figured amongst the patrons of the Order. All this is the mere stock-in-trade of the secret society leader as of the fraudulent company promoter, to whom the first essentials are a glowing

---

[1] *Lexicon of Freemasonry*, p. 142. See also Oliver's *Historical Landmarks of Freemasonry*, I. 26, where the Illuminati are rightly included amongst the enemies of Masonry. Nevertheless, both Mackey and Oliver proceed to revile Barruel and Robison as enemies of Masonry, and in order to substantiate this accusation Oliver descends to the most flagrant misquotation. For if we look up in the original the passages he quotes on page 382 from Robison and on page 573 from Barruel as evidence of their calumnies on Masonry, we shall find that they refer respectively to the Rose-Croix Cabalists and the Illuminati and not to the Freemasons at all! See Robison's *Proofs of a Conspiracy*, p. 93, and Barruel's *Mémoires sur le Jacobinisme* (1818 edition), II. 244.

prospectus and a long list of highly respectable patrons who know nothing whatever about the inner workings of the concern. These methods, pursued as early as the ninth century by Abdullah ibn Maymūn, enter largely into the policy of Frederick the Great, Voltaire, and his " brothers " in philosophy—or in Freemasonry.

The resemblances between Weishaupt's correspondence and that of Voltaire and of Frederick the Great are certainly very striking. All at moments profess respect for Christianity whilst working to destroy it. Thus just as Voltaire in one letter to d'Alembert expresses his horror at the publication of an anti-Christian pamphlet, *Le Testament de Jean Meslier*,[1] and in another urges him to have it circulated in thousands all over France,[2] so Weishaupt is careful in general to exhibit the face of a benign philosopher and even of a Christian evangelist; it is only at moments that he drops the mask and reveals the grinning satyr behind it.

Accordingly in the published statutes of the Illuminati no hint of subversive intentions will be found; indeed the " Obligation " expressly states that " nothing against the State, religion, or morals is undertaken."

Yet what is Weishaupt's real political theory? No other than that of modern Anarchy, that man should govern himself and rulers should be gradually done away with. But he is careful to deprecate all ideas of violent revolution—the process is to be accomplished by the most peaceful methods. Let us see how gently he leads up to the final conclusion:

The first stage in the life of the whole human race is savagery, rough nature, in which the family is the only society, and hunger and thirst are easily satisfied, . . . in which man enjoys the two most excellent goods, Equality and Liberty, to their fullest extent. . . . In these circumstances . . . health was his usual condition. . . . Happy men, who were not yet enough enlightened to lose their peace of mind and to be conscious of the unhappy mainsprings and causes of our misery, love of power . . . envy . . . illnesses and all the results of imagination.

The manner in which man fell from this primitive state of felicity is then described:

As families increased, means of subsistence began to lack, the nomadic life ceased, property was instituted, men established

---

[1] *Œuvres Complètes de Voltaire* (1818 edition), Vol. XLI. p. 153.
[2] Ibid., pp. 165, 168.

themselves firmly, and through agriculture families drew near each other, thereby language developed and through living together men began to measure themselves against each other, etc. . . . But here was the cause of the downfall of freedom; equality vanished. Man felt new unknown needs. . . .[1]

Thus men became dependent like minors under the guardian-ship of kings; the human must attain its majority and become self-governing:

Why should it be impossible that the human race should attain to its highest perfection, the capacity to guide itself? Why should anyone be eternally led who understands how to lead himself?[2]

Further, men must learn not only to be independent of kings but of each other:

Who has need of another depends on him and has resigned his rights. So to need little is the first step to freedom; therefore savages and the most highly enlightened are perhaps the only free men. The art of more and more limiting one's needs is at the same time the art of attaining freedom. . . .[3]

Weishaupt then goes on to show how the further evil of Patriotism arose:

With the origin of nations and peoples the world ceased to be a great family, a single kingdom: the great tie of nature was torn. . . . Nationalism took the place of human love. . . . Now it became a virtue to magnify one's fatherland at the expense of whoever was not enclosed within its limits, now as a means to this narrow end it was allowed to despise and outwit foreigners or indeed even to insult them. This virtue was called Patriotism. . . .[4]

And so by narrowing down affection to one's fellow-citizens, the members of one's family, and even to oneself:

There arose out of Patriotism, Localism, the family spirit, and finally Egoism. . . . Diminish Patriotism, then men will learn to know each other again as such, their dependence on each other will be lost, the bond of union will widen out. . . .[5]

---

[1] *Nachtrag von . . . Originalschriften*, II. 54-57.
[2] Ibid., p. 82.   [4] Ibid., p. 63.
[3] Ibid., p. 59.   [5] Ibid., p. 65.

It will be seen that the whole of Weishaupt's theory was in reality a new rendering of the ancient secret tradition relating to the fall of man and the loss of his primitive felicity; but whilst the ancient religions taught the hope of a Redeemer who should restore man to his former state, Weishaupt looks to man alone for his restoration. " Men," he observes, " no longer loved men but only such and such men.   The word was quite lost. . . ."[1]   Thus in Weishaupt's masonic system the " lost word " is " Man," and its recovery is interpreted by the idea that Man should find himself again. Further on Weishaupt goes on to show how " the redemption of the human race is to be brought about "·

These means are secret schools of wisdom, these were from all time the archives of Nature and of human rights, through them will Man be saved from his Fall, princes and nations will disappear with-out violence from the earth, the human race will become one family and the world the abode of reasonable men.   Morality alone will bring about this change imperceptibly.   Every father of a family will be, as formerly Abraham and the patriarchs, the priest and unfettered lord of his family, and Reason will be the only code of Man.   This is one of our greatest secrets. . . .[2]

But whilst completely eliminating any idea of divine power outside Man and framing his system on purely political lines, Weishaupt is careful not to shock the susceptibilities of his followers by any open repudiation of Christian doctrines; on the contrary, he invokes Christ at every turn and sometimes even in language so apparently earnest and even beautiful that one is almost tempted to believe in his sincerity.   Thus he writes:

This our great and unforgettable Master, Jesus of Nazareth, appeared at a time in the world when it was sunk in depravity. . . . The first followers of His teaching are not wise men but simple, chosen from the lowest class of the people, so as to show that His teaching should be possible and comprehensible to all classes and conditions of men. . . . He carries out this teaching by means of the most blameless life in conformity with it, and seals and confirms this with His blood and death.   These laws which He shows as the way to salvation are only two: love of God and love of one's neighbour; more He asks of no one.[3]

[1] *Nachtrag von . . . Originalschriften,* II. 67.
[2] Ibid., pp. 80, 81.
[3] Ibid., pp. 98, 99.

So far no Lutheran pastor could have expressed himself better. But one must study Weishaupt's writings as a whole to apprehend the true measure of his belief in Christ's teaching.

Now, as we have already seen, his first idea was to make Fire Worship the religion of Illuminism; the profession of Christianity therefore appears to have been an after-thought. Evidently Weishaupt discovered, as others have done, that Christianity lends itself more readily to subversive ideas than any other religion. And in the passages which follow we find him adopting the old ruse of representing Christ as a Communist and as a secret-society adept. Thus he goes on to explain that " if Jesus preaches contempt of riches, He wishes to teach us the reasonable use of them and prepare for the community of goods introduced by Him,"[1] and in which, Weishaupt adds later, He lived with His disciples.[2] But this secret doctrine is only to be apprehended by initiates:

No one . . . has so cleverly concealed the high meaning of His teaching, and no one finally has so surely and easily directed men on to the path of freedom as our great master Jesus of Nazareth. This secret meaning and natural consequence of His teaching He hid completely, for Jesus had a secret doctrine, as we see in more than one place of the Scriptures.[3]

Weishaupt thus contrives to give a purely political interpretation to Christ's teaching:

The secret preserved through the Disciplinam Arcani, and the aim appearing through all His words and deeds, is to give back to men their original liberty and equality. . . . Now one can understand how far Jesus was the Redeemer and Saviour of the world.[4]

The mission of Christ was therefore by means of Reason to make men capable of freedom[5]: " When at last reason becomes the religion of man, so will the problem be solved."[6]

---

[1] *Nachtrag von . . . Originalschriften*, II. 100-101.
[2] Ibid., p. 105: " He Himself lived with His disciples in community of goods."
[3] Ibid , p. 101. This was one of the earliest heresies of the Christian era refuted by Origen: " Moreover, he [Celsus] frequently calls the Christian doctrine a secret system, we must refute him on this point . . . to speak of the Christian doctrine as a secret system is altogether absurd."— Origen, *Contra Celsum*, in *The Ante-Nicene Christian Library*, p. 403 (1869).
[4] Ibid., p. 106.
[5] Ibid., p. 113.
[6] Ibid., p. 96.

Weishaupt goes on to show that Freemasonry can be inter-preted in the same manner. The secret doctrine concealed in the teaching of Christ was handed down by initiates who " hid themselves and their doctrine under the cover of Free-masonry,"[1] and in a long explanation of Masonic hieroglyphics he indicates the analogies between the Hiramic legend and the story of Christ. " I say then Hiram is Christ," and after giving one of his reasons for this assertion, adds: " Here then is much ground gained, although I myself cannot help laughing at this explanation [*obwohl ich selbst über diese Explication im Grund lachen muss*]."[2] Weishaupt then proceeds to give further interpretations of his own devising to the masonic ritual, including an imaginary translation of certain words supposed to be derived from Hebrew, and ends up by saying.: " One will be able to show several more resemblances between Hiram and the life and death of Christ, or drag them in by the hair."[3] So much for Weishaupt's respect for the Grand Legend of Freemasonry!

In this manner Weishaupt demonstrates that " Freemasonry is hidden Christianity, at least my explanations of the hiero-glyphics fit this perfectly; and in the way in which I explain Christianity no one need be ashamed to be a Christian, for I leave the name and substitute for it Reason."[4]

But this is of course only the secret of what Weishaupt calls " real Freemasonry "[5] in contradistinction to the official kind, which he regards as totally unenlightened: " Had not the noble and elect remained in the background . . . new depravity would have broken out in the human race, and through Regents, Priests, and Freemasons Reason would have been banished from the earth."[6]

In Weishaupt's masonic system, therefore, the designs of the Order with regard to religion are not confided to the mere Freemasons, but only to the Illuminati. Under the heading of " Higher Mysteries " Weishaupt writes:

The man who is good for nothing better remains a Scottish Knight. If he is, however, a particularly industrious co-ordinator [*Sammler*], observer, worker, he becomes a Priest. . . . If there are amongst these [Priests] high speculative intellects, they become Magi. These collect and put in order the higher philosophical system and work at the People's Religion, which the Order will next

[1] *Nachtrag von . . . Originalschriften*, II. 111.
[2] Ibid., II. 123.
[3] Ibid., II. 124.
[4] Ibid., I. 68.
[5] Ibid., II. 113.
[6] Ibid., II. 115.

give to the world. Should these high geniuses also be fit to rule the world, they become Regents. This is the last degree.[1]

Philo (the Baron von Knigge) also throws an interesting light on the religious designs of the Illuminati. In a letter to Cato he explains the necessity of devising a system that will satisfy fanatics and freethinkers alike: " So as to work on both these classes of men and unite them, we must find an explanation to the Christian religion . . . make this the secret of Freemasonry and turn it to our purpose."[2] Philo continues:

We say then: Jesus wished to introduce no new religion, but only to restore natural religion and reason to their old rights. Thereby he wished to unite men in a great universal association, and through the spread of a wiser morality, enlightenment, and the combating of all prejudices to make them capable of governing themselves; so the secret meaning of his teaching was to lead men without revolution to universal liberty and equality. There are many passages in the Bible which can be made use of and explained, and so all quarrelling between the sects ceases if one can find a reasonable meaning in the teaching of Jesus—be it true or not. As, however, this simple religion was afterwards distorted, so were these teachings imparted to us through Disciplinam Arcani and finally through Freemasonry, and all masonic hieroglyphics can be explained with this object. Spartacus has collected very good data for this and I have myself added to them, . . . and so I have got both degrees ready. . . .

Now therefore that people see that we are the only real and true Christians, we can say a word more against priests and princes, but I have so managed that after previous tests I can receive pontiffs and kings in this degree. In the higher Mysteries we must then (a) disclose the pious fraud and (b) reveal from all writings the origin of all religious lies and their connexion. . . .[3]

So admirably did this ruse succeed that we find Spartacus writing triumphantly:

You cannot imagine what consideration and sensation our Priest's degree is arousing. The most wonderful thing is that great Protestant and reformed theologians who belong to ⊙ [Illuminism] still believe that the religious teaching imparted in it contains the true and genuine spirit of the Christian religion. Oh! men, of

---

[1] *Nachtrag von . . . Originalschriften*, II. 13, 14.
[2] Ibid., I. 104.
[3] Ibid., I. 104-106.

what cannot you be persuaded? I never thought that I should become the founder of a new religion.[1]

It is on the " illuminized " clergy and professors that Weishaupt counts principally for the work of the Order.

Through the influence of the Brothers [he writes], the Jesuits have been removed from all professorships, and the University of Ingoldstadt has been quite cleansed of them. . . .[2]

Thus the way is cleared for Weishaupt's adepts.

The Institute of Cadets also comes under the control of the Order:

All the professors are members of the Illuminati, . . . so will all the pupils become disciples of Illuminism.[3]

Further:

We have provided our clerical members with good benefices, parishes, posts at Court.

Through our influence Arminius and Cortez have been made professors at Ephesus.

.   .   .   .   .   .

The German schools are quite under [the influence of] ⊙ and now only members have charge of them.

The charitable association is also directed by ⊙ .

.   .   .   .   .

Soon we shall draw over to us the whole Bartholomew Institute for young clergymen; the preparations have already been made and the prospects are very good, by this means we shall be able to provide the whole of Bavaria with proper priests.[4]

But religion and Freemasonry are not the only means by which Illuminism can be spread.

We must consider [says Weishaupt], how we can begin to work under another form. If only the aim is achieved, it does not matter under what cover it takes place, and a cover is always necessary. For in concealment lies a great part of our strength. For this reason we must always cover ourselves with the name of another society. The lodges that are under Freemasonry are in the meantime

[1] *Nachtrag von . . . Originalschriften*, I. 76.   [3] Ibid., p. 9.
[2] *Originalschriften*, p. 8.   [4] Ibid., p. 10.

the most suitable cloak for our high purpose, because the world is already accustomed to expect nothing great from them which merits attention. . . . As in the spiritual Orders of the Roman Church, religion was, alas! only a pretence, so must our Order also in a nobler way try to conceal itself behind a learned society or something of the kind. . . . A society concealed in this manner cannot be worked against. In case of a prosecution or of treason the superiors cannot be discovered. . . . We shall be shrouded in impenetrable darkness from spies and emissaries of other societies.[1]

In order to give a good appearance to the Order, Weishaupt particularly indicates the necessity for enlisting esteemed and " respectable " persons,[2] but above all young men whom he regards as the most likely subjects. " I cannot use men as they are," he observes, " but I must first form them."[3] Youth naturally lends itself best to this process. " Seek the society of young people," Weishaupt writes to Ajax, " watch them, and if one of them pleases you, lay your hand on him."[4] " Seek out young and already skilful people. . . . Our people must be engaging, enterprising, intriguing, and adroit. Above all the first."[5]

If possible they should also be good-looking—"' beautiful people, *cæteris paribus*. . . .*"

Such people have generally gentle manners, a tender heart, and are, when well practised in other things, of the greatest use in undertakings, for their first glance attracts; but their spirit *n'a pas la profondeur des physiognomies sombres*. They are, however, also less disposed to riots and disturbances than the darker physiognomies. That is why one must know how to use one's people. Above all, the high, soulful eye pleases me and the free, open brow.*

With these novices the adept of Illuminism is to proceed slowly, talking backwards and forwards:

One must speak, first in one way, then in another, so as not to commit oneself and to make one's real way of thinking impenetrable to one's inferiors.*

---

[1] *Neuesten Arbeiten des Spartacus und Philo*, pp. 143, 163.
[2] *Nachtrag von . . . Originalschriften*, I. 3.
[3] *Originalschriften*, p. 215.
[4] Ibid., p. 173.
[5] Ibid., p. 175.
* Ibid., pp. 237-8.
* *Nachtrag von . . . Originalschriften*, I. 12.

THE BAVARIAN ILLUMINATI

THE BAVARIAN ILLUMINATI

THE BAVARIAN ILLUMINATI 221

Weishaupt also insists on the importance of exciting the candidate's curiosity and then drawing back again, after the manner of the Fatimite *dais*:

> I have no fault to find with your [methods of] reception ["Spartacus" writes to "Cato"], except that they are too quick. . . . You should proceed gradually in a roundabout way by means of suspense and expectations, so as first to arouse indefinite, vague curiosity, and then when the candidate declares himself, present the object, which he will then seize with both hands.[1]

By this means his vanity will also be flattered, because one will arouse the pleasure of "knowing something which everyone does not know, and about which the greater part of the world is groping in darkness."[2]

For the same reason the candidate must be impressed with the importance of secret societies and the part they have played in the destinies of the world:

> One illustrates this by the Order of the Jesuits, of the Freemasons, by the secret associations of the ancients, one asserts that all events in the world occur from a hundred secret springs and causes, to which secret associations above all belong; one arouses the pleasure of quiet, hidden power and of insight into hidden secrets.[3]

At this point one is to begin to "'show glimpses and to let fall here and there remarks that may be interpreted in two ways," so as to bring the candidate to the point of saying: "If I had the chance to enter such an association, I would go into it at once." "These discourses," says Weishaupt, "are to be often repeated."[4]

In the discourse of reception to the "Illuminatus Dirigens," the appeal to love of power plays the most important part:

> Do you realize sufficiently what it means to rule—to rule in a secret society? Not only over the lesser or more important of the populace, but over the best men, over men of all ranks, nations, and religions, to rule without external force, to unite them indissolubly, to breathe one spirit and soul into them, men distributed over all parts of the world? . . .[5]

[1] *Originalschriften,* p. 231.
[2] *Nachtrag von . . . Originalschriften,* II. 2.
[3] *Originalschriften,* p. 51.
[4] Ibid., p. 52.
[5] *Nachtrag von . . . Originalschriften,* II. 45.

And finally, do you know what secret societies are? what a place they occupy in the great kingdom of the world's events? Do you really think they are unimportant, transitory appearances?[1] etc.

But the admission of political aims is reserved only for the higher grades of the Order. " With the beginner," says Weishaupt, " we must be careful about books on religion and the State. I have reserved these in my plan for the higher degrees."[2] Accordingly the discourse to the " Minerval " is expressly designed to put him off the track. Thus the initiator is to say to him:

After two years' reflection, experience, intercourse, reading of the graduated writings and information, you will necessarily have formed the idea that the final aim of our Society is nothing less than to win power and riches, to undermine secular or religious government, and to obtain the mastery of the world, and so on. If you have represented our Society to yourself from this point of view or have entered it in this expectation, you have mightily deceived yourself. . . .[3]

The initiator, without informing the Minerval of the real aim of the Society, then goes on to say that he is now free to leave it if he wishes. By this means the leaders were able to eliminate ambitious people who might become their rivals to power and to form their ranks out of men who would submit to be led blindly onward by unseen directors. " My circumstances necessitate," Spartacus writes to Cato, " that I should remain hidden from most of the members as long as I live. I am obliged to do everything through five or six persons."[4] So carefully was this secret guarded that until the papers of the Illuminati were seized in 1786 no one outside this inner circle knew that Weishaupt was the head of the Order. Yet if we are to believe his own assertions, he had been throughout in supreme control. Again and again he impresses on his *intimes* the necessity for unity of command in the Order: " One must show how easy it would be for one clever head to direct hundreds and thousands of men,"[5] and he

[1] *Nachtrag von . . . Originalschriften*, II. 51.
[2] *Originalschriften*, p. 210.
[3] Ibid., p. 72.
[4] Ibid., p. 271.
[5] Ibid., p. 50.

illustrates this system by the table reproduced on the next page, to which he appends the following explanation:

I have two immediately below me into whom I breathe my whole spirit, and each of these two has again two others, and so on. In this way I can set a thousand men in motion and on fire in the simplest manner, and in this way one must impart orders and operate on politics.[1]

Thus, as in the case of Abdullah ibn Maymūn's society, " the extraordinary result was brought about that a multitude of men of divers beliefs were all working together for an object known only to a few of them."

Enough has now been quoted from the correspondence of the Illuminati to show their aims and methods according to their own admissions. We shall now see how far their apologists are justified in describing them as " men of the strictest morality and humanity."[2] Doubtless there were many excellent people in the outer ranks of the Order, but this is not the contention of Mr. Gould, who expressly states that " all the prominent members of this association were estimable men both in public and in private life." These further extracts from their correspondence may be left to speak for themselves.

CHARACTER OF THE ILLUMINATI

In June 1782 Weishaupt writes to " Cato " as follows:
Oh, in politics and morality you are far behind, my gentlemen. Judge further if such a man as Marcus Aurelius[3] finds out how wretched it [Illuminism] appears in Athens [Munich]; what a collection of immoral men, of whoremongers, liars, debtors, boasters, and vain fools they have amongst them. If he saw all that, what do you suppose the man would think? Would he not be ashamed to find himself in such an association, in which the leaders arouse the greatest expectations and carry out the best plan in such a miserable manner? And all this out of caprice, expediency, etc. Judge whether I am not right.[4]

From Thebes [Freysing] I hear fatal news; they have received into the lodge the scandal of the whole town, the dissolute debtor Propertius, who is trumpeted abroad by the whole " personnel " of Athens [Munich], Thebes and Erzerum [Eichstadt]; D. also

[1] *Nachtrag von . . . Originalschriften,* I. 32.
[2] *Royal Masonic Cyclopædia,* article on Illuminati.
[3] Feder, a preacher at the Court who had joined the Illuminati.
[4] *Nachtrag von . . . Originalschriften,* I. 42.

32

mit ich indeſſen ſpeculiren, und die Leute ge-
ſchickt rangieren kann; denn davon hängt alles
ab. Ich werde in dieſer Figur mit ihnen operieren.

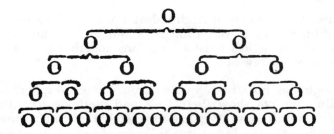

Ich habe zwey unmittelbar unter mir, wel-
chen ich meinen ganzen Geiſt einhauche, und von
dieſen zweyen hat wieder jeder zwey andere, und
ſo fort. Auf dieſe Art kann ich auf die einfach-
ſte Art tauſend Menſchen in Bewegung und
Flammen ſetzen. Auf eben dieſe Art muß man
die Ordres ertheilen, und im Politiſchen operieren.

Es iſt ein Kunſt dabey, dem Pythagoras et-
was aus dem Ill. min. vorzuleſen. Ich habe
ihn ja nicht: ich habe keinen einzigen Grad in
Handen, nicht einmal meine eigene Aufſätze.

Ich habe auch in des Philo Provinzen eine
Art von Eid, Verſicherung oder Betheuerung:
bey der Ehre des ☉: beym ☉, einge-
führt. Man gebraucht ſie nur, um ſie nicht
zu profaniren, bey den wichtigſten Vorfällen.

Wer

Diagram of Weishaupt's System. From *Nachtrag von weitern
Originalschriften der Illuminatensekte*, p. 32. München, 1787.

appears to be a bad man. Socrates who would be a capital man [*ein Capital Mann*] is continually drunk, Augustus in the worst repute, and Alcibiades sits the whole day with the innkeeper's wife sighing and pining: Tiberius tried in Corinth to rape the sister of Democedes and the husband came in. In Heaven's name, what are these for Areopagites! We upper ones, write, read and work ourselves to death, offer to ☉ our health, fame and fortune, whilst these gentlemen indulge their weaknesses, go a whoring, cause scandals and yet are Areopagites and want to know about everything.[1]

Concerning Arminius there are great complaints. . . . He is an unbearable, obstinate, arrogant, vain fool![2]

Let Celsus, Marius, Scipio, and Ajax do what they will . . . no one does us so much harm as Celsus, no one is less to be reasoned with than Celsus, and perhaps few could have been so much use to us as Celsus. . . . Marius is obstinate and can see no great plan, Scipio is negligent, and of Ajax I will not speak at all. . . . Confucius is worth very little: he is too inquisitive and a terrible chatterer [*ein grausamer Schwatzer*].[3]

Agrippa must be quite struck off our list, for the rumour goes round . . . that he has stolen a gold and silver watch together with a ring from our best fellow-worker Sulla.

It will doubtless be suggested at this point that all these letters merely portray the lofty idealist sorrowing over the frailties of his erring disciples, but let us hear what Weishaupt has to say about himself. In a letter to Marius (Hertel) he writes:

And now in the strictest confidence, a matter near my heart, which robs me of all rest, makes me incapable of anything and drives me to despair. I stand in danger of losing my honour and my reputation which gave me so much power over our people. Think, my sister-in-law is expecting a child.[5] I have for this purpose sent to Euriphon in Athens to solicit the marriage licence and Promotorial from Rome, you see how much depends on this and that no time must be lost; every minute is precious. But if the dispensation does not arrive, what shall I do? How shall I make amends to the person since I alone am to blame? We have already tried several ways to get rid of the child; she herself was resolved for anything. But Euriphon is too timid and yet I

[1] *Nachtrag von . . . Originalschriften*, I. 39, 40.
[2] Ibid., I. 47.
[3] *Originalschriften*, pp. 370, 371.
[4] Ibid., pp. 257, 258.
[5] Given in the cypher of the Illuminati: "Denken sie, meine 18. 10. 5. 21. 12. 6. 8. 17. 4. 13. ist 18. 10. 5. 21. 12. 13. 6. 8. 17. (meine Schwägerin ist schwanger)." See cypher on p. 1 of *Originalschriften*.

see no other expedient. ıı ɪ could ensure the silence of Celsus he could help me and indeed he already promised me this three years ago. . . .¹ If you can help me out of this dilemma, you will give me back life, honour, peace and power to work. . . . I do not know what devil led me astray, I who always in these circumstances took extreme precautions.²

A little later Weishaupt writes again:

All fatalities happen to me at the same time. Now there is my mother dead! Corpse, wedding, christening all in a short time, one on the top of the other. What a wonderful mix-up [*mischmasch*]!³

So much for what Mr. Gould calls the "rare qualities" of Weishaupt's heart. Let us now listen to the testimony of Weishaupt's principal coadjutor, Philo (the Baron von Knigge), to whom the "historian of Freemasonry" refers as "a lovable enthusiast." In all subversive associations, whether open or secret, directed by men who aim at power, a moment is certain to arrive when the ambitions of the leaders come into conflict. This is the history of every revolutionary organization during the last 150 years. It was when the inevitable climax had been reached between Weishaupt and Knigge that "Philo" wrote to "the most loving Cato" in the following terms:

It is not Mahomed and A. who are so much to blame for my break with Spartacus, as the Jesuitical conduct of this man which has so often turned us against each other in order to rule despotically over men, who, if they have not perhaps such a rich imagination as himself, also do not possess so much cuteness and cunning, etc.⁴

In a further letter Philo goes on to enumerate the services he has rendered to Weishaupt in the past:

At the bidding of Spartacus I have written against ex-Jesuits and Rosicrucians, persecuted people who never did me any harm, thrown the *Stricte Observance* into confusion, drawn the best amongst them to us, told them of the worthiness of ☉, of its power, its age, the excellence of its Chiefs, the blamelessness of its higher leaders, the importance of its knowledge, and given great ideas of the uprightness of its views; those amongst us who are

¹ Note, then, that this was no sudden lapse on the part of Weishaupt.
² *Nachtrag von . . . Originalschriften,* I. 14-16.
³ Ibid., I. 21.
⁴ Ibid., I. 99.

now working so actively for us but cling much to religiousness [*sehr an Religiosität kleben*] and who feared our intention was to spread Deism, I have sought to persuade that the higher Superiors had nothing less than this intention. Gradually, however, I shall work it as I please [*nach und nach wirke ich doch was ich will*]. If I now were to . . . give a hint to the Jesuits and Rosicrucians as to who is persecuting them . . . if I were to make known (to a few people) the Jesuitical character of the man who leads perhaps all of us by the nose, uses us for his ambitious schemes, sacrifices us as often as his obstinacy requires, [if I were to make known to them] what they have to fear from such a man, from such a machine behind which perhaps Jesuits may be concealed or might conceal themselves; if I were to assure those who seek for secrets that they have nothing to expect; if I were to confide to those who hold religion dear, the principles of the General; . . . if I were to draw the attention of the lodges to an association behind which the Illuminati are concealed; if I were again to associate myself with princes and Freemasons . . . but I shrink from the thought, vengeance will not carry me so far. . . .[1]

We have now seen enough of the aims and methods of the Illuminati and the true characters of their leaders from their own admissions. To make the case complete it would be necessary also to give a résumé of the confessions made by the ex-Illuminati, the four professors Cosandey, Grünberger, Utzschneider, and Renner, as also of the further published works of the Illuminati—but space and time forbid. What is needed is a complete book on the subject, consisting of translations of the most important passages in all the contemporary German publications.

From the extracts given above, can it, however, be seriously contended that Barruel or Robison exaggerated the guilt of the Order? Do my literal translations differ materially in sense from the translations and occasional paraphrases given by the much-abused couple?

Even those contemporaries, Mounier and the member of the Illuminati[2] who set out to refute Barruel and Lombard de Langres, merely provide further confirmation of their views. Thus Mounier is obliged to confess that the real design of Illuminism was "to undermine all civil order,"[3] and "Ancien Illuminé" asserts in language no less forcible

---

[1] *Nachtrag von . . . Originalschriften*, I. 112.
[2] Author of the very interesting work *La Vérité sur les Sociétés Secrètes en Allemagne*, par un Ancien Illuminé (Paris, 1819).
[3] *De l'Influence attribuée aux Philosophes, aux Francs-Maçons et aux Illuminés sur la Révolution de France*, par J. J. Mounier (1822), p. 181.

than Barruel's own that Weishaupt " made a code of Machiavellism," that his method was " a profound perversity, flatter-
ing everything that was base and rancorous in human nature
in order to arrive at his ends," that he was not inspired by " a
wise spirit of reform " but by a " fanatical enmity inimical to
all authority on earth." The only essential points on which
the opposing parties differ is that whilst Mounier and " Ancien
Illuminé " deny the influence of the Illuminati on the French
Revolution and maintain that they ceased to exist in 1786,
Barruel and Lombard de Langres present them as the inspirers
of the Jacobins and declare them to be still active after the
Revolution had ended. That on this point, at any rate, the
latter were right, we shall see in a further chapter.

The great question that presents itself after studying the
writings of the Illuminati is: what was the motive power
behind the Order? If we admit the possibility that Frederick
the Great and the Stricte Observance, working through an
inner circle of Freemasons at the Lodge St. Theodore, may
have provided the first impetus and that Kölmer initiated
Weishaupt into Oriental methods of organization, the source
of inspiration from which Weishaupt subsequently drew his
anarchic philosophy still remains obscure. It has frequently
been suggested that his real inspirers were Jews, and the
Jewish writer Bernard Lazare definitely states that " there were
Jews, Cabalistic Jews, around Weishaupt."[1] A writer in *La
Vieille France* went so far as to designate these Jews as Moses
Mendelssohn, Wessely, and the bankers Itzig, Friedlander, and
Meyer. But no documentary evidence has ever been produced
in support of these statements. It is therefore necessary to
examine them in the light of probability.

Now, as I have already shown, the theosophical ideas of
the Cabala play no part in the system of Illuminism; the only
trace of Cabalism to be found amongst the papers of the
Order is a list of recipes for procuring abortion, for making
aphrodisiacs, Aqua Toffana, pestilential vapours, etc., headed
" Cabala Major."[2] It is possible, then, that the Illuminati
may have learnt something of " venefic magic " and the use
of certain natural substances from Jewish Cabalists; at the
same time Jews appear to have been only in rare cases admitted
to the Order. Everything indeed tends to prove that Weishaupt
and his first coadjutors, Zwack and Massenhausen, were pure

[1] It has several times been stated that Weishaupt was himself a Jew. I
cannot find the slightest evidence to this effect.
[2] *Originalschriften*, pp. 107-10.

Germans. Nevertheless there is between the ideas of Weishaupt and of Lessing's " Falk " a distinct resemblance; both in the writings of the Illuminati and in Lessing's *Dialogues* we find the same vein of irony with regard to Freemasonry, the same design that it should be replaced by a more effectual system,[1] the same denunciations of the existing social order and of bourgeois society, the same theory that " men should be self-governing," the same plan of obliterating all distinctions between nations, even the same simile of the bee-hive as applied to human life[2] which, as I have shown elsewhere, was later on adopted by the anarchist Proudhon. It may, however, legitimately be urged that these ideas were those of the inner masonic circle to which both Lessing and Weishaupt belonged, and that, though placed in the mouth of Falk, they were in no sense Judaic.

But Lessing was also the friend and admirer of Moses Mendelssohn, who has been suggested as one of Weishaupt's inspirers. Now, at first sight nothing seems more improbable than that an orthodox Jew such as Mendelssohn should have accorded any sympathy to the anarchic scheme of Weishaupt. Nevertheless, certain of Weishaupt's doctrines are not incompatible with the principles of orthodox Judaism. Thus, for example, Weishaupt's theory—so strangely at variance with his denunciations of the family system—that as a result of Illuminism " the head of every family will be what Abraham was, the patriarch, the priest, and the unfettered lord of his family, and Reason will be the only code of Man,"[3] is essentially a Jewish conception.

It will be objected that the patriarchal system as conceived by orthodox Jews could by no means include the religion of Reason as advocated by Weishaupt. It must not, however, be forgotten that to the Jewish mind the human race presents a dual aspect, being divided into two distinct categories—the privileged race to whom the promises of God were made, and the great mass of humanity which remains outside the pale.

---

[1] " Foresight indicates," says Falk, " that an end must be made to the whole of the present scheme of Freemasonry [*dem ganzen jetzigen Schema der Freimaurerei ein Ende zu machen*]," and he goes on to show that this must be done by picked men in the secret societies who know the true secrets of Masonry. This is precisely Weishaupt's idea.

[2] In 1779 Spartacus writes to Marius and Cato suggesting that instead of Illuminati the Order should be called the " Order of Bees [Bienenorden oder Bienengesellschaft]," and that all the statutes should be clothed in this allegory.—*Originalschriften*, p. 320.

[3] *Nachtrag von . . . Originalschriften*, II. 81.

Whilst strict adherence to the commands of the Talmud and the laws of Moses is expected of the former, the most indefinite of religious creeds suffices for the nations excluded from the privileges that Jewish birth confers. It was thus that Moses Mendelssohn wrote to the pastor Lavater, who had sought to win him over to Christianity:

Pursuant to the principles of my religion, I am not to seek to convert anyone who is not born according to our laws. This proneness to conversion, the origin of which some would fain tack on to the Jewish religion, is, nevertheless, diametrically opposed to it. Our rabbis unanimously teach that the written and oral laws which form conjointly our revealed religion are obligatory on our nation only. "Moses commanded us a law, even the inheritance of the congregation of Jacob." We believe that all other nations of the earth have been directed by God to adhere to the laws of nature, and to the religion of the patriarchs. Those who regulate their lives according to the precepts of this *religion of nature and of reason*[1] are called virtuous men of other nations and are the children of eternal salvation.[2] Our rabbis are so remote from Proselytomania, that they enjoin us to dissuade, by forcible remonstrances, everyone who comes forward to be converted. (The Talmud says . . . "proselytes are annoying to Israel like a scab.")[3]

But was not this " religion of nature and of reason " the precise conception of Weishaupt?

Whether, then, Weishaupt was directly inspired by Mendelssohn or any other Jew must remain for the present an open question. But the Jewish connexions of certain other Illuminati cannot be disputed. The most important of these was Mirabeau, who arrived in Berlin just after the death of Mendelssohn and was welcomed by his disciples in the Jewish salon of Henrietta Herz. It was these Jews, "ardent supporters of the French Revolution "[4] at its outset, who prevailed on Mirabeau to write his great apology for their race under the form of a panegyric of Mendelssohn.

To sum up, I do not so far see in Illuminism a Jewish con-

---

[1] My italics.
[2] Where are they called this?   The Cabala distinctly states that Israel alone is to possess the future world (Zohar, section Vayschlah, folio 177b), whilst the Talmud even excludes the lost tribes: "the ten tribes have no share in the world to come" (Tract Sanhedrim, Rodkinson's translation, p. 363).
[3] *Memoirs of Moses Mendelssohn*, by M. Samuels, pp. 56, 57 (1827).
[4] Letter to the *Jewish Chronicle*, September 1, 1922, quoting Henrietta Herz.

spiracy to destroy Christianity, but rather a movement finding
its principal dynamic force in the ancient spirit of revolt against
the existing social and moral order, aided and abetted perhaps
by Jews who saw in it a system that might be turned to their
own advantage. Meanwhile, Illuminism made use of every
other movement that could serve its purpose. As the contemporary de Luchet has expressed it:

The system of the Illuminés is not to embrace the dogmas of
a sect, but to turn all errors to its advantage, to concentrate in
itself everything that men have invented in the way of duplicity
and imposture.

More than this, Illuminism was not only the assemblage of
all errors, of all ruses, of all subtleties of a theoretic kind, it
was also an assemblage of all practical methods for rousing men
to action. For in the words of von Hammer on the Assassins,
that cannot be too often repeated:

Opinions are powerless so long as they only confuse the brain
without arming the hand. Scepticism and free-thinking as long as
they occupied only the minds of the indolent and philosophical have
caused the ruin of no throne. . . . It is nothing to the ambitious
man what people believe, but it is everything to know how he
may turn them for the execution of his projects.

This was what Weishaupt so admirably understood; he knew
how to take from every association, past and present, the
portions he required and to weld them all into a working
system of terrible efficiency—the disintegrating doctrines of
the Gnostics and Manicheans, of the modern philosophers
and Encyclopædists, the methods of the Ismailis and the
Assassins, the discipline of the Jesuits and Templars, the
organization and secrecy of the Freemasons, the philosophy
of Machiavelli, the mystery of the Rosicrucians—he knew
moreover, how to enlist the right elements in all existing
associations as well as isolated individuals and turn them to
his purpose. So in the army of the Illuminati we find men of
every shade of thought, from the poet Goethe[1] to the meanest

[1] Goethe was initiated into Freemasonry on St. John's Eve, 1780. *The
Royal Masonic Cyclopædia* observes: "There exist two great classical
Masonic writers, Lessing and Goethe." Dr. Stauffer, in *New England and
the Bavarian Illuminati* (p. 172), points out further that Goethe's connexion
with the Illuminati is fully established by both Engel (*Geschichte des Illuminatenordens*, pp. 355 and following) and by Le Forestier (*Les Illuminés de
Bavière*, pp. 396 and following). It is possible that *Faust* may be the history
of an initiation by a disillusioned Illuminatus.

intriguer—lofty idealists, social reformers, visionaries, and at the same time the ambitious, the rancorous, and the disgruntled, men swayed by lust or embittered by grievances, all these differing in their aims yet by Weishaupt's admirable system of watertight compartments precluded from a knowledge of these differences and all marching, unconsciously or not, towards the same goal.

Although this was not the invention of Weishaupt but had been foreshadowed many centuries earlier in the East, it was Weishaupt, so far as we know, who reduced it to a working system for the West—a system which has been adhered to by succeeding groups of world-revolutionaries up to the present day. It is for this reason that I have quoted at length the writings of the Illuminati—all the ruses, all the hypocrisy, all the subtle methods of camouflage which characterized the Order will be found again in the insidious propaganda both of the modern secret societies and the open revolutionary organizations whose object is to subvert all order, all morality, and all religion.

I maintain, therefore, with greater conviction than ever the importance of Illuminism in the history of world-revolution. But for this co-ordination of methods the philosophers and Encyclopædists might have gone on for ever inveighing against thrones and altars, the Martinistes evoking spirits, the magicians weaving spells, the Freemasons declaiming on universal brotherhood—none of these would have " armed the hand " and driven the infuriated mobs into the streets of Paris; it was not until the emissaries of Weishaupt formed an alliance with the Orléaniste leaders that vague subversive theory became active revolution.

10

THE CLIMAX

THE first Masonic body with which the Illuminati formed an alliance was the Stricte Observance, to which the Illuminati Knigge and Bode both belonged. Cagliostro had also been initiated into the Stricte Observance near Frankfurt and was now employed as agent of the combined order. According to his own confession his mission " was to work so as to turn Freemasonry in the direction of Weishaupt's projects "; and the funds he drew upon were those of the Illuminati.[1] Cagliostro also formed a link with the Martinistes, whose doctrines, though derided by Weishaupt, were useful to his plan in attracting by their mystical character those who would have been repelled by the cynicism of the Illuminati. According to Barruel, it was the Martinistes who—following in the footsteps of the Rosicrucians—had suggested to Weishaupt the device of presenting Christ as an " Illuminatus " which had led to such triumphant results amongst the Protestant clergy.

But if Weishaupt made use of the various masonic associations, they on their account found in him a valuable ally. The fact is that by this time both French and German Freemasons were very much at sea with regard to the whole subject of Masonry and needed someone to give a point to their deliberations., Thus at the Congress of Wilhelmsbad convened on July 16, 1782, and attended by representatives of masonic bodies from all over the world, the first question propounded by the Grand Master of the Templars (i.e. the Stricte Observance) was: " *What is the real object of the Order and its true origin?*" So, says Mirabeau in relating this incident, " this same Grand Master and all his assistants had worked for more than twenty years with incredible ardour at a thing of which they knew neither the real object nor the origin."[2]

[1] Henri Martin, *Histoire de France*, Vol. XVI. p. 531.
[2] *Historie de la Monarchie prussienne*, V. 73.

Two years later the Freemasons of France do not appear to have been any less in the dark on this matter, for we find them writing to General Rainsford, one of the English Masons who had been present at the Congress of Wilhelmsbad, as follows:

Since you say that Masonry has never experienced any variation in its aim, do you then know with certainty what this unique object is? Is it useful for the happiness of mankind? . . . Tell us if it is of an historical, political, hermetical, or scientific nature? . . . Moral, social, or religious? . . . Are the traditions oral or written?[1]

But Weishaupt had a very definite object in view, which was to gain control of all Freemasonry, and though he himself was not present at the Congress, his coadjutor Knigge, who had been travelling about Germany proclaiming himself the reformer of Freemasonry, presented himself at Wilhelmsbad, armed with full authority from Weishaupt, and succeeded in enrolling a number of magistrates, savants, ecclesiastics, and ministers of state as Illuminati and in allying himself with the deputies of Saint-Martin and Willermoz. Vanquished by this powerful rival, the Stricte Observance ceased temporarily to exist and Illuminism was left in possession of the field.

On February 15, 1785, a further congress took place in Paris, convened this time by the Philalèthes, at which the Illuminati Bode (alias Amelius) and the Baron de Busche (alias Bayard) were present, also—it has been stated—the " magician " Cagliostro, the magnetiser Mesmer, the Cabalist Duchanteau, and of course the leaders of the Philalèthes, Savalette de Langes, who was elected President, the Marquis de Chefdebien, and a number of German members of the same Order. This congress led to no very practical results, and a further and more secret one was convened in the following year at Frankfurt, where a Grand Lodge had been established in 1783. It was here that the deaths of Louis XVI and Gustavus III of Sweden are said to have been decreed.

But already in this same year of 1785 the first act of the revolutionary drama had been played out. The famous " Affair of the Necklace " can never be understood in the pages of official history; only an examination of the mechanism provided by the secret societies can explain that extraordinary episode, which, in the opinion of Napoleon, contributed more than any other cause to the explosion of 1789. In its double attack on Church and Monarchy the Affair of the Necklace

[1] *Ars Quatuor Coronatorum*, Vol. XXVI. p. 98.

fulfilled the purpose of both Frederick the Great and of the Illuminati. Cagliostro, we know, received both money and instructions from the Order for carrying out the plot, and after it had ended in his own and the Cardinal de Rohan's exoneration and exile, we find him embarking on fresh secret-society work in London, where he arrived in November of the same year. Announcing himself as the Count Sutkowski, member of a society at Avignon, he " visited the Swedenborgians at their Theosophical Society meeting in rooms in the Middle Temple and displayed minute acquaintance with their doctrines, whilst claiming a superior knowledge."[1] According to a generally received opinion, Cagliostro was the author of a mysterious proclamation which appeared at this moment in the *Morning Herald* in the cypher of the Rose-Croix.[2]

But in the year before these events an extraordinary thing had happened. An evangelist preacher and Illuminatus named Lanze had been sent in July 1785 as an emissary of the Illuminati to Silesia, but on his journey he was struck down by lightning. The instructions of the Order were found on him, and as a result its intrigues were conclusively revealed to the Government of Bavaria.[3] A searching enquiry followed, the houses of Zwack and Bassus were raided, and it was then that the documents and other incriminating evidence referred to in the preceding chapter of this book were seized and made public under the name of *The Original Writings of the Order of the Illuminati* (1787). But before this the evidence of four ex-Illuminati, professors of Munich, was published in two separate volumes.[4]

The diabolical nature of Illuminism now remained no longer a matter of doubt, and the Order was officially suppressed. The opponents of Barruel and Robison therefore declare that Illuminism came finally to an end. We shall see later by documentary evidence that it never ceased to exist, and that twenty-five years later not only the Illuminati but Weishaupt himself were still as active as ever behind the scenes in Freemasonry.

But for the present we must follow its course from the moment of its apparent extinction in 1786. This course can

---

[1] " Notes on the Rainsford Papers " in *A.Q.C.*, Vol. XXVI. p. 111.
[2] *Morning Herald* for November 2, 1786.
[3] Eckert, *La Franc-Maçonnerie dans sa véritable signification*, Vol. II. p. 92.
[4] *Drei merkwürdige Aussagen*, etc., evidence of Grünberger, Cosandey, and Renner (Munich, 1786); *Grosse Absichten des Ordens der Illuminaten*, etc., Ditto, with Utzschneider (Munich, 1786).

be traced not only through the "German Union," which is believed to have been a reorganization of the original Illuminati, but through the secret societies of France. Illuminism in reality is less an Order than a principle, and a principle which can work better under cover of something else. Weishaupt himself had laid down the precept that the work of Illuminism could best be conducted "under other names and other occupations," and henceforth we shall always find it carried on by this skilful system of camouflage.

The first cover adopted was the lodge of the "Amis Réunis" in Paris, with which, as we have already seen, the Illuminati had established relations. But now in 1787 a definite alliance was effected by the aforementioned Illuminati, Bode and Busche, who in response to an invitation from the secret committee of the lodge arrived in Paris in February of this year. Here they found the old Illuminatus Mirabeau—who with Talleyrand had been largely instrumental in summoning these German Brothers—and, according to Gustave Bord,[1] two important members of the Stricte Observance, the Marquis de Chefdebien d'Armisson (*Eques a Capite Galeato*) and an Austrian, the Comte Leopold de Kollowrath-Krakowski (*Eques ab Aquila Fulgente*) who also belonged to Weishaupt's Order of Illuminati in which he bore the pseudonym of Numenius.

It is important here to recognize the peculiar part played by the Lodge of the *Amis Réunis*. Whilst the *Loge des Neuf Sœurs* was largely composed of middle-class revolutionaries such as Brissot, Danton, Camille Desmoulins, and Champfort, and the *Loge de la Candeur* of aristocratic revolutionaries— Lafayette as well as the Orléanistes, the Marquis de Sillery, the Duc d'Aiguillon, the Marquis de Custine, and the Lameths —*the Loge du Contrat Social* was mainly composed of honest visionaries who entertained no revolutionary projects but, according to Barruel, were strongly Royalist. The rôle of the "Amis Réunis" was to collect together the subversives from all other lodges—Philalèthes, Rose-Croix, members of the *Loge des Neuf Sœurs* and of the *Loge de la Candeur* and of the most

---

[1] Gustave Bord, *La Franc-Maçonnerie en France*, etc., p. 351 (1908). This Australian Count is referred to in the correspondence of the Illuminati more as an agent than as an adept. Thus Weishaupt writes: "I must attempt to cure him of theosophy and bring him round to our views" (*Nachtrag von . . . Originalschriften*, I. 71); and Philo, before the Congress of Wilhelmsbad, observes: "Numenius is not yet of much use. I am only taking him up so as to stop his mouth at the Congress [*um ihn auf dem Convente das Maul zu stopfen*]; still, if he is well led we can make something out of him" (ibid., p. 109).

secret committees of the Grand Orient, as well as deputies from the *Illuminés* in the provinces. Here, then, at the lodge in the Rue de la Sourdière, under the direction of Savalette de Langes, were to be found the disciples of Weishaupt, of Swedenborg, and of Saint-Martin, as well as the practical makers of revolution—the agitators and demagogues of 1789.

The influence of German Illuminism on all these heterogeneous elements was enormous. From this moment, says a further Bavarian report of the matter, a complete change took place in the Order of the "Amis Réunis." Hitherto only vaguely subversive, the Chevaliers Bienfaisants became the Chevaliers Malfaisants, the Amis Réunis became the Ennemis Réunis. The arrival of the two Germans, Bode and Busche, gave the finishing touch to the conspiracy. "The avowed object of their journey was to obtain information about magnetism, which was just then making a great stir," but in reality, "taken up with the gigantic plan of their Order," their real aim was to make proselytes. It will be seen that the following passage exactly confirms the account given by Barruel:

As the Lodge of the *Amis Réunis* collected together everything that could be found out from all other masonic systems in the world, so the way was soon paved there for Illuminism. It was also not long before this lodge together with all those that depended on it was impregnated with Illuminism. The former system of all these was as if wiped out, so that from this time onwards the framework of the Philalèthes quite disappeared and in the place of the former Cabalistic-magical extravagance [*Schwärmerei*] came in the philosophical-political.[1]

It was therefore not Martinism, Cabalism, or Freemasonry that in themselves provided the real revolutionary force. Many non-illuminized Freemasons, as Barruel himself declares, remained loyal to the throne and altar, and as soon as the monarchy was seen to be in danger the Royalist Brothers of the *Contrat Social* boldly summoned the lodges to coalesce in defence of King and Constitution; even some of the upper Masons, who in the degree of Knight Kadosch had sworn hatred to the Pope and Bourbon monarchy, rallied likewise to the royal cause. "The French spirit triumphed over the masonic spirit in the greater number of the Brothers. Opinions

---

[1] *Die Neuesten Arbeiten des Spartacus und Philo in dem Illuminaten-Orden*, p. viii (1794).

as well as hearts were still for the King." It needed the devastating doctrines of Weishaupt to undermine this spirit and to turn the " degrees of vengeance " from vain ceremonial into terrible fact.

If, then, it is said that the Revolution was prepared in the lodges of Freemasons—and many French Masons have boasted of the fact—let it always be added that it was *Illuminized Freemasonry* that made the Revolution, and that the Masons who acclaim it are illuminized Masons, inheritors of the same tradition introduced into the lodges of France in 1787 by the disciples of Weishaupt, " patriarch of the Jacobins."

Many of the Freemasons of France in 1787 were thus not conscious allies of the Illuminati. According to Cadet de Gassicourt, there were in all the lodges only twenty-seven real initiates; the rest were largely dupes who knew little or nothing of the source whence the fresh influence among them derived. The amazing feature of the whole situation is that the most enthusiastic supporters of the movement were men belonging to the upper classes and even to the royal families of Europe. A contemporary relates that no less than thirty princes—reigning and non-reigning—had taken under their protection a confederation from which they stood to lose everything and had become so imbued by its principles that they were inaccessible to reason.[1] Intoxicated by the flattery lavished on them by the priests of Illuminism, they adopted a religion of which they understood nothing. Weishaupt, of course, had taken care that none of these royal dupes should be initiated into the real aims of the Order, and at first adhered to the original plan of excluding them altogether; but the value of their co-operation soon became apparent and by a supreme irony it was with a Grand Duke that he himself took refuge.

But if the great majority of princes and nobles were stricken with blindness at this crisis, a few far-seeing spirits recognized the danger and warned the world of the impending disaster. In 1787 Cardinal Caprara, Apostolic Nuncio at Vienna, addressed a confidential memoir to the Pope, in which he pointed out that the activities carried on in Germany by the different sects of Illuminés, of Perfectibilists, of Freemasons, etc., were increasing.

The danger is approaching, for from all these senseless dreams of Illuminism, of Swedenborgianism, or of Freemasonry a frightful

[1] De Luchet, *Essai sur la Secte des Illuminés*, p. vii.

reality will emerge. Visionaries have their time; the revolution they forebode will have its time also.[1]

A more amazing prophecy, however, was the *Essai sur la Secte des Illuminés,* by the Marquis de Luchet,[2] a Liberal noble who played some part in the revolutionary movement, yet who nevertheless realized the dangers of Illuminism. Thus, as early as 1789, before the Revolution had really developed, de Luchet uttered these words of warning:

> Deluded people . . . learn that there exists a conspiracy in favour of despotism against liberty, of incapacity against talent, of vice against virtue, of ignorance against enlightenment. . . . This society aims at governing the world. . . . Its object is universal domination. This plan may seem extraordinary, incredible—yes, but not chimerical . . . no such calamity has ever yet afflicted the world.

De Luchet then goes on to foretell precisely the events that were to take place three and four years later; he describes the position of a king who has to recognize masters above himself and to authorize their " abominable régime," to become the plaything of an ambitious and fanatical horde which has taken possession of his will.

> See him condemned to serve the passions of all that surround him . . . to raise degraded men to power, to prostitute his judgement by choices that dishonour his prudence. . . .

All this was exactly fulfilled during the reign of the Girondin ministry of 1792. The campaign of destruction carried out in the summer of 1793 is thus foretold:

> We do not mean to say that the country where the Illumines reign will cease to exist, but it will fall into such a degree of humiliation that it will no longer count in politics, that the population will diminish, that the inhabitants who resist the inclination to pass into a foreign land will no longer enjoy the happiness of consideration, nor the charms of society, nor the gifts of commerce.

---

[1] Crétineau Joly, *L'Église Romaine en face de la Révolution,* I. p. 93.

[2] In my *World Revolution* I accepted erroneously the opinion of several well-known writers who attribute this pamphlet to Mirabeau. The fact that it was printed at the end of Mirabeau's *Histoire Secrète de la Cour de Berlin* and that a further edition revised by Mirabeau was published in 1792 no doubt gave rise to this supposition. But apart from the fact that Mirabeau as an Illuminatus was unlikely himself to denounce the Order, the proof that he was not the author may be found at the British Museum, where the copy of the 1792 edition bears on the title-page the words in ink " Donné par l'auteur," and Mirabeau died in the spring of the preceding year.

And de Luchet ends with this despairing appeal to the powers of Europe:

Masters of the world, cast your eyes on a desolated multitude, listen to their cries, their tears, their hopes. A mother asks you to restore her son, a wife her husband, your cities for the fine arts that have fled from them, the country for citizens, the fields for cultivators, religion for forms of worship, and Nature for beings of which she is worthy.

Five years after these words were written the countryside of France was desolate, art and commerce were destroyed, and women following the tumbril that carried Fouquier-Tinville to the guillotine cried out: "Give me back my brother, my son, my husband!" So was this amazing prophecy fulfilled. Yet not one word has history to say on the subject! The warning of de Luchet has fallen on deaf ears amongst posterity as amongst the men of his own day.

De Luchet himself recognizes the obstacle to his obtaining a hearing: there are too many "passions interested in support-ing the system of the Illuminés," too many deluded rulers imagining themselves enlightened ready to precipitate their people into the abyss, whilst "the heads of the Order will never relinquish the authority they have acquired nor the treasure at their disposal." In vain de Luchet appeals to the Freemasons to save their Order from the invading sect. "Would it not be possible," he asks, "to direct the Freemasons themselves against the Illuminés by showing them that whilst they are working to maintain harmony in society, those others are everywhere sowing seeds of discord" and preparing the ultimate destruc-tion of their Order? So far it is not too late; if only men will believe in the danger it may be averted: "from the moment they are convinced, the necessary blow is dealt to the sect." Otherwise de Luchet prophesies "a series of calamities of which the end is lost in the darkness of time, . . . a subter-ranean fire smouldering eternally and breaking forth periodi-cally in violent and devastating explosions." What words could better describe the history of the last 150 years?

The *Essai sur la Secte des Illuminés* is one of the most extra-ordinary documents of history and at the same time one of the most mysterious. Why it should have been written by the Marquis de Luchet, who is said to have collaborated with Mirabeau in the *Galerie de Portraits* published in the follow-ing year, why it should have been appended to Mirabeau's *His-toire Secrète de la Cour de Berlin,* and accordingly attributed to Mirabeau himself, why Barruel should have denounced it as dust thrown in the eyes of the public, although it entirely corroborated his own point of view, are questions to which I can find no reply. That is was written seriously and in all good faith it is impossible to doubt; whilst the fact that it appeared before, instead of after, the events described, renders it even more valuable evidence of the reality of the conspiracy than Barruel's own admirable work. What Barruel saw, de Luchet foresaw with equal clearness. As to the rôle of Mirabeau at this crisis, we can only hazard an explanation on the score of his habitual inconsistency. At one moment he was seeking interviews with the King's ministers in order to warn them of the coming danger, at the next he was energetically stirring up insurrection. It is therefore not impossible that he may have encouraged de Luchet's exposure of the conspiracy, although meanwhile he himself had entered into the scheme of destruction. Indeed, according to a pamphlet published in 1791 entitled *Mystères de la Conspiration*,[1] the whole plan of revolution was found amongst his papers. The editor of this *brochure* explains that the document here made public, called *Croquis ou Projet de Révolution de Monsieur de Mirabeau,* was seized at the house of Madame Lejai, the wife of Mirabeau's publisher, on October 6, 1789. Beginning with a diatribe against the French monarchy, the document goes on to say that "in order to triumph over this hydra-headed monster these are my ideas ":

We must overthrow all order, suppress all laws, annul all power, and leave the people in anarchy. The laws we establish will not perhaps be in force at once, but at any rate, having given back the power to the people, they will resist for the sake of their liberty which they will believe they are preserving. We must caress their vanity, flatter their hopes, promise them happiness after our work has been in operation; we must elude their caprices and their systems at will, for the people as legislators are very dangerous, they only establish laws which coincide with their passions, their want of knowledge would besides only give birth to abuses. But as the people are a lever which legislators can move at their will, we must necessarily use them as a support, and render hateful to them everything we wish to destroy and sow illusions in their path; we must also buy all the mercenary pens which propagate our methods and which will instruct the people concerning their enemies whom we attack. The clergy, being the most powerful through public opinion, can only be destroyed by ridiculing religion,

---

[1] British Museum press-mark F. 259 (14).

rendering its ministers odious, and only representing them as hypocritical monsters, for Mahomet in order to establish his religion first defamed the paganism which the Arabs, the Sarmathes, and the Scythians professed. Libels must at every moment show fresh traces of hatred against the clergy. To exaggerate their riches, to make the sins of an individual appear to be common to all, to attribute to them all vices; calumny, murder, irreligion, sacrilege, all is permitted in times of revolution.

We must degrade the *noblesse* and attribute it to an odious origin, establish a germ of equality which can never exist but which will flatter the people; [we must] immolate the most obstinate, burn and destroy their property in order to intimidate the rest, so that if we cannot entirely destroy this prejudice we can weaken it and the people will avenge their vanity and ·their jealousy by all the excesses which will bring them to submission.

After describing how the soldiers are to be seduced from their allegiance, and the magistrates represented to the people as despots, "since the people, brutal and ignorant, only see the evil and never the good of things," the writer explains they must be given only limited power in the municipalities.

Let us beware above all of giving them too much force; their despotism is too dangerous, we must flatter the people by gratuitous justice, promise them a great diminution in taxes and a more equal division, more extension in fortunes, and less humiliation. These phantasies [*vertiges*] will fanaticise the people, who will flatten out all resistance. What matter the victims and their numbers? spoliations, destructions, burnings, and all the necessary effects of a revolution? nothing must be sacred and we can say with Machiavelli: "What matter the means as long as one arrives at the end?"

Were all these the ideas of Mirabeau, or were they, like the other document of the Illuminati found amongst his papers, the programme of a conspiracy? I incline to the latter theory. The plan of campaign was, at any rate, the one followed out by the conspirators, as Chamfort, the friend and confidant of Mirabeau, admitted in his conversation with Marmontel:

The nation is a great herd that only thinks of browsing, and with good sheepdogs the shepherds can lead it as they please. . . . Money and the hope of plunder are all-powerful with the people. . . Mirabeau cheerfully asserts that with 100 louis one can make quite a good riot.[1]

---

[1] *Œuvres posthumes de Marmontel*, IV. 77.

Another contemporary thus describes the methods of the leaders:

Mirabeau, in the exuberance of an orgy, cried one day: "That *canaille* well deserves to have us for legislators!" These professions of faith, as we see, are not at all democratic; the sect uses the populace as revolution fodder [*chair à révolution*], as prime material for brigandage, after which it seizes the gold and abandons generations to torture. It is veritably the code of hell.[1]

It is this "' code of hell " set forth in the " Projet de Révolution " that we shall find repeated in succeeding documents throughout the last hundred years—in the correspondence of the " Alta Vendita," in the *Dialogues aux Enfers entre Machiavel et Montesquieu* by Maurice Joly, in the Revolutionary Catechism of Bakunin, in the Protocols of the Elders of Zion, and in the writings of the Russian Bolsheviks to-day.

Whatever doubts may be cast on the authenticity of any of these documents, the indisputable fact thus remains that as early as 1789 this Machiavellian plan of engineering revolution and using the people as a lever for raising a tyrannical minority to power, had been formulated; further, that the methods described in this earliest " Protocol " have been carried out according to plan from that day to this. And in every outbreak of the social revolution the authors of the movement have been known to be connected with secret societies.

It was Adrien Duport, author of the " Great Fear " that spread over France on July 22, 1789, Duport, the inner initiate of the secret societies, " holding in his hands all the threads of the masonic conspiracy," who on May 21, 1790, set forth before the Committee of Propaganda the vast scheme of destruction.

M. de Mirabeau has well established the fact that the fortunate revolution which has taken place in France must and will be for all the peoples of Europe the awakening of liberty and for Kings the sleep of death.

But Duport goes on to explain that whilst Mirabeau thinks it advisable at present not to concern themselves with anything outside France, he himself believes that the triumph of the French Revolution must lead inevitably to " the ruin

[1] Lombard de Langres, *Histoire des Jacobins*, p. 31 (1820).

of all thrones. . . . Therefore we must hasten among our neighbours the same revolution that is going on in France."[1]

The plan of illuminized Freemasonry was thus nothing less than world-revolution.

It is necessary here to reply to a critic who suggested that in emphasizing the rôle of the secret societies in *World Revolution* I had abandoned my former thesis of the Orléaniste conspiracy. I wish therefore to state that I do not retract one word I wrote in *The French Revolution* on the Orléaniste conspiracy, I merely supply a further explanation of its efficiency by enlarging on the aid it received from the party I referred to as the Subversives—outcome of the masonic lodges. It was because the Orléanistes held the whole masonic organization at their disposal that they were able to carry out their plans with such extraordinary skill and thoroughness, and because they had at their back men bent solely on destruction that they could enlist a following which would not have rallied to a mere scheme of usurpation. Even Montjoie, who saw in the Revolution principally the work of the Duc d'Orléans, indicates in a very curious passage of a later work the existence of the still darker intrigue behind the conspiracy he had spent his energies in unveiling:

I will not examine whether this wicked prince, thinking he was acting in his personal interests, was not moved by that invisible hand which seems to have created all the events of our revolution in order to lead us towards a goal that we do not see at present, but which I think we shall see before long.[2]

Unfortunately, after this mysterious utterance Montjoie never again returns to the subject.

At the beginning of the Revolution, Orléanism and Freemasonry thus formed a united body. According to Lombard de Langres:

France in 1789 counted more than 2,000 lodges affiliated to the Grand Orient; the number of adepts was more than 100,000. The first events of 1789 were only Masonry in action. All the revolutionaries of the Constituent Assembly were initiated into the

---

[1] Deschamps, *Les Sociétés Secrètes et la Société*, II. 151, quoting document amongst the papers of Cardinal Bernis entitled: *Discours prononcé au comité de la Propagande par M. Duport, un de ses mémoires, le 21 mai 1790.*

[2] Galart de Montjoie, *Histoire de Marie Antoinette de Lorraine*, p. 156 (1797).

third degree. We place in this class the Duc d'Orléans, Valence, Syllery, Laclos, Sièyes, Pétion, Menou, Biron, Montesquiou, Fauchet, Condorcet, Lafayette, Mirabeau, Garat, Rabaud, Dubois-Crancé, Thiébaud, Larochefoucauld, and others.[1]

Amongst these others were not only the Brissotins, who formed the nucleus of the Girondin party, but the men of the Terror—Marat, Robespierre, Danton, and Desmoulins.

It was these fiercer elements, true disciples of the Illuminati, who were to sweep away the visionary Masons dreaming of equality and brotherhood. Following the precedent set by Weishaupt, classical pseudonyms were adopted by these leaders of the Jacobins, thus Chaumette was known as Anaxagoras, Clootz as Anacharsis, Danton as Horace, Lacroix as Publicola, and Ronsin as Scaevola[2]; again, after the manner of the Illuminati, the names of towns were changed and a revolutionary calendar was adopted. The red cap and loose hair affected by the Jacobins appear also to have been foreshadowed in the lodges of the Illuminati.[3]

Yet faithfully as the Terrorists carried out the plan of the Illuminati, it would seem that they themselves were not initiated into the innermost secrets of the conspiracy. Behind the Convention, behind the clubs, behind the Revolutionary Tribunal, there existed, says Lombard de Langres, that " most secret convention [*convention sécrétissime*] which directed everything after May 31, an occult and terrible power of which the other Convention became the slave and which was composed of the prime initiates of Illuminism. This power was above Robespierre and the committees of the government, . . . it was this occult power which appropriated to itself the treasures of the nation and distributed them to the brothers and friends who had helped on the great work."[4]

What was the aim of this occult power? Was it merely the plan of destruction that had originated in the brain of a Bavarian professor twenty years earlier, or was it something far older, a live and terrible force that had lain dormant through the centuries, that Weishaupt and his allies had not created but only loosed upon the world? The Reign of

---

[1] Lombard de Langres, *Histoire des Jacobins*, p. 117 (1820).
[2] Ibid., p. **236.**
[3] See *Die Neuesten Arbeiten des Spartacus und Philo*, p. 71, where the Illuminati are described as wearing " fliegende Haare und kleine vierekte rothe samtne Hüte." An alternative theory is, however, that the " cap of liberty " was copied from that of the galley-slaves.
[4] *Histoire des Jacobins*, p. 117.

Terror, like the outbreak of Satanism in the Middle Ages, can be explained by no material causes—the orgy of hatred, lust, and cruelty directed not only against the rich but still more against the poor and defenceless, the destruction of science, art, and beauty, the desecration of the churches, the organized campaign against all that was noble, all that was sacred, all that humanity holds dear, what was this but Satanism?

In desecrating the churches and stamping on the crucifixes the Jacobins had in fact followed the precise formula of black magic: "For the purpose of infernal evocation . . . it is requisite . . . to profane the ceremonies of the religion to which one belongs and to trample its holiest symbols under foot."[1] It was this that formed the prelude to the "Great Terror," when, to those who lived through it, it seemed that France lay under the sway of the powers of darkness.

So in the "great shipwreck of civilization," as a contemporary has described it, the projects of the Cabalists, the Gnostics, and the secret societies which for nearly eighteen centuries had sapped the foundations of Christianity found their fulfilment. Do we not detect an echo of the Toledot Yeshu in the blasphemies of the Marquis de Sade concerning "the Jewish slave" and "the adulterous woman, the courtesan of Galilee?" And in the imprecations of Marat's worshippers, "Christ was a false prophet!" a repetition of the secret doctrine attributed to the Templars: "Jesus is not the true God; He is a false prophet; He was not crucified for the salvation of humanity, but for His own misdeeds"? Are these resemblances accidental, or are they the outcome of a continuous plot against the Christian faith?

What, then, was the rôle of Jews in the Revolution? In this connexion it is necessary to understand the situation of the Jews in France at this period.

After the decree of banishment issued by Charles VI in 1394, Jewry, as a body, had ceased to exist; but towards the end of the fifteenth century a certain number of Jews, driven out of Spain and Portugal, were allowed to settle in Bordeaux. These Spanish and Portuguese Jews, known as *Sephardim*, appeared to acquiesce in the Christian religion and were not officially regarded as Jews, but enjoyed considerable privileges conferred on them by Henri II. It was not until the beginning of the eighteenth century, during the Regency, that Jews

[1] A. E. Waite, *The Mysteries of Magic*, p. 215.

began to reappear in Paris. Meanwhile, the annexation of Alsace at the end of the previous century had added to the population of France the German Jews of that province known as the *Ashkenazim.*

It is important to distinguish between these two races of Jews in discussing the question of Jewish emancipation at the time of the Revolution. For whilst the Sephardim had shown themselves good citizens and were therefore subject to no persecutions, the Ashkenazim by their extortionate usury and oppressions had made themselves detested by the people, so that rigorous laws were enforced to restrain their rapacity. The discussions that raged in the National Assembly on the subject of the Jewish question related therefore mainly to the Jews of Alsace. Already, in 1784, the Jews of Bordeaux had been accorded further concessions by Louis XVI; in 1776 all Portuguese Jews had been given religious liberty and the permission to inhabit all parts of the kingdom. The decree of January 28, 1790, conferring on the Jews of Bordeaux the rights of French citizens, put the finishing touch to this scheme of liberation. But the proposal to extend this privilege to the Jews of Alsace evoked a storm of controversy in the Assembly and also violent insurrections amongst the Alsatian peasants. It was thus on behalf of the people that several deputies protested against the decree. " The Jews," said the Abbé Maury, " have traversed seventeen centuries without mingling with other nations. They have never done anything but trade with money, they have been the scourge of agricultural provinces, not one of them has known how to ennoble his hands by guiding the plough." And he went on to point out that the Jews " must not be persecuted, they must be protected as individuals and not as Frenchmen, since they cannot be citizens. . . . Whatever you do, they will always remain foreigners in our midst."

Monseigneur de la Fare, Bishop of Nancy, adopted the same line of argument:

They must be accorded protection, safety, liberty; but should we admit into the family a tribe that is foreign to it, that turns its eyes unceasingly towards a common country, that aspires to abandon the land that bears it? . . . My *cahier* orders me to protest against the motion that has been made to you. The interest of the Jews themselves necessitates this protest. The people have a horror of them; they are often in Alsace the victims of popular risings.[1]

[1] *Moniteur,* Vol. II., séance du 23 décembre, 1789.

In all this, as will be seen, there is no question of persecution, but of precautions against a race that wilfully isolates itself from the rest of the community in order to pursue its own interests and advantages. The Jews of Bordeaux indeed recognized the odium that the German Jews were calculated to bring on the Jewish cause, and in an address to the Assembly on January 22, 1790, dissociated themselves from the aggressive claims of the Ashkenazim:

> We dare to believe that our condition in France would not to-day be open to discussion if certain demands of the Jews of Alsace, Lorraine, and the Trois Evêchés [i.e. Metz, Toul, and Verdun] had not caused a confusion of ideas which appears to reflect on us. We do not yet know exactly what these demands are, but to judge by the public papers they appear to be rather extraordinary since these Jews aspire to live in France under a special régime, to have laws peculiar to themselves, and to constitute a class of citizens separated from all the others.

> As for us, our condition in France has long since been settled. We have been naturalized French since 1550; we possess all kinds of properties, and we enjoy the unlimited right to acquire estates. We have neither laws, tribunals, nor officers of our own[1]

In adopting this attitude the Sephardim created a precedent which, if it had been followed henceforth consistently by their co-religionists, might have gone far to allay prejudice against the Jewish race. It was the solidarity generally presented by the Jews towards the rest of the community which excited alarm in the minds of French citizens. Thirty years earlier the merchants of Paris, in a petition against the admission of the Jews to their corporations, indicated by an admirable simile the danger this solidarity offered to free commerce.

> The French merchant carries on his commerce alone; each commercial house is in a way isolated, whilst the Jews are particles of quicksilver, which at the least slant run together into a block.[2]

But in spite of all protests, the decree emancipating the Jews of Alsace was passed in September 1791, and hymns of praise were sung in the synagogues.

What part was actually played by the Jews in the tumults of the Revolution it is impossible to determine, for the reason

---

[1] Théophile Malvezin, *Histoire des Juifs à Bordeaux*, p. 262 (1875).
[2] *Requête des six corps de marchands et négociants de Paris contre l'admission des Juifs* in Archives Nationales, quoted by Henri Delassus, *La Question Juive*, p. 60 (1911).

that they are seldom designated as such in the writings of contemporaries. On this point Jewish writers appear to be better informed than the rest of the world, for Monsieur Léon Kahn in his panegyric on the part played by his co-religionists in the Revolution[1] finds Jews where even Drumont failed to detect them. Thus we read that it was a Jew, Rosenthal, who headed the legion known by his name, which was sent against La Vendée but took to flight,[2] and which was the subject of complaint when employed to guard the Royal Family at the Temple[3]; that amongst those who worked most energetically to deprive the clergy of their goods was a Jewish ex-old-clothes seller, Zalkind Hourwitz; that it was a Jew named Lang who murdered three out of the five Swiss guards at the foot of the staircase in the Tuileries on August 10 [4]; that Jews were implicated in the theft of the crown jewels on September 16, 1792, and one named Lyre was executed in consequence; that it was Clootz and the Jew Pereyra, and not, as I had stated, Hébert, Chaumette, and Momoro, who went to the Archbishop Gobel in November 1793 and induced him by means of threats to abjure the Christian faith.[5]

All these facts were unknown to me when I wrote my account of these events; it will be seen then that, far from exaggerating the rôle of the Jews in *The French Revolution*, I very much underrated it. Indeed the question of their complicity had not occurred to me at all when I wrote this book, and the only Jew to whom I referred was Ephraïm—sent to France by the Illuminati Frederick William II and Bischoffswerder— whom M. Kahn indicates as playing an even more important part than I had assigned to him.

But illuminating as these incidents may be, it is yet open to question whether they prove any concerted attempt on the part of the Jews to bring about the overthrow of the French monarchy and the Catholic religion. It is true, nevertheless, that they themselves boasted of their revolutionary ardour. In an address presenting their claims before the National Assembly in 1789, they declare:

Regenerators of the French Empire, you would not wish that we should cease to be citizens, since for already six months we have assiduously performed all duties as such, and the recompense for

[1] Léon Kahn, *Les Juifs de Paris pendant la Révolution* (1898).
[2] Ibid., p. 167. Cf. Arthur Chuquet, *La Légion Germanique,* p. 139 (1904).
[3] Archives Nationales, F⁷. 2486.
[4] My *French Revolution,* p. 274.
[5] Kahn, op. cit., pp. 140, 141, 170, 201, 241.

the zeal we have shown in accelerating the revolution will not be to condemn us to participate in none of its advantages now that it has been consummated. . . . Nosseigneurs, we are all very good citizens, and in this memorable revolution we dare to say that there is not one of us who has not proved himself.[1]

In all these activities, however, religious feeling appears to have played an entirely subordinate part; the Jews, as has been said, were free before the Revolution to carry on the rites of their faith. And when the great anti-religious campaign began, many of them entered whole-heartedly into the attack on all religious faiths, their own included. Thus on the 21st Brumaire, whilst the Feasts of Reason were taking place in the churches of Paris, we find " a deputation of Israelites " presenting themselves at the National Assembly and "depositing on the bosom of the Mountain the ornaments of which they had stripped a little temple they had in the Faubourg Saint-Germain." At the same moment—

A revolutionary committee of the Réunion brings to the general council crosses, suns, chalices, copes, and quantities of other ornaments of worship, and a member of this committee observes that several of these effects belong to individuals of the Jewish race. A minister of the religion of Moses, Abraham, and Jacob asks in the name of his co-religionists that the said effects should not be regarded as belonging to such and such a sect, . . . this citizen is named Benjamin Jacob. . . . Another member of the same committee pays homage to the patriotic zeal of the citizens heretofore Jews, . . . almost all have forestalled the wish of the revolutionary committee by themselves bringing their reliquaries and ornaments, amongst others the famous cope said to have belonged to Moses.[2]

On the 20th Frimaire at " the Temple of Liberty," formerly the church of the Benedictines, " the citizen Alexandre Lambert fils, a Jew brought up in the prejudices of the Jewish religion," uttered a violent harangue against all religions:

I will prove to you, citizens, that all forms of worship are impostures equally degrading to man and to divinities; I will not prove it by philosophy, I do not know it, but only by the light of reason.

After denouncing the iniquities of both the Catholic and Protestant faiths, Lambert demonstrates " the absurdities of

---

[1] *Nouvelle Adresse des Juifs à l'Assemblée Nationale,* le 24 décembre, 1789.
[2] *Moniteur,* Vol. XVIII., séances of 21st and 22nd Brumaire, An 2 (November, 1793).

THE CLIMAX 251

the Jewish religion, of this domineering religion "; he thunders
against Moses " governing a simple and agrarian people like
all' clever impostors," against " the servile respect of the Jews
for their kings . . . the ablutions of women," etc. Finally
he declares:

The bad faith, citizens, of which the Jewish nation is accused does
not come from themselves but from their priests. Their religion,
which would allow them only to lend to those of their nation at
5 per cent., tells them to take all they can from Catholics; it is
even hallowed as a custom in our morning prayers to solicit God's
help in catching out a Christian. There is more, citizens, and it is
the climax of abomination: if any mistake is made in commerce
between Jews, they are ordered to make reparation; but if on 100 louis
a Christian should have paid 25 too much, one is not bound to
return them to him. What an abomination! What a horror! And
where does that all come from but from the Rabbis? Who have
excited proscriptions against us? Our priests! Ah, citizens, more
than anything in the world we must abjure a religion which, . . .
by subjecting us to irksome and servile practices, makes it impossible
for us to be good citizens.[1]

The encouragement accorded by the Jews to the French
Revolution appears thus to have been prompted not by
religious fanaticism but by a desire for national advantage.
That they gained immensely by the overthrow of the Old
Order is undeniable, for apart from the legislation passed on
their behalf in the National Assembly, the disorder of the
finances in 1796 was such that, as M. Léon Kahn tells us, a
contemporary journal enquired: " Has the Revolution then
been only a financial scheme? a speculation of bankers?"[2] We
know from Prudhomme to what race the financiers who principally profited by this disorder belonged.[3]

But if the rôle of the Jews in the Revolution remains obscure
there can be no doubt of the part played by the secret societies
in the revolt against all religion, all moral laws, and social
order, which had been reduced to a system in the councils of
the Illuminati.

It was this conspiracy that reasserted itself in the Babouviste
rising of 1796 which was directly inspired by the secret

[1] *Discours de morale, prononcé le 2ième décadi, 20 frimaire, l'an 2ième de
la république . . . au temple de la Vérité, ci-devant l'église des bénédictins à
Angely Boutonne . . . fait par le citoyen Alexandre Lambert, fils, juif et élevé
dans les préjugés du culte judaïque* (1794), British Museum press-mark F.
1058 (4).
[2] Kahn, op. cit., p. 311.
[3] *Crimes de la Révolution*, III. 44.

societies. After the death of Babeuf, his friend and inspirer Buonarotti with the aid of Marat's brother founded a masonic lodge, the *Amis Sincères*, which was affiliated to the *Phila delphes*, at Geneva, and as " Diacre Mobile " of the " Order of Sublime and Perfect Masons " created three new secret degrees, in which the device of the Rose-Croix I.N.R.I. was interpreted as signifying " Justum necare reges injustos."[1]

The part to be assigned to each intrigue in preparing the world-movement of which the French Revolution was the first expression is a question on which no one can speak with certainty. But, as at the present moment, the composite nature of this movement must never be lost to sight. Largely perhaps the work of Frederick the Great, it is probable that but for the Orléanistes the plot against the French monarchy might have come to nought; whilst again, but for his position at the head of illuminized Freemasonry it is doubtful whether the Duc d'Orléans could have commanded the forces of revolution. Further, how far the movement, which, like the modern Bolshevist conspiracy, appears to have had unlimited funds at its disposal, was financed by the Jews yet remains to be discovered. Hitherto only the first steps have been taken towards elucidating the truth about the French Revolution.

In the opinion of an early nineteenth-century writer the sect which engineered the French Revolution was absolutely international:

The authors of the Revolution are not more French than German, Italian, English, etc. They form a particular nation which took birth and has grown in the darkness, in the midst of all civilized nations, with the object of subjecting them to its domination.[2]

It is curious to find almost precisely the same idea expressed by the Duke of Brunswick, formerly the " Eques a Victoria " of the Stricte Observance, " Aaron " of the Illuminati, and Grand Master of German Freemasonry, who, whether because the Revolution had done its work in destroying the French monarchy and now threatened the security of Germany, or whether because he was genuinely disillusioned in the Orders to which he had belonged, issued a Manifesto to all the lodges in 1794, declaring that in view of the way in which Masonry

---

[1] Archives Nationales, *Pièce remise par le Cabinet de Vienne* (1824), F⁷. 7566.
[2] Chevalier de Malet, *Recherches politiques et historiques*, p. 2 (1817).

had been penetrated by this great sect the whole Order must be temporarily suppressed. It is essential to quote a part of this important document verbatim:

Amidst the universal storm produced by the present revolutions in the political and moral world, at this period of supreme illumination and of profound blindness, it would be a crime against truth and humanity to leave any longer shrouded in a veil things that can provide the only key to past and future events, things that should show to thousands of men whether the path they have been made to follow is the path of folly or of wisdom. It has to do with you, VV. FF. of all degrees and of all secret systems. The curtain must at last be drawn aside, so that your blinded eyes may see that light you have ever sought in vain, but of which you have only caught a few deceptive rays. . . .

We have raised our building under the wings of darkness; . . . the darkness is dispelled, and a light more terrifying than darkness itself strikes suddenly on our sight. We see our edifice crumbling and covering the ground with ruins; we see destruction that our hands can no longer arrest. And that is why we send away the builders from their workshops. With a last blow of the hammer we overthrow the columns of salaries. We leave the temple deserted, and we bequeath it as a great work to posterity which shall raise it again on its ruins and bring it to completion.

Brunswick then goes on to explain what has brought about the ruin of the Order, namely, the infiltration of Freemasonry by secret conspirators:

A great sect arose which, taking for its motto the good and the happiness of man, worked in the darkness of the conspiracy to make the happiness of humanity a prey for itself. This sect is known to everyone: its brothers are known no less than its name. It is they who have undermined the foundations of the Order to the point of complete overthrow; it is by them that all humanity has been poisoned and led astray for several generations. The ferment that reigns amongst the peoples is their work. They founded the plans of their insatiable ambition on the political pride of nations. Their founders arranged to introduce this pride into the heads of the peoples. They began by casting odium on religion. . . . They invented the rights of man which it is impossible to discover even in the book of Nature, and they urged the people to wrest from their princes the recognition of these supposed rights. The plan they had formed for breaking all social ties and of destroying all order was revealed in all their speeches and acts. They deluged the world with a multitude of publications; they recruited apprentices of every rank and in every position; they deluded the most perspicacious men by falsely alleging different intentions. They sowed in the hearts of youth the seed of covetousness, and they excited it with the bait of the most insatiable passions. Indomitable pride, thirst of power, such were the only motives of this sect: their masters had nothing less in view than the thrones of the earth, and the government of the nations was to be directed by their nocturnal clubs.

This is what has been done and is still being done. But we notice that princes and people are unaware how and by what means this is being accomplished. That is why we say to them in all frankness: The misuse of our Order, the misunderstanding of our secret, has produced all the political and moral troubles with which the world is filled to-day. You who have been initiated, you must join yourselves with us in raising your voices, so as to teach peoples and princes that the sectarians, the apostates of our Order, have alone been and will be the authors of present and future revolutions. We must assure princes and peoples, on our honour and our duty, that our association is in no way guilty of these evils. But in order that our attestations should have force and merit belief, we must make for princes and people a complete sacrifice; so as to cut out to the roots the abuse and error, we must from this moment dissolve the whole Order. This is why we destroy and annihilate it completely for the time; we will preserve the foundations for posterity, which will clear them when humanity, in better times, can derive some benefit from our holy alliance.[1]

Thus, in the opinion of the Grand Master of German Freemasonry, a secret sect working within Freemasonry had brought about the French Revolution and would be the cause of all future revolutions. We shall now pursue the course of this sect after the first upheaval had ended.

Three years after the Duke of Brunswick issued his Manifesto to the lodges, the books of Barruel, Robison, and others appeared, laying bare the whole conspiracy. It has been said that all these books " fell flat."[2] This is directly contrary to the truth. Barruel's book went into no less than eight editions, and I have described elsewhere the alarm that his work and Robison's excited in America. In England they led to the very tangible result that a law was passed by the English Parliament in 1799 prohibiting all secret societies with the exception of Freemasonry.

It is evident, then, that the British Government recognized the continued existence of these associations and the danger

[1] Eckert, *La Franc-Maçonnerie dans sa véritable signification,* II. 125.
[2] Mr. Lucien Wolf, " The Jewish Peril," article in the *Spectator* for June 12, 1920.

they presented to the world. This fact should be borne in mind when we are assured that Barruel and Robison had conjured up a bogey which met with no serious attention from responsible men. For the main purpose of Barruel's book is to show that not only had Illuminism and Grand Orient Masonry contributed largely to the French Revolution, but that three years after that first explosion they were still as active as ever. This is the great point which the champions of the " bogey " theory are most anxious to refute. " The Bavarian Order of the Illuminati," wrote Mr. Waite, " was founded by Adam Weishaupt in 1776, and it was suppressed by the Elector of Bavaria in 1789. . . . Those who say that ' it was continued in more secret forms ' have never produced one item of real evidence."[1] Now, as we have seen, the Illuminati were not suppressed by the Elector of Bavaria in 1789, but in 1786—first error of Mr. Waite. But more extraordinary confusion of mind is displayed in his *Encyclopædia of Freemasonry*, where, in a Masonic Chronology, he gives, this time under the date of 1784, " Suppression of the Illuminati," but under 1793: " J. J. C. Bode joined the Illuminati under Weishaupt." At a matter of fact, this was the year Bode died. These examples will serve to show the reliance that can be placed on Mr. Waite's statement concerning the Illuminati.

We shall now see that not only the Illuminati but Weishaupt himself still continued to intrigue long after the French Revolution had ended.

Directly the Reign of Terror was over, the masonic lodges, which during the Revolution had been replaced by the clubs, began to reopen, and by the beginning of the nineteenth century were in a more flourishing condition than ever before. " It was the most brilliant epoch of Masonry," wrote the Freemason Bazot in his History of Freemasonry. Nearly 1,200 lodges existed in France under the Empire; generals, magistrates, artists, savants, and notabilities in every line were initiated into the Order.[2] The most eminent of these was Prince Cambacérès, pro Grand Master of the Grand Orient.

It is in the midst of this period that we find Weishaupt once more at work behind the scenes of Freemasonry. Thus in the remarkable masonic correspondence published by

[1] A. E. Waite, " Occult Freemasonry and the Jewish Peril," in *The Occult Review* for September, 1920.
[2] Deschamps, op. cit., II. 197, quoting *Tableau historique de la Maçonnerie*, p. 38.

M. Benjamin Fabre in his *Eques a Capite Galeato*—of which, as has already been pointed out, the authenticity is admitted by eminent British Freemasons—a letter is reproduced from Pyron, representative in Paris of the Grand Orient of Italy, to the Marquis de Chefdebien, dated September 9, 1808, in which it is stated that "a member of the sect of Bav." has asked for information on a certain point of ritual.

On December 29, 1808, Pyron writes again: "By the words sect of B. . . .' I meant W. . . ."; and on December 3, 1809, puts the matter quite plainly: "The other word remaining at the end of my pen refers enigmatically to Weis = pt."

So, as M. Fabre points out:

There is no longer any doubt that it is a question here of Weishaupt, and yet one observes that his name is not yet written in all its letters. It must be admitted here that Pyron took great precautions when it was a matter of Weishaupt! And one is led to ask what could be the extraordinary importance of the rôle played at this moment in the Freemasonry of the First Empire by this Weishaupt, who was supposed to have been outside the masonic movement since Illuminism was brought to trial in 1786![1]

But the Marquis de Chefdebien entertained no illusions about Weishaupt, whose intrigues he had always opposed, and in a letter dated May 12, 1806, to the Freemason Rœttiers, who had referred to the danger of isolated masonic lodges, he asks:

In good faith, very reverend brother, is it in isolated lodges that the atrocious conspiracy of Philippe [the Duc d'Orléans] and Robespierre was formed? Is it from isolated lodges that those prominent men came forth, who, assembled at the Hôtel de Ville, stirred up revolt, devastation, assassination? And is it not in the lodges bound together, co- and sub-ordinated, that the monster Weishaupt established his tests and had his horrible principles prepared?[2]

If, then, as M. Gustave Bord asserts, the Marquis de Chefdebien had himself belonged to the Illuminati before the Revolution, here is indeed Illuminist evidence in support of Barruel! Yet disillusioned as the "Eques a Capite Galeato" appears to have been with regard to Illuminism, he still retained his allegiance to Freemasonry. This would tend to prove that, however subversive the doctrines of the Grand

[1] *Eques a Capite Galeato*, pp. 362, 364, 366.
[2] Ibid., p. 423.

Orient may have been—and indeed undoubtedly were—it was not Freemasonry itself but Illuminism which organized the movement of which the French Revolution was the first manifestation. As Monsignor Dillon has expressed it:

Had Weishaupt not lived, Masonry might have ceased to be a power after the reaction consequent on the French Revolution. He gave it a form and character which caused it to outlive that reaction, to energize to the present day, and which will cause it to advance until its final conflict with Christianity must determine whether Christ or Satan shall reign on this earth to the end.[1]

If to the word Masonry we add Grand Orient—that is to say, the Masonry not of Great Britain, but of the Continent—we shall be still nearer to the truth.

In the early part of the nineteenth century Illuminism was thus as much alive as ever. Joseph de Maistre, writing at this period, constantly refers to the danger it presents to Europe. Is it not also to Illuminism that a mysterious passage in a recent work of M. Lenôtre refers? In the course of conversation with the friends of the false Dauphin Hervagault, Monsignor de Savine is said to have " made allusions in prudent and almost terrified terms to some international sect . . . a power superior to all others . . . which has arms and eyes everywhere and which governs Europe to-day."[2]

When in *World Revolution* I asserted that during the period that Napoleon held the reins of power the devastating fire of Illuminism was temporarily extinguished, I wrote without knowledge of some important documents which prove that Illuminism continued without break from the date of its foundation all through the period of the Empire. So far, then, from overstating the case by saying that Illuminism did not cease in 1786, I understated it by suggesting that it ceased even for this brief interval. The documents in which this evidence is to be found are referred to by Lombard de Langres, who, writing in 1820, observes that the Jacobins were invisible from the 18th Brumaire until 1813, and goes on to say:

Here the sect disappears; we find to guide us during this period only uncertain notions, scattered fragments; the plots of Illuminism lie buried in the boxes of the Imperial police.

[1] *The War of Anti-Christ with the Church and Christian Civilization*, p. 30 (1885).
[2] G. Lenôtre, *Le Dauphin* (Eng. trans.), p. 307.

But the contents of these boxes no longer lie buried; transported to the Archives Nationales, the documents in which the intrigues of Illuminism are laid bare have at last been given to the public. Here there can be no question of imaginative abbés, Scotch professors, or American divines conjuring up a bogey to alarm the world; these dry official reports prepared for the vigilant eye of the Emperor, never intended and never used for publication, relate calmly and dispassionately what the writers have themselves heard and observed concerning the danger that Illuminism presents to all forms of settled government.

The author of the most detailed report[1] is one François Charles de Berckheim, special commissioner of police at Mayence towards the end of the Empire, who as a Freemason is naturally not disposed to prejudice against secret societies. In October 1810 he writes, however, that his attention has been drawn to the Illuminati by a pamphlet which has just fallen into his hands, namely the *Essai sur la Secte des Illuminés*, which, like many contemporaries, he attributes originally to Mirabeau. He then goes on to ask whether the sect still exists, and if so whether it is indeed " an association of frightful scoundrels who aim, as Mirabeau assures us, at the overthrow of all law and all morality, at replacing virtue by crime in every act of human life." Further, he asks whether both sects of *Illuminés* have now combined in one and what are their present projects. Conversations with other Freemasons further increase Berckheim's anxiety on the subject; one of the best informed observes to him: " I know a great deal, enough at any rate to be convinced that the *Illuminés* have vowed the overthrow of monarchic governments and of all authority on the same basis."

Berckheim thereupon sets out to make enquiries, with the result that he is able to state that the *Illuminés* have initiates all over Europe, that they have spared no efforts to introduce their principles into the lodges, and " to spread a doctrine " subversive of all settled government . . . under the pretext of the regeneration of social morality and the amelioration of the lot and condition of men by means of laws founded on principles and sentiments unknown hitherto and contained only in the heads of the leaders." " Illuminism," he declares, " is becoming a great and formidable power, and I fear, in my conscience, that kings and peoples will have much to suffer

[1] Archives Nationales, F⁷ 6563.

from it unless foresight and prudence break its frightful mechanism [*ses affreux ressorts*]."

Two years later, on January 16, 1813, Berckheim writes again to the Minister of Police:

Monseigneur, they write to me from Heidelberg . . . that a great number of initiates into the mysteries of Illuminism are to be found there.

These gentlemen wear as a sign of recognition a gold ring on the third finger of the left hand; on the back of this ring there is a little rose, in the middle of this rose is an almost imperceptible dint; by pressing this with the point of a pin one touches a spring, by this means the two gold circles are detached. On the inside of the first of these circles is the device: "Be German as you ought to be "; on the inside of the second of these circles are engraved the words "Pro Patria."

Subversive as the ideas of the Illuminati might be, they were therefore not subversive of German patriotism. We shall find this apparent paradox running all through the Illuminist movement to the present day.

In 1814 Berckheim drew up his great report on the secret societies of Germany, which is of so much importance in throwing a light on the workings of the modern revolutionary movement, that extracts must be given here at length.[1] His testimony gains greater weight from the vagueness he displays on the origins of Illuminism and the rôle it had played before the French Revolution; it is evident, therefore, that he had not taken his ideas from Robison or Barruel—to whom he never once refers—but from information gleaned on the spot in Germany. The opening paragraphs finally refute the fallacy concerning the extinction of the sect in 1786.

The oldest and most dangerous association is that which is generally known under the denomination of the *Illuminés* and of which the foundation goes back towards the middle of the last century.

Bavaria was its cradle; it is said that it had for founders several chiefs of the Order of the Jesuits; but this opinion, advanced perhaps at random, is founded only on uncertain premises; in any case, in a short time it made rapid progress, and the Bavarian Government recognized the necessity of employing methods of repression against it and even of driving away several of the principal sectaries.

But it could not eradicate the germ of the evil. The *Illuminés*

---
[1] Archives Nationales F⁷ 6563 No. 2449, Série 2, No. 49.

who remained in Bavaria, obliged to wrap themselves in darkness so as to escape the eye of authority, became only the more formidable: the rigorous measures of which they were the object, adorned by the title of persecution, gained them new proselytes, whilst the banished members went to carry the principles of the Association into other States.

Thus in a few years Illuminism multiplied its hotbeds all through the south of Germany, and as a consequence in Saxony, in Prussia, in Sweden, and even in Russia.

The reveries of the Pietists have long been confounded with those of the Illuminés. This error may arise from the denomination of the sect, which at first suggests the idea of a purely religious fanaticism and of mystic forms which it was obliged to take at its birth in order to conceal its principles and projects; but the Association always had a political tendency. If it still retains some mystic traits, it is in order to support itself at need by the power of religious fanaticism, and we shall see in what follows how well it knows to turn this to account.

The doctrine of Illuminism is subversive of every kind of monarchy; unlimited liberty, absolute levelling down, such is the fundamental dogma of the sect; to break the ties that bind the Sovereign to the citizen of a state, that is the object of all its efforts.

No doubt some of the principal chiefs, amongst whom are numbered men distinguished for their fortune, their birth, and the dignities with which they are invested, are not the dupes of these demagogic dreams: they hope to find in the popular emotions they stir up the means of seizing the reigns of power, or at any rate of increasing their wealth and their credit; but the crowd of adepts believe in it religiously, and, in order to reach the goal shown to them, they maintain incessantly a hostile attitude towards sovereigns.

Thus the *Illuminés* hailed with enthusiasm the ideas that prevailed in France from 1789 to 1804. Perhaps they were not foreign to the intrigues which prepared the explosions of 1789 and the following years; but if they did not take an active part in these manœuvres, it is at least beyond doubt that they openly applauded the systems which resulted from them; that the Republican armies when they penetrated into Germany found in these sectarians auxiliaries the more dangerous for the sovereigns of the invaded states in that they inspired no distrust, and we can say with assurance that more than one general of the Republic owed a part of its success to his understanding with the *Illuminés*.

It would be a mistake if one confounded Illuminism with Freemasonry. These two associations, in spite of the points of resemblance they may possess in the mystery with which they surround themselves, in the tests that precede initiation, and in other matters of form, are absolutely distinct and have no kind of connexion with each other. The lodges of the Scottish Rite number, it is true, a few *Illuminés* amongst the Masons of the higher degrees, but these adepts are very careful not to be known as such to their brothers in Masonry or to manifest ideas that would betray their secret.

Berckheim then goes on to describe the subtle methods by which the Illuminati now maintain their existence; learning wisdom from the events of 1786, their organization is carried on invisibly, so as to defy the eye of authority:

It was thought for a long while that the association had a Grand Mastership, that is to say, a centre point from which radiated all the impulsions given to this great body, and this primary motive power was sought for successively in all the capitals of the North, in Paris and even in Rome. This error gave birth to another opinion no less fallacious: it was supposed that there existed in the principal towns lodges where initiations were made and which received directly the instructions emanating from the headquarters of the Society.

If such had been the organization of Illuminism, it would not so long have escaped the investigations of which it was the object: these meetings, necessarily thronged and frequent, requiring besides, like masonic lodges, appropriate premises, would have aroused the attention of magistrates: it would not have been difficult to introduce false brothers, who, directed and protected by authority, would soon have penetrated the secrets of the sect.

This is what I have gathered most definitely on the Association of the *Illuminés*:

First I would point out that by the word hotbeds [foyers] I did not mean to designate points of meeting for the adepts, places where they hold assemblies, but only localities where the Association counts a great number of partisans, who, whilst living isolated in appearance, exchange ideas, have an understanding with each other, and advance together towards the same goal.

The Association had, it is true, assemblies at its birth where receptions [i.e. initiations] took place, but the dangers which resulted from these made them feel the necessity of abandoning them. It was settled that each initiated adept should have the right without the help of anyone else to initiate all those who, after the usual tests, seemed to him worthy.

The catechism of the sect is composed of a very small number of articles which might even be reduced to this single principle:

" To arm the opinion of the peoples against sovereigns and to work by every method for the fall of monarchic governments in order to found in their place systems of absolute independence." Everything that can tend towards this object is in the spirit of the Association. . . .

Initiations are not accompanied, as in Masonry, by phantasmagoric trials, . . . but they are preceded by long moral tests which guarantee in the safest way the fidelity of the catechumen; oaths, a mixture of all that is most sacred in religion, threats and imprecations against traitors, nothing that can stagger the imagination is spared; but the only engagement into which the recipient enters is to propagate the principles with which he has been imbued, to maintain inviolable secrecy on all that pertains to the association, and to' work with all his might to increase the number of proselytes.

It will no doubt seem astonishing that there can be the least accord in the association, and that men bound together by no physical tie and who live at great distances from each other can communicate their ideas to each other, make plans of conduct, and give grounds of fear to Governments; but there exists an invisible chain which binds together all the scattered members of the association. Here are a few links:

All the adepts living in the same town usually know each other, unless the population of the town or the number of the adepts is too considerable. In this last case they are divided into several groups, who are all in touch with each other by means of members of the association whom personal relations bind to two or several groups at a time.

These groups are again subdivided into so many private coteries which the difference of rank, of fortune, of character, tastes, etc., may necessitate: they are always small, sometimes composed of five or six individuals, who meet frequently under various pretexts, sometimes at the house of one member, sometimes at that of another; literature, art, amusements of all kinds are the apparent object of these meetings, and it is nevertheless in these confabulations [*conciliabules*] that the adepts communicate their private views to each other, agree on methods, receive the directions that the intermediaries bring them, and communicate their own ideas to these same intermediaries, who then go on to propagate them in other coteries. It will be understood that there may be uniformity in the march of all these separated groups, and that one day may suffice to communicate the same impulse to all the quarters of a large town. . . .

These are the methods by which the *Illuminés,* without any apparent organization, without settled leaders, agree together from the banks of the Rhine to those of the Neva, from the Baltic to the Dardanelles, and advance continually towards the same goal, without leaving any trace that might compromise the interests of the association or even bring suspicion on any of its members; the most active police would fail before such a combination. . . .

As the principal force of the *Illuminés* lies in the power of opinions, they have set themselves out from the beginning to make proselytes amongst the men who through their profession exercise a direct influence on minds, such as *littérateurs,* savants, and above all professors. The latter in their chairs, the former in their writings, propagate the principles of the sect by disguising the poison that they circulate under a thousand different forms. These germs, often imperceptible to the eyes of the vulgar, are afterwards developed by the ad·pts of the Societies they frequent, and the most obscure wording is thus brought to the understanding of the least discerning. It is above all in the Universities that Illuminism has always found and always will find numerous recruits. Those professors who belong to the Association set out from the first to study the character of their pupils. If a student gives evidence of a vigorous mind, an ardent imagination, the sectaries at once get hold of him, they sound in his ears the words Despotism—Tyranny—Rights of the People, etc., etc. Before he can even attach any meaning to these words, as he advances in age, reading chosen for him, conversations skilfully arranged, develop the germs deposited in his youthful brain; soon his imagination ferments, history, traditions of fabulous times, all are made use of to carry his exaltation to the highest point, and before even he has been told of a secret Association, to contribute to the fall of a sovereign appears to his eyes the noblest and most meritorious act. . . .

At last, when he has been completely captivated, when several years of testing guarantee to the society inviolable secrecy and absolute devotion, it is made known to him that millions of individuals distributed in all the States of Europe share his sentiments and his hopes, that a secret link binds firmly all the scattered members of this immense family, and that the reforms he desires so ardently must sooner or later come about.

This propaganda is rendered the easier by the existing associations of students who meet together for the study of literature, for fencing, gaming, or even mere debauchery. The Illuminés insinuate themselves into all these circles and turn them into hot-beds for the propagation of their principles.

Such, then, is the Association's continual mode of progression from its origins until the present moment; it is by conveying from childhood the germ of poison into the highest classes of society, in feeding the minds of students on ideas diametrically opposed to that order of things under which they have to live, in breaking the ties that bind them to sovereigns, that Illuminism has recruited the largest number of adepts, called by the state to which they were born to be the mainstays of the Throne and of a system which would ensure them honours and privileges.

Amongst the proselytes of this last class there are some no doubt whom political events, the favour of the prince or other circumstances, detach from the Association; but the number of these deserters is necessarily very limited: and even then they dare not speak openly against their old associates, whether because they are in dread of private vengeances or whether because, knowing the real power of the sect, they want to keep paths of reconciliation open to themselves; often indeed they are so fettered by the pledges they have personally given that they find it necessary not only to consider the interests of the sect, but to serve it indirectly, although their new circumstances demand the contrary. . . .

Berckheim then proceeds to show that those writers on Illuminism were mistaken who declared that political assassinations were definitely commanded by the Order:

There is more than exaggeration in this accusation; those who put it forward, more zealous in striking an effect than in seeking the truth, may have concluded, not without probability, that men who surrounded themselves with profound mystery, who propagated a doctrine absolutely subversive of any kind of monarchy, dreamt only of the assassination of sovereigns; but experience has shown (and all the documents derived from the least suspect sources confirm this) that the *Illuminés* count a great deal more on the power of opinion than on assassination; the regicide committed on Gustavus III is perhaps the only crime of this kind that Illuminism has dared to attempt, if indeed it is really proved that this crime was its work; moreover, if assassination had been, as it is said, the fundamental point in its doctrine, might we not suppose that other regicides would have been attempted in Germany during the course of the French Revolution, especially when the Republican armies occupied the country?

The sect would be much less formidable if this were its doctrine, on the one hand because it would inspire in most of the *Illuminés* a feeling of horror which would triumph even over the fear of vengeance, on the other hand because plots and conspiracies always leave some traces which guide the authorities to the footsteps of the prime instigators; and besides, it is the nature of things that out of twenty plots directed against sovereigns, nineteen come to light before they have reached the point of maturity necessary to their execution.

The *Illuminés'* line of march is more prudent, more skilful, and consequently more dangerous; instead of revolting the imagination by ideas of regicide, they affect the most generous sentiments: declamations on the unhappy state of the people, on the selfishness of courtiers, on measures of administration, on all acts of authority that may offer a pretext to declamations as a contrast to the seductive pictures of the felicity that awaits the nations under the systems they wish to establish, such is their manner of procedure, particularly in private. More circumspect in their writings, they usually disguise the poison they dare not proffer openly under obscure metaphysics or more or less ingenious allegories. Often indeed texts from Holy Writ serve as an envelope and vehicle for these baneful insinuations. . . .

By this continuous and insidious form of propaganda the imagination of the adepts is so worked on that if a crisis arises, they are ready to carry out the most daring projects.

Another Association closely resembling the *Illuminés*, Berckheim reports, is known as the *Idealists*, whose system is founded on the doctrine of perfectibility; these kindred sects " agree in seeing in the words of Holy Scripture the pledge of universal regeneration, of an absolute levelling down, and it is in this spirit that the sectarians interpret the sacred books."

Berckheim further confirms the assertion I made in *World Revolution*—contested, as usual, by a reviewer without a shred of evidence to the contrary—that the Tugendbund derived from the Illuminati. " The League of Virtue," he writes, " was directed by the secondary chiefs of the *Illuminés*. . . . In 1810 the Friends of Virtue were so identified with the *Illuminés* in the North of Germany that no line of demarcation was seen between them."

But it is time to turn to the testimony of another witness on the activities of the secret societies which is likewise to be found at the Archives Nationales.[1] This consists of a document transmitted by the Court of Vienna to the Government of France after the Restoration, and contains the interrogatory of a certain Witt Doehring, a nephew of the Baron d'Eckstein, who, after taking part in secret society intrigues, was summoned before the judge Abel at Bayreuth in February, 1824. Amongst secret associations recently existing in Germany, the witness asserted, were the " Independents " and the " Absolutes "; the latter " adored in Robespierre their most perfect ideal, so that the crimes committed during the French Revolution by this monster and the Montagnards of the Convention were in their eyes, in accordance with their moral system, heroic actions ennobled and sanctified by their aim." The same document goes on to explain why so many combustible elements had failed to produce an explosion in Germany:

The thing that seemed the great obstacle to the plans of the Independents . . . was what they called the servile character and the dog-like fidelity [*Hundestreue*] of the German people, that is to say, that attachment—innate and firmly impressed on their minds without even the aid of reason—which that excellent people everywhere bears towards its princes.

[1] *Pièce remise par le Cabinet de Vienne*, F⁷ 7566.

A traveller in Germany during the year 1795 admirably summed up the matter in these words:

The Germans are in this respect [of democracy] the most curious people in the world . . . the cold and sober temperament of the Germans and their tranquil imagination enable them to combine the most daring opinions with the most servile conduct. That will explain to you . . . why so much combustible material accumulating for so many years beneath the political edifice of Germany has not yet damaged it. Most of the princes, accustomed to see their men of letters so constantly free in their writings and so constantly slavish in their hearts, have not thought it necessary to use severity against this sheeplike herd of modern Gracchi and Brutuses. Some of them [the princes] have even without difficulty adopted part of their opinions, and Illuminism having doubtless been presented to them as perfection, the complement of philosophy, they were easily persuaded to be initiated into it. But great care was taken not to let them know more than the interests of the sect demanded.[1]

It was thus that Illuminism, unable to provoke a blaze in the home of its birth, spread, as before the French Revolution, to a more inflammable Latin race—this time the Italians. Six years after his interrogatory at Beyreuth, Witt Doehring published his book on the secret societies of France and Italy, in which he now realized he had played the part of dupe, and incidentally confirms the statement I have previously quoted, that the Alta Vendita was a further development of the Illuminati.

This infamous association, with which I have dealt at length elsewhere,[2] constituted the Supreme Directory of the Carbonari and was led by a group of Italian noblemen, amongst whom a prince, " the profoundest of initiates, was charged as Inspector-General of the Order " to propagate its principles throughout the North of Europe. " He had received from the hands of. Kingge [i.e. Knigge, the ally of Weishaupt?] the cahiers of the last three degrees." But these were of course unknown to the great majority of Carbonari, who entered the association

---

[1] *Lettres d'un Voyageur à l'Abbé Barruel*, p. 30 (1800).

[2] *World Revolution*, pp. 86 and following, where extracts from the correspondence of the Alta Vendita (or Haute Vente Romaine) were given. This correspondence will be found in *L'Église Romaine en face de la Révolution*, by Crétineau Joly, who published it from the documents seized by the Pontifical Government at the death of one of the members. The documents were communicated to Crétineau Joly by the Pope Grégoire XVI, and published with the approval of Pius IX. Their authenticity has never been questioned. They are still in the secret archives of the Vatican, or at any rate were there at the beginning of the present year.

in all good faith. Witt Doehring then shows how faithfully the system of Weishaupt was carried out by the Alta Vendita. In the three first degrees, he explains—

It is still a question of the morality of Christianity and even of the Church, for which those who wish to be received must promise to sacrifice themselves. The initiates imagine, according to this formula, that the object of the association is something high and noble, that it is the Order of those who desire a purer morality and a stronger piety, the independence and the unity of their country. One cannot therefore judge the Carbonari *en masse*; there are excellent men amongst them. . . . But everything changes after one has taken the three degrees. Already in the fourth, in that of the *Apostoli*, one promises to overthrow all monarchies, and especially the kings of the race of the Bourbons. But it is only in the seventh and last degree, reached by few, that revelations go further. At last the veil is torn completely for the Principi Summo Patriarcho. Then one learns that the aim of the Carbonari is just the same as that of the *Illuminés*. This degree, in which a man is at the same time prince and bishop, coincides with the Homo Rex of the latter. The initiate vows the ruin of all religion and of all positive government, whether despotic or democratic; murder, poison, perjury, are all at their disposal. Who does not remember that on the suppression of the *Illuminés* was found, amongst other poisons, a *tinctura ad abortum faciendum*. The *summo maestro* laughs at the zeal of the mass of Carbonari who have sacrificed themselves for the liberty and independence of Italy, neither one nor the other being for him a goal but a method.[1]

Witt Doehring, who had himself reached the degree of P.S.P., thereupon declares that, having taken his vows under a misapprehension, he holds himself to be released from his obligations and conceives it his duty to warn society. "The fears that assail governments are only too well founded. The soil of Europe is volcanic."[2]

It is unnecessary to go over the ground already traversed in *World Revolution* by relating the history of the successive eruptions which proved the truth of Witt Doehring's warning. The point to emphasize again is that every one of these eruptions can be traced to the work of the secret societies, and that, as in the eighteenth century, most of the prominent revolutionaries were known to be connected with some secret association. According to the plan laid down by Weishaupt, Freemasonry was habitually adopted as a cover. Thus Louis

---

[1] Jan Witt, dit Buloz, *Les Sociétés Secrètes de France et d'Italie*, pp. 20, 21 (1830).
[2] Ibid., p. 6.

Amis de la Vérité, numbering Bazard and Buchez amongst Blanc, himself a Freemason, speaks of a lodge named the its founders, " in which the solemn puerilities of the Grand Orient only served to mask political action."[1] Bakunin, companion of the Freemason Proudhon,[2] " the father of Anarchy," makes use of precisely the same expression. Freemasonry, he explains, is not to be taken seriously, but " may serve as a mask " and " as a means of preparing something quite different."[3]

I have quoted elsewhere the statement of the Socialist Malon that " Bakunin was a disciple of Weishaupt," and that of the Anarchist Kropotkine that between Bakunin's secret society— the *Alliance Sociale Démocratique*—and the secret societies of 1795 there was a direct affiliation; I have quoted the assertion of Malon that " Communism was handed down in the dark through the secret societies " of the nineteenth century; I have quoted also the congratulations addressed by Lamartine and the Freemason Crémieux to the Freemasons of France in 1848 on their share in this revolution as in that of 1789; I have shown that the organization of this later outbreak by the secret societies is not a matter of surmise, but a fact admitted by all well-informed historians and by the members of the secret societies themselves.

So, too, in the events of the Commune, and in the founding of the First Internationale, the rôle of Freemasonry and the secret societies is no less apparent. The Freemasons of France have indeed always boasted of their share in political and social upheavals. Thus in 1874, Malapert, orator of the Supreme Council of the Ancient and Accepted Scottish Rite, went so far as to say: "' In the eighteenth century Freemasonry was so widespread throughout the world that one can say that since that epoch nothing has been done without its consent."

The secret history of Europe during the last two hundred years yet remains to be written. Until viewed in the light of the *dessous des cartes,* many events that have taken place during this period must remain for ever incomprehensible.

But it is time to leave the past and consider the secret forces at work in the world to-day.

[1] Louis Blanc, *Histoire de Dix Ans,* I. 88, 89.
[2] Deschamps, *Les Sociétés Secrètes et la Société,* II. 534, quoting the *Monde Maçonnique* for July, 1867.
[3] *Correspondance de Michel Bakounine,* published by Michael Dragomanov, pp. 73, 209 (1896).

PART II
THE PRESENT

11

MODERN FREEMASONRY

In the foregoing portion of this book we have followed the history of Freemasonry in the past and the various interpretations that have been placed on its rites and ceremonies. The question now arises: what is the rôle of Freemasonry to-day?

The fundamental error of most writers on this question, whether Masonic or anti-Masonic, is to represent all Freemasons as holding a common belief and animated by a common purpose. Thus on one hand the panegyrics by Freemasons on their Order as a whole, and on the other hand the sweeping condemnations of the Order by the Catholic Church, are equally at fault.

The truth is that Freemasonry in a generic sense is simply a system of binding men together for any given purpose, since it is obvious that allegories and symbols, like the x and y of algebra, can be interpreted in a hundred different manners. Two pillars may be said to represent strength and stability, or man and woman, or light and darkness, or any other two things we please. A triangle may signify the Trinity, or Liberty, Equality, and Fraternity, or any other triad. To say that any of these symbols have an absolute meaning is absurd.

The allegories of Freemasonry are equally capable of various interpretations. The building of the Temple of Solomon may signify the progress of any undertaking and Hiram the victim of its opponents. So also with regard to the " secret tradition " of Freemasonry concerning " a loss which has befallen humanity "[1] and its ultimate recovery. Any body of people working for an object may be said to have experienced a loss and to aim at its recovery.

In the same way the whole organization of Freemasonry, the plan of admitting candidates to successive degrees of

[1] A. E. Waite, *The Secret Tradition in Freemasonry*, Vol. I. p. ix.

initiation, of binding them to secrecy by fearful oaths, is one that can be employed for any purpose, social, political, philanthropic, or religious, for promoting that which is good or for disseminating that which is evil. It may be used to defend a throne or to overthrow it, to protect religion or to destroy it, to maintain law and order or to create anarchy.

Now, there was, as we have seen, from the beginning, besides the written charges, an *oral tradition* in Masonry, after the manner of the Cabala, on which the guidance of the society depended. The true character of any form of Freemasonry is thus not to be judged only by its printed ritual, but by the oral instruction of the initiates and the interpretations placed on the symbols and ritual. Naturally these interpretations vary in different countries and at different periods. Freemasonry is described in its Ritual as " a peculiar system of morality, veiled in allegory and illustrated by symbols." But what code of morality? In studying the history of the Order we shall find that the same code was by no means common to all masonic bodies, nor is it to-day. Some maintain a very high standard of morals; others appear to possess no standard at all. Mr. Waite observes that " the two doctrines of the unity of God and the immortality of the soul constitute ' the philosophy of Freemasonry.' " [1] But these doctrines are by no means essential to the existence of Freemasonry; the Grand Orient has renounced both, but it still ranks as Freemasonry.

M. Paul Nourrisson is therefore perfectly right in saying: " There are as many Masonries as countries; there is no such thing as universal Masonry."[2] Broadly, however, modern Freemasonry may be divided into two kinds: the variety worked in the British Empire, in America, Holland, Sweden, Denmark, etc., and Grand Orient Masonry, which prevails in Catholic countries and of which the most important centre is the Grand Orient of Paris.

CONTINENTAL MASONRY

The fact that Masonry in Protestant countries is neither revolutionary nor anti-religious is frequently used by Catholic writers to show that Protestantism identifies itself with the aims of Masonry, and by Freemasons to prove that the tyranny of the Church of Rome has driven Masonry into an attitude

[1] *The Real History of the Rosicrucians*, p. 403.
[2] Paul Nourrisson, *Les Jacobins au Pouvoir*, pp. 202, 215 (1904).

hostile to Church and State. The point overlooked in both these contentions is the essential difference in the character of the two kinds of Masonry. If the Grand Orient had adhered to the fundamental principle of British Masonry not to concern itself with religion or politics, there is no reason why it should have come into conflict with the Church. But its duplicity on this point is apparent. Thus in one of its earlier manuals it declares, like British Masonry, that it " never interferes with questions of government or of civil and religious legislation, and that whilst making its members participate in the perfecting of all sciences, it positively excepts in the lodges two of the most beautiful, *politics* and *theology*, because these two sciences divide men and nations which Masonry constantly tends to unite."[1] But on a further page of the same manual from which this quotation is taken we find it stated that Masonry is simply " the political application of Christianity."[2] Indeed, during the last fifty years the Grand Orient has thrown off the mask and openly declared itself to be political in its aims. In October 1887 the Venerable Bro.·. Blanc said in a discourse which was printed for the lodges:

You recognise with me, my brothers, the necessity for Freemasonry to become a vast and powerful political and social society having a decisive influence on the resolutions of the Republican government.[3]

And in 1890 the Freemason Fernand Maurice declared " that nothing should happen in France without the hidden action of Freemasonry," and " if the Masons choose to organize, in ten years' time no one in France will be able to move outside us (*personne ne bougera plus en France en dehors de nous*)."[4]

This is the despotic power which the Grand Orient has established in opposition to both Church and Government.

Moreover, Grand Orient masonry is not only political but subversive in its political aims. Instead of the peaceful trilogy of British masonry, " Brotherly love, relief, and truth," it has throughout adhered to the formula which originated in the Masonic lodges of France and became the war-cry of the Revolution: " Liberty, Equality, Fraternity." " It is the law of equality," says Ragon, " that has always

[1] J. M. Ragon, *Cours philosophique . . . des Initiations*, etc., édition sacrée (5,842), p. 19.
[2] Ibid., p. 38.
[3] Copin Albancelli, *Le Pouvoir occulte contre la France*, p. 124 (1908).
[4] Ibid., p. 125.

endeared Masonry to the French," and " as long as equality really exists only in the lodges, Masonry will be preserved in France."[1] The aim of Grand Orient Masonry is thus to bring about universal equality as formulated by Robespierre and Babeuf. In the matter of liberty we read further that as men are all by nature free—the old fallacy of Rousseau and of the Declaration of the Rights of Man—therefore " no one is necessarily subjected to another nor has the right to rule him."[2] The revolutionary expresses the same idea in the phrase that " no man should have a master." Finally, by fraternity Grand Orient Masonry denotes the abolition of all national feeling.

It is to Masonry [Ragon says again] that we owe the affiliation of all classes of society, it alone could bring about this fusion which from its midst has passed into the life of the peoples. It alone could promulgate that humanitarian law of which the rising activity, tending to a great social uniformity, leads to the fusion of races, of different classes, of morals, codes, customs, languages, fashions, money, and measures. Its virtuous propaganda will become the humanitarian law of all consciences.[3]

The policy of the Grand Orient is thus avowedly International Socialism. Indeed in a further passage Ragon plainly indicates this fact:

Every generous reform, every social benefit derives from it, and if these survive it is because Masonry lends them its support. This phenomenon is due only to the power of its organization. The past belongs to it and the future cannot escape from it. By its immense lever of association it alone is able to realize by a productive communion (*communion génératrice*) that great and beautiful social unity conceived by Jaurez, Saint-Simon, Owen, Fourier. If Masons wish it, the generous conceptions of these philanthropic thinkers will cease to be vain Utopias.[4]

Who are the philanthropic thinkers enumerated here but the men derisively described by Karl Marx as the " Utopian Socialists " of the nineteenth century? Utopian Socialism is thus simply the open and visible expression of Grand Orient Freemasonry. Moreover, these Utopian Socialists were almost without exception Freemasons or members of other secret societies.

[1] Ragon, op. cit., p. 38, note 2.
[2] Ibid., p. 39.
[3] Ibid., p. 52.
[4] Ibid., p. 53.

The Freemason Clavel confirms the foregoing account by Ragon. Thus, like Ragon, he quotes, the principle expressed in a ritual for the initiation of a Master Mason:

It is expressly forbidden to Masons to discuss amongst themselves, either in the lodge or outside it, religious and political matters, these discussions having usually the effect of creating discord where formerly peace, union, and fraternity reigned. This masonic law admits of no exceptions.[1]

But Clavel also goes on to say.:

To efface amongst men the distinctions of colour, rank, creed, opinions, country; to annihilate fanaticism, and . . . the scourge of war; in a word, to make of the whole human race one and the same family united by affection, by devotion, by work and knowledge: that, my brother, is the great work which Freemasonry has undertaken, etc.[2]

Up to a point many a British Freemason reading these passages will declare himself completely in accord with the sentiments expressed. Humanitarianism, the obliteration of class distinctions, fraternization between men of all races, conditions, and religious creeds, enter of course largely into the spirit of British Masonry, but form simply the basis on which Masons meet together in the lodges and not a political system to be imposed on the world in general.

British Masonry thus makes no attempt to interfere with the existing social system or form of Government; the essence of its teaching is that each member of the Fraternity should seek to reform himself and not society. In a word, individual regeneration takes the place of the social reorganization advocated by the Grand Orient under the influence of Illuminism. The formula of the " United States of Europe " and of the " Universal Republic " first proclaimed by the Illuminatus, Anacharsis Clootz,[3] has long been the slogan of the French lodges.[4]

In the matter of religion, Grand Orient Masonry has entirely departed from the principle laid down by the British lodges. If the Catholic Church has shown itself hostile to Masonry,

[1] Clavel, *Histoire pittoresque de la Franc-Maçonnerie*, p. 21.
[2] Ibid., p. 23.
[3] In *La République universelle*, published in 1793.
[4] Georges Goyau, *L'Idée de Patrie et l'Humanitarisme*, p. 242 (1913), quoting speech of F. Troubat in 1886. A periodical called *Les États Unis de l'Europe* was published by Ferdinand Buisson in 1868. Ibid., p. 113.

it must be remembered that in Catholic countries Masonry has shown itself militantly anti-Catholic. "Freemasonry," one of its modern orators declared, "is the anti-Church, the anti-Catholicism, the Church of Heresy (*la contre Eglise, le contre Catholicisme, l'Eglise de l'Hérésie*)."[1] The *Bulletin* of the Grand Orient in 1885 officially declared: "We Freemasons must pursue the definite demolition of Catholicism."

But the Grand Orient goes further than this and attacks all forms of religion. Thus, as has been said, those "ancient landmarks" of British Masonry, belief in the Great Architect of the Universe and in the immortality of the soul, had never formed an integral part of its system, and it was only in 1849 that for the first time "it was distinctly formulated that the basis of Freemasonry is a belief in God and in the immortality of the soul, and the solidarity of Humanity." But in September 1877 the first part of this formula was deleted, all allusions to the Great Architect were omitted, and the statute now reads: "Its basis is absolute liberty of conscience and the solidarity of Humanity."[2] British Freemasonry, which does not admit liberty of conscience in the sense of Atheism, but demands that every Mason should profess belief in some form of religion and which insists that the Volume of the Sacred Law—in England the Bible, in Mohammedan countries the Koran, and so on—should be placed on the table in its lodges, thereupon broke off all relations with the Grand Orient. In March 1878 the following resolution was passed unanimously:

That the Grand Lodge, whilst always anxious to receive in the most fraternal spirit the Brethren of any foreign Grand Lodge whose proceedings are conducted according to the Ancient Landmarks of the Order, of which a belief in T.G.A.O.T.U. is the first and most important, cannot recognize as "true and genuine" Brethren any who have been initiated in lodges which either deny or ignore that belief.[3]

The Grand Orient, says M. Copin Albancelli, not content with renouncing the Great Architect whose glory it had celebrated on every possible occasion and whose praises had been incessantly sung in its lodges, demanded of its initiates that they should declare themselves to be absolutely convinced

[1] Copin Albancelli, *Le Pouvoir occulte contre la France*, p. 89.
[2] Gould, *History of Freemasonry*, III. 191, 192.
[3] Ibid., III. 26.

that the Great Architect was nothing but a myth.[1] More than this, violent anti-religious tirades have been permitted and even applauded in the lodges. Thus in 1902 the Freemason Delpech in his discourse at a masonic banquet uttered these words:

The triumph of the Galilean has lasted twenty centuries; he is dying in his turn. The mysterious voice which once on the mountains of Epirus announced the death of Pan, to-day announces the death of the deceiver God who had promised an era of justice and peace to those who should believe in him. The illusion has lasted very long; the lying God in his turn disappears; he goes to rejoin in the dust of ages the other divinities of India, Egypt, Greece, and Rome, who saw so many deluded creatures throw themselves at the food of their altars. Freemasons, we are pleased to state that we are not unconcerned with this ruin of false prophets. The Roman Church, founded on the Galilean myth, began to decline rapidly on the day when the masonic association was constituted. From the political point of view Freemasons have often varied. But in all times Freemasonry has stood firm on this principle: war on all superstitions, war on all fanaticism.[2]

How is it possible to reconcile this attitude towards religion in general and Christianity in particular with the fact that the Grand Orient still works the Rose-Croix degree? This degree—which, as we have seen, was first devised (whether in Scotland or in France) to give a Christian meaning to Masonry —was only incorporated into British Freemasonry in 1846 and in our country has retained its original character. Its ritual, centring around a lost word, signifies that the Old Testament dispensation has come to an end with the Crucifixion, and is so strongly Christian that no Jew, Mohammedan, or other non-Christian can be admitted to it. Moreover, since this degree, known as the eighteenth degree, forms in reality the first degree of the Ancient and Accepted Rite, as worked in this country, non-Christians are excluded from the whole of this Rite and can only take the degrees of Royal Arch, Mark Mason, Royal Ark Mariner, and finally Royal Select and Super-Excellent Master. Consequently the thirty-three Masons of the thirty-third degree who compose the Supreme Council which directs the Ancient and Accepted Rite are necessarily professing Christians. Exactly the opposite is the case in France; the Rose-Croix, worked by professing atheists and Jews, can only be parody of Christian mysteries.

[1] Copin Albancelli, *Le Pouvoir occulte contre la France*, p. 97.
[2] Ibid., p. 90.

Now, it is essential to realize that in France the anti-masonic camp is divided into two parties. Whilst the majority of Catholic writers regard Freemasonry itself as the source of all evil—" the Synagogue of Satan "—more impartial investigators have pronounced the opinion that it is not Freemasonry even of the Grand Orient variety but something concealed behind Freemasonry which constitutes the principal danger. This view is expressed by M. Copin Albancelli, whose book *Le Pouvoir occulte contre la France* is of the utmost importance to an understanding of the masonic danger, for here there can be no question of Catholic prejudice or of imaginary accusations made by a stranger to Masonry. M. Copin Albancelli entered the Grand Orient as an agnostic and has never returned to the bosom of the Church; yet as a Frenchman, a patriot, and a believer in law, morality, and Christian ethics he found himself obliged, after six years' experience in the lodges and after attaining the degree of Rose-Croix, to leave Freemasonry and, further, to denounce it.   From what he himself heard and observed M. Copin Albancelli declares the Grand Orient to be anti-patriotic, subversive of all morality and religious belief, and an immense danger to France

But further than this, M. Copin Albancelli declares the Grand Orient to be a system of deception by which members are enlisted in a cause unknown to themselves; even the initiates of the upper degrees are not all aware of the real aim of the Order or of the power behind it.   M. Copin Albancelli thus arrives at the conclusion that there are three Freemasonries one above the other: (1) Blue Masonry (i.e. the three Craft Degrees), in which none of the real secrets are revealed to the members and which serves merely as a sorting-ground for selecting likely subjects; (2) the Upper Degrees, in which most of the members, whilst imagining themselves to have been initiated into the whole secret of the Order and " bursting with importance " over their imaginary rôle of leaders, are only admitted to a partial knowledge of the goal to which they are tending; and (3) the inner circle, " the true masters," those who conceal themselves behind high-grade Masonry.   Admission to this inner circle may be, moreover, not a matter of degrees.   " Whilst in the lower Masonries the adepts are obliged to pass through all the degrees of the established hierarchy, the upper and invisible Freemasonry is certainly recruited not only amongst the thirty-three degrees but in all the groups of upper-degree Masonry, and perhaps even in certain exceptional cases outside these."[1] This inner and invisible Freemasonry is to a large extent *international*.

The most illuminating passage in the whole of M. Copin Albancelli's book is where he describes an experience that befell him after he had taken the degree of Rose-Croix. It was then that one of his superiors took him aside and addressed him in the following terms:

"You realize the power which Freemasonry has at its disposal. We can say that we hold France. It is not because of our numbers, since there are only 25,000 Freemasons in this country [this was in 1889]. Nor is it because we are the brains, for you have been able to judge of the intellectual mediocrity of the greater number of these 25,000 Freemasons. We hold France because we are organized and the only people who are organized. But above all, we hold France because we have an aim, this aim is unknown; as it is unknown, no obstacle can be put in its way; and finally, as no obstacle is put up, the way is wide open before us. This is logical, is it not?"

"Absolutely."

"Good. But what would you say of an association which instead of consisting of 25,000 nonentities as in Freemasonry, were composed of, say, only a thousand individuals, but a thousand individuals recruited in the manner that I will tell you."

And the Freemason went on to explain the way in which such individuals were selected, the months and years of observation, of supervision, to which they were subjected, so as to form a body of picked men inside Freemasonry capable of directing its operations.

"You can imagine the power at the command of such an association?"

"An association thus selected would do anything it chose. It could possess the world if it pleased."

Thereupon the higher adept, after asking for a further promise of secrecy, declared:

"Well, in exchange for this promise, Brother Copin, I am authorized to let you know that this association exists and that, further, I am authorized to introduce you into it.'"[2]

It was then that Monsieur Copin Albancelli understood that the point to which the conversation was leading up was not, as he had at first supposed, an invitation to take the next

[1] *Le Pouvoir occulte contre la France*, pp. 274-7.
[2] Ibid., pp. 284-6.

step in Freemasonry—the thirtieth degree of Knight Kadosch —but to enter through a side-door into an association concealed within Freemasonry and for which the visible organization of the latter served merely as a cover. A very curious resemblance will here be noticed between the method of sounding M. Copin Albancelli and that of the Illuminatus Cato in the matter of Savioli, described in a passage already quoted:

Now that he is a Mason I have . . . taken up the general plan of our ☉, and as this pleased him I said that such a thing really existed, whereat he gave me his word that he would enter it.

M. Copin Albancelli, however, did not give his word that he would enter it, but, on the contrary, checked further revelations by declaring that he would leave Freemasonry.

This experience had afforded him a glimpse of " a world existing behind the masonic world, more secret than it, unsuspected by it as by the outside world."[1] Freemasonry, then, " can only be the half-lit antechamber of the real secret society. That is the truth."[2] " There exists then necessarily a permanent directing Power. We cannot see that Power, therefore it is occult."[3]

For some time M. Copin Albancelli concluded this Power to be " the Jewish power," and elaborated the idea in a further work[4]; but the war has led him to develop his theories in yet another book, which will shortly appear.

That the lodges of the Grand Orient are largely controlled by Jews is, however, certain, and that they are centres of political propaganda is equally undeniable. We have only to glance at the following extracts—some of which are reproduced on the opposite page—from the programme of debates in the *Bulletin* of the Grand Orient for June 5, 1922, to recognize that the ideas they propagate are simply those of International Socialism:

Loge " Union et France ": Lecture du Rapport de notre T.·. C.·. F.·. Chardard sur " L'Exploitation des richesses nationales au profit de la collectivité."

Loge " Les Rénovateurs ": " Exploitation des Richesses nationales et des grosses Entreprises au profit de la collectivité." Conférence de notre F.·. Goldschmidt, Orat.·. adjoint sur la même question.

---

[1] *Le Pouvoir occulte contre la France*, p. 44.
[2] Ibid., p. 263.
[3] Ibid., p. 294.
[4] *La Conjuration juive contre le Monde Chrétien* (1909).

Mardi 20 Juin 1922

UNION ET FRANCE
Temple · 16, rue Cadet.

P∴V∴ et Corresp∴. — Init∴ du prof∴ GUILLE-PAIN.
Lecture du rapport de notre T∴ C∴ F∴ CHAR-DARD sur :

L'EXPLOITATION
DES RICHESSES NATIONALES
AU PROFIT DE LA COLLECTIVITE

Demandes d'augm∴ de sal∴. — Lecture du travail de notre T∴ C∴ F∴ CROCHEREAU.

Mardi 20 Juin 1922

CLARTÉ
Temple · 379, rue des Pyrénées.

Corresp∴ au Vén∴, F∴ LEYRE, 15, boul. St-Marcel

Ouv∴ des trav∴ à 20 h. 30. — P∴V∴ et Corresp∴. Pl∴ du Comité républ∴ des Quatre Sergents de La Rochelle. — Les Faits de la Quinzaine (F∴ DANAE).
Lecture des rapports sur le prof∴ KIRCH (Paul), adjudant au 5ᵉ bataillon cycliste, au Fort de Romy, 122, avenue Pasteur, à Bagnolet. — Init∴ s'il y a lieu. — Allocution de bienvenue au F∴ Orat∴
Instruction maç∴ au 1ᵉʳ degré par le F∴ ANJOU.

QUELQUES REFLEXIONS SUR
LES RELIGIONS
Courte causerie du F∴ PROST (Amédée)

Divers : Y a-t-il lieu d'élever une protestation contre les projets du Bloc national touchant à la liberté d'opinion des fonctionnaires?

Vendredi 23 Juin 1922

LES ZÉLÉS PHILANTHROPES
Temple : 94, avenue de Suffren.

Vén∴ d'hon∴ FF∴ Dʳ BOURY et CAUDEIRIER. Vén∴ F∴ René DUBOIS, 139, av. Félix-Faure, Paris-15ᵉ. Secrét∴ F∴ LAURENT, 65, rue Lecourbe, Paris-15ᵉ. Trés∴ F∴ AUBRY (André), 5, rue Doumier, Paris-16ᵉ.

Ouv∴ des trav∴ à 20 h. 30. — P∴V∴ de la dernière Ten∴ et Corresp∴ — Instruction maç∴ pour les FF∴ nouvellement initiés.

SUITE DE L'ETUDE CRITIQUE DE LA SOCIETE ACTUELLE

La Transformation de la Société actuelle s'impose-t-elle ?

Conférence par le T∴ C∴ F∴ Edmond COTTIN, membre de la R∴ L∴ La Fédération Maç∴, avocat à la Cour
Discussion générale contradictoire
Récréation de cinq minutes. — Circul∴ du tr∴ pour les Affamés russes.
Election des délégués au Convent. — Sortie champêtre du 2 juillet. — Rapports divers. — Clôt∴ des trav∴ à 23 h. 30.
Nota. — Le Vén∴ et les Off∴ invitent très frat∴ les FF∴ des trois Obéd∴ à assister à cette Ten∴ qui promet d'être fort intéressante, étant donnée la valeur du Conférn∴ Tous les FF∴ présents aux col∴ seront priés de prendre part à la discussion générale.

Mardi 20 Juin 1922

ISIS MONTHYON
ET CONSCIENCE ET VOLONTÉ
Temple : 16, rue Cadet.

Ouv∴ des trav∴ à 20 h 30 précises. — P∴V∴ et Corresp∴ — Sit∴ du Trés∴ et de l'Hospit∴
1ʳᵉ lecture des rapports sur les prof∴ en instance : KLOTZ (Roger), importateur, 11, rue de Marseille; MEIGNEL (Joseph), garçon de restaurant, 94, rue Blanche; RUEGER (André), représentant d'automobiles, 8, rue Cottes, à Bellencourt; SISCO (Félicien), cuisinier, 95, rue de Clignancourt. — Appel nominal
Les Faits du Mois, par le F∴ MASSE, m∴ de l'At∴

LA TERREUR ET LE PÉRIL FASCISTE EN ITALIE
Le Fascisme et la F∴-Maç∴ Italienne

Impressions de notre F∴ MAZZINI, de retour, après un séjour prolongé en Italie

N. B. — Les FF∴ italiens des deux Obéd∴ sont spécialement invités à assister à cette Tenue.
Prière à nos FF∴ en retard de se mettre en règle avec le Trés∴

Loge "Les Zélés Philanthropes": "La Transformation de la Société Actuelle s'impose-t-elle?" Conférence par le T.·. C.·. F.·. Edmond Cottin.

Loge "Paix-Travail-Solidarité": "Rôle de la Franc-Maçonnerie dans la politique actuelle" par le F.·. F.·..

Loge "Les Trinitaires": "Le Socialisme Français" par le T.·. Ill. F.·. Elie May.

Ten.·. Collective des L.·. "Emmanuel Arago" & "les Cœurs Unis indivisibles": "Comment propager notre Idéal Maçonnique dans le Monde profane." Conférence par le F.·. Jahia, de la R.·. L.·. Isis Monthyon.

Loge "Isis Monthyon et Conscience et Volonté": "La Terreur et le Péril Fasciste en Italie, le Fascisme et la F.·.-Maç.·. Italienne," impressions de notre F.·. Mazzini, de retour, après un séjour prolongé en Italie."

It will be seen by the last of these extracts that Grand Orient Masonry is the enemy of Fascismo, which saved Italy in her hour of peril. Indeed, the Italian Masons passed a resolution which was directly opposed to Fascist views, especially with regard to the religious policy of Mussolini, who has restored the crucifix to the schools and religious teaching to the curriculum. The Fascist *Giornale di Roma* declared that the principles announced by the Masons in this resolution were those which threatened to submerge the State and nation. Consequently Mussolini declared that Fascisti must either leave their lodges or leave Fascismo.[1]

In Belgium Freemasonry has taken the same political and anti-religious course. In 1856 the directing committee of the Belgian Grand Orient declared: " Not only is it the right but the duty of the lodges to supervise the actions in public life of those amongst its members whom it has placed in political posts, the right to demand explanations . . ."[2] When in 1866 at a funeral ceremony in honour of the deceased King Leopold I the Grand Orient of Belgium displayed the maxim, " The soul which has emanated from God is immortal," the Freemasons of Louvain entered a violent protest on the ground that " Free-thinking had been admitted by the Belgian lodges in 1864 as its fundamental principle," and that the Grand Orient had therefore violated the convictions of its members.[3]

In Spain and Portugal Freemasonry has played not merely

[1] *Morning Post* for February 1 and February 26, 1923.
[2] Copin Albancelli, *Le Pouvoir occulte contre la France*, p. 132.
[3] Gautrelet, *La Franc-Maçonnerie et la Révolution*, p. 87 (1872).

a subversive but an actively revolutionary and sanguinary rôle. The anarchist Ferrer, intimately concerned with a plot to murder the King of Spain, was at the same moment entrusted with negotiations between the Grand Orient of France and the Grand Lodge of Catalonia.[1] These murderous schemes, frustrated in Spain, met, however, in Portugal with complete success. The Portuguese revolutions from 1910 to 1921 were organized under the direction of Freemasonry and the secret society of Carbonarios. The assassination of King Carlos and his elder son had been prepared by the same secret organizations. In 1908 a pamphlet modelled on the libels published against Marie Antoinette was directed against Queen Amélie and her husband. A month later the assassination took place. Amongst the leaders of the new Republic was Magalhaes Lima, Grand Master of the Grand Orient of Portugal.[2]

The authorship of these disorders was, in fact, so clearly recognized that honest Freemasons forsook the lodges. An English Mason, unaware of the true character of Portuguese Freemasonry, when in Lisbon in August 1919, made himself known to several moderate Portuguese Masons, who, while glad to welcome him as a brother, refused to take him to a lodge, declaring that they had severed all connection with Masonry since it had passed under the control of assassins. They also added that the assassination of Señor Paes, the President in December 1918, was the work of certain Portuguese lodges. A special meeting had previously been held in Paris in conjunction with the Grand Orient of France, at which it had been decided that Paes was to be removed. This decision reached, the earliest opportunity of putting it into force was sought—with fatal results. The assassin was imprisoned in the Penitentiary but liberated by the revolution of 1921, and no attempt has been made to recapture him. The murder of Dr. Antonio Granjo in October 1921 was traced to the same agency. In the pocket of the murdered man was found a document from the " Lodge of Liberty and Justice "(!) warning him of the decision taken against him for having ordered the police to protect the British tramway company.[3]

The present Portuguese Government, indeed, makes no secret of its masonic character and prints the square and compass on its bank-notes.

But whilst in Spain and Portugal Freemasonry manifested

[1] Copin Albancelli, *Le Pouvoir occulte contre la France*, p. 85.
[2] Louis Dasté, *Marie Antinette et le Complot Maçonnique*, pp. 49-51 (1910).
[3] *Times* for December 30, 1921; *A Epoca*, November 28, 1921.

itself in Anarchist outrages, in the east of Europe the lodges, largely under the control of Jews, followed the line of Marxian Socialism. After the fall of the Bela Kun régime in Hungary a raid on the lodges brought to light documents clearly revealing the fact that the ideas of Socialism had been disseminated by the Freemasons. Thus in the minutes of meetings it was recorded that on November 16, 1906, Dr. Kallos had addressed the Gyor Lodge on Socialist ideals. " The ideal world which we call the masonic world," he declared, " will be also a Socialist world and the religion of Freemasonry is that of Socialism as well." Dr. Kallos then proceeded to acquaint the members with the theories of Marx and Engels, showing that no help was to be found in Utopias, as the interests of the proletarians were in absolute conflict with those of other classes, and these differences could only be settled by international class warfare. Nevertheless with that fear of the proletariat which has always characterized the democrats of revolutionary Freemasonry, Dr. Kallos declared later that " the social revolution must take place without bloodshed."[1] The Karolyi régime was the direct outcome of these illusions, and as in all revolutions paved the way for the more violent elements.

Still further east in Europe the lodges, though revolutionary, instead of following the International Socialist line of Hungarian Freemasonry, exhibited a political and nationalist character. The Young Turk movement originated in the masonic lodges of Salonica under the direction of the Grand Orient of Italy, which later contributed to the success of Mustapha Kemal. Moreover, as we approach the Near East, cradle of the masonic system, we find the Semitic influence not only of the Jews but of other Semite races directing the lodges. In Turkey, in Egypt, in Syria now, as a thousand years ago, the same secret societies which inspired the Templars have never ceased to exist, and in this mingling of the East and West it is possible that the Grand Orient may draw reinforcement from those sources whence it drew its system and its name.

Amongst the strange survivals of early Eastern sects are the Druses of Lebanon, who might indeed be described as the Freemasons of the East; their outer organization closely resembles that of the Craft Degrees in Western Masonry, yet such is their power of secrecy that few if any Europeans

[1] These documents were published in a book entitled *A Szabadkömivesseg Bünei* by Adorjan Barcsay.

have ever succeeded in discovering the secret doctrines. That their tendency is largely political admits of little doubt; in fact men intimately acquainted with the Near East have declared that the influence they exercise over the politics of that region is as far-reaching as that of the Grand Orient over the affairs of Europe and that they form the breeding-ground of all political ideas and changes. Though small in numbers this mysterious society is composed of past masters in the game of intrigue, who, whilst playing apparently a minor part at political meetings, secret or otherwise, or even remaining completely silent, contrive to influence decisions with startling results.

BRITISH MASONRY

We shall now consider the further ways in which British Masonry differs from the Grand Orient.

In the first place, whilst working the same degrees, its rituals, formulas, and ceremonies, as also the interpretation it places on words and symbols, are different in many essential points.

Secondly, British Masonry is essentially an honest institution. Whereas in the Grand Orient the initiate is led through a maze of ceremonies towards a goal unknown to him which he may discover too late to be other than he supposed, the British initiate, although admitted by gradual stages to the mysteries of the Craft, knows nevertheless from the beginning the general aim of the Order.

Thirdly, British Masonry is primarily philanthropic and the sums it devotes to charitable purposes are immense. Since the war the three principal masonic charities have collected annually over £300,000.

But the point to be emphasized here is that British Masonry is strictly non-political, not merely in theory but in practice, and that it enforces this principle on every occasion. Thus before the recent General Election, the Report of the Board of General Purposes, drawn up by Grand Lodge on December 5, 1923, recalled to the notice of the Craft that " ' all subjects of a political nature are strictly excluded from discussion in masonic meetings,' this being in accordance with long-established masonic tradition . . . it follows from this that Masonry must not be used for any personal or party purpose in connexion with an election." It further emphasized the distinct caution " that any attempt to bring the Craft into the electioneering arena would be treated as a serious masonic offence."

At the same time a fresh injunction was made with regard to the Grand Orient of France:

As recognition was withdrawn from that body by the United Grand Lodge of England in 1878, . . . it is considered necessary to warn all members of our lodges that they cannot visit any lodge under the obedience of a jurisdiction unrecognized by the United Grand Lodge of England; and further that under Rule 150 of the Book of Constitutions, they cannot admit visitors therefrom.

For the reasons given at the beginning of this section British Masonry stands rigidly aloof from all attempts to create an international system of Masonry. The idea was first suggested at the Masonic Congress of Paris in 1889, convened to celebrate the centenary of the first French Revolution, but led to nothing very definite until the Congress of Geneva in September 1902, at which the delegates of thirty-four lodges, Grand Lodges, Grand Orients, and Supreme Councils were present, and a proposal was unanimously adopted " tending towards the creation of an International Bureau for Masonic Affairs," to which twenty Powers, mostly Europeans, gave their adherence. Brother Desmons, of the Grand Orient of France, in an after-dinner speech declared it to have been always " the dream of his life " that " all democracies should meet and understand one another in such a way as one day to form the Universal Republic."[1]

According to the official report of the proceedings, " the representatives of Belgium, Holland, France, Germany, England, Spain, Italy, and Switzerland greeted with much feeling the dawn of this new era." The same Report goes on to observe that—

It is altogether a mistake . . . to believe that Freemasonry does not attack the defects of such and such a State, and that consequently it remains a stranger to party-strife and the tendencies of the times.

And again:

Freemasonry has imposed upon itself a task—a mission. It is a question of nothing less than the rebuilding of society on an entirely new basis, which shall be more in accordance with the present conditions of the means of communication, of situation, and pro-

---

[1] *Two Centuries of Freemasonry*, p. 79. Published by the International Bureau for Masonic Affairs, of Neuchatel, 1917.

duction, as well as of a reform of right, of a complete renewal of the principle of existence, especially of the principle of community and of the relations of men among one another.

The Report here quoted is, however, inaccurate in one important particular. No English delegates were present at the Geneva Congress or on any other occasion of the kind. There was a delegate from Adelaide who spoke a good deal, but the Chairman specifically mentioned England as taking no part in the movement. Later on, in a Report of the Board of General Purposes to Grand Lodge on March 2, 1921, a letter from Lord Ampthill, pro Grand Master, appears, declining an invitation from the Swiss Grand Lodge Alpina to British Freemasons to attend an International Masonic Congress in Geneva and quoting the following letter from the Grand Secretary as an earlier precedent for this refusal:

I am directed to state, in reply to the invitation to attend an International Masonic Conference in Switzerland during the coming autumn, that the United Grand Lodge of England will be unable to send representatives on the occasion. It never participates in a Masonic gathering in which are treated as an open question what it has always held to be ancient and essential Landmarks of the Craft, these being an express belief in the Great Architect of the Universe, and an obligatory recognition of the Volume of the Sacred Law. Its refusal to remain in fraternal association with such Sovereign Jurisdictions as have repudiated or made light of these Landmarks has long been upon record, and its resolve in this regard remains unshaken.

Lord Ampthill then went on to say:

A further consequence of certain happenings of the war is to make more firm our resolve to keep, as far as in us lies, Freemasonry strictly away from participation in politics, either national or international. This attitude of aloofness from necessarily controversial affairs of State, on which Brethren can legitimately and most properly differ, has ever been maintained by our Grand Lodge since it was first convened in 1717. Because of this, it held aloof from such international conferences as were summoned during the war; and never more than now has the necessity for the maintenance of this attitude been felt by British Freemasons. . . . For these reasons, the invitation to participate in the proposed International Conference of Freemasons at Geneva cannot be accepted. Such an assembly might be termed informal, but inevitably it would be regarded as opening a door to compromise on those things which this Grand Lodge has always held to be essentials. Such a compromise English Freemasonry will never contemplate. On these essentials we take the firm stand we have always done; we cannot detract from full recognition of the Great Architect of the Universe, and we shall continue to forbid the introduction of political discussion into our Lodges.

British Masonry has thus taken a firm stand against the Grand Orient. But it is regrettable that views so admirably expressed should be confined to masonic correspondence and not made more apparent to the world in general. On the Continent, outside masonic circles, the difference between British Masonry and the Grand Orient variety is *not* sufficiently known, and the reticence of leading British Masons on this subject has not only played into the hands of the intractable anti-Masons, who declare all Masonry to be harmful, but has strengthened the position of the revolutionaries who use Masonry for a subversive purpose. Thus in the Portuguese revolution of 1920 the Masons of that country who were directing the movement sheltered themselves behind the good name of England. " How can you accuse the lodges of being murder clubs," they said to the people, "when Masonry is directed by England and had King Edward for its Grand Master?"

However ludicrous all this may seem to the British public, yet for the honour of our country such accusations should not remain unrefuted. A witness of the disorders that took place in Portugal declared to the present writer that if only Grand Lodge of England would have published a notice in the Continental press disassociating itself from the Grand Orient in general and from Portuguese Freemasonry in particular, the power of the revolutionaries would have been immensely weakened and the anti-British and pro-German propaganda then circulating in the country defeated. But British Freemasonry preferred to maintain an attitude of aloofness, contenting itself with issuing periodical warnings against the Grand Orient privately to the lodges.

This policy has done much to damage not only the good name of England but of British Masonry in the eyes of the outside world, and particularly in those of Roman Catholics, which is the more regrettable since Freemasonry and the Roman Catholic Church are the only two organized bodies in this country which really exercise discipline over their members and forbid them to belong to subversive secret societies; hence they provide the two strongest bulwarks against the occult forces of revolution. For this reason, as we shall see later, they are the two bodies which are the most feared by the recruiting agents of these societies.

But in the case of Freemasonry the fact is unfortunately too little known to the world in general. As a singularly broad-minded Jesuit has recently expressed it:

> The anti-clerical and revolutionary activities of Continental Freemasonry did not begin when the Grand Orient finally abolished God. During a century and more these evil forces had been at work. Nevertheless English Masons only shrugged their shoulders and looked another way, though the true character of foreign Masonry was brought to their notice in such books as that of John Robison, *Proofs of a Conspiracy against all the Religions and Governments of Europe*. . . .

> No doubt [the same writer says again] there has been at times a deplorable amount of exaggeration among Continental Catholics in attributing all the moral and social evils of the world to the insidious workings of Freemasonry. . . . But so long as English Freemasons resolutely avert their gaze from the anti-religious and anti-social activities of their Continental brethren there can be no hope of any better understanding.[1]

It is impossible to deny the truth of these strictures. As has already been pointed out in the course of this book, British Freemasons have frequently not only ignored Robison's warning but vilified him as the enemy of Masonry, although he never attacked their Order but only the perverted systems of the Continent; too often also they have exonerated the most dangerous secret societies, notably the Illuminati, because, apparently from a mistaken sense of loyalty, they conceive it their duty to defend any association of a masonic character. This is simply suicidal. British Masonry has no bitterer enemies than the secret societies working for subversion, which, from the Illuminati onwards, have always regarded honest Masonry with contempt and used its doctrines for an ulterior purpose.

It is easy to see how these doctrines may be perverted to an end directly opposed to that which British Masons have in view. Thus, for example, the idea of the brotherhood of man in the sense of love for all humanity is the essence of Christianity—" Be kindly affectioned one to another with brotherly love; in honour preferring one another." In adopting

---

[1] Article on " The Popes and Freemasonry," by the Rev. Herbert Thurston, S.J., in *The Tablet* for January 27, 1923.

"brotherly love" as a part of their sacred trilogy British Masons adopt an entirely Christian standpoint. But if by the brotherhood of man is meant that men of every race are equally related and that therefore one owes the same duty to foreigners as to one's fellow-countrymen it is obvious that all national feeling must vanish. The British Freemason does not, of course, interpret the theory in this manner; he cannot seriously regard himself as the brother of the Bambute pygmy or the Polynesian cannibal, thus he uses the term merely in a vague and theoretical sense.

What indeed does the word "brother" literally mean? If we consult the dictionary we shall see it defined as "a male born of the same parents; anyone closely united with or resembling one another; associated in common interests, occupation," etc. It is therefore obviously absurd to say that men of such different races as those referred to are brothers; they are not born of the same kind of parents, they are not united in their aims, they do not remotely resemble one another, and they are not associated in common interests and occupations. Though these happen to be extreme cases, there are nevertheless essential differences between men of the same zone and climate. The Englishman and the Frenchman are not brothers because they do not see life from the same point of view, but that is no reason why they should not be close allies.

The brotherhood of man, if taken literally, is therefore a misleading term, nor is such a relationship necessary to the peace of the world. Cain and Abel were not better friends, for being brothers. David and Jonathan, on the other hand, were not brothers but devoted friends. In striving after universal brotherhood in a literal sense, Freemasons are therefore pursuing a chimera.

The most dangerous fallacy to which democracy, under the influence of Illuminized Freemasonry, has succumbed is that peace between nations can be brought about by means of Internationalism, that is to say, by the destruction of national feeling. Yet a man is not more likely to live at peace with his neighbours because he is devoid of natural affection; on the contrary, the good brother, the devoted father, is most likely to become the faithful friend. Permanent peace between nations will probably never be ensured, but the only basis on which such a situation can conceivably be established is the basis of sane Nationalism—an understanding between the patriotic and virile elements in every country which, because they value their own liberties and revere their own traditions, are able to respect those of other nations. Internationalism is an understanding between the decadent elements in each country—the conscientious objectors, the drawing-room Socialists, the visionaries—who shirk the realities of life and, as the Socialist Karl Kautsky in a description of Idealists has admirably expressed it, " see only differences of opinion and misapprehension where there are actually irreconcilable antagonisms." This is why at times of crisis Idealists are of all men the most dangerous and Pacifists the great promoters of wars. Understanding between nations is wholly desirable, but the destruction of the national spirit everywhere can only lead to the weakening of all countries where this process takes place and the triumph of the nations who refuse to accept the same principle.

It will perhaps be answered that Freemasons do not believe in the doctrine of brotherhood between all men, but only between Masons of all races. But this may lead no less to national disintegration if it creates a nation within each nation, an international fraternity independent of the countries to which its members belong. The logical outcome of this may be that a man will refuse to fight for his country against his brother Masons—it is what has happened in France. The Grand Orient was before the recent war the great breeding-ground of anti-patriotism, where all schemes for national defence were discouraged. Before 1870 the same thing took place, and it was in the masonic lodges that Germany found her most valuable allies.

In the same way the doctrine of the perfectibility of human nature lends itself to perversion. Nothing could be more desirable than that man should strive after perfection. Did not Christ enjoin His disciples: " Be ye therefore perfect, even as your Father which is in Heaven is perfect "? Man is there-fore acting in accordance with Christian principles in seeking after divine perfection. But when he comes to believe that he has already attained it he makes of himself a god. " If I justify myself," said Job, " mine own mouth shall condemn me; if I say I am perfect, it shall also prove me perverse." And St. John: " If we say we have no sin, we deceive ourselves, and the truth is not in us." More than this, if we seek per-fection in others we deceive ourselves equally and make gods of men. This is precisely the conclusion at which perverted

Freemasonry and the forms of Socialism deriving from it arrive. Human nature, they say, is itself divine; what need then for other divinities? The Catholic Church is consequently quite right in declaring that the doctrine of the perfectibility of human nature leads to the deification of humanity in that it puts humanity in the place of God. The Grand Orient, which definitely accepts this doctrine, has therefore logically erased the name of the Great Architect of the Universe from its ritual and has become an association of Freethinkers and Atheists.

Is it necessary to point out the folly as well as the crime of this delusion—the ludicrous inconsequence of men who divinize humanity yet revile what they call " society "? All the evils of the world, they declare, are not to be found in nature but in " man-made laws," in the institutions of " society." Yet what is society but the outcome of human wills, of human aspirations? Society may be, and no doubt is, in need of reformation, but are not its imperfections the creation of imperfect beings? It is true that to-day the world is in a state of chaos, industrial chaos, political chaos, social chaos, religious chaos. Everywhere men are losing faith in the causes they are supposed to represent; authority questions its own right to govern, democracy is rent with divisions, the ruling classes are abdicating in favour of unscrupulous demagogues, the ministers of religion barter their faith for popularity.

And what has brought the world to this pass? Humanity! Humanity, that all-wise, all-virtuous abstraction that needs no light from Heaven. Humanity that was to take the place of God! If ever there was a moment in the history of the world when the futility of this pretension should be apparent it is the present moment. All the ills, all the confusion, what are they but the outcome of human error and of human passions? It is not Capitalism that has failed, nor yet Democracy, nor yet even Socialism as a principle, it is not monarchy that has broken down, nor Republicanism, nor again religion; *it is humanity that has broken down*. The ills of Capitalism arise from the egoism of individual capitalists; Socialism has failed because, as Robert Owen discovered, the idle, the quarrelsome, the selfish have prevented its success. If men were perfect, Socialism might succeed, but so might any other system. A perfect capitalist would love his employee as himself, just as a perfect Socialist would be willing to work for the common good. It is the imperfections of human nature that prevent, and will always prevent, any system from being perfect. There will never be a Millennium of man's making. Only the application of Christian principles to human conduct can bring about a better order of things.

Grand Orient Masonry, in deifying human nature, thus not only builds upon the sand, but by its rejection of all religion takes away the sole hope of human progress. Meanwhile, by the support it lends to Socialism it encourages the class war instead of the brotherhood between men of all ranks and conditions which it professes to advocate. British Freemasonry, on the other hand, whilst not interpreting brotherhood in a political sense, nevertheless contributes to social peace. At the annual conference of the Labour Party in 1923 a proposal was made by the extreme section that " any person who is a Free mason should be excluded from any kind of office," it being suggested that " in cases where an understanding has been reached between Trade Union leaders and employers, thus preventing or limiting industrial trouble, the secret has been the bond of Freemasonry."[1] Whether this was the case or not, British Masonry, by taking its stand on patriotism and respect for religion, necessarily tends to unite men of all classes and therefore offers a formidable bulwark against the forces of revolution. Any attacks on British Masonry as at present constituted and directed are therefore absolutely opposed to the interests of the country. But at the same time it behoves Masons to beware of the insidious attempts that are being made by irregular secret societies to infiltrate the Craft and pervert its true principles. The present satisfactory condition of Freemasonry in England is owing not only to its established statutes, but to the character of the men who control it—men who are not, as in eighteenth-century France, mere figureheads, but the real directors of the Order. Should the control ever pass into the wrong hands and the agents of secret societies succeed in capturing a number of the lodges, this great stabilizing force might become a gigantic engine of destruction. How insidiously these efforts are being made we shall see in the next chapter.

[1] *Evening Standard*, June 26, 1923.

12

SECRET SOCIETIES IN ENGLAND

WE have seen that from the Illuminati onwards subversive societies have always sought recruits amongst orthodox Freemasons. The reason for this is obvious: not only do the doctrines of Freemasonry lend themselves to perversion, but the training provided in the Lodges makes an admirable preparation for initiation into other secret systems. The man who has learnt to maintain silence even on what may appear to him as trivialities, who is willing to submit to mystification, to ask no questions, and to recognize the authority of superiors whom he is in no way legally obliged to obey, who has, moreover, become imbued with the *esprit de corps* which binds him to his fellow-members in a common cause, is naturally a better subject for the secret society adept than the free lance who is liable to assert his independence at any moment. Perhaps the most important factor, however, is the nature of the masonic oaths. These terrible penalties, which many Freemasons themselves regret as a survival of barbarism and which have in fact been abolished in the higher degrees, have done much to create prejudice against Freemasonry, whilst at the same time they provide an additional incentive to outside intriguers. In the opinion of M. Copin Albancelli, the abolition of the oath would go far to prevent penetration of British Masonry by the secret societies.

Now, by their obligations British Freemasons are forbidden to join these irregular societies, not only because their principles are in conflict with those of orthodox Masonry, but because in most cases they admit women. According to the ruling of Grand Lodge, "any member working under the English Jurisdiction . . . violates his Obligation by being present at or assisting in assemblies professing to be Masonic which are attended by women." Warnings to this effect have been frequently given in the Lodges; on September 3, 1919, the Board of General Purposes issued the following report:

The Board's attention is being increasingly drawn to sedulous endeavours which are being made by certain bodies unrecognized as Masonic by the United Grand Lodge of England, to induce Freemasons to join in their assemblies. As all such bodies which admit women to membership are clandestine and irregular, it is necessary to caution Brethren against being inadvertently led to violate their Obligation by becoming members of them or attending their meetings. Grand Lodge, nine years since, approved the action of the Board in suspending from all Masonic rights and privileges two Brethren who had contumaciously failed to explain the grave Masonic irregularity to which attention is now again called; and it is earnestly hoped that no occasion will arise for having again to institute disciplinary proceedings of a like kind.

The idea of women Masons is, of course, not a new one. As early as 1730 lodges for women are said to have existed in France, and towards the end of the century several excellent women, such as the Duchesse de Bourbon and the Princesse de Lamballe, played a leading part in the Order. But this *Maçonnerie d'Adoption,* as it was called, retained a purely convivial character; a sham ceremonial, with symbols, pass words, and a ritual, was devised as a consolation to the members for their exclusion from the real lodges. These mummeries were, as Ragon observes, " only the pretexts for assemblies; the real objects were the banquet and the ball, which were their inevitable accompaniments."[1]

But this precedent, inaugurated as a society pastime and accompanied by all the frivolity of the age, paved the way for Weishaupt's two classes of women members, who, although never initiated into the secrets of the Order, were to act as useful tools " directed by men without knowing it." For this purpose they were to be divided into two classes, the " virtuous " to play the part of figureheads or decoys, and the " freer-hearted," who were to carry out the real designs of the Order.

The same plan was adopted nearly a hundred years later by Weishaupt's disciple Bakunin, who, however, did admit women as actual initiates into his secret society, the Alliance Sociale Démocratique, but, like Weishaupt, divided them into classes. The sixth category of people to be employed in the work of social revolution is thus described in his programme:

The sixth category is very important. They are the women, who must be divided into three classes: the first, frivolous women, without

[1] Ragon, *Cours des Initiations,* p. 33.

mind or heart, which we must use in the same manner as the third and fourth categories of men [i.e. by "getting hold of their dirty secrets and making them our slaves"]; the second, the ardent, devoted and capable women, but who are not ours because they have not reached a practical revolutionary understanding, without phrase—we must make use of these like the men of the fifth category [i.e. by "drawing them incessantly into practical and perilous manifestations, which will result in making the majority of them disappear while making some of them genuine revolutionaries"]; finally, the women who are entirely with us, that is to say completely initiated and having accepted our programme in its entirety. We ought to consider them as the most precious of our treasures, without whose help we can do nothing.[1]

The first and only woman to be admitted into real Masonry, if such a term can be applied to so heterogeneous a system, was Maria Deraismes, an ardent French Feminist celebrated for her political speeches and electioneering campaigns in the district of Pontoise and for twenty-five years the acknowledged leader of the anti-clerical and Feminist party.[2] In 1882 Maria Deraismes was initiated into Freemasonry by the members of the Lodge *Les Libres Penseurs,* deriving from the Grande Loge Symbolique Écossaise and situated at Pecq in the Department of Seine-et-Oise. The proceeding being, however, entirely unconstitutional, Maria Deraismes's initiation was declared by the Grande Loge to be null and void and the Lodge *Les Libres Penseurs* was disgraced.[3] But some years afterwards Dr. George Martin, an enthusiastic advocate of votes for women, collaborated with Maria Deraismes in founding the *Maçonnerie Mixte* at the first lodge of the Order named "Le Droit Humain." The *Suprême Conseil Universel Mixte* was founded in 1899.

The Maçonnerie Mixte was political and in no way theosophical or occult, and its programme, like that of the Grand Orient, was Utopian Socialism, whilst by its insistence on the supremacy of reason it definitely proclaimed its antagonism to all revealed religion. Thus in the involved language of Dr. George Martin himself:

The Ordre Maçonnique Mixte Internationale is the first mixed, philosophic, progressive, and philanthropic Masonic Power to be

[1] Alliance de la Démocratie Socialiste, etc., publié par l'ordre du Congrès International de la Haye, p. 93 (1873).
[2] *Histoire des Clubs de Femmes,* by the Baron Marc de Villiers, p. 380.
[3] René Guénon, *Le Théosophisme,* p. 245 (1921).

organized and constituted in the world, placed above all the pre-occupations of the philosophical or religious ideas which may be professed by those who ask to become members. . . . The Order wishes to interest itself principally in the vital interests of the human being on earth; it wishes above all to study in its Temples the means for realizing Peace between all nations and social Justice which will enable all human beings to enjoy during their lives the greatest possible sum of moral felicity and of material well-being. . . . Claiming no divine revelation and loudly affirming that it is only an emanation of human reason, this fraternal institution is not dogmatic, it is rationalist.[1]

Into this materialist and political club, erected under the guise of Freemasonry, entered Annie Besant with all the strange conglomeration of Eastern doctrines now known as Theosophy.

THEOSOPHY

Before entering on this question it is necessary to make my own position clear. Although I should much prefer not to introduce a personal note into the discussion, I feel that nothing I say will carry any weight if it appears to be an expression of opinion by one who has never considered religious doctrines from anything but the orthodox Christian point of view. I should explain, then, that I have known Theosophists from my early youth, that I have travelled in India, Ceylon, Burma, and Japan and seen much to admire in the great religions of the East. I do not believe that God has revealed Himself to one portion of mankind alone and that during only the last 1,900 years of the world's history; I do not accept the doctrine that all the millions of human beings who have never heard of Christ are plunged in spiritual darkness; I believe that behind all religions founded on a law of righteousness there lies a divine and central truth, that Ikhnaton, Moses and Isaiah, Socrates and Epictetus, Marcus Aurelius, Buddha, Zoroaster, and Mohammed were all teachers who interpreted to men the aspect of the divine as it had been vouchsafed to them and which in harmony with the supreme revelation given to man by Jesus Christ.

This conception of an affinity between all great religious faiths was beautifully expressed by an old Mohammedan to a friend of the present writer with whom he stood watching

---

[1] Guénon, op. cit., p. 248, quoting *La Lumière Maçonnique*, Nov.-Dec. 1912, p. 522.

a Hindu procession pass through an Indian village. In answer to the Englishman's enquiry, "What do you think of this?" the Mohammedan replied:

"Ah, sahib, we cannot tell. We know of three roads up the hill of endeavour to the gates of Paradise—the way of Mousa [Moses], the way of Issa [Jesus], and the way of Mahmoud, and there may be other roads of which you and I know nothing. I was born in the way of Mahmoud, and I believe it to be the best and the easiest to follow, and you were born in the way of Issa. And of this I am very sure: that if you will follow your guide on your road and I follow my guide on my road, when we have climbed the hill of endeavour, we shall salute one another again at the gates of Paradise."

If, then, in the following pages I attempt to show the errors of Theosophy, it is not because I do not recognize that there is much that is good and beautiful in the ancient religions from which it professes to derive.

But what is Theosophy? The word, as we have already seen, was used in the eighteenth century to denote the theory of the Martinists; it was known two centuries earlier when Haselmeyer in 1612 wrote of "the laudable Fraternity of the Theosophists of the Rosy Cross." According to Colonel Olcott, who with Madame Blavatsky founded the modern Theosophical Society in New York in 1875, the word was discovered by one of the members "in turning over the leaves of a Dictionary" and forthwith unanimously adopted.[1] Madame Blavatsky had arrived in America two years earlier, before which date she professed to have been initiated into certain esoteric doctrines in Thibet. Monsieur Guénon, who writes with inside knowledge of the movement, indicates, however, the existence of concealed superiors on the Continent of Europe by whom she was in reality directed.

What is very significant . . . is that Madame Blavatsky in 1875 wrote this: "I have been sent from Paris to America in order to verify phenomena and their reality and to show the deception of the Spiritualist theory." Sent by whom? Later she will say: by the "Mahatmas"; but then there was no question of them, and besides it was in Paris that she received her mission, and not in India or in Thibet.[2]

---

[1] Alice Leighton Cleather, *H. P. Blavatsky: her Life and Work for Humanity*, p. 17 (Thacker, Spink & Co., Calcutta, 1922).
[2] René Guénon, op. cit., p. 17.

Elsewhere Monsieur Guénon observes that it is very doubt
ful whether Madame Blavatsky was ever in Thibet at all. These
obvious attempts at concealment lead Monsieur Guénon therefore to the conclusion that in the background of Theosophy
there existed a mysterious centre of direction, that Madame
Blavatsky was simply " an instrument in the hands of individuals or occult groups sheltering behind her personality,"
and that " those who believe she invented everything, that
she did everything by herself and on her own initiative, are as
much mistaken as those who, on the contrary, believe her
affirmations concerning her relations with the pretended
Mahatmas."[1]

There is some reason to believe that the people under whom
Madame Blavatsky was working at this date in Paris were
Serapis Bey and Tuiti Bey, who belonged to " the Egyptian
Brothers." This might answer M. Guénon's question: " By
whom was she sent to America?" But another passage from
Madame Blavatsky's writings, on the person of Christ, that
M. Guénon quotes later, indicates a further source of inspira-
tion: " For me, Jesus Christ, that is to say the Man-God of
the Christians, copy of the Avatars of all countries, of the
Hindu Chrishna as of the Egyptian Horus, was never a *historical*
personage." Hence the story of His life was merely an allegory
founded on the existence of " a personage named Jehoshua born
at Lud." But elsewhere she asserted that Jesus may have lived
during the Christian era or a century earlier " *as the Sepher
Toldoth Jehoshua indicates*" (my italics). And Madame
Blavatsky went on to say of the savants who deny the historical
value of this legend, that they—

either lie or talk nonsense. *It is our Masters who affirm it* [my italics].
If the history of Jehoshua or Jesus Ben Pandera is false, then the
whole of the Talmud, the whole of the Jewish canon law, is false.
It was the disciple of Jehoshua Ben Parachia, the fifth President
of the Sanhedrim since Ezra, who re-wrote the Bible. . . . This story
is much truer than that of the New Testament, of which history does
not say a word.[2]

Who were the Masters whose authority Madame Blavatsky
here invokes? Clearly not the Trans-Himalayan Brotherhood
to whom she habitually refers by this term, and who can
certainly not be suspected of affirming the authenticity of

[1] René Guénon, op. cit., p. 30.
[2] Guénon, op cit., p. 193, quoting *Le Lotus* for December, 1887.

the Toldoth Yeshu. It is evident, then, that there were other
"Masters" from whom Madame Blavatsky received this
teaching, and that those other masters were Cabalists.

The same Judaic influence appears more strongly in a book
published by the Theosophical Society in 1903, where the
Talmud and the Toledot Yeshu are quoted at great length
and the Christians are derided for resenting the attacks on
their faith contained in these books, whilst the Jews are represented as innocent, persecuted victims. One passage will suffice
to give an idea of the author's point of view:

> The Christ [said the mystics] was born "of a virgin"; the
> unwitting believer in Jesus as *the* historical Messiah in the exclusive
> Jewish sense, and in his being *the* Son of God, nay God Himself,
> in course of time asserted that Mary was that virgin; whereupon
> Rabbinical logic, which in this case was simple and common logic,
> met this extravagance by the natural retort that, seeing that his
> paternity was unacknowledged, Jesus was therefore illegitimate, a
> bastard [*mamzer*].[1]

It is obviously, then, less from Thibetan Mahatmas, Hindu
Swamis, Sikh Gurus, or Egyptian Brothers than from Jewish
Cabalists that these leaders of Theosophy have borrowed their
ideas on Jesus Christ. As the Jewish writer Adolphe Franck
has truly observed: "Dès qu'il est question de théosophie,
on est sûr de voir apparaître la Kabbale."[2]   And he goes on
to show the direct influence of Cabalism on the modern Theosophical Society.

Mrs. Besant, without endorsing the worst blasphemies of the
Toledot Yeshu, nevertheless reflected this and other Judaic
traditions in her book *Esoteric Christianity*, where she related
that Jesus was brought up amongst the Essenes, and that later
He went to Egypt, where He became an initiate of the great
esoteric lodge—that is to say, the Great White Lodge—from
which all great religions derive. It will be seen that this is
only a version of the old story of the Talmudists and Cabalists,
perpetuated by the Gnostics, the Rosicrucians, and the
nineteenth-century *Ordre du Temple.*[3]   But according to
one of Mrs. Besant's Theosophical antagonists, her doctrine
"rests on a perpetual equivocation," and whilst allowing the
English public to believe that when she spoke of the coming

---

[1] I refrain from giving the name of this book as the author has now left
the Theosophical Society and may regret having written these words.
[2] Adolphe Franck, *La Kabbale*, pp. ii-iv.
[3] See *ante*, pp. 21, 66, 92.

Christ she referred to the Christ of the Gospels, she stated to
her intimates what Mr. Leadbeater taught in his book *The
Inner Life,* namely, that the Christ of the Gospels never existed,
but was an invention of the monks of the second century.[1]
It should be understood, however, that in the language of the
Theosophists, led by Mrs. Besant and Mr. Leadbeater, Jesus
and " the Christ " are two separate and distinct individualities,
and that when they now speak of " the Christ " they refer to
someone living in a bungalow in the Himalayas with whom
Mr. Leadbeater has interviews to arrange about his approaching advent.[2]   Portraits of this person have been distributed
amongst the members of " The Star in the East," an Order
founded at Benares in 1911 by Mr. Leadbeater and J. Krishnamurti for the purpose of preparing the world for the coming
of the Great Teacher.

But it is time to return to the alliance between Theosophy
and the Maçonnerie Mixte.   Whether Mrs. Besant, who had
begun her career as a Freethinker, retained some lingering
belief in her earlier creed at the time she entered into relations
with the Order, or whether she saw in this materialistic society
a valuable concrete organization for the dissemination of her
new esoteric theories, it is impossible to know.   At any rate,
she rose rapidly through the succeeding degrees and became
before long Vice President of the *Suprême Conseil,* which
appointed her its national delegate to Great Britain.   It was
in this capacity that she founded the English branch of the
Order under the name of Co-Masonry (that is, admitting both
sexes) at the Lodge " Human Duty " in London, which was
consecrated on September 26, 1902, and later founded another
lodge at Adyar in India, named " The Rising Sun."   The
number of lodges on the Grand Roll of Co-Masonry, including
those abroad, is now said to be no less than 442.

Co-Masonry thus receives a two-fold direction, for whilst
remaining in constant correspondence with the *Suprême
Conseil Universel Mixte,* situated at 5 Rue Jules-Breton
in Paris and presided over by the Grand Master Piron, with
Madame Amélie Gédalje, thirty-third degree, as Grand Secre-
tary-General, it receives further instructions from " the V.·.
Ill.·. Bro.·. Annie Besant 33°·" at Adyar.   In order not to
shock the susceptibilities of English adepts who might be

[1] Alice Leighton Cleather, *A Great Betrayal,* p. 13 (1922).
[2] See on this subject the ravings contained in the book *Christ and the
New Age* (1922), edited by G. Leopold, under the auspices of " The Star in
the East."

repelled by the rationalist tendencies of the Maçonnerie Mixte, Mrs. Besant has, however, borrowed the formulas of British Masonry together with its custom of placing the V.S.L. on the table in the lodges. These conflicting doctrines are blended in an amusing manner on the certificates of the Order, where at the top we find the French motto and initials:

Liberté   Égalité   Fraternité

À .·. L .·. G .·. D .·. L'H .·.

(i.e. à la gloire de l'Humanité)

and below, for the benefit of English members, the initials of the British masonic device, that does not of course appear on the diplomas of the French Order, which, like the Grand Orient, has rejected the Great Architect:

T .·. T .·. G .·. O .·. T .·. G .·. A .·. O .·. T .·. U .·.

(To the glory of the Great Architect of the Universe).

Our Co-Masons therefore enjoy the advantage of being able to choose whether they shall render glory to God or to Humanity. That the two devices are somewhat incompatible does not appear to strike the English initiates, nor do they probably realize the imposture practised on them by the further wording of the certificate, which, after announcing in imposing capitals " To all Masons dispersed over both Hemispheres, Greeting," goes on to say " We therefore recommend him (or her) as such to all Freemasons of the Globe, requesting them to recognize him (or her) in all the rights and privileges attached to this Degree, as we will do to all presenting themselves under similar circumstances."

Now, any British Mason will see at a glance that all this is a false pretension. No order of Masonry can recommend its members for rights and privileges to " all the Freemasons of the world," for the simple reason that, as has been said, there is no such thing as " Universal Masonry," so that even Grand Lodge of England—the most important Lodge in the world—could not, if it would, accord the right of entry for its members into Continental lodges. As an English Mason recently expressed it:

The impression among non-Masons generally appears to be that a British or Irish member of the Craft is able to enter a masonic lodge in any part of the world and take part in its deliberations and proceedings. To this belief an unqualified denial may at once be given. Nor may a member of a lodge under any Jurisdiction not in communion with the Grand Lodges of the United Kingdom be received as a visitor or as a Joining Member in any subsidiary lodge of the Grand Lodges of England, Ireland, or Scotland.[1]

But for Co-Masonry to make this claim is even more ridiculous, since at the time when the above quoted diploma was drawn up Co-Masonry and its parent, the Maçonnerie Mixte, were not recognized by any other order of Masonry except the " Droit Humain," and it is not only unrecognized but utterly repudiated by Grand Lodge of England. The British Mason, in fact, does not recognize the Co-Mason as a Mason at all, and would violate his obligations by discussing masonic secrets with him or her, so that there is no manner in which the Co-Mason could be accorded masonic rights and privileges by British Masons. In order, further, to keep up the illusion in the minds of its members that they are genuine Masons, Co-Masonry, in its quarterly organ, *The Co-Mason,* is careful to include masonic news relating to British Masonry as if it formed one and the same order.

With regard to the Grand Orient, an equally tortuous policy was pursued. As we have already seen, the Grande Loge disgraced the lodge that had admitted Maria Deraismes and did not officially recognize the Maçonnerie Mixte. The ritual adopted by the latter Order was, however, not that of British Masonry, and in most Co-Masonic Lodges the ritual employed contains variations derived from the Grand Orient[2]; indeed the Grand Orient character of Co-Masonry has always been generally recognized in masonic circles. This being so, I pointed out in *World Revolution* that Co-Masonry derives from the Grand Orient, but I received the following protest from a woman Co-Mason:

Are you aware that for twenty years the Grand Orient has refused to recognize it [Co-Masonry] as a legitimate body, just as the English Orthodox Masons do now? Also, we are distinctly told before joining that we shall not be recognized by that body. Also, we have nothing to do with Illuminati, or with Germany. As the Grand Orient have eliminated the Deity, it is rather a dreadful thing to a Mason to be connected in any way with that Order, and I cannot imagine a worse thing could be said about us.

[1] Dudley Wright, *Roman Catholicism and Freemasonry,* p. 221 (1922).
[2] In a few lodges the purely British ritual has been adopted under the name of the Verulam working, whilst recently a third ritual has been introduced by " Bishop Wedgwood," which in the opinion of a high British Mason " upsets the whole working of the Craft degrees and reduces it all to an absurdity."

This letter was dated March 6, 1922, and on the 19th of the preceding month of February an alliance between the Grand Orient and Co-Masonry had been finally celebrated at the Grand Temple of the Droit Humain in Paris! We find a report of this ceremony in the *Co-Mason* for the following April. It is evident, therefore, that members who were likely to be repelled by the idea of connexion with the Grand Orient were assured that no such connexion existed. But when this covert *liaison* developed into official recognition—although this did not include the right of entry to the lodges of the Grand Orient for women members—the triumphant manner in which the great event was announced in the *Co-Mason* suggests that the majority of members were likely to feel nothing but satisfaction at association with the Order that "had eliminated the Deity." It is true that a few members protested, and by this time Co-Masonry was too completely under the control of Mrs. Besant for any faction to question her dictates. Moreover, the opposition had been weakened by a schism which took place in the Order in 1908, when a number of members who objected to the introduction of Eastern occultism into Masonry and likewise disapproved of the Grand Orient, formed themselves into a separate body under Mrs. Halsey and Dr. Geikie Cobb, working only the Craft Degrees according to the Grand Lodge of England.

It has been shown by this brief résumé that Co-Masonry is a hybrid system deriving from two conflicting sources—the political and rationalist doctrines of the *Maçonnerie Mixte* and the Eastern occultism of Madame Blavatsky and Mrs. Besant.

As a professing Buddhist, Madame Blavatsky consistently dissociated herself from any schemes of material welfare. Thus in the early Constitution of the Theosophical Society it is stated:

"The Society repudiates all interference on its behalf with the Governmental relations of any nation or community, confining its attention exclusively to the matters set forth in the present document."[1]

These matters relate to the study of Occult Sciences. Again Madame Blavatsky herself wrote in the *Theosophist*:

Unconcerned about politics: hostile to the insane dreams of Socialism and Communism, which it abhors—as both are but disguised conspiracies of brutal force and selfishness against honest

[1] Alice Leighton Cleather, *H. P. Blavatsky: her Life and Work for Humanity*, p. 24 (Thacker, Spink & Co., Calcutta, 1922).

labour; the Society cares but little about the outward human management of the material world. The whole of its aspirations are directed towards the occult truths of the visible and invisible worlds.[1]

It will be seen that this declaration is diametrically opposed to that of the Maçonnerie Mixte. Nevertheless, Madame Blavatsky so far departed from her purely occult programme after her arrival in India in 1879 as to reconstruct the society on the basis of " Universal Brotherhood." This idea was completely absent from her first scheme; " the Brotherhood plank in the Society's future platform," wrote her coadjutor Colonel Olcott, " was not thought of." [2] It was over this plank, however, that Mrs. Besant was able to walk to the Supreme Council of the Maçonnerie Mixte, and adding Liberty and Equality to the principle of Fraternity to establish Co-Masonry on a definitely political basis as a preparation for the Socialist doctrines her teacher had " abhorred."

In the matter of esoteric doctrines Mrs. Besant again departed from the path laid down by Madame Blavatsky, whose aim had been to rehabilitate Buddhism in India, representing the teachings of Gautama Buddha as an advance on Hinduism.[3] Mrs. Besant, however, came to regard the doctrines of the Brahmins as the purer faith. Yet it was neither Buddhism nor Hinduism in a pure form that she introduced to the Co-Masons of the West, but an occult system of her own devising, wherein Mahatmas, Swamis, and Gurus were incongruously mingled with the charlatans of eighteenth-century France. Thus in the Co-Masonic lodges we find " the King " inscribed over the Grand Master's chair in the East, in the North the empty chair of " the Master "—to which, until recently, all members were required to bow in passing—and over it a picture, veiled in some lodges, of the same mysterious personage. Should the neophyte enquire, " Who is the King?" he may be told that he is the King who is to come from India—whether he is identical with the young Hindu Krishnamurti adopted by Mrs. Besant in 1909 is not clear—whilst the question " Who is the Master?" will probably be met with the reply that he is " the Master of all true Freemasons throughout the world," which the enquirer takes to mean the head of the religion to which he happens to belong—Christ, Mohammed, or another. But in the third degree the astonishing information is confided

[1] Alice Leighton Cleather, *H. P. Blavatsky : her Life and Work for Humanity*, p. 24 (Thacker, Spink & Co., Calcutta, 1922).
[2] Ibid., p. 14.   [3] Ibid., pp. 20, 311.

with an appearance of great secrecy that he is no other than the famous Comte de Saint-Germain, who did not really die in 1784, but is still alive to-day in Hungary under the name of Ragocsky. In yet a higher degree, however, the initiate may be told that the Master is in reality Prince Eugene of Austria.

It would be superfluous to describe in detail the wild nonsense that composes the creed of Co-Masonry, since a long series of articles was recently devoted to the subject in *The Patriot* and can be consulted by anyone who desires information concerning its ceremonies and the personnel directing it.[1] Suffice it to say here that its course, like that of most secret societies, has been marked by violent dissensions amongst the members—the Blavatsky-ites passionately denouncing the Besantites and the Besantites proclaiming the divine infallibility of their leader—whilst at the same time scandals of a peculiarly unsavoury kind have been brought to light. This fact has indeed created a serious schism in the ranks of the Theosophists, which shows that a number of perfectly harmless people are to be found amongst them. Yet the peculiar recurrence of such scandals in the history of secret societies leads one inevitably to wonder how far these are to be regarded as merely deplorable accidents or as the results of secret-society methods and of occult teaching. That the men against whom charges of sexual perversion were brought were not isolated examples of these tendencies is shown by a curious admission on the part of one of Madame Blavatsky's " chelas," or disciples, who relates:

I was a pupil of H. P. B. before Mrs. Besant joined the T.S. and saw her expel one of her most gifted and valued workers from the Esoteric Section for offences against the occult and moral law, similar to those with which Mr. Leadbeater's name has now been associated for nearly-twenty years. H. P. B. was always extremely strict on this particular point, and *many* [my itals.] would-be aspirants for chelaship were refused on this one ground alone, while others who had been accepted " on probation " failed almost immediately afterwards.[2]

It would appear, then, that these deplorable proclivities are peculiarly prevalent amongst aspirants to Theosophical knowledge.

It is unnecessary to enlarge at length on Mrs. Besant's connexion with the seditious elements in this country and in India,

[1] Nos. of January 11 to March 22, 1923.
[2] A. L. Cleather, *H. P. Blavatsky* a Great Betrayal, p. 69 (Thacker, Spink & Co., Calcutta, 1922).

since these have frequently been referred to in the press. It is true that the Theosophical Society, like the Grand Orient, disavows all political intentions and professes to work only for spiritual development, but the leaders appear to consider that a radical change must take place in the existing social system before true spiritual development can be attained. That this change would lie in the direction of Socialism is suggested by the fact that a group of leading Theosophists, including Mrs. Besant, were discovered in 1919 to be holding a large number of shares in the Victoria House Printing Company, which was financing the *Daily Herald* at that date[1]; indeed, Mrs. Besant in her lectures on Liberty, Equality, Fraternity, at the Queen's Hall in October of the same year, clearly indicated Socialism as the system of the coming New Era.[2] Since then the " Action Lodge " has been founded with the object of carrying " Theosophical ideals and conceptions into all fields of human activity "[3]—from which the political field appears not to be excluded, since this lodge has been known to co-operate with the promoters of a political meeting on the Indian question.[4] It is interesting to notice that a leading member of the " Action Lodge," and also of the " Order of the Star in the East," was recently reported in the press to have been long connected with the Labour Party and to have notified her intention of standing for it in Parliament.

This is, of course, not to say that all Theosophists are Socialists. The Theosophical Society of America, in an admirable series of articles[5] discussing the theory of world-revolution set forth in my books, pointed out that:

The pupils of the powers of evil work . . . untiringly to thwart every real advance of the human race, to pull down whatever civilization painfully builds, that makes for light and true development and spiritual growth. . . . It would not be difficult to suggest reasons why these pupils and co-workers of the powers of darkness choose the chief clauses of their creed: Internationalism, Communism, the destruction of the higher class through the despotic rule of the lowest class, the corruption of family life. The attack on religion hardly needs comment.

[1] *John Bull*, June 7, 1919; *The Patriot*, February 15, 1923.
[2] *The War and the Builders of the Commonwealth*, a lecture given at the Queen's Hall by Annie Besant on October 5, 1919, pp. 15, 18 (printed by the Theosophical Publishing Co.).
[3] Diary of the Theosophical Society for April-July, 1924, p. 43.
[4] On June 26, 1923.
[5] *The Theosophical Quarterly* for October 1920, April 1921, and April 1922 (published by the Theosophical Society, New York).

It will be seen, then, that Socialism and Internationalism are not an essential part of Theosophical teaching, and that the more enlightened Theosophists recognize the danger of these destructive doctrines. At a Special Convention in England on April 6 of this year, seven Lodges entered a protest against recent departures from the original policy of the Society. Amongst the resolutions put forward was one urging the President (Mrs. Besant) to establish a tribunal " to investigate matters affecting the good name of the Society, and the conduct of certain members "; this was lost by " an overwhelming majority." Another resolution regretted that " the Administration, the Magazine, and the influence of the Society have been used for controversial political ends and sectarian religious propaganda." Unhappily these resolutions were not met in the fraternal spirit that might be expected from a Society setting out to establish Universal Brotherhood and were stigmatized in a proposed amendment as " destructive motions . . . at variance with the objects for which the Society stands." This clause in the amendment was lost by a small majority, but a very large majority supported the further clauses in which the Special Convention affirmed " its complete confidence in the administration of the Society and its beloved and revered President Dr. Annie Besant, the chosen leader of whom it is justly proud," and sent " its cordial greetings to Bishop Leadbeater, F.T.S.," thanking him " for his invaluable work and his unswerving devotion to the cause of Theosophy and the service of the Theosophical Society."

There are, then, a certain number of Theosophists in this country who have the courage and public spirit to protest against the use of the Society for political ends and against infractions of the moral code which they believe certain members to have committed. But this party unfortunately constitutes only a small minority; the rest are prepared to render blind and unquestioning obedience to the dictates of Mrs. Besant and Mr. Leadbeater. In this respect the Theosophical Society follows the usual plan of secret societies. For although not nominally a secret society it is one in effect, being composed of outer and inner circles and absolutely controlled by supreme directors. The inner circle, known as the Esoteric Section, or rather the Eastern School of Theosophy—usually referred to as the E.S.—is in reality a secret society, consisting in its turn of three further circles, the innermost composed of the Mahatmas or Masters of the White Lodge, the second of the Accepted Pupils or Initiates, and the third of the Learners or ordinary members. The E.S. and Co-Masonry thus compose two secret societies within the open order controlled by people who are frequently members of both. Whether even these higher initiates are really in the secret is another question. Dr. Weller van Hook who is said to have been also a Rosicrucian and an important member of the Grand Orient once cryptically observed that " Theosophy is not the hierarchy," implying that it was only part of a world-organization, and darkly hinting that if it did not carry out the work allotted to it, the Rosicrucians would take control. That this is more than probable we shall see later.

The outer ranks of the Theosophical Society seem to be largely composed of harmless enthusiasts who imagine that they are receiving genuine instruction in the religions and occult doctrines of the East. That the teaching of the E.S. would not be taken seriously by any real Orientalist and that they could learn far more by studying the works of recognized authorities on these subjects at a University or at the British Museum does not occur to them for a moment. Nor would this fulfil the purpose of the leaders. For the Theosophical Society is not a study group, but essentially a propagandist society which aims at substituting for the pure and simple teaching of Christianity the amazing compound of Eastern superstition, Cabalism, and eighteenth-century charlatanism which Mrs. Besant and her coadjutors have devised. Yet even were the doctrines of Mrs. Besant those of true Buddhism or of Brahmanism, to what extent are they likely to benefit Western civilization? Setting the question of Christianity aside, experience shows that the attempt to orientalize Occidentals may prove no less disastrous than the attempt to occidentalize Orientals, and that to transport Eastern mysticism to the West is to vulgarize it and to produce a debased form of occultism that frequently ends in moral deterioration or mental derangement.[1] I attribute the scandals that have taken place amongst Theosophists directly to this cause.

[1] Syed Ameer Ali expresses the opinion that even to Eastern minds esoteric speculation presents a danger: "Sufism in the Moslem world, like to its counterpart in Christendom, has, in its practical effect, been productive of many mischievous results. In perfectly well-attuned minds mysticism takes the form of a noble type of idealistic philosophy; but the generality of mankind are more likely to unhinge their brains by busying themselves with the mysteries of the Divine Essence and our relations thereto. Every ignorant and idle specimen of humanity, who, despising real knowledge, abandoned the fields of true philosophy and betook himself to the domains of mysticism, would thus set himself up as one of the Ahl-i-Ma 'rifat."—*The Spirit of Islam*, p. 477.

But it is time to turn to another society in which this debased occultism plays a still more important part.

ROSICRUCIANISM

At the present time, as in the eighteenth century, the term " Rosicrucianism " is used to cover a number of associations differing in their aims and doctrines.

The first of these societies to be founded in England was the *Societas Rosicruciana in Anglia,* founded in 1867 by Robert Wentworth Little on instructions received from abroad. Only Master Masons are admitted—a procedure not condemned by Grand Lodge of England, which regards the S.R.I.A. as a perfectly innocuous body. Although neither polical nor anti-Christian, but, on the contrary, containing distinctly Christian elements and claiming to descend from Christian Rosenkreutz —a claim which must be dismissed as an absurdity—the S.R.I.A. is nevertheless largely Cabalistic,[1] dealing with the forces of Nature, alchemy, etc. If its progenitors are really to be traced further back than the Rosicrucians of the nineteenth century—Ragon, Eliphas Lévi, and Kenneth Mackenzie —they must be sought amongst certain esoteric Masons in Hungary and also amongst the French Martinistes, whose rituals doubtless derived from a kindred source. It will be remembered that Martines Pasqually bequeathed to his disciples a large number of Jewish manuscripts which were presumably preserved in the archives of the Martiniste Lodge at Lyons. The Order of Martinistes has never ceased to exist, and the President of the Suprême Conseil, Dr. Gérard Encausse, well known as " Papus," an avowed Cabalist, only died in 1916. To these archives another famous Cabalist, the renegade Abbé, Alphonse Louis Constant, who assumed the name of Eliphas Lévi, may well have had access. It is said that one of Eliphas Lévi's most distinguished disciples, the occultist Baron Spedalieri of Marseilles, was a member of the " Grand Lodge of Solitary Brethren of the Mountain," an " Illumined Brother of the Ancient Restored Order of Manicheans," a high member of the Grand Orient, and also a " High Illuminate of the Martinistes." Before his death in 1875 Eliphas Lévi announced that in 1879 a new political and religious " universal Kingdom " would be established, and that it would be possessed by " him who would have the keys of the East." The manuscript containing this prophecy was passed on by Baron Spedalieri to Edward Maitland, who in his turn gave it to a leading

[1] Confirmed by A.Q.C. 1. 54.

member of S.R.I.A., by whom it was published in English.[1]

But, as we have already seen, the principal centre of Cabalism was in Eastern Europe, whilst Germany was the principal home of Rosicrucianism, and it was from these directions that, a few years later, a new Rosicrucian Order in England derived its inspiration. It is curious to notice that the eighties of the last century were marked by a simultaneous recrudescence of secret societies and of Socialist organizations. In 1880 Leopold Engel reorganized Weishaupt's Order of Illuminati, which, according to M. Guénon, played thenceforth "an extremely suspect political rôle," and soon after this in 1884 it is said that a strange incident took place in London.[2] The Rev. A. F. A. Woodford, a F.·. M.·., happened to be turning over the contents of a second-hand bookstall in Farringdon Street when he came upon some cypher MSS., attached to which was a letter in German saying that if the finder were to communicate with Sapiens Dominabatur Astris, c/o Fraulein Anna Sprengel, in Germany, he would receive further interesting information.

This, at any rate, is the story told to initiates of the Order which came to be founded according to the instructions given in the cypher. But when we remember that precisely the same story was told by Cagliostro concerning his discovery of a MS. in London by the mysterious George Cofton on which he had founded his Egyptian rite, we begin to wonder whether the placing of a MS. in a spot where it is certain to be discovered by precisely the people qualified to decipher it forms one of the traditional methods of secret-society adepts for extending their sphere of influence without betraying their identity or revealing the centre of direction.

In this case it certainly succeeded admirably, for by a fortunate coincidence the clergyman who found the cypher MSS. was acquainted with two prominent members of the S.I.R.A.,

[1] Guénon, op. cit., p. 296. It would appear to be this MS. or a copy which was recently offered for sale by a Paris bookseller under the following description: "Manuscrit de Kabbale.—Spedalieri (Baron de. Le Sceau de Salomon. Traité sur les Séphiroth, en un in-f. de 16 pp. . . . le baron Spedalieri fut le disciple le plus instruit et le plus intime d'Eliphas Lévi.— Son traté kabalistique 'Le Sceau de Salomon' est fondé sur la tradition hébraïque et hindoue et nous révèle le sens occulte du grand pantacle mystique. Dans une étude sur les séphiroth, Eliphas Lévi annonçait que le temps venu il révèlerait à ses disciples ce grand mystère jusqu'ici caché.—Spedalieri entreprend cette révélation." Le Bibliophile ès Sciences Psychiques, No. 16 (1922). Librairie Emile Nourry, 62 ru des Ecoles, Paris, Ve.

Dr. Wynn Westcott and Dr. Woodman, to whom he took the documents, and by a further fortunate coincidence one of them happened to be the very person to whom Eliphas Lévi's prophecy had been given; These two men who now assumed the pseudonyms of S.A. (Sapere Aude) and M.E.V. (Magnus est Veritas), were able partially to decipher the manuscript; S.A., with the assistance of a German, then wrote to S.D.A. c/o Fraulein Anna Sprengel, saying that he and a friend had finished the deciphering and that they desired further information. In reply they were told to elaborate the notes, and that if diligent they would be allowed to form an elementary branch of the Rosicrucian Order in England. Finally S.D.A. wrote to S.A. authorising him to sign her (or his?) name to any warrant or document necessary for the constitution of an Order, and promising later on further rituals and advanced teachings if the preliminary Order proved successful. S.A. and M.E.V. now called in the aid of a third member of the S.I.R.A., Macgregor Mathers, henceforth known as D.D.C.F. (Deo Duce Comite Ferro), who, having more time at his disposal, was able, by means of long and arduous labour, to elaborate the rituals in Masonic style. On March 8, 1888, a warrant was then drawn up according to the design given in the cypher MSS. and was signed by S.A. for S.D.A., by M.E.V. and D.D.C.F., all three having received the honorary grade of 7-4 from S.D.A. so as to enable them to act as Chief of the New Temple. It is interesting to note that whilst the instructions in the cypher MSS. were in English and German, the name now given to the new Order "The Golden Dawn," was accompanied by its equivalent in Hebrew "Chebreth Zerech aur Bokher" that is to say "The Companions of the Rising Light of the Morning." Amongst the instructions we find: "Avoid Roman Catholics but with pity"; also these directions concerning the Obligation:

The candidate asking for Light is taken to the Altar and forced to take an Obligation to secrecy under penalty of expulsion and death or palsy from hostile current of will.

From the subsequent correspondence of the Order it is seen that this so-called "punitive current" was actually directed by the Chiefs against those who rebelled.

Although the members of the Golden Dawn later became linked up with the "Esoteric Masons" in Germany, neither the organization nor the ritual of the Order are masonic, but rather Martiniste and Cabalistic. For amidst all the confused phraseology of the Order, the phrases and symbols borrowed from Egyptian, Greek, or Hindu mythology, one detects the real basis of the whole system—the Jewish Cabala, in which all the three Chiefs were, or became, experts. Mathers in fact translated the famous book of Abraham the Jew from French into English with explanatory notes, and Wynn Westcott translated the Sepher Yetzirah from Hebrew. Lectures were given to the society on such subjects as the Tarot Cards, Geomantic Talismans, and the Schemhamphorasch or Tetragrammaton.

The Order was at first absolutely governed by the three Chiefs, but after a time—owing to the death of Woodman and the resignation of Wynn Westcott—Mathers became the Sole Chief and professed to have obtained further instructions from the Hidden Chiefs through his wife—a sister of Bergson— by means of clairvoyance and clairaudience. But the real directors of the Order were in Germany and known as the " Hidden and Secret Chiefs of the Third Order." A curious resemblance will here be noted with the " Concealed Superiors " by whom members of the *Stricte Observance* in the eighteenth century declared themselves to be controlled.

Who these men were at the time the Order was founded remains a mystery not only to the outside world but even to the English initiates themselves. The identity of Sapiens Dominabatur Astris appears never to have been established, nor was anything more heard about the still more mysterious Anna Sprengel until her death in an obscure German village was reported in 1893. Indeed, one of the most active members of the Order, Dr. Robert Felkin, M.D., known as F.R. (Finem Respice), later declared that, although he had visited five temples of the Order in Germany and Austria, he had been unable to get into touch with the Hidden Chiefs, or to discover how the original MSS. came into the hands of the clergyman who handed them to Wynn Westcott and Woodman. According to Felkin's statement, all that he had been able to find out was that the MSS. were the notes of ceremonies made by a man who had been initiated into a Lodge in Germany, and that the temple from which they originated was " a special temple " working on the Cabala tree like the English branch of the Order. Further, he was told that none of the " big Three " who founded the Golden Dawn in England were real Rosicrucians at all.

The confusion of ideas which must inevitably result when,

as in secret societies or revolutionary organizations, a number
of people are being blindly led by hidden directors, naturally
brought about dissensions amongst the members, who mutually
accused each other of ignorance of the real aims of the Order.
Thus the London Lodge ended by breaking with Mathers,
who was in Paris, on account of his arrogance in claiming
supreme power through the mystery of the Hidden Chiefs, and
after two years of unsettled government, in 1902 elected three
new chiefs—Dr. Felkin (F.R. = Finem Respice), Bullock, a
solicitor (L.O. = Levavi Oculos) who resigned at the end of the
year, and Brodie Innes (S.S. = Sub Spe). But although Mathers
had been repudiated, his teachings were retained as emanating
from the Hidden Chiefs.

Two years earlier a dramatic incident had occurred. In 1898
a very sinister personage, Aleister Crowley, had been introduced
into the Order (on the recommendation of A. E. Waite (S.R. =
Sacramentum Regis) the well-known mystical writer. A man
of many aliases, Crowley followed the precedent of the " Comte
de Saint-Germain," the " Comte de Cagliostro," and the " Baron
von Offenbach " by ennobling himself and masquerading
under various titles in turn, such as " Count Svareff," " Lord
Boleskine," " Baron Rosenkreutz," but usually known in the
Order as " P " for " Perdurabo."

Crowley, who was a Cabalist, had written a book on Goetic
Magic and soon after becoming a member of the " Golden
Dawn " set to work with another " Frater " on magical experi-
ments, including evocations, the consecration and use of talismans, divination, alchemy, etc. In 1900 Crowley had joined
Mathers in Paris where the latter and his wife were living
under the assumed names of the " Comte and Comtesse of
Glenstrae " and engaged in reviving the mysteries of Isis at the
Bodinière Theatre. In this task they were joined by an extraordinary lady, the notorious Madame Horos (alias the Swami)
who claimed to be the real and authentic Sapiens Dominabatur
Astris. Crowley described her as " a very stout woman and very
fair " and " a vampire of remarkable power;" Mathers declared
her to be " probably the most powerful medium living," but
later, in a letter to another member of the " Golden Dawn "
observed: " I believe her and her accomplices to be emissaries
of a very powerful *secret occult order* who have been trying for
years to break up other Orders and especially my work." Incidentally this lady, who proved to be a false S.D.A., ended by
starting an Order in collaboration with her husband, in which

it was said that certain rituals of the Golden Dawn were adapted to an immoral purpose, with the result that the couple were brought to trial and finally condemned to penal servitude.

Whether owing to this disturbing experience, or because, as Crowley declared, he had "imprudently attracted to himself forces of evil too great and terrible for him to withstand, presumably Abramelin demons," Mathers' reason began to totter. This then was the situation at the time of his rupture with the Order, and the dramatic incident referred to was the sudden appearance of Crowley in London, who, whether acting as Mathers' envoy or on his own initiative, broke into the premises of the Order, with a black mask over his face, a plaid shawl thrown over his shoulders, an enormous gold (or gilt) cross on his breast, and a dagger at his side, for the purpose of taking over possession. This attempt was baffled with the prosaic aid of the police and Crowley was expelled from the Order. Eventually, however, he succeeded in obtaining possession of some of the rituals and other documents of the Golden Dawn, which he proceeded to publish in the organ of a new Order of his own. This magazine, containing a mixture of debased Cabalism and vulgar blasphemies, interspersed with panegyrics on haschish—for Crowley combined with sexual perversion an addiction to drugs—which might appear to express only the ravings of a maniac. But eccentricity has often provided the best cloak for dark designs, and the outbreak of war proved that there was a method in the madness of the man whom the authorities persisted in regarding merely as an irresponsible degenerate of a non-political kind. To quote the press report of his exploits after this date:

In November 1914 Crowley went to the United States, where he entered into close relations with the pro-German propagandists. He edited the New York *International,* a German propagandist paper run by the notorious George Silvester Viereck, and published, among other things, an obscene attack on the King and a glorification of the Kaiser. Crowley ran occultism as a side-line, and seems to have been known as the "Purple Priest." Later on he publicly destroyed his British passport before the Statute of Liberty, declared in favour of the Irish Republican cause, and made a theatrical declaration of "war" on England. . . . During his stay in America Crowley was associated with a body known as the "Secret Revolutionary Committee" which was working for the establishment of an Irish Republic. He is known also as the writer of a defeatest manifesto circulated in France in 1915.

But to return to the Golden Dawn. In 1903 a split occurred in the Order. A. E. Waite, an early member of it, seceded from it with a number of other members and carried off with him the name of " Golden Dawn," also the vault and other property of the Order. The original Order then took the name of " Stella Matutina," with Dr. Felkin as Chief.

In the preceding year the members of the London Lodge had again believed that they were in touch with the *Hidden Third Order* and revived their efforts to communicate with the Secret Chiefs in Germany. This state of uncertainty continued till about 1910, when Felkin and Meakin set forth for Germany, where they succeeded in meeting several members of the Third Order, who professed to be " true and genuine Rosicrucians " and to know of Anna Sprengel and the starting of the Order in England. They were not, it was believed, the Secret and Hidden Chiefs, but more probably Esoteric Masons of the Grand Orient. These Fratres, however, told them that in order to form a definite etheric link between themselves and the Order in Great Britain, it would be necessary for a British Frater to be under their instruction for a year. Accordingly Meakin remained in Germany for special training, so that he might act as the " etheric link " between the two countries. After a pilgrimage to the Near East, closely following the itinerary of Christian Rosenkreutz, Meakin returned to Germany, and it appears to have been now that he was able to get into touch with a certain high adept of occult science.

This remarkable personage, Rudolf Steiner, had earlier belonged to the Theosophical Society, and it has been suggested that at some period he may have been connected with the revived Illuminati of Leopold Engel. There is certainly some reason to believe that at one point in his career he came into touch with men who were carrying on the teachings of Weishaupt, the chief of whom was the President of a group of Pan-German secret societies, and it seems not improbable that the mysterious S.D.A., under whose directions the Golden Dawn was founded, might be located in this circle.

A few years before the war, Steiner, whilst still a Theosophist, started a society of his own, the Anthroposophical Society, a name borrowed from the work of the XVIIth century Rosicrucian, Thomas Vaughan, " Anthroposophica Magica." The ostensible leader of Rosicrucianism in Germany was Dr. Franz Hartmann, founder of the " Order of the Esoteric Rose Croix." Although in some way connected with Engel's Illuminati and more definitely with the Theosophical Society, Hartmann was believed to be a genuine Christian mystic. Steiner also made the same profession, and it seems probable that he formed one of the group of mysterious personages, including besides Grand Orient Masons, Baron von Knigge, great grandson of Weishaupt's coadjutor "Philo," who met together in secret conference at Ingoldstadt where the first Lodge of the Illuminati had been founded in 1776, and decided to revive Illuminism on Christian mystic lines used in a very elastic sense amongst occultists.   At the same time Steiner introduces into his teaching a strong vein of Gnosticism, Luciferianism, Johannism, and Grand Orient Masonry, whilst reserving Rosicrucianism for his higher initiates.   On this last point he is extremely reticent, preferring to call his teaching "occult science," since he recognizes that "real Rosicrucians never proclaim themselves as such"; it is therefore only in the inner circle of his society, on which no information is given to the public and into which members are admitted by much the same forms of initiation as those used by the Grand Orient, that Rosicrucianism is mentioned.   Some of Steiner's imitators in The Rosicrucian Fellowship at Oceanside, California, however, openly profess what they call Rosicrucianism and at the same time claim superior knowledge on the subject of Masonry.   Thus in a book by the leader of this group we find it solemnly stated that according to Max Heindl, Eve cohabited with serpents in the garden of Eden, that Cain was the offspring of her union with "the Lucifer Spirit Samael," and that from this "divine progenitor" the most virile portion of the human race descended, the rest being merely the "progeny of human parents."   Readers of the present work will recognize this as not the legend of Masonry but of the Jewish Cabala which has been already quoted in this context.[1]   Whether this also forms part of Steiner's teaching it is impossible to say, since his real doctrines are known only to his inner circle; even some of his admirers amongst the Steiner Matutina, whilst consulting him as an oracle, are not admitted to the secrets of his grades of initiation and have been unable to succeed in obtaining from him a charter.   Meanwhile they themselves do not disclose to the neophytes whom they seek to win over that they are members of any secret association.   This is quite in accordance with the methods of Weishaupt's "Insinuating Brothers."

The result of what Steiner calls "occult science" is thus described in a striking passage of one of his own works:

"This is the change which the occult student observes coming over himself—that there is no longer a connection between

[1] See ante, p. 34.

a thought and a feeling or a feeling and a volition, except when he creates the connection himself. No impulse drives him from thought to action if he does not voluntarily harbour it. He can now stand completely without feeling before an object which, before his training, would have filled him with glowing love or violent hatred; he can likewise remain actionless before a thought which heretofore would have spurred him to action as if by itself," etc.

I can imagine no clearer exposé of the dangers of occultism than this. Weishaupt had said: " I cannot use men as I find them; I must form them." Dr. Steiner shows how this transformation can be accomplished. Under the influence of so-called occult training, which is in reality simply powerful suggestion, all a man's native impulses and inhibitive springs of action may be broken; the pupil of the occultist will no longer react to the conceptions of beauty or ugliness, of right or wrong, which, unknown to himself, formed the law of his being. Thus not only his conscious deeds but his sub-conscious processes pass under the control of another. If this is indeed the method employed by Dr. Steiner and his adepts there would certainly seem to be some justification for the verdict of M. Robert Kuentz that " Steiner has devised occult exercises which render the mind incapable (rendent l'esprit anéanti), that he attacks the individual by deranging his faculties (il détraque les facultés." [1]

What is the real motive power behind such societies as the Stella Matutina and again behind Steiner? This remains a mystery, not only to the outside world but to the " initiates " themselves. The quest of the Hidden Chiefs, undertaken by one intrepid pilgrim after another, seems to have ended only in further meetings with Steiner. Yet hope springs eternal in the breast of the aspirant after occult knowledge, and astral messages spurred the Fratres to further efforts. One of these contained the exhortation: " Go on with Steiner, which is not the ultimate end of search, and we will come into contact with many serious students who will lead us to the real master of the Order, who will be so overpoweringly impressive as to leave no room for doubt."

A curious analogy with Co-Masonry will here be observed. For whilst the veiled picture of the Co-Masonic lodges is said to represent " the Master " in the person of Ragocsky or some

[1] Robert Kuentz, *Le Dr Steiner et la Théosophie actuelle*," series of articles in the review *Le Feu* for October, November and December 1913 and reprinted in pamphlet form.

other personage in Austria or Hungary, so it is likewise in Austria and Germany that the members of Stella Matutina seek their Hidden Chiefs and the " real Master " of their Order. Moreover, whilst the Co-Masons await the coming of the great " World Teacher," King, or Messiah in 1926, it is also in 1926 that the Stella Matutina expect Christian Rosenkreutz to appear again.[1] There are many other points of resemblance between the phraseology of the two Orders, as, for example, the idea of the " Astral Light," " the Great White Lodge," and also " the GREAT WORK " by which both Orders denote the supreme object of their aspirations—" the union of the East and the West." It is therefore impossible not to suspect that, although the members of Co-Masonry and of the Stella Matutina imagine their respective Orders to be entirely unconnected and indeed appear to be hardly aware of each other's existence, there may be nevertheless some point of junction in the background and even a common centre of direction.

In this connexion it is interesting to notice the political tendencies of the societies in question. Although the outcome of the *Maçonnerie Mixte,* and nominally under the jurisdiction of headquarters in Paris, Co-Masonry does not appear to be pro-French in its sympathies. On the contrary, the Co-masonic lodges in this country, as also the head lodge in the Rue Jules-Breton, seem to have adopted that form of universal brotherhood which principally redounds to the benefit of Germany.

The Stella Matutina, whilst professing to be solely concerned in occult science and warning its members against Co-Masonry on account of the political tendencies of the latter, is nevertheless still more imbued with German influence, since, as we have seen, it has ever since it first came into existence been secretly under Germany direction. Indeed, during the war this influence became so apparent that certain patriotic members, who had entered the society in all good faith with the idea of studying occult science, raised an energetic protest and a schism took place. Thus, just as in the case of Co-Masonry, the more clear-sighted recognized the imprudence of placing themselves under foreign control. That this was no imaginary danger is shown by a correspondence which had taken place some years earlier and has recently been brought to light. It will be remembered that the great aim of Weishaupt and the Illuminati of the eighteenth century was

---

[1] The year of the General Strike.

to obtain control over all existing masonic and occult Orders. This also became the dream of Rudolf Steiner and his allies in other countries, whose plan was to form what they called an "International Bund." The idea of an International Bureau for Masonic Affairs had already, as we have seen, been started in Switzerland; this was the same idea applied to occult groups, so that all such societies as Rosicrucianism, Theosophy with its various ramifications of Co-Masonry, etc., Hermetic Orders, isolated occultists, and so on, were to be placed under German control. The audacity of the proposal seems to have been too much even for some of the most internationally minded members of the Stella Matutina, and in the discussion that took place it was pointed out that admirable as the scheme might be, there was nevertheless some British spirit amongst these Orders to be reckoned with. Even Mrs. Besant's followers, headed by the Co-Masons, described as a group which "attracts a large number of idle women who have leisure to take a little occultism with their afternoon tea," might be liable to ask, "Who are these Germans to interfere?" But the real obstacle to success was held to be British Freemasonry, to which a certain number of students of occult science, including all the members of the S.R.I.A., belonged. "English Masonry," it was remarked, "boasts the Grand Lodge of 1717, the Mother Lodge of the World. They are a proud, jealous, autocratic body. Co-Masonry derives from the Grand Orient of France, an illegitimate body according to English ruling. No English Mason can work with Co-Masons. . . . If the English Grand Lodge hears of anything called 'Esoteric Masonry' derived from such sources, under chiefs once T.S. [Theosophical Society] members, under a head in Berlin, it will not enquire who Dr. Steiner is or what is the nature of his work, it will simply say, 'No English Masons of the Free and Accepted Masons may join any Society working pseudo-Masonic rites, i.e. no one of ordinary accepted Freemasonry can attend any meetings or attend any grades in this illegitimate body.' Finis! . . . If a lodge of the Continental Order is to be established in England, Dr. Steiner will be faced with the Masonic difficulty. This is really serious. . . ."[1]

Here then is one of the finest tributes ever paid to British Masonry, for it shows that as at present constituted and controlled it provides the most formidable barrier against the infiltration of this country by alien or subversive secret

[1] Letter from Meakin to Baron Walleen, a Dane and member of the S.M.

societies.   Thus the Freemasons and the Roman Catholics
are recognized as the principal obstacles to success.   The
Freemasons, however, would do well to realize the attempts
that are made to break down this resistance by traitors in the
Masonic camp, who, after violating their obligations by
belonging to an irregular secret society, act as recruiting agents
in the lodges.   For the author of these remarks was a British
Freemason who, in collusion with a foreign adept, proposed to
penetrate Freemasonry by the process known in revolutionary
language as " boring from within."   To quote his own words,
" *They must be got at from within, not from without.*"   This
was to be accomplished in various ways—by adepts of the Continental Order getting themselves initiated into orthodox
Masonry and then spreading their own doctrines in the lodges,
or by enlisting recruits amongst orthodox Masons and using
them as propagandists among their brother-Masons.   It was
also suggested that in order not to rouse suspicion it would
be better to avoid the name " Esoteric Masonry," to adopt one
of the rituals used in England, and to employ as " officers "
a " mixed group " drawn from various secret societies.   This
plan has been carried out with considerable success, and at a
recent conference held by a high Continental adept under the
most distinguished patronage, it was interesting to notice the
various secret societies represented by certain of the promoters,
who of course to the general public appeared to be merely
isolated individuals interested in philosophical speculation.
But it is time to pass on to the question of yet another secret
association, for amongst those present at the Conference
referred to were members of the group Clarté.

This society, of which the name as well as its avowed aims
are singularly reminiscent of Illuminism, was first heard of
in France and was led by men who carried on active anti-
patriotic propaganda throughout the war.   Amongst these was
Henri Barbusse, author of *Le Feu,* a defeatest novel which was
received with acclamations from " illuminated " reviewers in
the press of this country.   Yet although outwardly a French
organization, the real inspiration and teaching of *Clarté* is
essentially German-Jewish and a great number of Jews are to
be found amongst its members, particularly in Central Europe.
At the inaugural meeting of the Austrian group it was stated
that 80 per cent. of those present were of the Jewish race.   The
keynote of *Clarté* is Internationalism—abolition of nationality,
destruction of frontiers, and pacifism or rather the substitution

of class warfare for war between nations. For this purpose it is willing to make use of all subversive doctrines, to whatever school of thought they may belong. Hence, although the creed of the leaders is professedly Socialism, they readily co-operate with Syndicalists, Anarchists, or revolutionaries of any brand, carrying on propaganda in Trade Unions and various workers' organizations; some are secretly in the ranks of the Communists. In fact members of *Charté* have succeeded in penetrating into almost every subversive group, even as far afield as New Zealand, where the society has an agency in Wellington and disseminates the most violent revolutionary teaching and literature.

But whilst thus making use of the " proletariat " to further its ends, the point of view of *Clarté* is fundamentally un-democratic—for the real grievances of the workers it has no use at all. The plan of this group—who were recently de-scribed in the French press as " the finest specimens of cannibals smeared with humanitarianism (les plus beaux spécimens de cannibales barbouillés d'humanitairerie) "—is to constitute a sort of International Hierarchy of Intellectual Socialists, whose influence is to make itself invisibly felt in literary, educational, and artistic circles all over the world. For the members of *Clarté* are as careful as were the adepts of Weis-haupt to preserve their incognito and not to be known as " Illuminati." Thus the public in our own country and else-where, reading the diatribes of certain well-known authors against the existing order of society, may vaguely wonder why men living amidst all the amenities of civilization should desire its destruction, but do not dream that all this is not the outcome of an individual brain but propaganda put out by a company which, having largely primed such writers with ideas, is able, owing to the high position of many of its leading members and its influence with the literary world, to ensure the success of any publication that will further its ends.

The organization of *Clarté* thus approximates more nearly to the system of Weishaupt than that of the other societies described in this chapter. Although in the strictest sense a secret society, it is in no sense occult and therefore possesses no ritual of its own, but, like the earlier Illuminati, recognizes the utility of working through Freemasonry. *Clarté,* in fact, forms an adjunct of the Grand Orient and owns a lodge under its jurisdiction in Paris. It would be interesting, how-ever, to know whether the idea of the alliance with the Grand

Orient occurred as an afterthought to the *Clarté* group or whether the original inspiration of ,*Clarté* emanated from an inner circle of the Grand Orient. We shall return to the question of this inner circle in a later chapter.

Such, then, are the principal secret societies at work in Great Britain, but amongst minor secret or semi-secret movements may be mentioned the strange sect the Faithists, said to have some affinity with the Druses, inhabiting a singularly unromantic London suburb, whose " Ancient Founder " is the author of a series of tracts urging man not to be misled by false Gods, but to worship " Jehovih the Creator only," and at the same time advocating nationalization as a cure for all social ills; or again The Institute for the Harmonious Development of Man at Fontainebleau, led by Gurdjieff and Uspenski which combines esoteric meditation with an extremely meagre diet and strenuous manual labour. It is interesting, by the way, to notice that the art of movement known as Eurhythmy—not to be confounded with the system of M. Dalcroze which is known in England only as Eurhythmics—forms an important part of the curriculum of the last society, as also of Herr Steiner's Order, of the Stella Matutina, and of the Russian Bolsheviks.[1]

The one question that presents itself to the judicial mind after examining all these movements, is inevitably: Are they of any real importance? Can a few hundreds, or even thousands, of men and women, drawn largely by curiosity or want of occupation into societies of which the very names are hardly known to the general public, exercise any influence on the world at large? It would certainly be an error to overestimate the power that each of these societies individually can wield; to do so would be, in fact, to play into the hands of the leaders, whose plan, from Weishaupt onwards, has always been to represent themselves as directing the destinies of the universe. This claim to power is the bait laid for neophytes, who are made to believe that " the Order will one day rule the world." But, whilst recognizing the folly of this pretension, we should be mistaken in underrating their importance, for the reason that they provide evidence of a larger organization in the background. The Stella Matutina may be only an obscure Fraternity, even the Theosophical

[1] Bertrand Russell, *The practice and Theory of Bolshevism*, p. 65 (1920).

Society with all its ramifications[1] may not be of great importance in itself, but will anyone with a knowledge of European affairs seriously maintain that the Grand Orient is a small or unimportant organization? And have we not seen that investigations into the smaller secret societies frequently lead back to this greater masonic power? Secret societies are of importance, because they are, moreover, symptomatic, and also because, although the work actually carried out in their lodges or councils may be of a trivial character, they are able by the power of association and the collective force they generate to influence public opinion and to float ideas in the outside world which may have far-reaching consequences.

At any rate, the fact that they exist finally disposes of the contention that secret societies of a subversive and even of an abominable kind are things of the past. These amazing cults, these strange perverted rites which we associate with the dark ages, are going on around us to-day. Illuminism, Cabalism, and even Satanism are still realities. In 1908 Monsieur Copin Albancelli stated that circumstances had afforded him the proof that—

certain Masonic societies exist which are Satanic, not in the sense that the devil comes to preside at their meetings, as that romancer of a Leo Taxil pretended, but in that their initiates profess the cult of Lucifer. They adore him as the true God, and they are animated by an implacable hatred against the Christian God, whom they declare to be an impostor. They have a formula which sums up their state of mind; it is no longer: "To the glory of the Great Architect of the Universe," as in the two lower Masonries; it is G.·. E.·. A.·. A.·. L.·. H.·. H.·. H.·. A.·. D.·. M.·. M.·. M.:., which means "Gloire et Amour à Lucifer! Haine! haine! haine! au Dieu maudit! maudit! maudit! (Glory and Love for Lucifer! Hatred! hatred! hatred! to God, accursed, accursed, accursed!)

It is professed in these societies that all that the Christian God commands is disagreeable to Lucifer; that all that He forbids is, on the contrary, agreeable to Lucifer; that in consequence one must do all that the Christian God forbids and that one must shun like fire all that He commands. I repeat that with regard to all that, I have the proofs under my hand. I have read and studied hundreds of documents relating to one of these societies, documents that I have not permission to publish and which emanate from the

[1] Amongst the "subsidiary activities" of the Theosophical Society may be mentioned the Liberal Catholic Church, the Guild of the Citizens of Tomorrow, the Order of the Brothers of Service, the Golden Chain, the Order of the Round Table, the Bureau of Social Reconstruction, the Braille League, the Theosophical Educational Trust, etc.

members, men and women, of the group in question.[1]

I do not say that any society in England consciously practices this cult of Satan, but I too have seen dozens of documents relating to occult groups in this country which practise rites and evocations that lead to illness, moral perversion, mental derangement, and even in some cases to death. I have heard from the lips of initiates themselves accounts of the terrible experiences through which they have passed; some have even urged me to bring the matter before the attention of the authorities. But unfortunately no department exists for the investigation of subversive movements. Yet since all these movements are intimately connected with revolutionary agitation they are well worth the attention of Governments that desire to protect law, order, and public morality. The fact is that the very extravagance of their doctrines and practices seems to ensure their immunity. Nevertheless, whether the power at work behind them is of the kind we are accustomed to call "supernatural," or whether it is merely the outcome of the human mind, there can be no doubt of its potency for evil and of its very definite effects in the obliteration of all sense of truth and in sexual perversion.

In the opinion of an initiate who belonged for years to the Stella Matutina, the dynamic force employed known as "Kundalini" is simply an electro-magnetic force, of which the sex-force is a part, on which the adepts know how to play, and "the unseen hand behind all the seeming Spiritism of these Orders is a system of very subtle and cunning hypnotism and suggestion." Further, "the aim of this group like that of all subversive Esoteric Orders, is, by means of such processes as eurhythmics, meditations, symbols, ceremonies, and formulas, to awaken this force and produce false " Illumination " for the purpose of obtaining " Spiritual Seership," which is at most clairvoyance, clairaudience, etc. The ceremonies of the Order are hypnotic, and by suggestion create the necessary mental and astral atmosphere, hypnotize and prepare the members to be the willing tools in the hands of the controlling adepts. The same initiate has communicated to me the following conclusions concerning the group in question, with the permission to quote them verbatim:

I have been convinced that we, as an Order, have come under the power of some very evil occult Order, profoundly versed in science both occult and otherwise, though not infallible, their methods being

[1] *Le Pouvoir Occulte contre la France*, p. 291.

BLACK MAGIC, that is to say, electro-magnetic power, hypnotism, and powerful suggestion.

We are convinced that the Order is being controlled by some SUN Order after the nature of the Illuminati, if not by that Order itself.

The reason why they (the leaders of all such Orders) insisted so much upon the Church and Sacrament, especially before the initiation, is, I think, for the same reason as the use of the consecrated Host in Black Magic. The Christian consecration and the use of the sacraments renders the building or person more powerful as a material basis for black magic even as in white magic—"for the Great Good or the Great Evil." When the initiation is accomplished and the domination of the person complete, there is no further need for Church or Sacrament.

We are told at the Initiation: "There is nothing incompatible with your civil, moral, or religious duties in this obligation." We now are convinced that this Order is contrary absolutely to our civil, moral, and religious duties; which being so, our obligations are null and void.

We are told that all that has taken place in Russia and elsewhere is due to these International Occult Forces set in motion by Subversive Esoteric Lodges. Yet it is known that we have several branches of these same Esoteric Masonic Lodges carrying on their deadly work in our midst. England, as well as Europe, seems to be drifting along in a hypnotic sleep, and even our soundest politicians seem paralysed and all that they attempt is turned to foolishness. Is there no one in authority who understands these things and realizes the danger both to the country and to individuals from these forces working for disruption and world revolution?

How in the face of these declarations, coming from those inside the movement, can anyone maintain that Illuminism is dead and that secret societies present no danger to Christian civilization?

13

OPEN SUBVERSIVE MOVEMENTS

ALTHOUGH the sceptical reader who has reached this stage of the present work will perhaps be willing to admit that some connexion may be traced between hidden forces and open subversive movements, the objection he will still raise against the general thesis here set forth will probably be expressed somewhat in the following manner:

" It is quite possible that secret societies and other unseen agencies may have played a part in revolutions, but to attribute the continued revolt against the existing social order to these causes is absurd. Poverty, unemployment, inadequate housing, and above all the inequalities of human life are quite sufficient to produce a revolutionary spirit without the aid of secret instigators. Social revolution is simply a rising of the ' have-nots ' against the ' haves,' and requires no further cause to explain it."

Let it be at once admitted that the injustices here enumerated are real. The working classes throughout the nineteenth century had very genuine reasons for complaints. Wages were far too low, the rich sometimes showed themselves indifferent to the sufferings of the poor, employers of labour often made profits out of all proportion to the remuneration paid to the workers. Nor, in spite of the immense reforms introduced during the last hundred years, have all these grievances been redressed. The slums of our great cities still constitute a blot upon our civilization. Profiteering since the beginning of the war has been more flagrant than ever. " Rings " and combines provide fabulous wealth for individuals or groups at the expense of vast numbers of consumers. And in all classes of the community, just as before the French Revolution, people feast and dance whilst others live on the border-line of starvation.

But let us see how far the Socialist movement can be regarded as the spontaneous revolt of the "people" against this condition of things. Dividing the people after the manner of

Marx into the non-revolutionary and the "revolutionary proletariat," we shall find that the former category, by far the larger, combines with a strong respect for tradition a perfectly reasonable desire for social reform. Briefly it asks for adequate wages, decent housing, and a fair share of the good things of life. For State interference in the affairs of everyday life it feels nothing but abhorrence. The ideal of Communism as formulated by Lenin, wherein "the getting of food and clothing shall be no longer a private affair,"[1] would meet with stronger opposition from working men—and still more from working women, to whom "shopping" is as the breath of life—than from any other section of the population. Even such apparently benign Socialist schemes as "communal dining-rooms" or "communal kitchens" appeal less to the working-class mentality than to the upper-class mind that devises them.

Turning to the "revolutionary proletariat," we shall find this individualistic instinct quite as strongly developed. It is not the Socialist idea of placing all wealth and property in the hands of the State, but the Anarchist plan of "expropriation," of plunder on a gigantic scale for the benefit of the revolutionary masses, which really appeals to the disgruntled portion of the proletariat. The Socialist intellectual may write of the beauties of nationalization, of the joy of working for the common good without hope of personal gain; the revolutinary working man sees nothing to attract him in all this. Question him on his ideas of social transformation, and he will generally express himself in favour of some method by which he will acquire something he has not got; he does not want to see the rich man's motor-car socialized by the State—he wants to drive about in it himself. The revolutionary working man is thus in reality not a Socialist but an Anarchist at heart. Nor in some cases is this unnatural. That the man who enjoys none of the good things of life should wish to snatch his share must at least appear comprehensible. What is not comprehensible is that he should wish to renounce

[1] "The struggle to instil into the masses the idea of the Soviet State control, and accounting, that this idea may be realised and a break be made with the accursed past, which accustomed the people to look upon the work of getting food and clothing as a 'private' affair and on purchase and sale as something that 'concerns only myself'—this is a most momentous struggle, of universal historical significance, a struggle for Socialist consciousness against bourgeois-anarchistic 'freedom.'"—Lenin, *The Soviets at Work*, p. 22 (The Socialist Information and Research Bureau, 196 St. Vincent Street, Glasgow, 1919).

all hope of ever possessing anything. Modern Socialist propagandists are very well aware of this attitude of the working classes towards their schemes, and therefore that as long as they explain the real programme they mean to put into operation, which is nothing but the workhouse system on a gigantic scale, they can meet with no success. As a life-long Socialist has frequently observed to me, " Socialism has never been a working-class movement; it was always we of the middle or upper classes who sought to instil the principles of Socialism into the minds of working men." Mr. Hyndman's candid confessions of the failures to enlist the sympathies even of slum-dwellers in his schemes of social regeneration bear out this testimony.

Less honest Socialist orators as the result of long experience have therefore adopted the more effectual policy of appealing to the predatory instincts of the crowd. From Babeuf onwards, Socialism has only been able to make headway by borrowing the language of Anarchy in order to blast its way to power.

Socialism is thus essentially a system of deception devised by middle-class theorists and in no sense a popular creed. Had the revolutionary movement of the past 150 years really proceeded from the people, it would inevitably have followed the line laid down by one of the two sections of the proletariat indicated above, that is to say, it would either have taken the form of a continuous and increasing agitation for social reforms which would have enlisted the sympathy of all right-thinking men and must therefore in the end have proved irresistible, or it would have followed the line of Anarchy, organizing brigandage on a larger and yet larger scale, until, all owners of wealth having been exterminated and their expropriators in their turn exterminated by their fellows, the world would have been reduced to a depopulated desert.

But the world revolution has followed neither of these lines. Always the opponent of sane social reforms which Socialists deride as " melioration " or as futile attempts to shore up an obsolete system, it has consistently disassociated itself from such men as Lord Shaftesbury, who did more to better the conditions of the working classes than anyone who has ever lived. Anarchy, on the other hand, has been used by them merely as a means to an end; for genuine revolutionary sentiment they have no use at all. In Russia the Anarchists became the first objects of Soviet vengeance. The cynical attitude of Socialists towards the revolutionary proletariat was illustrated by Mr. Bernard Shaw, who in December 1919 openly boasted that he had helped to organize the railway strike,[1] and two years later wrote about the miners' strike in the following terms:

A Socialist State would not tolerate such an attack on the community as a strike for a moment. If a Trade Union attempted such a thing, the old Capitalist law against Trade Unions as conspiracies would be re-enacted within twenty-four hours and put ruthlessly into execution. Such a monstrosity as the recent coal strike, during which the coal-miners spent all their savings in damaging their neighbours and wrecking the national industries, would be impossible under Socialism. It was miserably defeated, as it deserved to be.[2]

Now, if this had been written by the Duke of Northumberland in the *National Review* instead of by Mr. Bernard Shaw in the *Labour Monthly*, one can imagine the outcry there would have been in the Socialist press. But the leaders of what is called democracy may always use what language they please in speaking of the people. " Our peasants," Maxim Gorky openly declared, " are brutal and debased, hardly human. I hate them."[3] It will be noticed that in descriptions of the French Revolution references to the savageries of the people are never resented by the Liberal or Socialist press; the persons of the leaders alone are sacred. It is clearly not the cause of democracy but of demagogy that these champions of " liberty " are out to defend.

The world-revolution is therefore not a popular movement but a conspiracy to impose on the people a system directly opposed to their real demands and aspirations, a system which, moreover, has proved disastrous every time an attempt has been made to put it into practice.

Russia has provided a further example of its futility. The fact that the more responsible leaders in this country do not advocate violence, does not affect the ultimate issue. Whilst Bolshevism sets out to destroy Capitalism at a blow, Socialism prefers a more gradual process. It is the difference between clubbing a man on the head and bleeding him to death—that is all.

The fact is that all Socialism leads to Communism in the

---

[1] Mr. Bernard Shaw on " Railway Strike Secrets," reported in *Morning Post* for December 3, 1919.
[2] Mr. Bernard Shaw in the *Labour Monthly* for October 1921.
[3] Report of interview with Maxim Gorky in *Daily News* for October 3, 1921.

long run[1] and therefore to disaster. The Bolshevist régime brought ruin and misery to Russia not because of the brutality of its methods, but because it was founded on the gigantic economic fallacy that industry can be carried on without private enterprise and personal initiative. The same theory applied by constitutional methods would produce precisely the same results. If the Socialists are ever allowed to carry out their full programme, England may be reduced to the state of Russia without the shedding of a drop of blood.

But how are we to explain the fact that in spite of the failure of Socialism in the past, in spite of the gigantic fiasco presented by Russia, in spite, moreover, of the declaration by the Bolsheviks themselves that Communism had failed and must be replaced by "a new economic policy," that is to say by a return to "Capitalism," [2] there should still be a large and increasing body of people to proclaim the efficacy of Socialism as the remedy for all social ills? In any other field of human experiment, in medicine or mechanical invention, failure spells oblivion; the prophylactic that does not cure, the machine that cannot be made to work, is speedily relegated to the scrap-heap. What indeed should we say of the bacteriologist, who, after killing innumerable patients with a particular serum, were to advertise it as an unqualified success? Should we not brand such a man as an unscrupulous charlatan or at best as a dangerous visionary? If, moreover, we were to find that large bands of agents backed by unlimited funds, were engaged in pressing his remedy upon the public and carefully avoiding all reference to the fatalities it had caused, should we not further conclude that there was "something behind all this"—some powerful company "running" the concern with a view to advancing its own private interests?

Why should not the same reasoning be applied to Socialism? For not only has Socialism never been known to succeed, but all its past failures are carefully kept dark by its exponents. Who, then, stands to gain by advocating it? And further, who provides the vast sums spent on propaganda? If in reality Socialism is a rising of the "have-nots" against the "haves," how is it that most of the money seems to be on

---

[1] Opinion expressed to me in conversation with a Socialist. Cf. Keir Hardie, "Communism, the final goal of Socialism" (*Serfdom to Socialism,* p. 36).

[2] "By the decree of May 22, 1922, the right of private ownership of means of production and for production itself was re-established." See article by Krassin on "The New Economic Policy of the Soviet Government" in *Reconstruction* (the monthly review edited by Parvus) for September 1922.

the side of the "have-nots"? For whilst organizations working for law and order are hampered at every turn for funds, no financial considerations ever seem to interfere with the activities of the so-called "Labour movement." Socialism, in fact, appears to be a thoroughly "paying concern," into which a young man enters as he might go into the City, with the reasonable expectation of "doing well." It is only necessary to glance at the history of the past hundred years to realize that "agitation" has provided a pleasant and remunerative career for hundreds of middle-class authors, journalists, speakers, organizers, and dilettantes of all kinds who would otherwise have been condemned to pass their lives on office-stools or at schoolmasters' desks. And when we read the accounts of the delightful treats provided for these "devoted workers" in the cause of the proletariat as given in the records of the First Internationale or the pages of Mrs. Snowden, we begin to understand the attractions of Socialism as a profession.[1]

But again I repeat: *Who provides the funds for this vast campaign?* Do they come out of the pockets of the workers or from some other mysterious reservoir of wealth? We shall return to this point in a later chapter.

How is it possible at any rate to believe in the sincerity of the exponents of equality who themselves adopt a style of living so different from that of the proletariat whose cause they profess to represent? If the doctrinaires of Socialism formed a band of ascetics who had voluntarily renounced luxury and amusement in order to lead lives of poverty and self-sacrifice—as countless really devoted men and women *not* calling themselves Socialists have done—we should still doubt the soundness of their economic theories as applied to society in general, but we should respect their disinterestedness. But with very few exceptions Socialist Intellectuals dine and sup, feast and amuse themselves with as few scruples of conscience as any unregenerate Tories.

With people such as these it is obviously as futile to reason as it would be to attempt to convince the agent of a quack medicine company that the nostrums he presses on the public will not effect a cure. He is very well aware of that already. Hence the efforts of well-meaning people to set forth in long, well-reasoned arguments the "fallacies of Socialism" produce little or no result. All these so-called "fallacies" have been

[1] See Guillaume's *Documents de l'Internationale* and Mrs. Snowden's *A Political Pilgrim in Europe*.

exposed repeatedly by able writers and disproved by all experience, so that if based merely on ignorance or error they would long since have ceased to obtain credence. The truth is that they are not fallacies but lies, deliberately devised and circulated by men who do not believe in them for a moment and who can therefore only be described as unscrupulous charlatans exploiting the credulity of the public.

But if this description may be legitimately applied to the brains behind Socialism and to certain of its leading doctrinaires, there are doubtless thousands of honest visionaries to be found in the movement. A system that professes to cure all the ills of life inevitably appeals to generous minds that feel but do not reason. In reality many of these people, did they but know it, are simply social reformers at heart and not Socialists at all, and their ignorance of what Socialism really means leads them to range themselves under the banner of a party that claims a monopoly of ideals. Others again, particularly amongst the young intelligentsia, take up Socialism in the same spirit as they would adopt a fashion in ties or waistcoats, for fear of being regarded as " reactionaries." That in reality, far from being " advanced," the profession of Socialism is as retrogressive as would be a return to the side-whiskers and plaid trousers of the last century, does not occur to them. The great triumph of Mussolini was to make the youth of Italy realize that to be a Communist was to be a " back number," and that progress consisted in marching forward to new ideas and aspirations. The young men of Cabet's settlement discovered this sixty years ago when they formed themselves into a band of " Progressives " in opposition to the old men who still clung to the obsolete doctrine of Communism.

Socialism at the present moment is in reality less a creed than a cult, founded not on practical experience but on unreal theory. It is here we find a connexion with secret societies. M. Augustin Cochin in his brilliant essays on the French Revolution[1] has described that " World of the Clouds " of which the Grand Orient was the capital, peopled by the precursors of the French Revolution. " Whilst in the real world the criterion of all thought lies in putting it to the test," there in the World of the Clouds the criterion is opinion. " They

[1] *Les Sociétés de Pensée et la Démocratie* (1921). M. Augustin Cochin collaborated with M. Charles Charpentier in throwing new light on the French Revolution, and triumphantly refuted M. Aulard in 1908. Unhappily his work was cut short by the war and he was killed at the front in July 1916, leaving his great history of the Revolution unfinished.

are there to talk, not to do; all this intellectual agitation, this immense traffic in speeches, writings, correspondence, leads not to the slightest beginning of work, of real effort." We should be wrong to judge them harshly; their theories on the perfectibility of human nature, on the advantages of savagery, which appear to us " dangerous chimeras," were never intended to apply to real life, only to the World of the Clouds, where they present no danger but become, on the contrary, " the most fecund truths."

The revolutionary explosion might well have finally shattered these illusions but for the Grand Orient. We have already seen the identity of theory between French Masonry and French Socialism in the nineteenth century. It was thus that, although in France one experiment after another demonstrated the unreality of Socialist Utopias, the lodges were always there to reconstruct the mirage and lead humanity on again across the burning desert sands towards the same phantom palm-trees and illusory pools of water.

Whatever the manner in which these ideas penetrated to this country—whether through the Radicals of the last century, adorers of the Encyclopædist Masons of France, or through the British disciples of German Social Democrats from the time of the First Internationale onwards—it is impossible to ignore the resemblance between the theories not only of French but of modern British Socialism and the doctrines of illuminized Freemasonry. Thus the idea running through Freemasonry of a Golden Age before the Fall, when man was free and happy, and which through the application of masonic principles is to return once more, finds an exact counterpart in the Socialist conception of a past halcyon era of Liberty and Equality, which is to return not merely in the form of a regenerated social order, but as a complete Millennium from which all the ills of human life have been eliminated. This idea has always haunted the imagination of Socialist writers from Rousseau to William Morris, and leads directly up to the further theory—the necessity for destroying civilization.

I cannot find in Mr. Lothrop Stoddart's conception of the revolutionary movement as the revolt of the " Under Man " against civilization, the origin of this campaign. In reality the leaders of world-revolution have not been " Under Men," victims of oppression or of adverse fate, nor could they be ranged in this category on account of physical or mental inferiority. It is true that most revolutionary agitators have been in some way abnormal and that the revolutionary army has largely been recruited from the unfit, but the real inspirers of the movement have frequently been men in prosperous circumstances and of brilliant intellect who might have distinguished themselves on other lines had they not chosen to devote their talents to subversion. To call Weishaupt, for example, an " Under Man " would be absurd. But let us see what is the idea on which the plan of destroying civilization is ostensibly founded.

It will be remembered that Rousseau like Weishaupt held that the Golden Age of felicity did not end in the garden of Eden, as is popularly supposed, but was prolonged into tribal and nomadic life. Up to this moment Communism was the happy disposition under which the human race existed and which vanished with the introduction of civilization. Civilization is therefore the *fons et origo mali* and should be done away with. Let no one exclaim that this theory died out either with Rousseau or with Weishaupt; the idea that " civilization is all wrong " runs all through the writings and speeches of our Intellectual Socialists to-day. I have referred elsewhere to Mr. H. G. Wells's prediction that mankind will more and more revert to the nomadic life, and Mr. Snowden has recently referred in tones of evident nostalgia to that productive era when man " lived under a system of tribal Communism."[1] The children who attend the Socialist Schools are also taught in the " Red Catechism " the advantages of savagery, thus :

Question. Do savages starve in the midst of plenty?

Answer. No; when there is plenty of food they all rejoice, feast, and make merry.[2]

That when there is not plenty of food they occasionally eat each other is not mentioned.

Here, then, is the theory on which this yearning for a return to nature is based. For it is quite probable that if a Golden Age ever existed it was Communistic; it is also true that certain primitive tribes have found it possible to continue the same system, for the simple reason that when and where

[1] Mr. Philip Snowden in debate on Socialism in the House of Commons on March 20, 1923: " By far the greatest time that man has been upon this globe he has lived not under a system of private enterprise, not under capitalism, but under a system of tribal communism, and it is well worth while to remember that most of the great inventions that have been the basis of our machinery and our modern discoveries were invented by men who lived together in tribes."

[2] *The Red Catechism*, by Tom Anderson, p. 3.

the earth was very thinly populated it brought forth, without the artificial aid of agriculture, more than enough to supply each man's needs. There was therefore no need for laws to protect property, since every man could help himself freely to all that he required. If at the present time a dozen people were shipwrecked on a fertile island some miles in area, the institution of property would be equally superfluous; if, however, several hundred were to share the same fate, it would at once become necessary to institute some system of cultivation which in its turn would necessitate either the institution of property, by which each man would depend on his own plot of land for his existence, or a communal system, by which all would be obliged to work for the common good and force applied to those who refused to do their allotted share.

Peaceful Communism is thus simply a matter of population; the conditions under which men can sit in the sun and enjoy the fruits of the earth with little effort must be transformed with the multiplication of the human species into a system which recognizes private property, or a communal State which enforces compulsory labour by means of overseers with whips. It was perhaps an appreciation of this truth that impelled the practical exponents of Rousseau's doctrines, the Terrorists of 1793, to embark on their " plan of depopulation " by way of establishing Communism on a peaceful basis.

But our Intellectual Socialists deny this necessity on the ground that under the benign régime of Socialism all men would be good and happy and would work joyfully for the welfare of the community. The fact that this has not proved the case even in voluntary Communist settlements does not daunt them, because, as has been said, their creed is founded not on practical experiment, but on theory, and it is here that we again find the inspiration of Grand Orient Freemasonry. The assumption that under an ideal social order all human failings would vanish derives directly from the two masonic doctrines which the Grand Orient, under the influence of Illuminism, has brought to a *reductio ad absurdum*—the perfectibility of human nature and universal brotherhood. The whole philosophy of Socialism is built upon these false premises.

Indeed the actual phraseology of illuminized Freemasonry has now passed into the language of Socialism; thus the old formulæ of " the United States of Europe " and " the Universal Republic " have been adopted not only by Mrs. Besant and her followers[1] as the last word in modern thought, but have also reappeared as a brilliant inspiration under the pen of Mr. H. G. Wells in the slightly varied form of the " World State." It would be amusing, for anyone who had the time, to discover how many of the ideas of our so-called advanced thinkers might be found almost verbatim in the writings of Weishaupt, the *République Universelle* of Anacharsis Clootz, and in the speeches of Grand Orient orators during the last century.

Moreover, the world-revolution is not only founded on the doctrines of illuminized Freemasonry, but has adopted the same method of organization. Thus, after the plan of the secret societies, from the Batinis onward, we shall find the forces of revolution divided into successive grades—the lowest consisting of the revolutionary proletariat, the *chair à révolution* as Marx expressed it, knowing nothing of the theory of Socialism, still less of the real aims of the leaders; above this the semi-initiates, the doctrinaires of Socialism, comprising doubtless many sincere enthusiasts; but above these again further grades leading up to the real initiates, who alone know whither the whole movement is tending.

For the final goal of world-revolution is not Socialism or even Communism, it is not a change in the existing economic system, it is not the destruction of civilization in a material sense; the revolution desired by the leaders is a moral and spiritual revolution, an anarchy of ideas by which all standards set up throughout nineteen centuries shall be reversed, all honoured traditions trampled under foot, and above all the Christian ideal finally obliterated.

It is true that a certain section of the Socialist movement proclaims itself Christian. The Illuminati made the same profession, so have the modern Theosophists and Rosicruciahs. But, as in the case of these secret societies, we should ask of so-called Christian Socialists: What do they means by Christ? What do they mean by Christianity-? On examination it will be found that their Christ is a being of their own inventing,

---

[1] E.g. the following extract from an address by Miss Esther Bright to the Esoteric School of Theosophy quoted in *The Patriot* for March 22, 1923: " The hearty and understanding co-operation between E.S.T. members of many nations will form a nucleus upon which the nations may build the big brotherhood which we hope may become the United States of Europe. United States! What a fine sound it has when one looks at the Europe of to-day!" A review named *Les États-Unis d'Europe* existed as early as 1868, and M. Goyau shows that this formula and also that of the " République Universelle " were slogans current amongst the pacifists before and during the war of 1870 which they signally failed to avert.—*L'Idée de Patrie et l'Humanitarisme*, pp. 113, 115.

that their Christianity is a perversion of Christ's real teaching.

The Christ of Socialism invoked in the interests of Pacifism as the opponent of force and in the interests of class warfare as a Socialist, a revolutionary, or even an " agitator," bears no resemblance to the real Christ. Christ was not a Pacifist when He told His disciples to arm themselves with swords, when He made a scourge of cords and drove the money-changers from the Temple. He did not tell men to forgive the enemies of their country or of their religion, but only their private enemies. Christ was not a Socialist when He declared that " a man's life consisteth not in the abundance of the things that he possesseth." Socialism teaches that a man must never rest content as long as another man possesses that which he has not. Christ did not believe in equality of payment when He told the parable of the ten talents and the unprofitable servant. Socialism would reduce all labour to the pace of the slowest. Above all, Christ was not a Socialist when He bade the young man who had great possessions sell all that he had and give it to the poor. *What School of Socialism has ever issued such a command?* On the contrary, Socialists are enjoined by their leaders not to give their money away in charity lest they should help by this means to prolong the existence of the present social system. The truth is that, as I showed in connexion with the fallacy of representing Christ as an Essene, there is no evidence to show that He or His disciples practised even the purest form of Communism. Christ did not advocate any economic or political system; He preached a spirit which if applied to any system would lead to peace among men. It is true that He enjoined His disciples to despise riches and that He denounced many of the rich men with whom He came into contact, but it must not be forgotten that His immediate mission was to a race that had always glorified riches, that had worshipped the golden calf, and by which wealth was regarded as the natural reward of godliness.[1] Christ came to teach men not to look for present reward in the form of increased material welfare, but to do good out of love to God and one's neighbour.

I do not doubt that in the past such men as Kingsley and

---

[1] How bitterly this attitude is still resented by the Jews is shown in the article on Jesus in the *Jewish Encyclopædia*, which observes that: " In almost all of his public utterances he was harsh, severe, and distinctly unjust . . . toward the ruling and well-to-do classes. After reading his diatribes against the Pharisees, the Scribes, and the rich, it is scarcely to be wondered at that these were concerned in helping to silence him " (vol. vii, p. 164).

J. F. D. Maurice sincerely imagined that they were following in the footsteps of the Master by describing themselves as Christian Socialists, but that the present leaders of Socialism in England are Christians at heart is impossible to believe in view of their attitude towards the campaign against Christianity in Russia. Never once have they or their allies, the Quakers, officially denounced the persecution not only of the priests but of all who profess the Christian faith in Russia.[1] Listen to this voice from the abyss of Russia:

We very much ask for prayer for the Church of Russia; it is passing through great tribulation and it is a question whether spiritual or earthly power will triumph. Many are being executed for not denying God. . . . Those placed by God at the helm need all the prayer and help of Christians all over the earth, because their fate is partly theirs too, for it is a question of faith triumphing over atheism, and it is a tug-of-war between those two principles.[2]

And again:

I look upon the persecution of the Russian Church as an effort to overthrow Christianity in general, for we are governed just now by the power of darkness, and all that we consider sinful seems to get the upper hand and to prosper.[3]

Yet it is for this power that the Socialist Party of Great Britain have for years been demanding recognition. Even the appeals for help from their fellow-Socialists in Russia have left them cold. "We would suggest," ran one such appeal—

1. That the British Labour Party issue an official protest against the Soviet Government's inhuman treatment of its political opponents in general and the political prisoners in particular.

2. That meetings of protest should be organized in the industrial towns of Great Britain.

3. That the British Labour Party make an official representation to the Soviet Government directly, urging the latter to put a stop to the persecutions of the Socialists in Russia.[3]

And it was of this régime that Mr. Lansbury wrote:

Whatever their faults, the Communist leaders of Russia have hitched their wagon to a star—the star of love, brotherhood, comradeship.[4]

---

[1] The execution of Monseigneur Butkievitch, the Roman Catholic Archbishop of Petrograd, was condoned by the *Daily Herald*, the *New Statesman*, and the *Nation*. See the *Daily Herald* for April 7, 1923.
[2] Letters from a friend of the present writer in Russia, dates of August 1922 and February 1923.
[3] *Daily Herald* for February 21, 1922.   [4] Ibid., March 18, 1920.

The callous indifference displayed by British Socialists, with the honourable exception of the Social Democratic Federation,[1] towards the crimes of the Bolsheviks offers indeed a painful contrast to the attitude of the other Socialists of Europe. At the conference of the Labour and Socialist International at Hamburg in May 1923, a resolution was passed condemning the persecution by the Soviet Government. When the resolution was put to the congress, 196 voted for, 2 against it, and 39, including the 30 British delegates, abstained.

I ask, then: Why should the Socialists of Great Britain be differentiated from the Bolsheviks of Russia? In every question of importance they have always lent them their support. In the great war on Christianity they have acted as the advance guard by the institution of Socialist Sunday-schools, from which all religious teaching is excluded. Socialists are very anxious to disassociate these from the " Proletarian " Sunday-schools which teach atheism. But from ignoring the existence of God to denying it is but a step; moreover, it will be noticed that the Socialists have never issued any protests against the blasphemies of the Proletarian schools. The real attitude of the Socialist Party towards religion may perhaps be gauged by the notice, reproduced on page 341, which once appeared in its official organ the *Daily Herald,* of which Mr. Lansbury, widely advertised as a fervent Christian, was once editor and is now managing director.

It was to the party controlling this organ that 700 clergymen of the Church of England and the Episcopal Church of Scotland saw fit to offer their congratulations by means of a memorial presented to Mr. Ramsay MacDonald in March 1923. Shall we yet see the scene of Brumaire 1793 repeated and a procession of prelates presenting themselves at Westminster to lay down their rings and crosses and declare that " henceforth there shall be no other worship than that of liberty and holy equality "?

Already the desecration of the churches has begun. The red flag was recently carried into the City Temple by a band of unemployed, although several of their number objected to its presence in the church. An attempt to sing " The Red Flag " was also suppressed by a section of the unemployed

---

[1] See Report of Annual Conference of the Social Democratic Federation in *Morning Post* for August 6, 1923, where it is said that " Whole-hearted denunciation of Sovietism was the chief feature of the day's discussion," etc.

Books We All Pretend to Have Read

The Bible is a real book, although during the whole of the nineteenth century the Churches turned a blind eye to the fact that it was a free translation by Jacobean clergymen of a Greek text of doubtful authenticity and of multiple authorship. The Bible is as divinely inspired as Shakespeare, or Milton, or Anatole France. But it is not as " pure " as the texts of these authors, for it is :—

(1) A miscellaneous collection of folk-tales and traditional history bound together and described as the " Old Testament," and

(2) " The New Testament," a collection of Eastern theological doctrines centralized in the figure of a great Syrian mystic religious teacher, Jesus.

Those who will go to the Bible with an unprejudiced mind will discover that it is one of the great books of the world, full of beauty, humour, and aspiration, and disfigured, as great books often are, by occasional brutalities and crudities.
—*Daily Herald*, February 7, 1923.

---

themselves, who had apparently retained some sense of decency.[1]

Weishaupt's design of enlisting the clergy in the work of world-revolution has been carried out according to plan. Those Catholic priests in Ireland who inflamed popular passions acted as the tools of the International Atheist conspiracy and found at last the movement turning against themselves. The Protestant clergymen who profess " Christian Socialism " are playing the same part. Doubtless without knowing it, they act as the agents of the Continental Illuminati and pave the way, as did the emissaries of Weishaupt, for the open attack on all forms of religion. It is not a mere accident that the blasphemous masquerades of the French Revolution have

---

[1] *Evening Standard* for January 15, 1924.

recently been repeated in Russia. The horrible incidents described in the press[1] were simply the outward manifestation of a continuous conspiracy of which evidence was seen some years ago in Portugal under the influence of the Carbonarios, led by Alfonso Costa, whose utterances at times bore a striking resemblance to those of Anacharsis Clootz. The late Duchess of Bedford thus described the war on religion which inaugurated the new Republic:

> One of the most zealous enterprises of this great society [the Carbonarios] is, in their own words, to exterminate "the Christian myth" in the minds of the nation of Portugal. The little children in the schools have badges pinned into their clothes with the words "No God! No religion!" and a British tourist who made a journey throughout the country of Portugal met bands of innocent babes carrying banners, on which the inscription was "We have no need of God."[2]

Is it only a coincidence that last year a Socialist and Communist meeting in Trafalgar Square displayed a red banner bearing the motto: "No King, no God, no Law"?[3]

I repeat: It is not an economic revolution which forms the plan of the real directors of the movement, it is neither the "dictatorship of the proletariat" nor the reorganization of society by the Intelligentsia of "Labour"; it is the destruction of the Christian idea. Socialist orators may inveigh against corrupt aristocracy or "bloated Capitalists," but these are not in reality the people who will suffer most if the aim of the conspiracy is achieved. The world-revolution has always shown itself indulgent towards selfish and corrupt aristocrats, from the Marquis de Sade and the Duc d'Orléans onwards; it is the gentle, the upright, the benevolent, who have fallen victims to revolutionary fury.

Socialism with its hatred of all superiority, of noble virtues —loyalty and patriotism—with its passion for dragging down instead of building up, serves the purpose of the deeper conspiracy. If the Christian Intelligentsia can be destroyed or won over and the nation deprived of all its natural leaders, the world-revolutionaries reckon that they will be able to

---

[1] *Daily Telegraph* for January 8, 1923; *Daily Mail* for January 24, 1923.
[2] Report of speech by Adeline, Duchess of Bedford, at a public meeting to protest against the treatment of political prisoners in Portugal, April 22, 1913, quoted in *Portuguese Political Prisoners*, p. 89 (published by Upcott Gill & Son).
[3] *Evening Standard*, May 14, 1923.

mould the proletariat according to their desires. This being so, the thing we now call Bolshevism forms only one phase of the movement which is carried on by countless different methods, apparently disconnected but all tending towards the same end. We have only to look around us in the world to-day to see everywhere the same disintegrating power at work—in art, literature, the drama, the daily press—in every sphere that can influence the mind of the public. Just as in the French Revolution a play on the massacre of St. Bartholomew was staged in order to rouse the passions of the people against the monarchy, so our modern cinemas perpetually endeavour to stir up class hatred by scenes and phrases showing " the injustice of kings," " the sufferings of the people," the selfishness of " aristocrats," regardles of whether these enter into the theme of the narrative or not.[1] And in the realms of literature, not merely in works of fiction but in manuals for schools, in histories and books professing to be of serious educative value and receiving a skilfully organized boom throughout the press, everything is done to weaken patriotism, to shake belief in all existing institutions by the systematic perversion of both contemporary and historical facts, whilst novels and plays calculated to undermine all ideas of morality are pressed upon the public as works of genius which, in order to maintain a reputation for intellect, it is essential to admire. I do not believe that all this is accidental; I do not believe that the public asks for the anti-patriotic or demoralizing books and plays placed before it; on the contrary, it invariably responds to an appeal to patriotism and simple healthy emotions. The heart of the people is still sound, but ceaseless efforts are made to corrupt it.

This conspiracy has long been apparent to Continental observers. Some years before the war, Monsieur de Lannoy, a member of an anti-masonic association in France, at a conference on " the influence of judæo-masonic sects in the theatre, in literature, in the fashions," showed how " orders

[1] That this use of the cinema for revolutionary propaganda is deliberate was proved to me by personal experience. A man who had been struck with the dramatic possibilities of something I had written wrote to ask if he might place it before a certain well-known film producer in America. I gave my consent, and some time later he informed me that the producer in question regretted he could not film my work as it might appear to be anti-Bolshevist propaganda. Soon after this the same producer brought out a film on the same subject with the moral turned round the other way, so as to make the whole thing subtly revolutionary, and brought this over to England, where he advertised it as anti-Bolshevist propaganda! This is typical of the duplicity displayed by these propagandists.

of things which appear to have no connexion with each other are skilfully bound up together and directed by a single methodical movement towards a common end. This common end is the paganization of the universe, the destruction of all Christianity, the return to the loosest morals of antiquity."[1] Robison saw in the indecent dress of the period of the Directory the result of Weishaupt's teaching, and traces to the same cause the ceremony which took place in Notre Dame when a woman of loose morals was held up to the admiration of the public.[2] The same glorification of vice has found exponents amongst the modern Illuminati in this country. In *The Equinox—the Journal of Scientific Illuminism,* it is proposed that prostitutes should be placed on the same level as soldiers who have served their country and be honoured and pensioned by the State.[3] The community of women was not an idea that originated with the Russian Bolsheviks, but one that has run through all the revolutionary movements of the past.

The attempt to pervert all conceptions of beauty in the sphere of art serves to pave the way for moral perversion. In the *New York Herald* two years ago there appeared a circular protesting against the so-called Modernistic cult in art as " world-wide Bolshevist propaganda." The circular went on to declare:

This aims to overthrow and destroy all existing social systems, including that of the arts. This modernistic degenerate cult is simply the Bolshevist philosophy applied in art. The triumph of Bolshevism therefore means the destruction of the present æsthetic system, the transportation of all æsthetic values, and the deification of ugliness.

The whole propaganda of the movement was said to be organized by " a coterie of European art-dealers "—elsewhere described as German—who had flooded the market with the works of artists who began as " a small group of neurotic ego-maniacs in Paris styling themselves worshippers of Satan, the God of Ugliness." Some of these men were suffering from the " visual derangement " of the insane, whilst " many of the pictures exhibited another form of mania. The system of this is an incontrollable desire to mutilate the human body." Sadism, as we know, played a prominent part in both the

---

[1] Quoted in *Le Problème de la Mode,* by the Baronne de Montenach, p. 30 (1913).
[2] Robison, *Proofs of a Conspiracy,* pp. 251, 252 (1798).
[3] Article by A. Quiller in *The Equinox* for September 1910, p. 338.

French and Russian revolutions. The most important point in all this is not that degenerates should be found to perpetrate these abominations, but what the circular describes as the " Machiavellian campaign organized for the unloading of these works. Editions de luxe . . . were published and sold by the picture dealers; . . . every crafty device known to the picture trade was resorted to in order to discredit and destroy the heretofore universally accepted standards of æsthetics."[1]

This process of reversing all accepted standards may also be brought about by subtler methods. We have already seen that occult practices may lead to the obliteration of all sense of truth and of normal sexual instincts. Under the influence of so-called occult science, which is, in reality, simply powerful suggestion or self-hypnotism, all a man's natural impulses and inhibitive springs of action may be broken; he will no longer react to the conceptions of beauty or ugliness, or right or wrong, which, unknown to himself, formed the law of his being. Thus not only his conscious deeds but his subconscious mental processes may pass under the control of another, or become entirely deranged.

Much the same consequences may result from the Freud system of Psycho-Analysis, which, particularly by its insistence on sex, tends to subordinate the will to impulses of a harmful kind. An eminent American neuro-psychiatrist of New York has expressed his opinion on this subject in the following words:

The Freud theory is anti-Christian and subversive of organized society. Christianity teaches that the individual can resist temptation and Freudism teaches that the matter of yielding to or resisting temptation is one for which the individual is not wilfully responsible. Freudism makes of the individual a machine, absolutely controlled by subconscious reflexes. . . . It would of course be difficult to prove that psycho-analysis has been evolved as a destructive propaganda measure, but in one sense the point is immaterial. Whether conscious or unconscious, it makes for destructive effect.[2]

In general, the art of the conspiracy is not so much to create movements as to capture existing movements, often innocuous and even admirable in themselves, and turn them to a subversive purpose. Thus birth control, which—if combined with the restriction of alien immigration and carried out under proper direction—would provide a solution to the frightful

---

[1] *New York Herald* for September 6 and 7, 1921.
[2] Private communication to the author.

problem of over-population, can without these provisos become a source of national weakness and demoralization. It is easy to see how a limitation of the native population would serve the cause of England's enemies by reducing her fighting forces and by making room for undesirable aliens. That the birth-control campaign may also be used for evil purposes is suggested by the fact that it has not been confined to our own overcrowded island, but has been carried on in France, where under-population has long constituted a tragedy. In 1903 and 1904 the " Ligue de la Régéneration Humaine," founded by Monsieur Paul Robin, in its organ *L'Émancipateur* issued not only instructions on " the means how to avoid large families," but also pamphlets on " free love and free maternity." [1] The campaign of race-suicide was thus combined with the undermining of morality ; legal families were to be limited and illegal births encouraged. This was quite in accord with the doctrines of the Grand Orient, in whose Temples, Monsieur Copin Albancelli points out, the principle of " la libre maternité "—known in this country as " the right to motherhood "—was advocated.

It is curious to notice that the apparently innocent invention of Esperanto receives support from the same quarter. This is not surprising since we know that the idea of a universal language has long haunted the minds of Freemasons. I have myself seen a document emanating from a body of French Masons stating that Esperanto is directly under the control of the three masonic powers of France—the Grand Orient, the Grande Loge Nationale, and the Droit Humain.

That it is largely used for promoting Bolshevism has been frequently stated. In July 1922, M. Bérard, Minister of Education, issued a circular " to the heads of all French Universities, academies, and colleges, calling on them not to help in any way in the teaching of Esperanto on the ground that Bolsheviks use it as one of their dangerous forms of propaganda." [2] A correspondent points out to me that another universal language, Ido, is used for propaganda by the Anarchists, and that several journals distributed by revolutionary societies, written in Ido, are " frankly and baldly Anarchical." The writer adds :

Last week I received a copy of *Libereso* (Liberty), monthly organ of the Anarchist Section of the " Emancipating Star "—" Cosmopolitan Union of Labour-class Idists." It commands carrying out

---

[1] Paul Bureau, *La Crise morale des Temps nouveaux*, p. 108 (1907).
[2] *Daily Mail*, July 14, 1922.

Anarchistic principles to their extreme limits; commends "La Ruzo" (ruse); is sarcastic regarding Socialism and Democracy. . . . It contains an appeal for help (in money) for the Anarchists imprisoned in Russia . . . written by Alexander Berkmann and signed by him with Emma Goldmann and A. Schapiro."

Here, then, we have a revolutionary movement which is anti-Socialist and even anti-Bolshevist, which tends to prove the opinion I have already expressed, that Bolshevism is only one phase of the world-conspiracy. But if we explain this by the old antagonism between the opposing revolutionary camps of Anarchy and Socialism, how are we to account for the fact that the same destructive purpose animates people who are neither Anarchist nor Socialist, but can only be ranged in the category of extreme reaction? Of this phase of the movement Nietzsche provides the supreme example. In his imprecations against "the Crucified," the advocate of autocracy and militarism rivals the most infuriated of revolutionary Socialists. The whole spirit of perversion is contained in the description of Nietzsche by his friend Georges Brandes: "His thoughts stole inquisitively along forbidden paths: 'This thing passes for a value. Can we not turn it upside-down? This is regarded as good. Is it not rather evil?'" What is this but Satanism? The case of Nietzsche is not to be explained away by the fact that he died raving mad, since a number of apparently sane people still profess for him unbounded admiration, and whilst deriding Socialism and even attacking Bolshevism join in the war against Christian civilization. The conspiracy therefore exists apart from so-called democratic circles.

Not long ago I picked up an Italian novel by an anti-Socialist containing precisely the same diatribes against "Christian-bourgeois society" that are to be found in Anarchist and Bolshevist literature. "The family," says the author, "is the kernel of contemporary society and its base. Whoever would really reform or subvert must begin by reforming and subverting the family. . . . The family . . . is the principal path of all unhappiness, of all vice, of all hypocrisy, of all moral ugliness, . . ." and he goes on to show that the two countries which have proved themselves the sanest and the strongest are Germany and America, because they have advanced by long strides towards free love.[1]

The writer of these words may be of no importance, but

---

[1] *Le Smorfie dell' Anima,* by Mario Mariani (1919).

they should be noted because they are symptomatic and help us to locate certain centres of infection.

It is impossible to observe all these miscellaneous movements going on all around us without being struck by the similarity of aim between them ; each seems to form part of a common plan, which, like the separate pieces of a jig-saw puzzle, convey no meaning, but when fitted together make up a perfectly clear design. That there is somewhere in the background a point of contact is suggested by the fact that we find members of the different groups playing a double and a treble rôle, the same name occurring in the list of patrons in a Birth Control paper and in a revolutionary secret society, amongst the exponents of Psycho-Analysis and the members of an Irish Republican Committee.

With the open as with the secret forces the great method of warfare is the capture of public opinion. A hidden influence behind the press contributes powerfully to this end. Some of the subtlest disintegrating propaganda during the last seven years has emanated from the so-called " Capitalist press." The *Daily Herald* is only the brass band of the Revolution. It is to the journals inspired and patronized by the Intelligentsia that we must turn to find the doctrines of Illuminism set forth with the most persuasive eloquence.[1]

More than eighty years ago a Frenchman endowed with extraordinary prophetic instinct foretold not only the danger that would one day come from Russia, but that the press would facilitate the destruction of civilization :

When our cosmopolitan democracy, bearing its last fruits, shall have made of war a thing odious to whole populations, when the nations calling themselves the most civilized on earth shall have finished enervating themselves in their political debaucheries, . . . the floodgates of the North will open on us once again, then we shall undergo a last invasion not of ignorant barbarians but of cunning and enlightened masters, more enlightened than ourselves, for they will have learnt from our own excesses how we can and must be governed.

It is not for nothing that Providence piles up so many inactive forces in the East of Europe. One day the sleeping giant will arise and force will put an end to the reign of words. In vain, then, distracted equality will call the old aristocracy to the help

---

[1] A leader writer in one of the most important literary Constitutional journals in this country observed to me in conversation that " all such nonsense as patriotism ought to be done away with " ; another writer for the same paper told me he would not in the least regret to see the British Empire broken up.

of liberty; the weapon grasped again too late and wielded by hands too long inactive will have become powerless. Society will perish for having trusted to words void of sense or contradictory; then the deceitful echoes of public opinion, the newspapers, wishing at all costs to keep their readers, will push [the world] to ruin if only to have something to relate for a month longer. They will kill society to live upon its corpse.[1]

To-day the newspapers, no longer the echoes of public opinion but its supreme directors, throw open their columns to every form of disintegrating doctrine and close them to arguments that could effectually arrest the forces of destruction.

What is the hidden influence behind the press, behind all the subversive movements going on around us? Are there several Powers at work? Or is there one Power, one invisible group directing all the rest—the circle of the *real Initiates*?

[1] Astolphe de Custine, *La Russie en* 1839, I. 149 (1843).

14

PAN-GERMANISM

WE have seen in the course of this book that the idea of a secret power working for world-revolution through both open movements and secret societies, is not a new one, but dates from the eighteenth century. In order to appreciate the continuity of this idea, let us recapitulate the testimonies of contemporaries, some of which have been already quoted in their context, but which when collected together and placed in chronological order make up a very remarkable chain of evidence.

In 1789 the Marquis de Luchet warned France of the danger of the Illuminati, whose object was world-domination.[1] In consequence of this " gigantic project " de Luchet foresees " a series of calamities of which the end is lost in the darkness of time, like unto those subterranean fires of which the insatiable activity devours the bowels of the earth and which escape into the air by violent and devastating explosions."[2]

In 1794 the Duke of Brunswick in his manifesto to the German lodges said:

A great sect arose, which, taking for its motto "the good and happiness of man," worked in the darkness of the conspiracy to make the happiness of humanity a prey for itself. This sect is known to everyone: its brothers are known no less than its name. . . . The plan they had formed for breaking all social ties and of destroying all order was revealed in their speeches and acts. . . . Indomitable pride, thirst of power, such were the only motives of this sect: their masters had nothing less in view than the thrones

---

[1] *Essai sur la Secte des Illuminés* (1792 edition), p. 48. On p. 46 de Luchet expresses his idea in a curious passage which I find difficult to render in English: " Il s'est formé au sein des plus épaisses ténèbres, une société d'êtres nouveaux qui se connaissent sans s'être vus, qui s'entendent sans s'être expliqués, qui se servent sans amitié. Cette société a le but de gouverner le monde. . . ."
[2] Ibid., p. 171.

PAN-GERMANISM 351

of the earth, and the government of the nations was to be directed by their nocturnal clubs.[1]

In 1797 Montjoie, writing of the Orléaniste conspiracy, to which in an earlier work he had attributed the whole organization of the French Revolution in its first stages, observed:

I will not examine whether this wicked prince, thinking he was acting in his personal interests, was not moved by that *invisible hand*[2] which seems to have created all the events of our revolution in order to lead us towards a goal that we do not see at present, but which I think we shall see before long.[3]

In 1801 Monsignor de Savine "made allusions in prudent and almost terrified terms to some international sect . . . a power superior to all others . . . which has arms and eyes everywhere and which governs Europe to-day."[4]

In 1817 the Chevalier de Malet declared that " the authors of the Revolution are not more French than German, Italian, English, etc. They form a particular nation which took birth and has increased in the dark amidst all civilized nations with the object of subjecting them all to its domination."[5]

In 1835 the Carbonaro, Malegari, wrote to another member of the Carbonari:

We form an association of brothers in all points of the globe, we have desires and interests in common, we aim at the emancipation of humanity, we wish to break every kind of yoke, yet there is one that is unseen, that can hardly be felt, yet that weighs on us. Whence comes it? Where is it? No one knows, or at least no one tells. The association is secret, even for us, the veterans of secret societies.[6]

In 1852 Disraeli wrote:

It was neither parliaments nor populations, nor the course of nature, nor the course of events, that overthrew the throne of Louis Philippe . . . the throne was surprised by the Secret Societies, ever prepared to ravage Europe. . . . Acting in unison with a great popular movement they may destroy society, as they did at the end of the last century.[7]

[1] Eckert, *La Franc-Maçonnerie dans sa véritable signification,* translated by the Abbé Gyr (1854), II. 133, 134.
[2] My italics.
[3] Galart de Montjoie, *Histoire de Marie Antoinette,* p. 156 (1797).
[4] G. Lenôtre, *The Dauphin,* Eng. trans., p. 307.
[5] *Recherches politiques et historiques sur l'existence d'une secte révolutionnaire,* p. 2 (1817).
[6] J. Crétineau-Joly, *L'Église Romaine en face de la Révolution,* II. 143 (1859).
[7] *Lord George Bentinck, A Political Biography,* pp. 552-4 (1852).

In 1874 Père Deschamps, after his exhaustive study of secret societies, thus propounded the question:

We have now to ask ourselves whether there is anything but an identity of doctrines and personal communications between the members of the different sects, whether there is really a unity of direction which binds together all the secret societies, including Free Masonry. Here we touch on the most mysterious point of the action of secret societies, on that which these national Grand Orients who declare themselves independent of each other and sometimes even excommunicate each other conceal most carefully beneath a veil.[1]

Finally Deschamps is led to the conclusion that there is " a secret council which directs all masonic societies,"[2] that there are secret lairs where the chiefs of the sects agree together on their work of destruction."[3]

It would be easy to multiply quotations of this kind taken from many different sources. Whether the men who expressed these opinions were, as we are frequently told, suffering from delusions or not, the fact remains that the idea of a hidden hand behind world-revolution has existed for at least 135 years. And when we compare these utterances with Monsieur Copin Albancelli's description of an inner circle secretly directing the activities of the Grand Orient, and with the conclusions reached by members of other secret societies, that such a circle exists behind all occult and masonic societies of a subversive kind, we are necessarily led to enquire: is there one circle or rather one Power behind both open and secret organizations working for the overthrow of the existing social order and Christian civilization? If so, what is this power?

Now, to leave speculation for the moment and come to known facts, everyone who has seriously studied these matters is aware that there are at the present moment five principal organized movements at work in the world with which ordered government has to contend, that may be summarized as follows:

1. Grand Orient Freemasonry.
2. Theosophy with its innumerable ramifications.
3. Nationalism of an aggressive kind, now represented by Pan-Germanism.
4. International Finance.
5. Social Revolution.

[1] *Les Sociétés Secrètes et la Société*, I. 91.
[2] Ibid., II. 243.   [3] Ibid., II. 521.

It will be seen that, with the exception of the fourth, these movements are those of which I have endeavoured to trace the course throughout the earlier part of this book. It is a highly significant fact that it was only when I had reached this stage of my work I discovered there were independent investigators who had arrived at precisely the same conclusions as myself.

The problem that now confronts us is therefore this: if there is indeed one power directing all subversive movements, is it one of the five movements here enumerated or is it yet another power more potent and more invisible? In order to discover this, it is necessary to consider whether these movements, although apparently divergent in their ultimate purpose, have nevertheless any ideas or any aims in common. One fundamental point of similarity will certainly be found between them. All desire to dominate the world and to direct it along lines and according to rules of their own devising; more than this, each desires to direct it solely for the benefit of one class of people—social, intellectual, or national as the case may be—to the entire exclusion of every human being outside that class. Thus in reality each aspires to the dictatorship of the world.

Besides this, it will be noticed that not only these principal movements, but also the minor subversive movements described in the last chapter, have in the main (1) a pro-German tendency —none, at any rate, are pro-French nor do they encourage British patriotism, (2) all contain a Jewish element—none, at least, are " anti-Semite," and (3) all have a more or less decided antagonism to Christianity. If then, there is a single power behind them, is it the Pan-Germanic Power? Is it the Jewish Power? Or is it the Anti-Christian Power? Let us examine each of these possibilities in turn.

Viewed under the aspect of exaggerated Nationalism, the spirit of Pan-Germanism is nothing new. The dream of world-domination has haunted the imagination of many races from the time of Alexander the Great to Napoleon I, but nowhere has the plan been carried out by the Machiavellian methods which have characterized Prussian foreign policy and diplomacy from the days of Frederick the Great onwards. It is not Prussian militarism that constitutes the crime of modern Germany. Militarism in the sense of courage, patriotism, discipline, and devotion to duty is a splendid thing. But the spirit of Pan-Germanism differs from the British conception of patriotism in that it overrides the rights of all other peoples and seeks to establish its domination over the whole world. Under German domination every German would be free and every other human being a slave. England, whilst seeking conquests, has, on the other hand, always allowed the inhabitants of conquered territories to develop along their own lines and has made use of legislation largely to protect them from each other. The preference of the native of India for an English judge to one of his own race is evidence of this fact. But it is further the abandonment of all principle, the acceptance of the doctrine that everything is allowable—lying, treachery, calumny, and bad faith—in order to achieve its end, that has placed Germany outside the comity of nations. Robison describes the system of the Illuminati as leading to the conclusion that " nothing would be scrupled at, if it could be made appear that the Order would derive advantage from it, because the great object of the Order was held as superior to every consideration."[1] Change the word Order to State, and one has the whole principle of modern German Imperialism.

Now, it is interesting to notice that the founders of German Illuminism and of German Imperialism drew certain of their ideas from the same source. Both Weishaupt and Frederick the Great were earnest students of Machiavelli—and both out-did their master. This form of Machiavellism, carried to a point probably never dreamt of by the Italian philosopher, has run through the whole struggle of Prussia for supremacy and at the same time through each outbreak of world revolution in which Prussian influence has played a part. Thus the Ems telegram in 1870, the false report that tricked Russia into mobilization in 1914,[2] the violation of treaties and of all the laws of civilized warfare during the recent war, were the direct outcome of doctrines that may be found in embryo in *The Prince*. So also the most striking characteristic of the French Revolution under the inspiration of Weishaupt's emissaries and the agents of Prussia, and of the present revolutionary movement inaugurated by Karl Marx and Friedrich Engels, is not so much its violence as its Machiavellian cunning. The art popularly known to-day as *camouflage*—of dressing-up one design under the guise of something quite different, of making black appear white by glorifying the most ignoble

---

[1] Robison's *Proofs of a Conspiracy*, p. 107.
[2] A good account of this was contained in a letter to *The Times* of January 23, 1924.

actions, of making white appear black by holding up all honourable traditions to contempt and ridicule, in a word *perversion*—has been reduced to a system by the secret directors of world revolution. It is here that we can detect the non-proletarian character of the movement. The working-man of all countries is the least Machiavellian of beings; his weakness lies in the fact that he is too inarticulate, that he does not know how to put his case even when he has a good one, still less to make a bad one appear plausible. It was not until world revolution was taken over by the faction described by Bakunin as " the German-Jew Company " that it reassumed its Machiavellian character and gradually became the formidable organization it is to-day.

A few extracts from *The Prince* will show how closely both the Prussians and the Terrorists of France and Russia have followed Machiavelli's manual for despots:

" He who usurps the government of any State is to execute and put in practice all the cruelties which he thinks material at once, that he may have no occasion to renew them often," etc.[1] (Vide the German principle of " frightfulness " to be exercised against the inhabitants of invaded territory and the plan of the French and Russian Terrorists in suppressing " counter-revolutionaries.")

" It is of such importance to a prince to take upon him the nature and disposition of a beast; of all the whole flock he ought to imitate the lion and the fox."[2] (Vide Frederick the Great and the demagogues of France and Russia.)

" A prince . . . who is wise and prudent, cannot or ought not to keep his parole, when the keeping of it is to his prejudice, and the causes for which he promised removed."[3] (Vide Germany's doctrine of the scrap of paper and the promises of the Bolshevist Trade Delegation in London to refrain from propaganda.)

" Because the whole multitude which submits to your government is not capable of being armed, if you be beneficial and obliging to those you do arm, you may make the bolder with the rest, for the difference of your behaviour to the soldier binds him more firmly to your service," etc.[4] (Vide the insolent behaviour permitted to officers of the German Imperial Army and the feeding of the Red Army in Russia at the expense of the rest of the population.)

" The prince . . . is obliged . . . at convenient times in the

---

[1] *The Prince*, Eng. trans. by Henry Morley, p. 61.
[2] Ibid., p. 110.   [3] Ibid., p. 110.   [4] Ibid., p. 131.

year to entertain the people by feastings and plays and spectacles of recreation ... and give them some instance of his humanity and magnificence." [1] (Vide the important part played by " spectacles" in the French Revolution and by the theatre and opera in Soviet Russia. Always the same plan of " *panem et circenses !* ")

Just after the fall of Napoleon I a French writer published a book describing the " methodic perversity " of the revolutionary leaders and the Revolution as the beginning of a Machiavellian régime.[2] How did this system come to be established in France unless under the guidance of Weishaupt's emissaries and the agents of Frederick the Great and of the Illuminatus Frederick William II ?

Germany was well able, however, to defend herself against the devastating doctrines of Illuminism. Always the home of secret societies, she became by the end of the nineteenth century the spiritual home of Socialism. Yet although this might appear to present a danger to German Imperialism, no country has remained so free as Germany from serious agitation. It has been well said that the Germans are theoretically more Socialistic than other nations, but they are far less revolutionary.

The truth is that the rulers of Germany have always known that they could count not merely on the servility of the people but on their ardent national spirit. A strong vein of patriotism ran through all the secret societies even of the most subversive variety, and it was the German Student Orders, whence the Illuminati drew their disciples, that became also the recruiting-ground for the German Imperialist idea. Instead of combating subversive forces, German Imperialism adopted the far more skilful expedient of enlisting them in its service.

It was thus that in Germany Freemasonry became a powerful aid to Prussian aggrandizement. From 1840 onwards the word of command to all the lodges went out from Berlin,[3] and in the revolution of 1848 the Freemasons of Germany showed themselves the most ardent supporters of German unity under the aegis of Prussia. Later, Bismarck with superb ingenuity enlisted not only Freemasons and members of secret societies but Socialists and democrats in the same cause. Lassalle and

[1] *The Prince*, Eng. trans. by Henry Morley, pp. 143, 144.
[2] M. Mazères, *De Machiavel et de l'influence de sa doctrine sur les opinions, les mœurs et la politique de la France pendant la Révolution* (1816).
[3] Deschamps, *Les Sociétés Secrètes, etc.*, I. p. xcii., quoting " Discours du F.·. Malapert à la Loge Alsace-Lorraine " in *La Chaîne d'Union*, pp. 88, 89 (1874); cf. Eckert, *La Franc-Maçonnerie dans sa véritable signification*, II. 293.

Marx contributed powerfully to the cause of pan-Germanism. Dammer, who succeeded Lassalle as head of the Socialist party, instructed his successor Fritsche that " in the meetings which took place in Saxony, whilst putting forward Socialist claims, they must not fail to demand the unity of Germany under the domination of Prussia. Fritsche was personally to render an account to Bismarck of the results obtained at these meetings."[1]

Even as far afield as Italy, Bismarck succeeded in imposing the policy of German autocracy on men who were ostensibly marching in the vanguard of " liberty." " I believe in the unity of Germany," Mazzini wrote to Bismarck in 1867, " and I desire it as I desire that of my own country. I abhor the empire and supremacy that France arrogates to herself over Europe."[2]

Before 1870 Freemasonry everywhere on the Continent helped the cause of Germany. " The Occult Power preached pacifism and humanitarianism in France by means of French Freemasonry whilst it preached patriotism in Germany by means of German Freemasonry."[3] So although throughout the nineteenth century the rulers of Germany permitted the dissemination of ideas antagonistic to religion, until by the dawn of the following century the very idea of God was rooted out of the minds of many German children, the Imperial Government was careful that nothing should be allowed to weaken patriotism. Indeed, the Pan-German obsession into which German patriotism became transformed under the influence of such men as Treitschke and Bernhardi was, no less than revolutionary Socialism, fortified by irreligion because founded on the law of force and the absence of all moral scruple. It is thus not " militarism " in the accepted sense that has rendered Germany a menace to the world, but the Machiavellian plan of using for export doctrines sternly repressed within her own borders.

I shall not enlarge here on the crime of the German Imperial Staff in sending Lenin and his fellow-Bolsheviks to Russia, because I have already dealt at length with this question in a controversy that appeared in the *Morning Post* two years ago.[4] But whilst acknowledging the fair and courteous line

[1] Deschamps, op. cit., II. 681.
[2] *Politica Segreta Italiana,* by Diamilla Muller, p. 346 (1891).
[3] Copin Albancelli, *Le Pouvoir occulte contre la France,* p. 388.
[4] Series of article entitled " Boche and Bolshevik " by Nesta H. Webster and Herr Kurt Kerlen, which appeared in the *Morning Post* for April 26, 27, June 10, 11, 15, 16, 1922. Reprinted in book form by the Beckwith Company of New York.

of argument adopted by my German opponent, with which on certain points I found myself completely in agreement. I was obliged to recognize that the bar to any real understanding between us lay in the impossibility of persuading him to recognize the principle that all means are not justifiable in order to obtain one's ends.   This is how he expresses himself on the subject :

If Mrs. Webster . . . reproaches Germany for having employed seditious propaganda in the countries of the Allies, it may simply be brought to mind that all is fair in love and war.   In a war, in a fight concerning life and death, one does not look at the weapons which one takes, nor at the values which are destroyed by using the arms.   The only adviser [sic] is, first of all, the success of the fight, the salvation of one's independence.[1]

Until Germany abandons this Machiavellian doctrine it will be impossible to treat her as a civilized Power.

But Herr Kerlen accuses England of pursuing the same Machiavellian policy of encouraging sedition abroad.   Undoubtedly England did propagate Pacifism in Germany and other enemy countries and hoped to bring about a political revolution, that is to say, a rising of the German people against the rulers who had led them into war.   (It should be remembered that all the friends of Germany in this country always declared that the German people did not want the war and were dragged into it unwillingly by the military caste.)   But is there any evidence to show that England ever attempted to engineer a social revolution, to undermine morality and all belief in ordered government, in a word to promote Bolshevism in Germany or elsewhere ?   Herr Kerlen cites the sympathy accorded in this country to the Kerensky revolution.   But England, largely through the influence of the Liberals, had always entertained an exaggerated idea of " Tzarist tyranny," and honestly sympathized with all efforts, however misguided, to " liberate " the Russian people.   Further, throughout the war the Tzar and Tzarina had been ceaselessly represented as faithless to the Allies—a story that we now know to have been an infamous calumny circulated doubtless by enemy agents.   This idea even obtained credence in Conservative circles, misled by false information on the situation in Russia. One must have lived through the spring of 1917 in London to realize how completely not only the public but the authorities were deluded.   What else could be expected when the

[1] *Boche and Bolshevik*, p. 39.

opinion of Socialists was accepted on the matter? I know from personal experience that two of the most important Government departments were completely mistaken even on the subject of Bolshevism, with the result that measures were not taken which might have checked its spread into this country.

In a word, then, the essential difference between the attitude of Germany and England to Russia was that whilst England imagined that the Kerensky revolution would be for the good of Russia as well as for the advantage of the Allies, Germany deliberately introduced into Russia what she knew to be a poison.

Always faithful to the maxim of *divide et impera*, Germany, after bringing Russia to ruin, has at last succeeded in causing dissensions between the Allies. This policy she pursued unremittingly throughout the war. Thus whilst on one hand she was assuring the French that " the English would fight to the last breath of the last Frenchman," General Ludendorff was instructing the Imperial Chancellor that: " We must again and again rub in the sentence in Kuhlmann's speech to the effect that the question of Alsace-Lorraine is the only one which stands in the way of peace. And we must lay special emphasis on the fact that the English people are shedding their blood for an Imperialistic war-aim."[1]

So skilfully was this propaganda carried on after the war had ended that whilst English officers returning to England from the occupied areas were declaring that the friendliness of the Germans convinced them that Germany was really our friend and that we should have an " entente " with her rather than with France, French officers returning to France said that the Germans had assured them that they were their best friends, that England was the real enemy, and that it would be better to break the Entente and form an alliance with Germany. At the same time no less than three lines of propaganda concerning the causes of the war were going out from Germany, one laying all the blame on the English, one on the French, and one on the Jews, and pamphlets embodying these conflicting theories were despatched broadcast to likely subjects in the countries of the Allies.[2]

---

[1] *The General Staff and its Problems,* II. 556.

[2] One of the pamphlets emanating from the first of these lines and entitled "England's War Guilt" reached the present writer. Its purport is to show that " England alone was the chief agent of the war," and that Lord Haldane and Sir Edward Grey, by encouraging Germany to believe that England would not intervene, led her into a trap.

The greatest triumph for Imperial Germany lay in her success in enlisting the very elements amongst the Allies which might most be expected to oppose her. Although there was no country in the world where monarchy was so adored, militarism so universally admired, where rank and birth played so important a part, and the working classes, though cared for, so rigidly kept in subjection, Germany from the time of Bismarck onwards has always been the " spiritual home " of British Socialists, democrats, and pacifists, just as in France she has always found her principal allies in the masonic lodges. And this although the German Socialists and Freemasons have never attempted to use their influence in favour of the masonic and Socialist ideal of universal brotherhood and world-peace, but, on the contrary, at every crisis have thrown in their lot with the military party. Thus before the Franco-Prussian War, whilst French Freemasons of the Loge Concordia and the Socialists of the First Internationale were urging their brothers to rely on German Socialism to avert a conflict, the Prussian lodges were shouting Hoch ! to the national colours and chanting the praises of King William and " the Prussian sword," and the German Social Democrats were applauding the cause of German unity.[1]

Exactly the same thing happened before the recent war, when Jaurès assured his fellow-Socialists that at the first sign of conflict he had only to communicate with Berlin in order to enlist German Socialism in the interests of peace ; yet on the declaration of war the German Socialists voted solidly for war credits, whilst the British Socialists opposed participation in the war and even in some instances expressed sympathy with Germany. And let it never be forgotten, it was not Socialist Germany but Imperial Germany that won the allegiance of our so-called democrats.

In spite of this betrayal by the Socialists of Germany, in spite of the fact that they have contributed nothing to the cause of International Socialism or of world-peace, the British " Labour " Party never until its accession to office wavered in its policy of publicly advocating the cause of Germany. With the exception of the Social Democratic Federation, every Socialist body in this country has proclaimed pro-German sentiments, and *Justice* alone, of all Socialist organs, has expressed its sympathy for the

[1] Georges Goyau, *L'Idée de Patrie et l'Humanitarisme*, p. 111 (1913).

sufferings of France. In fact, any Socialist who dared to champion the cause of France immediately lost his influence and position in Socialist circles. As to the *Daily Herald,* had it been edited in Berlin it could not more faithfully have supported German interests. When Alsace-Lorraine was restored to France, it published an article showing how deeply the inhabitants of this province resented being transferred from the German Empire to the French Republic[1]; when a general strike threatened this country, it seized the opportunity to come out with an appeal in enormous capitals to revise the Versailles Treaty; in the matter of reparations its efforts to let Germany off altogether have been, as it itself observed, " unceasing." " The plain fact is," it declared on December 17, 1921, " that these fantastic reparation demands cannot be met; and that every payment by which Germany attempts to meet them will only work further havoc to our own commerce and our own industry. We have urged that ceaselessly for three years. To-day even the Premier begins to see that we were right, that the interests of this country demand the scrapping of *the whole bad business of ' making Germany pay.'* " [2]

Indeed, when the interests of Germany were concerned, this paper, which Lenin has described as "our own organ," but which might still more truly be claimed by Ludendorff and Stinnes, was quite ready to throw Socialism to the winds and plead the cause of capital. At the very moment that it was advocating the Labour policy of a capital levy on all fortunes exceeding £5,000 in this country, the *Daily Herald* waxed almost tearful over the iniquity of France in attempting to touch the pockets of German multi-millionaires whose profits, it went on to explain elaborately, were not nearly as huge as might appear in view of the decline in the purchasing power of the mark. The decline in the purchasing power of the pound had, however, never been taken into account when assessing the profits of British employers of labour.[3]

---

[1] August 19, 1919.

[2] My italics.

[3] *Daily Herald* for January 26, 1923. So tender a regard did the *Daily Herald* entertain for the feelings of German magnates that its susceptibilities were deeply shocked at the correspondent of another paper, who, after lunching with Herr Thyssen, was so " ungentlemanly " as to comment afterwards on the display of wealth he had witnessed (*Daily Herald* for February 2, 1923). Yet the *Daily Herald* reporter had seen nothing ungentlemanly in attending a garden party at Buckingham Palace and publishing a sneering account of it afterwards under the heading of " Pomp and Farce in the Palace " (date of July 21, 1921).

We have only to follow point by point the policy of the British Labour Party since the war to recognize that whilst the measures it advocated might be of doubtful benefit to the workers, there could be no doubt whatever of the benefit they would confer on Germany. With a million and a quarter unemployed and large numbers of the working classes unable to find homes, the professed representatives of Labour have persistently clamoured for the removal of restrictions on alien immigration and alien imports. So although through the Trade Unions the British worker was to be rigorously protected against competition from his fellow-Briton, no obstacles were to be placed in the way of competition by foreign, and frequently underpaid, labour. That this glaring betrayal of their interests should not have raised a storm of resentment amongst the working classes is surely evidence that the Marxian doctrine " the emancipation of the working classes must be brought about by the working classes themselves "[1] has so far led to no great results. Emerson truly observed: " So far as a man thinks, he is free." The working classes can never be free until they learn to think for themselves instead of allowing their thinking to be done for them by the middle-class exploiters of Labour.

The hand of Germany behind Socialism must be apparent to all those who do not deliberately shut their eyes to the fact, and it is significant to notice that the nearer Socialism approaches to Bolshevism the more marked this influence becomes. Thus although certain Socialist groups, such as the Social Democratic Federation in England and the Socialist Party in France, have not become Germanized, the avowed Communists in all the Allied countries are strongly pro-German. This is the case even in France, where the Bolsheviks find fervent supporters in the group led by Marcel Cachin, Froissart, and Longuet, grandson of Karl Marx.

The organization of the Bolshevist movement has indeed throughout owed a great deal of its efficiency to German co-operation, provided not only by the Socialist but by the Monarchist elements in Germany. It is necessary in this connexion to understand the dual character of the German Monarchist party since the ending of the war. The great majority of its adherents, animated by nothing more reprehensible than the spirit of militarism and an aggressive form of patriotism that clings to the old formula of *Deutschland über*

---

[1] Karl Marx in his *Preamble of the Provisional Rules of the Internationale* (1864).

alles, are probably strangers to any intrigues, but behind this mass of honest Imperialists, and doubtless unknown to a great number, there lurk those sinister organizations the Pan-German secret societies.

Many of these, as for example the *Ostmarkenverein,* ostensibly instituted for the defence of German interests on the Russian frontier, existed before the war; indeed, there is little doubt that they have continued without a break since the days of the Tugendbund and have always preserved their masonic and " illuminized " character. But since the beginning of the Great War, and still more since the Armistice, their numbers have increased until in 1921 they were estimated to run into three figures. Moreover, as in the time of Weishaupt, Bavaria is still a centre for secret-society intrigue, and it was here that Escherich founded the *Einwohnerwehr* sometimes known as the *Orgesch* or Organization Escherich, with Munich as its headquarters. The Orgesch was followed by the formidable murder club known to all the world as the Organization C or " Consul," named after its founder, the famous Captain Ehrhardt, whose nickname was " *der Herr Consul.*" During the year 1921 no less than 400 political assassinations were reported in Germany and said to be the work of secret societies. Amongst the crimes attributed to the initiative of Organization C were the murders of Herr Erzberger and the attempt on the life of Herr Scheidemann. Eighty persons arrested for complicity in the murder of Herr Rathenau were also said to be members of the same society.[1]

But as in the case of all secret societies, the visible leaders were not the real hierarchy; behind this active body there existed an inner circle organised on masonic lines, the Druidenorden, a name unknown to the public, and behind this again another and still more secret circle which appears to be nameless. It is these inner rings which, whilst remaining Monarchist in Germany, work for other ends abroad, and are connected with the world-revolutionary movement.

This alliance between the two extremes of ardent Monarchism and revolutionary Socialism existed at the beginning of the war or even earlier, and, as is now well known, it was the Jewish Social Democrat, Israel Lazarewitch, alias Helphandt alias Parvus, who arranged with the German General Staff

[1] *The Times,* June 30, 1922; the *Morning Post,* June 26 and 30, 1922. A very curious and well-informed article, from which some of these details are taken, appeared in the *West Coast Leader,* Lima, Peru, of December 14, 1921.

12e

for the passage of Lenin from Switzerland to Russia, accompanied by Karl Radek, the Austrian Jew deserter, and a number of other Jews.

Now, Switzerland has been for hundreds of years a centre of revolutionary and secret-society intrigue. As early as the sixteenth century the Pope, writing to the Kings of France and Spain, warned them that Geneva was " un foyer éternel de révolution," and Joseph de Maistre, quoting this letter in 1817, declared Geneva to be the metropolis of the revolutionaries, whose art of deception he describes as "the great European secret."[1] Elsewhere, a year earlier, he had referred to Illuminism as the root of all the evil at work. It is now known that at the moment de Maistre wrote these words an inner ring of revolutionaries, claiming direct descent from Weishaupt and even from an earlier sect existing at the end of the fifteenth century, profited by the fall of Napoleon I to reconstruct its organization and took up its headquarters in Switzerland with branch offices in London and Paris. The same secret ring of Illuminati is believed to have been intimately connected with the organization of the Bolshevist revolution, although none of the leading Bolsheviks are said to have been members of the innermost circle, which is understood to consist of men belonging to the highest intellectual and financial classes whose names remained absolutely unknown. Outside this absolutely secret ring there existed, however, a semi-secret circle of high initiates of subversive societies drawn from all over the world and belonging to various nationalities—German, Jewish, French, Russian, and even Japanese. This group, which might be described as the active ring of the inner circle, appears to have been in touch with, if not in control of, a committee which met in Switzerland to carry out the programme of the Third Internationale.

It was thus in Switzerland that at the same time high initiates of Pan-German secret societies foregathered and that an active centre of pro-German, anti-Entente, and even Bolshevist propaganda was established. These Germans, although Monarchists themselves, co-operated with the secret revolutionary forces in stirring up trouble in the countries of the Allies. At the same time the conferences of the Second Internationale, attended by members of the British I.L.P. took place in Switzerland, and at one of these—the Berne Conference of 1919—the delegates were entertained by a

---

[1] *Lettres inédites de Joseph de Maistre*, p. 415 (1851).

mysterious "American" millionaire, John de Kay, living himself in great style, paying for press service at the rate of 2,000 francs a day, lavishing money on the conference, and at the same time subsidizing a Pacifist and Defeatest paper named *La Feuille*.

It is impossible, then, to ignore the rôle of Germany in the present outbreak of world revolution. In the British White Paper on Bolshevism in Russia we find it stated by an Englishman who had been through the whole of the Revolution in that country that:

The Germans initiated disturbances in order to reduce Russia to chaos. They printed masses of paper money to finance their schemes; the notes, of which I possess specimens, can be easily recognized by a special mark.[1]

What has Germany to say to all this? Simply that the promotion of Bolshevism was a military "necessity" in order to bring about the downfall of her opponents, but that the propaganda utilized by her was in reality of Jewish origin, and that Jewry, not Germany, was the real author of world revolution.

It is easy to see how such a theory can be made to serve the cause of Pan-Germanism. For if Germany can persuade us that the Jews alone were responsible for the war and were also the sole authors of Bolshevism, we shall naturally be led to the conclusion that Germany is, after all, innocent of the crimes attributed to her, and that our only safety lies in forgoing reparations, restoring her to her former power, and coalescing with her against a common enemy. We shall therefore do well to accept with extreme caution advice on the Jewish question emanating from German sources, and to test the sincerity of the spirit in which it is offered by considering the relations which have hitherto existed between the Germans and the Jews.

Now, Germany has long been the home of modern "anti-Semitism." Although in every country and at every period, but more particularly in the East of Europe during the last century, the Jews have suffered from unpopularity, it was Germany that organized this aversion into a definite plan of campaign. If in Russia, Galicia, and Poland the Jews have met with sporadic violence at the hands of the peasants, in Germany they have been systematically held up by the

[1] Letter from the Rev. B. S. Lombard to Lord Curzon, March 23, 1919.

authorities to hatred and contempt. Luther, Kant, Fichte, Schopenhauer, Treitschke, successively inveighed against the Jewish race. Jews were denied admission to masonic lodges and to the rank of officers in the army, whilst society excluded them up to the outbreak of war.

Yet the extraordinary fact remains that of all nations the Germans have always been the favourites of the Jews. Throughout the whole movement for the unification of Germany under the ægis of Prussia, Jews played a leading part, and in the recent war Germany found in them some of her most valuable allies. As Maximilian Harden recently pointed out: " The services of the Jews to Germany during the war were enormous. The patriotism of the Jews was beyond reproach, in many cases even ludicrous and offensive in its intensity." And in spite of " anti-Semitism," Harden declares: " There is a strong affinity between the German and the Jew."[1] To the Ashkenazim Germany even more than Palestine has appeared the Land of Promise. Thus some years before the war Professor Ludwig Geiger, leader of the Liberal Jews of Berlin, denounced " Zionist sophisms " in the words: " The German Jew who has a voice in German literature must, as he has been accustomed to for the last century and a half, look upon Germany alone as his fatherland, upon the German language as his mother-tongue, and the future of that nation must remain the only one upon which he bases his hopes."[2]

How are we to explain this unrequited devotion? Simply by the German policy of enlisting every dynamic force in her service. She has known how to use the Jews just as she has known how to use the Freemasons, the Illuminati, and the Socialists for the purpose of Pan-Germanism. From Frederick the Great, who employed the Jew Ephraim to coin false money, to William II, who kept in touch with Rathenau by means of a private telephone wire, the rulers of Germany have always allowed them to co-operate in their schemes of world-domination. As the allies of Bismarck, who used them freely to fill his war-chests, the Jews directed the power of the secret societies in the interests of Germany; in 1871 the Jew Bloechreider acted as adviser to the new German Empire as to the best method of wresting indemnities from France. And Germany, whilst heaping insults on the Jews, nevertheless fulfils certain conditions essential to Jewish enterprise. Unlike England and France, she has never allowed herself to be seriously weakened

---

[1] *Jewish Guardian* for January 18, 1924.
[2] *Jewish Encyclopædia,* article on Zionism.

by democratic ideas, and therefore to the Jews—as to British believers in autocracy—she represents the principle of stability.

Moreover, Germany as the home of militarism offers a wide field for Jewish speculation. We have only to couple together an aphorism of Mirabeau's with one of Werner Sombart's to perceive the bond of union between the two races, thus: " War is the national industry of Prussia " and " Wars are the Jews' harvests." As long ago as 1793 Anacharsis Clootz, the apostle of universal brotherhood and defender of the Jewish race, declared that if Germany were to be prevented from going to war the Jews must be persuaded to withdraw their support from her military adventures:

War could not begin or last in Germany without the activity, the intelligence, and the money of the Jews. Magazines and munitions of all kinds are provided by Hebrew capitalists and all the subaltern agents of military provisionment are of the same nation. We have only to come to an understanding with our brothers, the Rabbis, to produce astonishing, miraculous results.[1]

Mr. Ford, the American motor-car manufacturer, appears to have arrived at much the same conclusion expressed in the words recently attributed to him: " We don't need the League of Nations to end war. Put under control the fifty most wealthy Jewish financiers, who produce wars for their own profit, and wars will cease."[2]

On another occasion Mr. Ford is reported to have said that the Jews who voyaged with him in the Peace ship in 1915 " went out of their way to convince " him of " the direct relations between the International Jew and the war ": they " went into details to tell me the means by which the Jews controlled the war—how they had the money, how they had cornered all the basic materials needed to fight the war," etc.[3]

Without in any way absolving Germany from the crime of the war, it is necessary to take this secondary factor into consideration if peace between the nations is to be established. For as long as the lust of war lingers in the hearts of the Germans and the lust of gain at the price of human suffering lingers in the hearts of the Jews, both races will remain necessary to each other and the hideous nightmare of war will continue to brood over the world.

[1] *La République universelle,* p. 186 note (1793).
[2] *Daily Mail,* September 21, 1923.
[3] Reported in the *Jewish World,* January 5, 1922.

There is then a great deal of truth in the Socialist phrase " Capitalists' Wars," although not in the sense they attribute to it. For it will be noticed that the Capitalists who are most instrumental in making wars are precisely those whom the Socialists are always careful to shield from blame. The following incident will illustrate this point.

At a meeting of the Social Democratic Federation Mr. Adolphe Smith moved a resolution appealing to the organized workers of Great Britain—

Not to permit themselves in the supposed interests of their fellow-workers in other countries, to be used by sinister financial and militarist influences merely to weaken the Entente nations in the present critical situation, and urging them to keep careful watch against such manœuvres on the part of pro-German international financiers, who were able to exercise considerable reactionary influence among the wealthy and official classes in this country.[1]

Mr. Hyndman added that " the most serious danger by which we were threatened was from the most powerful group of capitalists in Europe headed by Hugo Stinnes and backed by Hindenburg, Ludendorff, and the militarist party in Germany." This resolution was opposed by a member of the Parliamentary Labour Party and eventually withdrawn.

The connexion between German Imperialism, International Finance, Illuminism, Bolshevism, and certain sections of British Socialism is thus apparent. Is Germany then the secret power behind the thing we call Bolshevism ? Are Illuminism and Pan-Germanism one and the same thing ? To this hypothesis two objections present themselves : firstly, that the spirit of Illuminism and Bolshevism existed, as we have seen in earlier chapters of this book, long before modern Germany came into existence ; and secondly, that Germany herself is not entirely free from the contagion. For although the danger of Bolshevism in Germany has been doubtless greatly exaggerated in order to prevent the Allies from pressing their demands for disarmament and reparations, nevertheless Bolshevism under its illuminated name of Spartacism cannot be regarded as a movement entirely staged for the deception of Europe. Moreover, just as in the countries of the Allies it has shown itself, under the guise of Pacifism, savagely anti-national and pro-German, so in Germany, as also in Hungary,

[1] *Morning Post* for August 1, 1921.

it turned Pacifism to the opposite purpose by professing sympathy at moments with the Allies.

It is clear, then, that besides Pan-Germanism there is another power at work, a power far older, that seeks to destroy all national spirit, all ordered government in every country, Germany included. What is this power? A large body of opinion replies: the Jewish power.

15

THE REAL JEWISH PERIL

IN considering the immense problem of the Jewish Power, perhaps the most important problem with which the modern world is confronted, it is necessary to divest oneself of all prejudices and to enquire in a spirit of scientific detachment whether any definite proof exists that a concerted attempt is being made by Jewry to achieve world-domination and to obliterate the Christian faith.

That such a purpose has existed amongst the Jews in the past has been shown throughout the earlier chapters of this book. The conception of the Jews as the Chosen People who must eventually rule the world forms indeed the basis of Rabbinical Judaism.

It is customary in this country to say that we should respect the Jewish religion, and this would certainly be our duty were the Jewish religion founded, as is popularly supposed, solely on the Old Testament. For although we do not consider ourselves bound to observe the ritual of the Pentateuch, we find no fault with the Jews for carrying out what they conceive to be their religious duties. Moreover, although the Old Testament depicts the Jews as a favoured race—a conception which we believe to have been superseded by the Christian dispensation, whereby all men are declared equal in the sight of God—nevertheless it does contain a very lofty law of righteousness applicable to all mankind. It is because of their universality that the books of Job and Ecclesiastes, as also many passages in the Psalms, in Isaiah, and the minor prophets, have made an undying appeal to the human race. But the Jewish religion now takes its stand on the Talmud rather than on the Bible. "The modern Jew," one of its latest Jewish translators observes, "is the product of the Talmud."[1] The Talmud itself accords to the Bible only a secondary place. Thus the Talmudic treatise Soferim says: "The Bible is like

[1] Michael Rodkinson (i.e. Rodkinssohn), in Preface to translation of the Talmud, Vol. I. p. x.

water, the Mischna is like wine, and the Gemara is like spiced wine."

Now, the Talmud is not a law of righteousness for all mankind, but a meticulous code applying to the Jew alone. No human being outside the Jewish race could possibly go to the Talmud for help or comfort. One might look through its pages in vain for any such splendid rule of life as that given by the prophet Micah: " He hath shewed thee, O man, what is good; and what doth the Lord require of thee, but to do justly, and to love mercy, and to walk humbly with thy God?" In the Talmud, on the contrary, as Drach points out, " the precepts of justice, of equity, of charity towards one's neighbour, are not only not applicable with regard to the Christian, but constitute a crime in anyone who would act differently. . . . The Talmud expressly forbids one to save a non-Jew from death, . . . to restore lost goods, etc., to him, to have pity on him."[1]

How far the Talmud has contributed to the anti-social tendencies of modern Judaism is shown by the fact that the Karaites living in the south of Russia, the only body of Jews which takes its stand on the Bible, and not on the Talmud, —of which it only accepts such portions as are in accordance with Bible teaching—have always shown themselves good subjects of the Russian Empire, and have therefore enjoyed equal rights with the Russian people around them. Catherine the Great particularly favoured the Karaites.

Thus even the Jews are not unanimous in supporting the Talmud; indeed, as we have already seen, many Jews have protested against it as a barrier between themselves and the rest of the human race.

But it is in the Cabala, still more than in the Talmud, that the Judaic dream of world-domination recurs with the greatest persistence. The Zohar indeed refers to this as a *fait accompli*, explaining that " the Feast of Tabernacles is the period when Israel triumphs over the other people of the world; that is why during this feast we seize the Loulab [branches of trees tied together] and carry it as a trophy to show that we have conquered all the other peoples known as ' populace ' and that we dominate them."[2] God is, however, asked to accord these other peoples a certain share of blessings, " so that

[1] Drach, *De l'Harmonie entre l'Élise et la Synagogue*, I. 167, quoting the treatise Aboda-Zara, folio 13 verso, and folio 20 recto; also treatise Baba Kamma, folio 29 verso. Drach adds: " We could multiply these quotations almost to infinity."

[2] Zohar, section Toldoth Noah, folio 63b (de Pauly's trans., I. 373).

occupied with this share they shall not participate nor mingle with the joy of Israel when he calls down blessings from on high." The situation may thus be compared with that of a king who, wishing to give a feast to his special friends, finds his house invaded by importunate governors demanding admittance. " What then does the king do? He orders the governors to be served with beef and vegetables, which are common food, and then sits down to table with his friends and has the most delicious dishes served."[1]

But this is nothing to the feasting that is to take place when the Messianic era arrives. After the return of the Jews from all nations and parts of the world to Palestine, the Messiah, we are told in the Talmud, will entertain them at a gorgeous banquet, where they will be seated at golden tables and regaled with wine from Adam's wine-cellar. The first course is to consist of a roasted ox named Behemoth, so immense that every day it eats up the grass upon a thousand hills; the second of a monstrous fish Leviathan; the third of a female Leviathan boiled and pickled; the fourth of a gigantic roast fowl known as Barjuchne, of which the egg alone was so enormous that when it fell out of the nest it crushed three hundred tall cedars and the white overflowed threescore villages. This course is to be followed up by " the most splendid and pompous Dessert " that can be procured, including fruit from the Tree of Life and " the Pomegranates of Eden which are preserved for the Just."

At the end of the banquet " God will entertain the company at a ball "; He Himself will sit in the midst of them, and everyone will point Him out with his finger, saying: " Behold, this is our God: we have waited for Him, we will be glad and rejoice in His salvation."[2]

The eighteenth-century commentator, whose summary of these passages we quote, goes on to observe:

But let us see a little after what manner the Jews are to live in their ancient Country under the Administration of the Messiah. In the First Place, the strange Nations, which they shall suffer to live, shall build them Houses and Cities, till them Ground, and

[1] Zohar, section Toldoth Noah, folio 64b (de Pauly's trans., I. 376).
[2] J. P. Stehelin, *The Traditions of the Jews*, II. 215-20, quoting Talmud treatises Baba Bathra folio 74b, Pesachim folio 32, Bekhoroth folio 57, Massektoth Ta'anith folio 31. The Zohar also refers to the female Leviathan (section Bô, de Pauly's trans., III. 167). Drach shows that amongst the delights promised by the Talmud after the return to Palestine will be the permission to eat pork and bacon.—*De l'Harmonie entre l'Église et la Synagogue*, I. 265, 276, quoting treatise Hullin, folio 17, 82.

plant them Vineyards; and all this, without so much as looking for any Reward of their Labour. These surviving Nations will likewise voluntarily offer them all their Wealth and Furniture: And Princes and Nobles shall attend them; and be ready at their Nod to pay them all Manner of Obedience; while they themselves shall be surrounded with Grandeur and Pleasure, appearing abroad in Apparel glittering with Jewels like Priests of the Unction, consecrated to God. . . .

In a word, the felicity of this Holy Nation, in the Times of the Messiah, will be such, that the exalted Condition of it cannot enter into the Conception of Man; much less can it be couched in human Expression. This is what the Rabbis say of it. But the intelligent reader will doubtless pronounce it the Paradise of Fools.[1]

It is interesting to notice that this conception of the manner in which the return to Palestine is to be carried out has descended to certain of the modern colonists. Sir George Adam Smith, after watching Zionism at work in 1918, wrote:

On visiting a recently established Jewish colony in the north-east of the land, round which a high wall had been built by the munificent patron, I found the colonists sitting in its shade gambling away the morning, while groups of *fellahin* at a poor wage did the cultivation for them. I said that this was surely not the intention of their patron in helping them to settle on land of their own. A Jew replied to me in German: " Is it not written: The sons of the alien shall be your ploughmen and vinedressers?" I know that such delinquencies have become the exception in Jewish colonization of Palestine, but they are symptomatic of dangers which will have to be guarded against.

The fellahin may, however, consider themselves lucky to be allowed to live at all, for, according to several passages in the Cabala, all the *goyim* are to be swept off the face of the earth when Israel comes into its own. Thus the Zohar relates that the Messiah will declare war on the whole world and all the kings of the world will end by declaring war on the Messiah. But " the Holy One, blessed be He, will display His force and exterminate them from the world."[3] Then:

Happy will be the lot of Israel, whom the Holy One, blessed be He, has chosen from amongst the *goyim* of whom the Scriptures

[1] Stehelin, op. cit., II. 221-4.
[2] The Very Rev. Sir George Adam Smith, *Syria and the Holy Land*, p. 49 (1918).
[3] Zohar, section Schemoth, folio 7 and 9b; section Beschalah, folio 58b (de Pauly's trans., III. 32, 36, 41, 260).

say: "Their work is but vanity, it is an illusion at which we must laugh; they will all perish when God visits them in His wrath." At the moment when the Holy One, blessed be He, will exterminate all the *goyim* of the world, Israel alone will subsist, even as it is written: "The Lord alone will appear great on that day."[1]

The hope of world-domination is therefore not an idea attributed to the Jews by "anti-Semites," but a very real and essential part of their traditions. What then of their attitude to Christianity in the past? We have already seen that hatred of the person and teaching of Christ did not end at Golgotha, but was kept alive by the Rabbis and perpetuated in the Talmud and the Toledot Yeshu. The Cabala also contains passages referring both to Christ and to Mohammed so unspeakably foul that it would be impossible to quote them here.

But it will be urged: the Jews of Western Europe to-day know nothing of the Cabala. This may be so, yet imperceptibly the Cabala has moulded the mind of the Jew. As a modern Jewish writer has declared:

[Kabbalism] has contributed to the formation of modern Judaism, for, without the influence of the Kabbala, Judaism to-day might have been one-sided, lacking in warmth and imagination. Indeed, so deeply has it penetrated into the body of the faith that many ideas and prayers are now immovably rooted in the general body of ortho-dox doctrine and practice. This element has not only become in-corporated, but it has fixed its hold on the affections of the Jews and cannot be eradicated.[2]

It is thus not in the law of Moses thundered from Sinai, not in the dry ritual of the Talmud, but in the stupendous imaginings of the Cabala, that the real dreams and aspirations of Jewry have been transmitted through the ages. Belief in the coming Messiah may burn low, but faith in the final triumph of Israel over the other nations of the world still glows in the hearts of a race nurtured on this hope from time immemorial. Even the free-thinking Jew must unconsciously react to the promptings of this vast and ancient ambition. As a modern French writer has expressed it:

Assuredly sectarian Freethinkers swarm, who flatter themselves on having borrowed nothing from the synagogue and on hating

---

[1] Ibid., section Vayschlah, folio 177*b* (de Pauly's trans., II. p. 298).
[2] Hastings' *Encyclopædia of Religion and Ethics*, article on the Kabbala by H. Loewe.

equally Jehovah and Jesus. But the modern Jewish world is itself also detached from any supernatural belief, and the Messianic tradition, of which it preserves the cult, reduces itself to considering the Jewish race as the veritable Messiah.[1]

Some colour is lent to this statement by an article which recently appeared in the Jewish press, in which it is explained that, according to the teaching of the " Liberal Jewish Synagogue," the beautiful passages in the fifty-third chapter of Isaiah concerning " the Man of Sorrows acquainted with grief," usually supposed by Christians to relate to the promised Messiah, are interpreted to modern Jewish youth as relating to Israel and signifying that Israel's " sufferings were caused by the sins of other nations," who thus " escaped the suffering they deserved." Consequently " Israel has suffered for the sake of the whole world."[2] How this amazing pretension can be maintained in view of the perpetual denunciations of the Israelites throughout the whole of the Old Testament is difficult to imagine. On their entry into Canaan they were distinctly told by Moses that the Lord their God had not given them " this good land " on account of their righteousness or the uprightness of their hearts[3]; long afterwards Daniel declared that all Israel had transgressed the law of God[4]; Nehemiah showed that on account of their rebellion and disobedience they had been delivered into the hands of their enemies.[5] Isaiah spoke of the iniquities of Judah in burning words:

Ah sinful nation, a people laden with iniquity, a seed of evil-doers, children that are corruptors! . . . Wash your, make you clean; put away the evil of your doings from before Mine eyes; cease to do evil; learn to do well, etc.

Thus even the Word of God itself is powerless to mitigate the immense megalomania of the Jewish race. It is doubtful indeed whether by the majority of Jews the Bible is now regarded as divinely inspired. " The ten commandments which *we* gave to mankind "[7] is a phrase typical of the manner in which Israel now arrogates to itself the sole authorship of the Scriptures. The deification of humanity by the Freemasons of the Grand Orient finds its counterpart in the deification of Israel by the modern Jew.

[1] Eugène Tavernier, *La Religion Nouvelle*, p. 265 (1905).
[2] *Jewish Guardian* for January 25, 1924.
[3] Deuter. ix. 5.   [4] Dan. ix. 11.   [5] Neh. ix. 26.
[6] Isa. i. 1-17. See also Ezek. xx. 13.
[7] *Jewish Guardian* for October 1, 1920.

It is here that we must surely see the cause of much of the suffering the Jews have endured in the past. No one of course would justify the cruelty with which they have frequently been treated; nevertheless to maintain there was no provocation on the part of the Jews would be absurd. A race that has always considered itself entitled to occupy a privileged position amongst the nations of the world must inevitably meet with resentment, and in a primitive age or population resentment is apt to find a vent in violence shocking to the civilized mind. Moreover, to represent the Jews as a gentle long-suffering people, always the victims but never the perpetrators of violence, is absolutely contrary to historic fact. In the dark ages of the past the Jews showed themselves perfectly capable of cruelties not only towards other races but towards each other. One of the first pogroms recorded in the Christian era was carried out by the Jews themselves. The Jewish historian Josephus describes the reign of "lawlessness and barbarity" that was inaugurated about the middle of the first century A.D. by the band of assassins known as the Sicarii, who infested the country round Jerusalem and, by means of little daggers that they wore concealed beneath their garments, "slew men in the daytime and in the midst of the city, especially at the festivals when they mixed with the multitude." During one night raid on the small town of Engaddi they massacred more than seven hundred women and children.[1] And Josephus goes on to say:

Somehow, indeed, that was a time most fertile in all manner of wicked practices among the Jews, insomuch that no kind of villainy was then left undone; nor could anyone so much as devise any bad thing that was new if he wished. So deeply were they all infected, both privately and publicly, and vied with one another who should run the greatest lengths in impiety towards God, and in unjust actions towards their neighbours, men in power oppressing the multitude, and the multitude earnestly endeavouring to destroy men in power.[2]

It is futile then to maintain as do the Jews and their friends —for the pro-Jew is frequently *plus royaliste que le roi*—that all the faults of the modern Jew are to be attributed to bitterness engendered by persecution. Judaism has always contained an element of cruelty[3] which finds expression in the

[1] Josephus, *The Jewish War* (Eng. trans.), IV. 170, 334.
[2] Ibid., V. 152.
[3] See, for example, the descriptions of the horrible cruelty practised in the Jewish schools of Poland in the eighteenth century, given in *The Autobiography of Solomon Maimon* (Eng. trans., 1888), p. 32.

Talmud. It is from the Talmud, not from the Mosaic law, that the inhuman methods of Jewish slaughtering are derived.[1] The Talmud likewise gives the most horrible directions for carrying out capital punishment, particularly with regard to women, by the methods of stoning, burning, choking, or slaying with the sword. The victim condemned to be burnt is to have a scarf wound round his neck, the two ends pulled tightly by the executioners whilst his mouth is forced open with pincers and a lighted string thrust into it " so that it flows down through his inwards and shrinks his entrails."[2]

It will be said that all this belongs to the past. True, the practice here described may be considered obsolete, but the spirit of cruelty and intolerance that dictated it is still alive. One has only to study the modern Jewish press to realize the persecution to which Jews are subjected from members of their own race should they infringe one fraction of the Jewish code.

If, then, " the modern Jew is the product of the Talmud," it is here that we must see the principal obstacle to Jewish progress. It is said that Isaac Disraeli, the father of Lord Beaconsfield, gave as his reason for withdrawing from the Synagogue that Rabbinical Judaism with its unyielding laws and fettering customs " cuts off the Jews from the great family of mankind."[3] Such a system is indeed absolutely incompatible not only with Christian teaching but with the secular ideas of Western civilization. The attitude it adopts towards women would be in itself sufficient to justify this assertion. The Jewish daily prayer, " Blessed be Thou, O Lord our God, King of the universe, that Thou has not made me a woman! "[4] is a ludicrous anachronism in the present age. According to the Talmud a service can take place in the Synagogue only if ten persons are present, which number ensures the presence of God in the assembly. Drach explains however that these persons must all be men. " If then there were nine men and a million women there could be no assembly, for the reason that women are nothing. But there arrives [on the scene] only one small boy of thirteen years and a day,

---

[1] Treatise Hullin, folio 27a.
[2] Talmud, treatise Sanhedrim (Rodkinson's trans., p. 156).
[3] *Encyclopædia Britannica* (1911 edition), article on Lord Beaconsfield.
[4] Drach, *De l'Harmonie entre l'Église et la Synagogue*, II. 336. This custom is still in force; see the very legitimate complaint of a Jewess in the *Jewish World* for December 21, 1923, that women are stil relegated to the gallery " to be hidden behind the grille, whence they may hear their menfolk bless the Almighty in strident tones that ' Thou hast not made me a woman.' "

at once there can be a holy assembly and, according to our
Doctors, it is permitted to God to be present."[1]

When therefore we say that we must respect the Jewish
religion we cannot, if we know anything about it, mean that
we respect that portion of it which is founded on the Rabbinical
traditions of the Talmud and the Cabala, but only that ethical
law set forth in the Old Testament, to which right-living Jews
have faithfully adhered and which is largely in accord with
Christian teaching.

Let us not forget that Rabbinical Judaism is the declared
and implacable enemy of Christianity. Hatred of Christianity
and of the person of Christ is not a matter of remote history,
nor can it be regarded as the result of persecution; it forms
an integral part of Rabbinical tradition which originated before
any persecution of the Jews by Christians had taken place,
and has continued in our country long after all such persecution
has ended.

It is here that we cannot fail to detect the origin of much
of that virulent anti-Christian teaching that is being disseminated in our midst to-day. This teaching will be observed to
follow three lines, of which the course has been traced throughout this book. These consist in desecrating the Christian
tradition by declaring that Christ was either (a) a myth,
(b) a purely human teacher endowed with superior virtue and
knowledge of natural laws, (c) a crazy fanatic[2] or a malefactor.
The first two theories are, as we have seen, those held by secret
societies; the last is essentially Jewish. It is true that
there is now a movement amongst the more enlightened Jews
to recognize Jesus as a great teacher; so far, unfortunately,
this is met by bitter hostility from the rest, and in the current
Jewish press contemptuous and even blasphemous references
to Christ and the Christian faith frequently occur. The fact
that here in England, for nearly three hundred years, the
Jews have been allowed to dwell in peace and carry out their
religious rites unmolested, that they have been admitted to
society, to masonic lodges, and to all offices of State and have
met with increasing tolerance and favour, has done nothing
to moderate that hatred of Christianity inculcated throughout

[1] Drach, op. cit., II. 335, 336, quoting Talmud, treatise Meghilla folio 23
verso, treatise Berachoth folio 21 verso, treatise Sanhedrim folio 2 recto,
Maimonides chap. viii. art 6; Schulchan Arukh, etc.
[2] In this connexion see article on "Jesus" in the *Jewish Encyclopædia*,
where the reader is referred to the work of O. Holtzmann (*War Jesus Eksta-
tiker?*), who "agrees that there must have been abnormal mental processes
involved in the utterances and behaviour of Jesus."

nineteen centuries of Rabbinical teaching. Thus, for example, under the heading of " What Christianity has Meant," we read in a modern Jewish periodical:

We are thinking of what Christianity as an institution has meant to us Jews. The twenty centuries of its existence have been coeval with the long-drawn tragedy of the Jew's dispersal among the nations. . . . What kindliness and consideration we have received at the hands of Christianity has for the most part been tendered with the lure of the baptismal font. To the extent to which Christianity's embodiment, the Church, has been puissant has the Jewish tragedy deepened. Only when and where the Church has been weak has life been tolerable for the Jew. . . . Hatred of the Jew, anti-Jewish outbursts and anti-Semitic campaigns, are traceable to nothing so surely as to antipathy to the Jew which has been inbred by Christianity. . . . There is thus precious little about which the Jew has for rejoicing and gladness in the institution of Christianity, etc.[1]

The most cursory study of history would reveal the falseness of this contention. Antipathy to the Jew began long before the Christian era; in Egypt, Persia, and Rome he became, whether just or not, the object of suspicion to rulers. The reason given by Pharaoh for oppressing the Israelites was that if they were allowed to grow too powerful they might join themselves to the enemy in time of war[2]; the Emperors of Rome regarded them as a turbulent element; Mohammed declared: " Their aim will be to abet disorder on the earth, but God loveth not the abettors of disorder."[3] Meanwhile, the antipathy shown by the " people " in every country was mainly based on economic grounds. It was not simply the possession of wealth—which according to the Socialist creed should justify any amount of hatred—but the manner in which it was acquired and the arrogance with which it was displayed that roused popular feeling against the Jews. An Arab Fakih, Abu Ishak of Elvira, thus warned his master of the growing power of the Jews in Spain in the middle of the eleventh century A.D.:

The Jews, contemptible outcasts, have become great lords, and their pride and arrogance know no bounds. . . . Take not such men for thy ministers, but abandon them to curses, for the whole earth crieth out against them—ere long it will quake and we shall all

---

[1] *Jewish World* for December 22, 1920.
[2] Exod. i. 10.
[3] Sura v. 60 (Everyman's Library edition, p. 493).

perish. Turn thine eyes to other lands and behold how the Jews are treated as dogs, and kept apart. . . .

I came to Granada, and there I beheld the Jews reigning. They had parcelled out the provinces and the capital between them: everywhere one of these accursed ruled. They collected the taxes, they made good cheer, they were sumptuously clad, while your garments, O Moslems, were old and worn-out. All the secrets of state were known to them; yet is it folly to put trust in traitors! While believers ate the bread of poverty, they dined delicately in the palace. . . . How can we thrive if we live in the shade and the Jews dazzle us with the glory of their pride?[1]

In mediæval France the chief cause for complaint against the Jews is that of not working with their hands but of enriching themselves by " excessive usury." In the fifteenth century the Strasbourg preacher Geyler asks: " Are the Jews above the Christians? Why will they not work with their hands? . . . practising usury is not working. It is exploiting others whilst remaining idle."[2] Such quotations as these might be multiplied *ad infinitum*.

To attribute the persecution of the Jews to Christianity is therefore ludicrous. That in a less enlightened age the Church should have adopted rigorous measures—although no more rigorous than their own laws demanded—against those Jews who practised magic and witchcraft must appear deplorable to the modern mind, but so must many other phases of mediæval life. Why then hark back perpetually to the past? If the Jews were persecuted in a less enlightened age, so were many other sections of the community. Catholics were persecuted, Protestants were persecuted, men were placed in the stocks for minor offences, scolding women were ducked in the village pond. But if all these cruelties of the dark ages are to be remembered and perpetuated on the plan of a tribal blood-feud, what peace can there be for the world? The disastrous results of this tendency were seen in the Irish Intellectuals, nourished from infancy on the story of Ireland's wrongs, who, instead of sanely facing present problems, unhinged their minds by brooding on historic grievances, thereby sealing their own doom and plunging their country into ruin. So, too, the enraged Feminists, harking back to injustices that had long ceased to exist, embittered their lives by proclaiming themselves the eternal enemies of Man. Emerson, the prophet of sanity, declared: " The only ballast I know is a respect to

---

[1] Reinhardt Dozy, *Spanish Islam* (Eng. trans.), p. 651.
[2] J. Denais-Darnays, *Les Juifs en France*, p. 17 (1907).

the present hour." It is for lack of this ballast that the Jews have become victims of a fanaticism in which Christians from a mistaken idea of kindness have frequently encouraged them. In reality nothing is more cruel than to encourage in the minds of a nervous race the idea of persecution; true kindness to the Jews would consist in urging them to throw off memories of past martyrdom and to enter healthfully into the enjoyment of their present blessings, which are the direct outcome of Christian civilization.

Let us consider what Christianity has in reality done for the Jews. If so much is to be said about the persecutions they have endured, what of the extraordinary indulgence shown them as the result of Christian respect for the Bible?   For hundreds of years Christian school children have been brought up on Old Testament history and Christian congregations have listened sympathetically to the story of Israel's sufferings and hopes of final restoration.   All the support lent to Zionism arose from this tradition.   Christianity, then, so reviled by the Jews, has been their greatest protection.   If Christianity goes, the whole theory that the Jews were once the Chosen People goes with it as far as Gentiles are concerned, and the Jewish race, divested of its halo of divine favour, will have to be judged on its own merits.

In our own country, the Chosen People theory has in fact been carried to the point of superstition—a superstition immensely advantageous to the Jews—which consists in interpreting the passage of Scripture containing the promise made to Abraham, " I will bless them that bless thee, and curse them that curseth thee," as meaning that favour shown to the Jews—who form merely a fraction of the seed of Abraham —brings with it peculiar blessings.   In reality it would be easier to show by history that countries and rulers who have protected the Jews have frequently met with disaster.   France banished the Jews in 1394 and again in 1615, and did not readmit them in large numbers till 1715-19, so that they were absent throughout the most glorious period in French history—the *Grand Siècle* of Louis XIV—whilst their return coincided with the Regency, from which moment the monarchy of France may be said to have declined.   England likewise banished the Jews in 1290, and it was during the three and a half centuries they remained in exile that she was known as " Merrie England."   The fact that their return in force in 1664 was followed the next year by the Great Plague and the year after by the Great Fire of London would not appear to indicate that the Jews necessarily bring good fortune to the land that protects them. The truth is, of course, that kindness to any portion of the human race brings its own reward in the form of moral improvement in the individual or nation that performs it, but no more benefit attaches to philanthropy when exercised towards the Jew than towards the Chinaman.

I would urge, then, that the Jewish problem should be approached neither in the spirit of superstitious pro-Semitism nor in the bitter spirit of " anti-Semitism," but with a sanity worthy of an enlightened age. To quote again the words of Bernard Lazare, let us enquire what part " the Jew, consider-ing his spirit, his character, the nature of his philosophy and his religion," may now be taking " in revolutionary processes and movements." Is there, then, any evidence that there exists amongst Jewry to-day an organized conspiracy having for its objects world-domination and the destruction of Chris-tianity such as the famous *Protocols of the Elders of Zion* suggest?[1]

The theory of a Jewish world-conspiracy does not, of course, rest on the evidence of Protocols. To judge by the pæans of joy that rang through the press after the publication of the *Times* articles, one would imagine that with the so-called " refutation " of this one document the whole case against the Jews had collapsed and that the " anti-Semites " must be for ever silenced. But the arguments of the Jews and their friends go further than this; not only do they claim that there is no Jewish conspiracy, but no world-plot of any kind. This contention they had indeed maintained from the begin-ning, and Mr. Lucien Wolf, in his earliest " refutation " of the Protocols, derided the exponents of the secret-society danger as vehemently as he derided the perfidious author of the Jewish Peril. It will in fact always be noticed that references to the Illuminati meet with almost as much resentment from the Jewish press as allusions of a directly " anti-Semitic " character. Barruel, who refused to incriminate the Jews, and de Malet, who never referred to them at all, are denounced by Mr. Lucien Wolf no less as scaremongers than Gougenot des Mousseaux or Chabauty. To suggest that any Hidden Hand has ever been at work in the world is to raise immediately a storm of Jewish protest.

Yet intelligent Jews must be well aware that, whether secret societies have contributed as much to past revolutions

[1] On the question of the Protocols, see Appendix II.

as these writers believed, their existence and their very real influence is not a matter of surmise but of historical fact. No one ever warned the British public more distinctly of the danger they presented or of the rôle the Jews were playing in them than Disraeli, whose famous words have been quoted so frequently in this connexion: " The world is governed by very different personages from what is imagined by those who are not behind the scenes." What is this but a clear recognition of the Hidden Hand? Why, then, is Disraeli not included with Barruel, Robison, de Malet, and Des Mousseaux in Mr. Wolf's list of scaremongers? Is it because Disraeli pointed the moral that, Jews being so dangerous, they should be employed?

If, then, leading Jews persist in villifying everyone who reiterates the warnings uttered by so eminent a member of their race, it is inevitable that they should come to be suspected of having some interest in suppressing further revelations.

Setting all such evidence as the Protocols completely aside, let us examine the reasons for believing in the exisence of a Jewish world-conspiracy. Now, we know for certain that the five powers before referred to—Grand Orient Masonry, Theosophy, Pan-Germanism, International Finance, and Social Revolution—have a very real existence and exercise a very definite influence on the affairs of the world. Here we are not dealing with hypothesis but with facts based on documentary evidence. We know in each case the names of many of the leaders, their methods of organization, their centres of direction, and the aims they are pursuing. But with regard to the Jewish power we cannot proceed with the same certainty. We cannot cite the names of the leaders or the centres of direction, we cannot produce documentary evidence as to their methods of organization or their final aims. The very existence of such a power, in the sense of a united and organized body of Jews working for the destruction of Christianity and the existing social system, is still a matter of speculation and not of known fact. Investigations into the activities of such groups as the B'nai B'rith, Poale Zion, the Jewish Bund, and the Weltverband (or Jewish International Union of Socialists), might however throw much light on this question. The custom of printing their pidgin German, known as Yiddish, in Hebrew characters provides the Jews with a more or less secret code by means of which their ideas and aspirations are concealed from the great mass of the Gentiles.

Whether then the Jewish power is unified or not, Jews are to be found co-operating with, if not directing, all the five powers of which the existence is known. Thus Jews have long played a leading part in Grand Orient Masonry[1] and predominate in the upper degrees. As we have already seen, Freemasonry is always said to be subversive in Roman Catholic countries. It will also be noticed that in countries where Freemasonry is subversive, Jews are usually less conspicuous in the revolutionary movement than in countries where Freemasonry is either non-existent or constitutional. Thus in France the masonic peril is much more generally recognized than the Jewish peril; in Italy the Freemasons have been banned by Mussolini, but the Jews are not regarded by him as a particular danger; in Portugal it was the Freemasons rather than the Jews who made the recent revolutions. In Hungary, however, the revolutionaries were principally both Jews and Freemasons. On the other hand, in England, Germany, and America, where Freemasonry is not subversive, the Jewish question is more apparent. All this would suggest that either Freemasonry is the cover under which the Jews, like the Illuminati, prefer to work, so that where the cover is not available they are obliged to come out more into the open, or that Grand Orient Masonry is the directing power which employs Jews as agents in those countries where it cannot work on its own account.

The preponderance of Jews in the ranks of " Aurora " has already been indicated, as also the influence of the Jewish Cabala in the teaching of Theosophy and Rosicrucianism. But it is important that the latter point should be further emphasized in connexion with the craze for occultism that is spreading through society. Ragon has said: " The Cabala is the key of all occult sciences "; therefore in this field of experiment the Gentile must always be at a disadvantage with the Jew. Indeed Mr. Waite, who certainly cannot be suspected of " anti-Semitism," goes so far as to suggest that the gift of ceremonial magic was " the answer of Jewry to Christendom as a counter-blast " to " centuries of persecution."[2] It would be well if every Gentile who has been tempted to dabble in occultism were to realize this source of inspiration.

The rôle of Jews in social revolution and particularly in Bolshevism hardly needs comment. Yet since the Jewish press has chosen to deny this last and very obvious fact and

[1] " Jews have been most conspicuous in connexion with Freemasonry in France since the Revolution."—*Jewish Encyclopædia*, article on Freemasonry.
[2] A. E. Waite, *The Secret Tradition in Freemasonry*, II. 115.

still persists in setting down to prejudice or " anti-Semitism "
a mere statement of facts, it may be well to quote here a few
official statements on the subject which admit of no denial.

First of all, it must be remembered that the founder and
patron saint of Bolshevism was the Jew Karl Marx, and that
it was the Anarchist Bakunin, not the Duke of Northumberland, who described him and his following in the Internationale
as " the German-Jew Company " and the " red bureaucracy."
It was therefore not surprising that when the " red bureaucracy," avowedly founded on the doctrines of Marx, came to
be set up in Russia, it should have been largely led by Jews.
This is what the official British White Paper has to say on the
matter:

*Extract from Report from the Netherlands Minister at Petro-
grad on the 6th of September, 1918, forwarded by Sir M.
Findlay, at Christiania, to Mr. Balfour:*

I consider that the immediate suppression of Bolshevism is the
greatest issue now before the world, not even excluding the war
which is still raging, and unless, as above stated, Bolshevism is
nipped in the bud immediately, it is bound to spread in one form
or another over Europe and the whole world, as it is organized and
worked by Jews who have no nationality, and whose one object
is to destroy for their own ends the existing order of things.[*1]

Mr. Alston to Lord Curzon, quoting statement from British
Consul at Ekaterinburg, January 23, 1919:

The Bolsheviks can no longer be described as a political party
holding extreme communistic views. They form a relatively small
privileged class which is able to terrorize the rest of the population
because it has a monopoly both of arms and of food supplies. This
class consists chiefly of workmen and soldiers, and includes a large
non-Russian element, such as Letts and Esthonians and Jews; the
latter are specially numerous in higher posts.

Lord Kilmarnock to Lord Curzon, quoting information given
by Frenchman from Petrograd, February 3, 1919:

The Bolsheviks comprised chiefly Jews and Germans, who were
exceedingly active and enterprising. The Russians were largely anti-
Bolshevik, but were for the most part dreamers, incapable of any
sustained action, who now, more than ever before, were unable to
throw off the yoke of their oppressors.[*1]

---

[1] It is significant to notice that in the second and abridged edition of the
white Paper issued by the Foreign Office these two most important passages
marked with an asterisk were omitted and the first edition was said to be
unobtainable.

Mr. Alston to Lord Curzon, forwarding Report from Consul at Ekaterinburg of February 6, 1919:

From examination of several labourer and peasant witnesses, I have evidence to the effect that very smallest percentage of this district were pro-Bolshevik, majority of labourers sympathizing with summoning of Constituent Assembly. Witnesses further stated that Bolshevik leaders did not represent Russian working classes, most of them being Jews.

The Rev. B. S. Lombard to Lord Curzon, March 23, 1919:

I have been for ten years in Russia, and have been in Petrograd through the whole of the revolution. . . . [I] had ample opportunity of studying Bolshevik methods. It originated in German propaganda, and was, and is being, carried out by international Jews. The Germans initiated disturbances in order to reduce Russia to chaos. They printed masses of paper money to finance their schemes, the notes, of which I possess specimens, can be easily recognized by a special mark.

As one of the results, the writer adds:

All business became paralysed, shops were closed, Jews became possessors of most of the business houses, and horrible scenes of starvation became common in the country districts.

In Hungary (where, as has been said, Socialism had been propagated by Jews in the masonic lodges[1]) the outbreak of Bolshevism was conducted under the auspices of the same race. To quote again an official document on this question, the Report on Revolutionary Activities issued by a Committee of the New York Legislature, headed by Senator Lusk[2]:

There was no organized opposition to Bela Kun. Like Lenin, he surrounded himself with commissars, having absolute authority. Of the thirty-two principal commissars, twenty-five were Jews, which was about the same proportion as in Russia. The most prominent of these formed a directorate of five: Bela Kun, Bela Varga, Joseph Pogany, Sigmund Kunfi, and one other. Other leaders

---

[1] On this point see also a very interesting pamphlet *From Behind the Vail*, published by Victor Hornyanszky (Budapest, 1920), also Madame Cécile Tormay, *The Diary of an Outlaw* (1923).
[2] *Revolutionary Radicalism, its History, Purpose, and Tactics, with an Exposition and Discussion of the Steps being taken and required to curb it, being the Report of the Joint Legislative Committee investigating Seditious Activities, filed April 24, 1920. in the Senate of the State of New York* (Albany, J. B. Lyon Company, Printers, 1920).

were Alpari and Samuely, who had charge of the Red Terror, and carried out the torturing and executing of the bourgeoisie, especially the groups held as hostages, the so-called counter-revolutionists and peasants.[1]

The same Report publishes a list of seventy-six men prosecuted by the Committee on the charge of criminal anarchy in America at the beginning of 1920, of which the overwhelming majority are seen by their names to be Jewish.[2]

These names speak for themselves and are published without comment on the obvious nationality of the majority of the persons concerned. So far indeed does the Lusk Committee appear to have been removed from " anti-Semitism," that nowhere in its vast Report, running to 2008 pages, is attention drawn to the preponderance of Jews concerned in the revolutionary movement, except in the one passage on Hungary quoted above. The Lusk Report must therefore be regarded as an absolutely impartial statement of facts.

In view of these official data, how is it possible for the Jewish press to pretend that a connexion between Jews and Bolshevism is a malicious invention of the " anti-Semites "? That all Jews are not Bolsheviks and that all Bolsheviks are not Jews is of course obvious; but that Jews are playing a preponderating part in Bolshevism it is absurd to deny.

An attempt has been made to show that Jews have suffered as much as the rest of the population in Russia under Bolshevism and that the Jewish religion has met with the same hostility as the Christian faith. Doubtless many Jews have suffered in Russia, since human violence, once allowed to go unchecked, is liable to express itself in various unexpected ways, and the resentment of the Russian " proletariat " towards the Jews was bound to break out under Lenin as under the Tzar. Again, a campaign against Christianity inevitably led in Russia, as in France, to a campaign against all forms of religion, and the Jewish Bolsheviks, being atheists themselves, were doubtless as ready as Lambert of the French Revolution to turn against the believers in the faith they had abandoned.

Yet that the Jewish religion suffered to the same extent as Christianity, or that any organized campaign was conducted against it by the Government, is effectually disproved by the lamentations of professing Jews on the death of Lenin.[3]

---

[1] *Revolutionary Radicalism*, Vol. I. p. 374.   [2] Ibid., p. 24.
[3] Among those who prominently showed their profound grief at the death of Lenin were Jews, and not merely Jews by origin but conforming Jews. Children from Jewish schools, we learn, joined in the procession, while

Indeed, as is generally recognized, the fall of the Soviet Government must mean the downfall of the Jews from the position of privilege they now occupy.

That in our own country Jews are playing a part in the background of Bolshevism is again evident. The *Patriot* recently published a series of articles giving inside information on the organization of the revolutionary movement in Great Britain, where it was stated the whole plot was directed by a group of twelve men. This group in turn was controlled by three of its members. These three men, as the key revealed, were all Jews, so also was " the fiend in human form whose psychological perversion produced this plot,"[1] and who was one of a group in America consisting of four Jews and a Jewess which controlled an outer revolutionary group of eighteen.[2] The Irish Republican Brotherhood also maintained close relations with a ring of revolutionary Jews in America. Incidentally, it is curious to notice that the language employed in some of the correspondence that has passed between members of an inner group bears a strong resemblance to that of Weishaupt and his fellow-Illuminati.

Jewish influence in the less extreme forms of Socialism in this country is no less apparent. If the Labour Party is solidly pro-German, it is also solidly pro-Jewish. Whilst loudly proclaiming pacifism and pressing for the reduction of armaments, it has never uttered a word of protest against the employment of British troops to defend Jewish interests against the Arabs in Palestine. The blessed word Mesopotamia may be freely mentioned in connexion with the withdrawal of troops from military adventures, but never the word Palestine. Again, the free admission of aliens and particularly of Jews into this country has always been one of the principal planks in the Labour platform. Even the Jewish capitalist meets with indulgence at the hands of our Socialist Intellectuals, who whilst inveighing against British owners of property, never include Jewish millionaires in their diatribes.

This may perhaps throw some light on the question frequently propounded: How can one believe that Jews advocate

the Hebrew Art Theatre (Habima) sent a banner with the inscription in Hebrew: ' You freed the nations; you will be remembered for ever.' In addition Rabbi Jacob Mase, of Moscow, the Jewish Relief Committee of that city and other Jewish bodies, sent telegrams of condolence; while the Association of Jewish Authors issued a special memorial magazine in Yiddish dedicated to the memory of Lenin."—*Jewish World* for January 21, 1924.

[1] *Patriot*, for April 26, 1923.   [2] Ibid., May 3, 1923.

Socialism since they stand to lose everything by it? The
fact remains that many Jews do advocate it. After the recent
accession of the Labour Party to office the *Jewish World*
observed:

> The result of the General Election in England is regarded as very
> gratifying by the Hebrew and Yiddish press. The Hebrew journals
> in Palestine, as well as the Hebrew and Yiddish organs in Europe
> and America, express satisfaction at the return to Parliament of
> men who have repeatedly assured the public of their intention to
> adhere to the Balfour declaration.[1]

A further reason is advanced by the *Jewish Courier* for
rejoicing at the downfall of the Conservative Government,
namely, that " the election results have wiped out anti-
Semitic remnants in England," for " the Conservative Government does include several members who are far from favourably disposed towards Jews."[2] The indulgence shown to the
Jews and the honours piled on them by Conservative statesmen
therefore availed nothing to the Conservative cause, and the
welfare of the whole country was subordinated to the interests
of the Jews alone.

It is difficult at first to understand how the programme of
the " Labour " Party, even when combined with ardent pro-
Semitism, could however be in accord with the interests of
the Jews, who have never displayed any hostility towards the
Capitalist system which Socialism sets out to destroy. Indeed,
we find the same Jewish paper which rejoiced at the advent
of the present Government to office offering birthday congratulations to the richest Jew in this country, whose wealth, it
goes on to observe with some complacency, " amounts to no
less than £12,000,000 sterling, and is constantly increasing,
apart from the interest that it brings, by the huge profits of
the concerns in which he is interested."[3]

It would seem, then, that in the eyes of Jewry all capitalists
are not to be regarded as monsters who should be mercilessly
expropriated.

But in considering the war on Capitalism it is essential to
bear in mind that capitalists are of two kinds: national industrial capitalists—largely Gentiles and usually men of brains and
energy who have built up flourishing businesses—and international loan-mongering capitalists, principally, though not

[1] *Jewish World* for January 10, 1924.
[2] Quoted in the *Jewish World* for January 10, 1924.
[3] *Jewish World* for November 9, 1922.

exclusively, Jews, who live by speculation. Whilst to the former, social unrest may prove fatal, to the latter any disturbances may provide opportunities for profit. As M. Georges Batault has well expressed it:

From the strictly financial point of view, the most disastrous events of history, wars or revolutions, never represent catastrophes; the manipulators of money and the wary business men can make profit out of everything, provided they know beforehand and are well-informed. . . . It is certain that the Jews dispersed over all the surface of the earth . . . are particularly favourably situated in this respect.[1]

It is significant to notice that the capitalists most attacked by the Socialists and Pacifists are not those who make profit out of wars and revolutions, but those who contribute to the prosperity of the country and provide work for millions of people. Here, then, the Jews and the Socialists seem to find a point of agreement. It is evident, at any rate, that many rich Jews consider that they have nothing to fear from the threatened Capital Levy and other features of expropriation. Are we not irresistibly reminded of the passage in the Protocols —where incidentally the Capital Levy is specifically mentioned —" Ours they will not touch, because the moment of attack will be known to us and we shall take measures to protect our own "?

But let us consider further how the Socialist plan for " the nationalization of all the means of production, distribution, and exchange " might be reconciled even with the interests of Jewish Industrial Capitalists. The more we examine this magic formula which is to transform the world into a Paradise for the workers, the more we shall see that it approximates to the system of Super-Capitalism, of which, as Werner Sombart has shown, the Jews were the principal inaugurators. Socialists are fond of explaining that " Capitalism " began with the introduction of steam; in reality, of course, Capitalism, in the sense of wealth accumulated in private hands, has always existed since the first savage made his store of winter food. What Socialists really mean by Capitalism is the modern system of Industrialism, which tends to concentrate all the means of production and distribution in the hands of individuals or groups, who, if they happen to be unscrupulous, are able by systematic sweating of the worker and bleeding of the consumer to conduct operations on so large a scale as to crush

[1] *Le Problème Juif*, pp. 41, 43.

all competition by the home worker or the small tradesman.

Obviously, however, with the growing demand of the workers for better conditions of life and the increasing support lent to them by enlightened public opinion this possibility cannot continue indefinitely, and unless a violent convulsion takes place the time will come when great industrial magnates will have to content themselves with moderate profits on their outlay. Thus although at first sight it might appear that the Super-Capitalist must desire to maintain the existing order of things, if he is far-seeing he must realize that profiteering under present conditions must soon cease.

It is therefore conceivable that even the Jewish Industrial Capitalist may see in the nationalization of industry a preferable alternative to the limitation of profits under private enterprise. The same financial acumen and skill in management which has enabled him to control rings and trusts in the past would ensure him a place at the head of nationalized industries, which in effect would be nothing but gigantic trusts nominally under State control but really, like all State enterprises, in the hands of a few men. Under Socialism the position of these trusts would be rendered impregnable. For whilst under the present system any individual or group may set out to break a trust, no such competition would be possible in a State where private enterprise had been made illegal. The men in control of nationalized industries would therefore be able to exercise absolute authority both over the worker and the consumer. Further, if the worker can be persuaded to accept the ultimate scheme of Communism, which is compulsory labour in return for no monetary remuneration, but merely a daily ration of food and the other necessaries of life whenever State officials decide that he requires them, the directors of Labour, like the overseers in a slave plantation, will be able, as in Russia, to impose any conditions they please.

The Jews may well hope to occupy these posts, not only because of their aptitude for organization on so large a scale, but because their international relations would facilitate the sale or barter of goods between countries. The cohesion which exists amongst them would speedily lead to the monopolization of all the higher posts by members of their race.

It is idle to dismiss such a possibility as a chimera. This is what happened in Russia and is happening in Germany to-day. Here, then, we may find perhaps the inner meaning of a remark attributed to a prominent member of the Labour Party, that under Socialism a certain well-known Jewish capitalist might well be worth £10,000 a year. Lenin expressed much the same idea when he said that the Russian Soviet Republic might require a thousand first-class specialists " to direct the work of the people," and that " these greatest ' stars ' must be paid 25,000 roubles each," or even four times that sum, supposing it were necessary to employ foreign specialists for the purpose.[1]

But the Jewish capitalists doubtless see further that in England, as in Russia, this condition of things would be merely a temporary phase, and that the institution of Socialism by dispossessing the present Gentile owners of wealth and property would pave the way for a Jewish and German plutocracy. In Russia wealth has not been altogether destroyed; it has simply changed hands, and a class of new rich has sprung up which meets with no hostility from the professed advocates of equality. Those Jews who see in the Christian Intelligentsia the main obstacle to their dream of world-power, therefore naturally find in the promoters of class-warfare their most valuable allies. For the Christian Intelligentsia is the sole bare to the enslavement of the proletariat; most of the movements to redress the wrongs of the workers, from Lord Shaftesbury's onwards, have arisen not amongst the workers themselves, but amongst the upper or middle classes[2]; once these were swept away an iron bureaucracy would have the workers at their mercy. I do not say this is the plan, but I do say that such a hypothesis provides a reason for the otherwise unaccountable indulgence displayed by Socialists everywhere towards wealthy Jews and at the same time for the huge funds the Socialists appear to have at their disposal.

If big financiers are not at their back, I repeat: where does all the money come from? It seems unlikely that it can be derived from the British owners of wealth and property whom the Socialists are openly out to dispossess; the only body of financiers which can therefore be suspected of contributing towards this end is the body known as " International Finance," which is mainly, though not exclusively, Jewish.

The influence of the Jews in all the five great powers at work

---

[1] Lenin, *The Soviets at Work*, p. 18.

[2] I do not here ignore the work of the Trade Unions; but the Trade Unions would have been powerless to better conditions without the support of upper and middle-class men in Parliament.

in the world—Grand Orient Masonry, Theosophy, Pan-Germanism, International Finance, and Social Revolution—is not a matter of surmise but of fact. Let us now examine what part they are playing in the minor subversive movements enumerated in an earlier chapter.

Freud, the inventor of the most dangerous form of Psycho-Analysis, is a Jew. In this connexion the eminent American neuro-psychiatrist before quoted writes:

Not only the Freud theory of psycho-analysis but a considerable quantity of pseudo-scientific propaganda of that type has for years been emanating from a group of German Jews who live and have their headquarters in Vienna. From its inception, psycho-analysis has been in Jewish hands. There are not half a dozen physicians in the whole world, recognized as authorities in this field, whose names are identified with this movement who are not Jews. This may have been an accident, but nevertheless it is a fact.[1]

I have already referred in an earlier chapter to the question of degenerate art defined in a circular to the *New York Herald* as " the deification of ugliness."[2] The originators of this cult are here described as a group of Satan worshippers in Paris, and the dealers by whom the movement was propagated as " Germans," but we note amongst the lenders to the exhibition at which these "works of art" were displayed several Jewish names. Of one well-known Jewish artist a critic has written:

Were these works the product of a man who had imperfect control over his material, who, in stumbling towards the light, dwelt inevitably upon much darkness, who sought for beauty and found ugliness, who looked for purity and found filth—even then one might be silent and hope for better things to come. But here, apparently, unless my whole reading is ludicrously wrong, he delights in deformity and glories in degradation. . . . He brings to the world of art a new gospel, a black gospel, a gospel in which everything is to be inverted and distorted. Whatsoever things are hideous, whatsoever things are of evil report, whatsoever things are sordid: if there be any unhealthiness or any degradation: think on these things.

What better résumé could be given of that tendency to perversion denounced by the prophet Isaiah in the words: " Woe unto them that call evil good, and good evil; that put darkness for light, and light for darkness "? An organ of the Jewish press, with that sense of solidarity which always rallies Jews

[1] Private communication to author. [2] See *ante*, p. 343.

to the defence of their compatriots however culpable, immediately detects in the critic's expression of opinion the insidious work of "anti-Semitism." A more enlightened Jew, Mr. Frank L. Emanuel, however, having come to the support of the Gentile critic, the Jewish journal is obliged to admit the justice of his contention that " it is lamentable to think of the undue proportion of young Jews " who " have joined the Revolutionary or sham ' Modern Art ' movement in this country."

The same influence will be noticed in the cinema world, where, as has already been pointed out, history is systematically falsified in the interests of class hatred, and everything that can tend, whilst keeping within the present law, to undermine patriotism or morality is pressed upon the public. And the cinema trade is almost entirely in the hands of the Jews.

In the drug traffic Jews are playing a prominent part both here and in America. An eminent New York doctor writes to me as follows:

Members of the Federal narcotic squad attached to the Treasury Department and having the function of enforcing the provisions of the Harrison Act have long been convinced that there is a direct relationship between Radicalism and narcotism. From seven to ten years ago this was thought to be a manifestation of pan-German propaganda. Activity was and still is greater on the part of the distributors and pedlars than is to be accounted for by the large profits, according to their story. Curiously enough, the traffic largely stopped for several weeks following the signing of the Armistice.

In one instance, seven regularly licensed physicians of the "East Side," all Jews, were arrested in succession during the summer of 1920 for illegitimate use of narcotic prescriptions, and every office raided had large quantities of Radical literature. Such associations are not uncommon.

As to the distribution, a recent investigation by *Hearst's Magazine* definitely revealed the fact that the illegitimate distributors were almost invariably of the Jewish race, and that the pedlars were exclusively Jewish and Italian.

Enough, then, has been said to show that, whether as agents or as principals, Jews are playing a part in all subversive movements. A Christian Jew, no renegade to his race but deeply concerned for their future development, said recently to the present writer: " The growing materialism amongst Jews has made them the most destructive force in the world. The only hope for them is to accept Christianity.

At present they are the greatest danger that Christian civilization has to face."

The recognition of all these facts does not of course imply the belief that all Jews are destructive. Undoubtedly there are good and loyal Jews—particularly in France, where the Sephardim predominate—who have absolutely identified themselves with the country of their adoption, and are sincerely opposed to Bolshevism. But these isolated individuals carry little weight compared to the massed forces of subversive Jewry. The same thing was observed in America, where a report privately communicated to the present writer in 1923 stated:

It appears not without significance that Radical literature is never anti-Semitic, but, on the contrary, manifestoes issued by the Executive Committee of the Communist Party are often emphatically pro-Jewish. So far as I know, there is not one exclusively Jewish organization in the United States which is openly and consistently fighting Radicalism. Conservative Judaism loyal to the United States and its institutions as conceived by its founders is unorganized and inarticulate.

When, therefore, the Jewish press protests at the injustice of associating Jews with Bolshevism it may be legitimately answered: What has Jewry done collectively to disassociate itself from Bolshevism?[1] What official protests has the Jewish press uttered against any subversive movement except when Jewish interests were threatened?[2] Has it not, on the contrary, denounced all patriotic efforts to oppose the forces of destruction whenever such efforts necessitated the exposure of the corrupt elements in Jewry?

But these tactics have not been confined to the Jewish press alone. The general press of this country, over which the Jews exercise an increasing control, has followed the same policy. This process of penetration began long ago on the Continent. As early as 1846 an English missionary to the Jews in Berlin wrote:

Independently of the fifteen exclusively Jewish journals of

[1] Madame Cécile Tormay, in her description of the Jewish Bolshevist régime in Hungary, eloquently observes: "It is said that only a misguided fraction of the Jews is active in the destruction of Hungary. If that be so, why do not the Jews who represent Jewry in London, in New York, and at the Paris Peace Conference disown and brand their tyrant co-religionists in Hungary? Why do they not repudiate all community with them? Why do they not protest against the assaults committed by men of their race?" (An Outlaw's Diary, p. 110, 1923).

[2] For example, when religious persecution in Russia was said to have turned against the Jews in the spring of 1923.

396 SECRET SOCIETIES

Germany, four of which have made their appearance since the beginning of the present year, the daily political press of Europe is very much under the dominion of the Jews; as literary contributors, they influence almost every leading Continental newspaper, and as controversy seems to be their native air, and they bring into the field mental energies of no ordinary stamp, they find no lack of employment, and if any literary opponent ventures to endeavour to arrest the progress of Judaism to political power, he finds himself held up to public notice, and exposed to attack after attack in most of the leading journals of Europe. Such . . . was the lot of a Roman Catholic priest of Prague, who lately wrote a pamphlet entitled *Guter Rath für Zeit der Noth,* directed against the advancing power of Judaism. And such is my conviction of the extent of the participation the Jews take in the everyday literature of Germany, that I never pass by a crowded reading-room, but what I think I see standing behind the scenes a Jew, causing new ideas to rise and stir, and develop themselves in the unsuspecting mind of the Gentile.[1]

Do we not see the same methods being pursued with still greater vigour to-day? It would not be an exaggeration to say that there is hardly a periodical in this country with the exception of *The Patriot* that dares to speak out freely on questions in which the interests of Jews are involved.

The fact is that the whole educational as well as the whole political and social world is permeated with Jewish influence. Every man in public life, every modern politician, to whatever party he belongs, seems to find it *de rigueur* to have his confidential Jewish adviser at his elbow, just as in the Middle Ages a prince had his Jewish doctor always at hand to mix his potions and ensure him long life. This appears to be owing not only to the utility of the Jew in financing projects, but to the almost universal belief in the superior intelligence of the Jewish race which the Jew has succeeded in implanting in the Gentile mind.

But the time has come to ask: Is the Jew really the superman we have been taught to consider him? On examination we shall find that in the present as in the past his talents are displayed principally along two lines—financial and occult. Usurers in the Middle Ages, financiers to-day, the Jews have always excelled in the making and manipulating of wealth. And just as at the former period they were the great masters of magic, so at the present time they are the masters of the

[1] *Jewish Intelligence, and Monthly Account of the Proceedings of the London Society for Promoting Christianity amongst the Jews,* April 1846, pp. 111, 112: Letter from the Rev. B. W. Wright.

almost magical art of gaining control over the mind both of the individual and of the public.

Yet in the realms of literature, philosophy, painting, sculpture, politics, and even science, Jews will be found frequently occupying the second or third ranks, and only very seldom the first. Heine may be cited as a poet of the first order, Spinoza as a philosopher, Disraeli as a statesman, but it would be difficult to prolong the list. On the stage and in music alone can the Jews be said to have proved absolutely the equals of their Gentile competitors. The fact is that the Jew is not usually a man of vast conceptions, nor is he endowed with great originality of mind; his skill consists rather in elaborating or in adapting other men's ideas and rendering them more effectual. Thus the most important inventions of modern times have not been made by Jews, but have been frequently improved by them. Neither James Watt, Stephenson, Marconi, Edison, Pasteur, nor Madame Curie were of the Jewish race, and the same might be said of nearly all the greatest' men who have lived since the dawn of our civilization. Napoleon was not a Jew, nor was Shakespeare, nor Bacon, nor Sir Isaac Newton, nor Michael Angelo, nor Leonardo da Vinci, nor Galileo, nor Dante, nor Descartes, nor Molière, nor Emerson, nor Abraham Lincoln, nor Goethe, nor Kant, nor even Machiavelli. Thrown on their own resources, what civilization were the Jews able to create? Whilst Egypt, Greece, and Rome have left immortal monuments, what monuments has Palestine bequeathed to the world?[1]

The Jews, then, provide a high average of cleverness, but have they ever during the last two thousand years produced one mighty genius? Moreover, against this high average of intelligence must be set an equally high average of mental derangement. On this point we have the evidence of the *Jewish Encyclopædia*:

The Jews are more subject to diseases of the nervous system than the other races and peoples among which they dwell. Hysteria and neurasthenia appear to be most frequent. Some physicians of large experience among Jews have even gone so far as to state that most of them are neurasthenic and hysterical. Tobler claims

[1] Gustave Le Bon goes so far as to say that "the Jews have never possessed either arts, sciences, or industries, or anything that constitutes a civilization. . . . At the time of their greatest power under the reign of Solomon it was from abroad that they were obliged to bring the architects, workmen, and artists, of which no rival then existed in Israel."—*Les Premières Civilisations*, p. 613 (1889). It should be remembered, however, that Hiram, the master-builder, was half, if not wholly, an Israelite.

that all the Jewish women in Palestine are hysterical; and Raymond says that in Warsaw, Poland, hysteria is very frequently met with among both Jewish men and Jewish women. The Jewish population of that city alone is almost exclusively the inexhaustible source for the supply of hysterical males for the clinics of the whole Continent (*L'Etude des Maladies du Système Nerveux en Russie*). As regards Austria and Germany, the same neurotic taint of the Jews has been emphasized by Krafft, Ebbing, etc. . . . In New York it has been shown by Collins that among 333 cases of neurasthenia which came under his observation, more than 40 per cent. were of Jewish extraction, etc.[1]

The same American neuro-psychiatrist already quoted attributes the predominance of Jews in the revolutionary movement in America largely to this cause:

Anarchists have been developed largely from the criminal classes, and a belief in anarchy, *per se*, is a psychopathic manifestation. A student of anarchy, therefore, would not only be obliged to cover the field of criminology, but its more significant and important background, psycho-pathology. Some anarchists are actually insane, while others show marked psychological deficiencies. Under our laws as they are now framed, they cannot be restrained unless they commit acts of violence.

As it is, our asylums are filled with this class, and that introduces another phase of the matter. Our asylum insane are largely recruited from the Jewish race, at least recruited in tremendous disproportion to their number in the population. The fact that the revolutionary movement is so largely made up of Jewish elements furnishes an interesting confirmation of what I have said.

The *Jewish World*, recently commenting on the " generally admitted " fact that " the percentage of mental disorders among Jews is much greater than among non-Jews," asks: " Is the cause inherent, that is to say, is there a racial disposition towards degeneracy, or is it the result of the external conditions and causes?" The writer goes on to refer to an article in the *Zukunft* which supports the view that the terrible experiences of the Jews in the Middle Ages have affected their nervous system, and therefore that the cause of mental derangement amongst them " is not due to racial disposition, is not an ethnic principle, but is the result of the tragic lot of the Jewish people."[2] It might perhaps be traced more surely to the habit of brooding on that tragic lot. At any rate, it

[1] *Jewish Encyclopædia*, article on Nervous Diseases.
[2] *Jewish World* for November 9, 1922.

is curious to notice that the two symptoms recognized in the first stages of " general paralysis of the insane,'" the mania that one is the object of persecution and " exalted ideas " (known in France as the *folie des grandeurs*), are the two obsessions that the Talmud and the Cabala with their dreams of world-domination under an avenging Messiah have inculcated in the mind of the Jew.

But whatever are the causes of this neurosis, it is surely un-desirable that a race which exhibits it should be allowed to control the destinies of the British Empire or indeed of any country. If " all the Jewish women in Palestine are hysterical," presumably many of their menkind suffer from the same disability, which certainly does not promise well for the luck-less Arab who is to live beneath their sway.   How much of the trouble that has occurred already in Palestine may be attributed to this cause it is impossible to know.   The in-creasing number of Jews in positions of authority in England presents, however, a far greater subject for alarm.   Jews and Arabs are at any rate both Semites and may be expected to have certain ideas in common, but to place a highly civilized Aryan race under Semitic control is another matter.   The time has come for every Briton to ask himself whether he seriously desires to see the traditions of his country, those great tradi-tions of honour, integrity, and justice which have made the name of England great, replaced by Oriental standards.   I do not say that there are no honourable and upright Jews, but I do maintain that the spirit of fair play which is the essence of the British character is not the characteristic of the Jewish race in general.   The complete absence of this spirit shown in the attempts of agitators to suppress free speech during elec-tions cannot be attributed to English working-men—whose " sporting " instinct is highly developed—and testifies to the alien character of the so-called Labour movement.   If England loses the spirit of fair play, she will have lost her most price-less national heritage.

Conservatism, which has always stood for these great tradi-tions, allows itself to be hypnotized by the memory of Disraeli and accepts his dictum that " the natural tendency of the Jews is to Conservatism "—hence the advisability of placing Jews in control of its interests.   The late Mr. Hyndman saw further when he warned us that " those who are accustomed to look upon all Jews as essentially practical and conservative, as certain, too, to enlist on the side of the prevailing social system, will be obliged to reconsider their conclusions."[1] The causes of the recent *débâcle* of the Conservative Government are still obscure, but the fact remains that it was precisely at a moment when Conservative organization had passed largely into Jewish hands that Conservatism met with the most astounding disaster in the whole of its history. If the manner in which Conservative propaganda was conducted at this moment was an example of Jewish efficiency, it might be well to consider whether on a future occasion the task should not be confided into the hands of simple Britons.

The only effectual way of combating Socialism is to show up the alien influences behind it. As long as the working man believes it to be the outcome of a genuine British labour movement, he will turn a deaf ear to all warnings and anti-Socialist propaganda will merely serve to drive more recruits into the Socialist camp. But let him once suspect that he is being made the tool of foreign intrigue, and all his national feeling will assert itself. We have only to ask him whether he wants his work taken from him by the import of alien goods, his housing accommodation appropriated by alien immigrants, finally to make him understand who are the people behind the scenes advocating a policy so disastrous to his true interests, in order to gain his support. The Secret Service has overwhelming evidence on this last point, which under a Conservative Government might have been made public, but unseen influences in high places have ordained its suppression. The slogan " Britain for the Britons," that would form the strongest counterblast to the false slogans of Socialism, has been barred from Conservative platforms and the very word " alien " avoided lest it should offend Jewish susceptibilities. Thus out of deference to the Jews, Conservatism allows its most powerful weapon to rust in its armoury.

In reality these tactics avail nothing to the Conservative cause. The great weight of Jewry will never be thrown into the scale of true Conservatism; only in so far as Conservatism abandons its patriotic traditions and compromises with the forces of Internationalism will it win any considerable Jewish support. We have but to follow the commitments on current politics in the Jewish press in order to realize that the only standard by which the Jews judge of any political party is the measure in which it will confer exclusive advantages on their own race. The Jewish question, therefore, does not

[1] H. M. Hyndman, " The Dawn of a Revolutionary Epoch," in *The Nineteenth Century* for January 1881.

turn on whether the Jews shall be accorded everywhere equal
rights with the rest of mankind, but whether they shall be
placed above the law, whether they shall be allowed to occupy
everywhere a privileged position.[1] Nothing less will satisfy
them, and any attempt to oppose this claim will always be
met by them with the cry of " persecution." Further, this
position of privilege represents to a section of Jewry merely
a stage on the road to world-domination. For if, as we have
seen by documentary evidence, this plan has always existed
in the past, is it likely that it has been abandoned at the
very moment which seems most propitious for its realization?
The trend of present events and the tone of the Jewish press
certainly do not warrant any such conclusion.

To sum up, then, I do not think that the Jews can be proved
to provide the sole cause of world-unrest. In order to establish
this contention we should be obliged to show the Jews to have
been the authors of every past social convulsion in the history
of modern civilization, to discover their influence behind the
heretical sects of Islam, as behind the Bavarian Illuminati and
the Anarchists of Russia. In the absence of any such conclusive evidence we must therefore recognize the existence
of other destructive forces at work in the world.

But this is not to underrate the importance of the Jewish
peril. Although the existence of an inner circle of Masonic
" Elders " remains problematical, Jewry in itself constitutes the
most effectual Freemasonry in the world. What need of
initiations, or oaths, or signs, or passwords amongst people who
perfectly understand each other and are everywhere working
for the same end? Far more potent than the sign of
distress that summons Freemasons to each other's aid at
moments of peril is the call of the blood that rallies the most
divergent elements in Jewry to the defence of the Jewish
cause.

The old complaint of the French merchants already quoted
would thus appear to be justified, that " the Jews are particles
of quicksilver, which at the least slant run together into a
block." One must therefore not be deceived by the fact

---

[1] A committee has recently been formed by the Jewish Board of Guardians
to sit on all " anti-Semitic " movements in this country. At a meeting of this
body it was complacently announced that " the Committee had obtained
the removal of the posters of an anti-Semitic paper from the walls of an
important establishment, and steps had been taken to get others removed."
—*Jewish Guardian*, February 22, 1924. We wonder whether the Welsh would
be able to obtain the removal of posters advertising literature of an anti-
Celtic nature. This comes perilously near to a fulfilment of the Protocols.

that they often appear disunited. There may be, and indeed is, very little unity amongst Jews, but there is immense solidarity.   A Jew named Morel, referring to the persecution of the converted Rabbi Drach by the Jews, observes:

> What can the wisest measures of the authorities of all countries do against *the vast and permanent conspiracy of a people* which, like a network as vast as it is strong, stretched over the whole globe, brings its force to bear wherever an event occurs that interests the name of Israelite?[1]

It is this solidarity that constitutes the real Jewish Peril and at the same time provides the real cause of " anti-Semitism." If in a world where all patriotism, all national traditions, and all Christian virtues are being systematically destroyed by the doctrines of International Socialism one race alone, a race that since time immemorial has cherished the dream of world-power, is not only allowed but encouraged to consolidate itself, to maintain all its national traditions, and to fulfil all its national aspirations at the expense of other races, it is evident that Christian civilization must be eventually obliterated. The wave of anti-Jewish feeling that during the last few years has been passing over this country has nothing in common with the racial hatred that inspires the " anti-Semitism " of Germany; it is simply the answer to a pretension that liberty-loving Britons will not admit. Those of us who, sacrificing popu-larity and monetary gain, dare to speak out on this question have no hatred in our hearts, but only love for our country. We believe that not only our national security but our great national traditions are at stake, and that unless England awakens in time she will pass under alien domination and her influence as the stronghold of Christian civilization will be lost to the world.

[1] Drach, *De l'Harmonie entre l'Église et la Synagogue,* I. 79 (1844). It is curious to notice that the Jewish writer Margoliouth makes use of the same expression where he says, " It was well remarked that the house [of Roths-child] ' was spread like a network over the nations.' "—*History of the Jews in Great Britain,* II. 161 (1851).

CONCLUSION

WE have now followed the course of associations working throughout nineteen centuries to undermine social and moral order and above all Christian civilization. We have also seen that although on the one hand the unholy spirit of destruction and on the other the natural spirit of revolt against oppression have always existed independently of any organization, it is to secret societies using and organizing these forces that the revolutionary movement has owed its success. Further, we have considered the possibility that behind both open and secret subversive societies there may exist a hidden centre of direction, and finally we have observed that at the present time many lines of investigation reveal a connexion between these groups and the Grand Orient, or rather with an invisible circle concealed behind that great masonic power. At the same time this circle is clearly not French in character since everywhere the activities of World Revolution are directed against France and England but seldom against Germany and never against the Jews. It would not be an exaggeration to say that no subversive movement in the world to-day is either pro-French, pro-British, or " anti-Semitic." We must conclude then that if one Power controls the rest it is either the Pan-German Power, the Jewish Power or what we can only call Illuminism.

This last hypothesis is one that deserves serious consideration. In the light of our present knowledge it does not appear impossible that if an inner circle of World Revolution exists it consists of a purely International group of men whose aim is that of Weishaupt—the destruction of the present system of society. That such an aim can be seriously entertained is shown by the fact that it is openly proclaimed by a whole school of writers and thinkers ranging from gentle Idealists to ferocious Anarchists who, whilst widely differing as to methods and the ultimate ends to be attained, are agreed on the common purpose expressed by Rabaud de Saint-Étienne in the words: " Everything, yes, everything must be destroyed, since everything must be re-made."

It is idle to say that so insane a project can present no danger to the world; the fact remains that an increasing number of people regard it with perfect equanimity. The phrase: " All civilizations have passed away; ours will doubtless pass away likewise," is continually to be heard on the lips of apparently sane men and women who, whether they advocate such an eventuality or not, seem prepared to accept it in a spirit of complete fatalism and to put up no resistance. The point they ignore is that when civilization existed only in isolated spots on the earth's surface it might pass away in one spot only to spring to life in another, but now that civilization is world-wide the dream of a return to nature and the joys of savagery conjured up by Rousseau and Weishaupt can never be realized. Yet if civilization in a material sense cannot be destroyed, it is none the less possible to take the soul out of it, to reduce it to a dead and heartless machine without human feelings or divine aspirations. The Bolsheviks continue to exist amidst tele-phones, electric light, and other amenities of modern life, but they have almost killed the soul of Russia. In this sense then civilization may pass away, not as the civilizations of the ancient world passed away, leaving only desert sands and crumbling ruins behind them, but vanishing imperceptibly from beneath the outward structure of our existing institutions. Here is the final goal of world revolution.

If, then, one inner circle exists, composed of Illuminati animated by a purely destructive purpose it is conceivable that they might find support in those Germans who desire to dis-integrate the countries of the Allies with a view to future con-quests, and in those Jews who hope to establish their empire on the ruins of Christian civilization—hence the superb organization and the immense financial resources at the dis-posal of the world revolutionaries. On the other hand it may be that the hidden centre of direction consists in a circle of Jews located in the background of the Grand Orient, or perhaps, like the early nineteenth-century Illuminati, located nowhere but working in accord and using both Pan-Germans and Gentile Illuminati as their tools.

On this point I think it would be dangerous at present to dogmatize. But that the problem is capable of elucidation

I have no doubt whatever. If the Secret Services of the world had chosen to co-ordinate and make public the facts in their possession the whole plot might long since have been laid bare. A " Department for the Investigation of Subversive Movements " should have had a place in every ordered government. This might have been created by the recent Conservative Government in England, but the same mysterious influence that protected the enemy during the Great War has throughout prevented disclosures that would have enlightened the country on the real nature of the peril confronting it. In the present state of European politics the only course open to those who would save civilization is to act independently of governments, and form a counter-organization in each country with unofficial bureaux of information maintaining relations with each other, yet each retaining its national character.

As far as this country is concerned I am convinced that only a great national movement can save us from destruction—a movement in which men of all classes and above all of the working-class will take part. Fascismo triumphed in Italy, because it was not, as it has been absurdly represented, a reactionary movement, but because it was essentially democratic and progressive, because by appealing to the noblest instincts in human nature, to patriotism and self-sacrifice, it rallied all elements in a disorganized and disunited nation around the standard of a common cause.

One cannot bring about any great movement without first kindling a sacred fire in the hearts of men; one cannot move masses of people merely by appealing to self-interest; they must have a cause to fight for, a cause that is not entirely their own. Socialism, whilst enlisting a large proportion of its following by appealing to their baser instincts, has nevertheless, by its false ideals and promises, been able to kindle a fire in many generous hearts, and to persuade deluded enthusiasts that they are working for the welfare of humanity. The only way to combat Socialism is to create counter enthusiasm for a true ideal.

Yet even Mussolini found that a purely secular ideal was not enough, and that the spirit of religious fervour was necessary to defeat the spirit of materialism and destruction. For behind the concrete forces of revolution—whether Pan-German, Judaic, or Illuminist—beyond that invisible secret circle which perhaps directs them all, is there not yet another force, still more potent, that must be taken into account? In looking back over the centuries at the dark episodes that have marked the history of the human race from its earliest origins—strange and horrible cults, waves of witchcraft, blasphemies, and desecrations—how is it possible to ignore the existence of an Occult Power at work in the world? Individuals, sects, or races fired with the desire of world-domination, have provided the fighting forces of destruction, but behind them are the veritable powers of darkness in eternal conflict with the powers of light.

APPENDIX

I

JEWISH EVIDENCE ON THE TALMUD

THE denunciation of the Talmud by the Jew Pfefferkorn in 1509 and the ex-Rabbi Drach in 1844 have been quoted in the course of this book. Graetz however, in his *History of the Jews,* quotes an earlier incident of this kind.[1] In the thirteenth century a converted Jew and former Talmudist Donin who, on his baptism, assumed the name of Nicholas, presented himself before the Pope, Gregory IX, "and brought charges against the Talmud, saying that it distorted the words of Holy Writ, and in the Agadic portions of it there were to be found disgraceful representations of God," that it contained many gross errors and absurdities, further that "it was filled with abuse against the founder of the Christian religion and the Virgin. Donin demonstrated that it was the Talmud which prevented the Jews from accepting Christianity, and that without it they would certainly have abandoned their state of unbelief." Again "he stated that the Talmudical writings taught it was a meritorious action to kill the best man among the Christians[2] . . . that it was lawful to deceive a Christian without any scruple; that it was permitted to Jews to break a promise made on oath." These Graetz describes as lying charges.

The Jews were accordingly ordered by the Pope to hand over all their copies of the Talmud to the Dominicans and Franciscans for examination, and if their judgment should corroborate the charges of Nicholas Donin, they were to burn the volumes of the Talmud (June 9, 1239).

In France Graetz goes on to relate that "the priest-ridden and weak-minded Louis IX"—that is to say, Saint Louis—pursued the same course. "The Talmud was put on its trial. Four distinguished Rabbis of North France were commanded by the King to hold a public disputation with Nicholas, either to refute the imputations levelled against the Talmud, or to make confession of

[1] Eng. trans., Vol. III. p. 591 ff.
[2] Confirmed by Werner Sombart, *The Jews and Modern Capitalism* (Eng. trans.), p. 203: "The Talmud says: 'Kill even the best of the Gentiles.'" The Zohar also says: "Tradition tells us that the best of the Gentiles deserves death."—Section Vaïqra, folio 14b (de Pauly's trans., Vol. V. p. 42).

407

the abuse against Christianity and the blasphemies against God
that it contained."

It is impossible to imagine a fairer decision, and the queen-
mother, Blanche de Castille, was careful to assure the first witness
summoned that if the lives of the Rabbis were in danger she
would protect them and that he was only required to answer
the questions that would be asked of him. Now, there would
have been nothing simpler than for the Rabbis to admit honestly
that these offensive passages existed, that they had been written
perhaps in moments of passion in a less enlightened age, that they
recognized the indelicacy of insulting the religion of the country
in which they lived, and that therefore such passages should henceforth be deleted. But instead of adopting this straightforward
course, which might have put an end for ever to attacks on the
book they held sacred, the Rabbis proceeded to deny the existence
of the "alleged blasphemous and immoral expressions" and to
declare that "the odious facts related in the Talmud concerning
a Jesus, the son of Pantheras, had no reference to Jesus of Nazareth,
but to one of a similar name who had lived long before him."
Graetz, who admits that this was an error and that the passages
in question did relate to the Jesus of the Christians, represents the
Rabbis as being merely "misled" on the question. But the King,
who was not misled by the Rabbis, ordered all copies of the
Talmud to be burnt, and in June 1242 these were committed to the
flames.[1]

The Talmud, however, continued to exist, and it was not until
1640 that, as we have already seen, the offending passages against
Christ were expunged by the Rabbis as a measure of expediency.
Now that they have been replaced, no further attempt is made
to deny that they refer to the founder of Christianity. As far as
I am aware they are not included in any English translation of the
Talmud, but may be found in an English version of Dr. Gustav H.
Dalman's book, *Jesus Christus im Talmud* (1891).

II

THE "PROTOCOLS" OF THE ELDERS OF ZION

Contrary to the assertions of certain writers, I have never affirmed
my belief in the authenticity of the Protocols, but have always
treated it as an entirely open question.[2] The only opinion to

[1] Professor H. Graetz, *The History of the Jews* (Eng. trans.), III. 591-6.
[2] See my *World Revolution*, pp. 296-307. The misapprehension referred
to above may have arisen from the resemblance between the title of my
book and the series of articles which appeared in the *Morning Post* under
the name of *The Cause of World Unrest*. In view of the fact that these
articles were on some points at variance with my own theories, it seems
hardly necessary to state that they were not my work. As a matter of fact,
I did not know of their existence until they were in print, and later I
contributed four supplementary articles signed by my name.

which I have committed myself is that, whether genuine, or not, the Protocols do represent the programme of world revolution, and that in view of their prophetic nature and of their extraordinary resemblance to the protocols of certain secret societies in the past, they were either the work of some such society or of someone profoundly versed in the lore of secret societies who was able to reproduce their ideas and phraseology.

The so-called refutation of the Protocols which appeared in the *Times* of August 1922, tends to confirm this opinion. According to these articles the Protocols were largely copied from the book of Maurice Joly, *Dialogues aux Enfers entre Machiavel et Montesquieu,* published in 1864. Let it be said at once that the resemblance between the two works could not be accidental, not only are whole paragraphs almost identical, but the various points in the programme follow each other in precisely the same order. But whether Nilus copied from Joly or *from the same source whence Joly derived his ideas* is another question. It will be noticed that Joly in his preface never claimed to have originated the scheme described in his book; on the contrary he distinctly states that it " personifies in particular a political system which has not varied for a single day in its application since the disastrous and alas! too far-off date of its enthronement." Could this refer only to the government of Napoleon III, established twelve years earlier? Or might it not be taken to signify a Machiavellian system of government of which Napoleon III was suspected by Joly at this moment of being the exponent? We have already seen that this system is said by M. de Mazères, in his book *De Machiavel et de l'influence de sa doctrine sur les opinions, les mœurs et la politique de la France pendant la Révolution,* published in 1816, to have been inaugurated by the French Revolution, and to have been carried on by Napoleon I against whom he brings precisely the same accusations of Machiavellism that Joly brings against Napoleon III. " The author of *The Prince,"* he writes, " was always his guide," and he goes on to describe the " parrot cries placed in the mouths of the people," the " hired writers, salaried newspapers, mercenary poets and corrupt ministers employed to mislead our vanity methodically "—all this being carried on by " the scholars of Machiavelli under the orders of his cleverest disciple." We have already traced the course of these methods from the Illuminati onwards.

Now precisely at the moment when Joly published his *Dialogues aux Enfers* the secret societies were particularly active, and since by this date a number of Jews had penetrated into their ranks a whole crop of literary efforts directed against Jews and secret societies marked the decade. Eckert with his work on Freemasonry in 1852 had given the incentive; Crétineau Joly followed in 1859 with *L'Eglise Romaine en face de la Révolution,* reproducing the documents of the Haute Vente Romaine; in 1868 came the book of the German anti-Semite Goedsche, and in the following year on a higher plane the work of Gougenot Des Mousseaux, *Le Juif, le Judaïsme, et la Judaïsation des Peuples Chrétiens*. Meanwhile in 1860 the *Alliance Israëlite Universelle* had arisen, having for its ultimate object " the great work of humanity, the annihilation of error and fanaticism, the union of human society in a faithful and solid fraternity "—a formula singularly reminiscent of Grand Orient philosophy; in 1864 Karl Marx obtained control of the two-year-old " International Working Men's Association," by which a number of secret societies became absorbed, and in the same year Bakunin founded his *Alliance Sociale Démocratique* on the exact lines of Weishaupt's Illuminism, and in 1869 wrote his *Polémique contre les Juifs* (or *Etude sur les Juifs allemands*) mainly directed against the Jews of the *Internationale*. The sixties of the last century therefore mark an important era in the history of the secret societies, and it was right in the middle of this period that Maurice Joly published his book.

Now it will be remembered that amongst the sets of parallels to the Protocols quoted by me in *World Revolution,* two were taken from the sources above quoted—the documents of the Haute Vente Romaine and the programme of Bakunin's secret society, the *Alliance Sociale Démocratique*. Meanwhile Mr. Lucien Wolf had found another parallel to the Protocols in Goedsche's book. " The Protocols," Mr. Wolf had no hesitation in asserting, " are, in short, an amplified imitation of Goedsche's handiwork "[1] and he went on to show that " Nilus followed this pamphlet very closely." The Protocols were then declared by Mr. Wolf and his friends to have been completely and finally refuted.

But alas for Mr. Wolfe's discernment! The *Times* articles came and abolished the whole of his carefully constructed theory. They did not, however, demolish mine; on the contrary, they supplied another and a very curious link in the chain of evidence. For is it not remarkable that one of the sets of parallels quoted by me appeared in the same year as Joly's book, and that within the space of nine years no less than four parallels to the Protocols should have been discovered? Let us recapitulate the events of this decade in the form of a table and the proximity of dates will then be more apparent:

1859. Crétineau Joly's book published containing documents of Haute Vente Romaine (parallels quoted by me).

1860. *Alliance Israëlite Universelle* founded.

1864. 1st *Internationale* taken over by Karl Marx.

,,   *Alliance Sociale Democratique* of Bakunin founded (parallels quoted by me).

,,   Maurice Joly's *Dialogue aux Enfers* published (parallels quoted by *Times*).

---

[1] *Spectator* for June 12, 1920.

1866.   1st Congress of Internationale at Geneva.

1868.   Goedsche's *Biarritz* (parallels quoted by Mr. Lucien Wolf).

1869.   Gougenot Des Mousseaux's *Le Juif*, etc.

,,   Bakunin's *Polémique contre les Juifs*.

It will be seen, then, that at the moment when Maurice Joly wrote his *Dialogues*, the ideas they embodied were current in many different circles.   It is interesting, moreover, to notice that the authors of the last two works referred to above, the Catholic and Royalist Des Mousseaux and the Anarchist Bakunin, between whom it is impossible to imagine any connexion, both in the same year denounced the growing power of the Jews whom Bakunin described as "the most formidable sect" in Europe, and again asserted that a leakage of information had taken place in the secret societies.   Thus in 1870 Bakunin explains that his secret society has been broken up because its secrets have been given away,[1] and that his colleague Netchaïeff has arrived at the conclusion that "in order to found a serious and indestructible society one must take for a basis the policy of Machiavelli."[2]   Meanwhile Gougenot Des Mousseaux had related in *Le Juif*, that in December 1865 he had received a letter from a German statesman saying:

> Since the revolutionary recrudescence of 1848, I have had relations with a Jew who, from vanity, betrayed the secret of the secret societies with which he had been associated, and who warned me eight or ten days beforehand of all the revolutions which were about to break out at any point of Europe.   I owe to him the unshakeable conviction that all these movements of "oppressed peoples," etc., etc., are devised by half a dozen individuals, who give their orders to the secret societies of all Europe.   The ground is absolutely mined beneath our feet, and the Jews provide a large contingent of these miners. . . ."[3]

These words were written in the year after the *Dialogues aux Enfers* were published.

It is further important to notice that Joly's work is dated from Geneva, the meeting-place for all the revolutionaries of Europe, including Bakunin, who was there in the same year, and where the first Congress of the *Internationale* led by Karl Marx was held two years later.   Already the revolutionary camp was divided into warring factions, and the rivalry between Marx and Mazzini had been superseded by the struggle between Marx and Bakunin. And all these men were members of secret societies.   It is by no means improbable then that Joly, himself a revolutionary, should during his stay in Geneva have come into touch with the members of some secret organization. who may have betrayed to him their

---

[1] James Guillaume, *Documents de l'Internationale,* I. 131.
[2] *Correspondance de Bakounine,* published by Michael Dragomanov, p. 325.
[3] *Le Juif,* etc., pp. 367, 368.

own secret or those of a rival organization they had reason to suspect of working under the cover of revolutionary doctrines for an ulterior end. Thus the protocols of a secret society modelled on the lines of the Illuminati or the Haute Vente Romaine may have passed into his hands and been utilized by him as an attack on Napoleon who, owing to his known connexion with the Carbonari, might have appeared to Joly as the chief exponent of the Machiavellian art of duping the people and using them as the lever to power which the secret societies had reduced to a system.

This would explain Maurice Joly's mysterious reference to the "political system which has not varied for a single day in its application since the disastrous and alas! too far-off date of its enthronement." Moreover, it would explain the resemblance between all the parallels to the Protocols from the writings of the Illuminati and Mirabeau's *Projet de Révolution* of 1789 onwards. For if the system had never varied, the code on which it was founded must have remained substantially the same. Further, if it had never varied up to the time when Joly wrote, why should it have varied since that date? The rules of lawn tennis drawn up in 1880 would probably bear a strong resemblance to those of 1920, and would also probably follow each other in the same sequence. The differences would occur where modern improvements had been added.

Might not the same process of evolution have taken place between the dates at which the works of Joly and Nilus were published? I do not agree with the opinion of the *Morning Post* that "the author of the Protocols must have had the *Dialogues* of Joly before him." It is possible, but not proven. Indeed, I find it difficult to imagine that anyone embarking on such an elaborate imposture should not have possessed the wit to avoid quoting passages verbatim— without even troubling to arrange them in a different sequence— from a book which might at any moment be produced as evidence against him. For contrary to the assertions of the *Times* the *Dialogues* of Joly is by no means a rare book, not only was it to be found at the British Museum but at the London Library and recently I was able to buy a copy for the modest sum of 15 francs. There was therefore every possibility of Nilus being suddenly confronted with the source of his plagiarism. Further, is it conceivable that a plagiarist so unskilful and so unimaginative would have been capable of improving on the original? For the Protocols are a vast improvement on the *Dialogues* of Joly. The most striking passages they contain are not to be found in the earlier work, nor, which is more remarkable, are several of the amazing prophecies concerning the future which time has realized. It is this latter fact which presents the most insuperable obstacle to the *Times* solution of the problem.

To sum up then, the Protocols are either a mere plagiarism of Maurice Joly's work, in which case the prophetic passages added by Nilus or another remain unexplained, or they are a revised edition of the plan communicated to Joly in 1864, brought up to date and supplemented so as to suit modern conditions by the continuers of the plot.

Whether in this case the authors of the Protocols were Jews or whether the Jewish portions have been interpolated by the people into whose hands they fell is another question. Here we must admit the absence of any direct evidence. An International circle of world revolutionaries working on the lines of the Illuminati, of which the existence has already been indicated, offers a perfectly possible alternative to the "Learned Elders of Zion." It would be easier, however to absolve the Jews from all suspicion of complicity if they and their friends had adopted a more straightforward course from the time the Protocols appeared. When some years ago a work of the same kind was directed against the Jesuits, containing what purported to be a "Secret Plan" of revolution closely resembling the Protocols,[1] the Jesuits indulged in no invectives, made no appeal that the book should be burnt by the common hangman, resorted to no fantastic explanations, but quietly pronounced the charge to be a fabrication. Thus the matter ended.

But from the moment the Protocols were published the Jews and their friends had recourse to every tortuous method of defence, brought pressure to bear on the publishers—succeeded, in fact, in temporarily stopping the sales—appealed to the Home Secretary to order their suppression, concocted one clinching refutation after another, all mutually exclusive of each other, so that by the time the solution now pronounced to be the correct one appeared, we had already been assured half a dozen times that the Protocols had been completely and finally refuted. And when at last a really plausible explanation had been discovered, why was it not presented in a convincing manner? All that was necessary was to state that the origin of the Protocols had been found in the work of Maurice Joly, giving parallels in support of this assertion. What need to envelop a good case in a web of obvious romance? Why all this parade of confidential sources of information, the pretence that Joly's book was so rare as to be almost unfindable when a search in the libraries would have proved the contrary? Why these allusions to Constantinople as the place "to find the key to dark secrets," to the mysterious Mr. X. who does not wish his real name to be known, and to the anonymous ex-officer of the Okhrana from whom by mere chance he bought the very copy of the *Dialogues* used for the fabrication of the Protocols by the Okhrana itself, although this fact was unknown

---

[1] *Revolution and War or Britain's Peril and her Secret Foes*, by Vigilant (1913). A great portion of this book exposing the subtle propaganda of Socialism and Pacifism is admirable; it is only where the author attempts to lay all this to the charge of the Jesuits that he entirely fails to substantiate his case.

to the officer in question? Why, further, should Mr. X., if he were a Russian landowner, Orthodox by religion and a Constitutional Monarchist, be so anxious to discredit his fellow Monarchists by making the outrageous assertion that " the only occult Masonic organization such as the Protocols speak of "—that is to say, a Machiavellian system of an abominable kind—which he had been able to discover in Southern Russia " was a Monarchist one "?

It is evident then that the complete story of the Protocols has not yet been told, and that much yet remains to be discovered concerning this mysterious affair.

INDEX

A&B Publishers Group
SELECTED TITLES

A BOOK OF THE BEGINNINGS VOL. I & II		40.00
AFRIKAN HOLISTIC HEALTH		15.9.
AFRICAN DISCOVERY OF AMERICA		10.00
ARAB INVASION OF EGYPT & THE FIRST 30 YEARS OF ROMAN DOMINION		14.9:
ANACALYPSIS (SET)		40.00
ANACALYPSIS VOL.. 1		25.00
ANACALYPSIS VOL.. 11		20.00
AIDS THE END OF CIVILIZATION		9.9:
BRITISH HISTORIANS & THE WEST INDIES	ERIC WILLIAMS	9.9.
CHRISTOPHER COLUMBUS & THE AFRICAN HOLOCAUST	JOHN HENRIK CLARKE	10.00
COLUMBUS CONSPIRACY		11.9.
DAWN VOYAGE:THE BLACK AFRICAN DISCOVERY OF AMERICA		11.9.
DOCUMENTS OF WEST INDIAN HISTORY	ERIC WILLIAMS	9.9.
EDUCATION OF THE NEGRO		9.9.
EGYPTIAN BOOK OF THE DEAD	E. W. BUDGE	9.9.
EGYPTIAN BOOK OF THE DEAD/ANCIENT MYSTERIES OF AMENTA	GERALD. MASSEY	9.9.
EVERYTHING YOU NEED TO KNOW ABOUT HAIRLOCKING		7.9.
FIRST COUNCIL OF NICE: A WORLD'S CHRISTIAN CONVENTION A.D. 325		9.9.
GOSPEL OF BARNABAS		8.9.
GERALD MASSEY'S LECTURES		9.9:
GLOBAL AFRIKAN PRESENCE	EDWARD SCOBIE	14.9.
HARLEM VOICES FROM THE SOUL OF BLACK AMERICA	JOHN HENRIK CLARKE	11.9.
HARLEM USA	JOHN HENRIK CLARKE	11.9
HEALTHY FOODS & SPIRITUAL NUTRITION HANDBOOK	KEITH WRIGHT	9.9.
HEAL THYSELF FOR HEALTH AND LONGEVITY	QUEEN AFUA	9.9
HEAL THYSELF COOKBOOK:HOLISTIC COOKING WITH JUICES	DIANE CICCONE	9.9
HISTORICAL JESUS & THE MYTHICAL CHRIST	GERALD MASSEY	9.9
HISTORY OF THE PEOPLE OF TRINIDAD & TOBAGO	ERIC WILLIAMS	14.9
LOST BOOKS OF THE BIBLE& THE FORGOTTEN BOOKS OF EDEN		11.9*
RAPE OF PARADISE: COLUMBUS AND THE BIRTH OF RACISM IN AMERICA	JAN CAREW	14.9
SIGNS & SYMBOLS OF PRIMORDIAL MAN		16.9.
VACCINES ARE DANGEROUS: A WARNING TO THE BLACK COMMUNITY		9.9
VITAMINS & MINERALS A TO Z	JEWEL POOKRUM	9.9.
FREEMASONRY INTERPRETED		12.9
FREEMASONRY & THE VATICAN		9.9.
FREEMASONRY & JUDAISM		9.9
FREEMASONRY:CHARACTER & CLAIMS		9.9.
FREEMASONRY EXPOSITION: EXPOSITION & ILLUSTRATIONS OF FREEMASONRY		9.9*
SECRET SOCIETY & SUBVERSIVE MOVEMENTS		13.9

SEND FOR OUR COMPLETE CATALOG NOW!